BY ELMER DAVIS

EDITED BY

ROBERT LLOYD DAVIS

Essay Index Reprint Series

BOOKS FOR LIBRARIES PRESS
FREEPORT, NEW YORK

PS 3507
A7165A6

The editor is grateful to the *New York Times* for its kind permission to quote from
Elmer Davis's Godfrey Gloom pieces, which first appeared in that newspaper.

INTERNATIONAL STANDARD BOOK NUMBER:

0-8369-1798-7

LIBRARY OF CONGRESS CATALOG CARD NUMBER:

77-117780

PRINTED IN THE UNITED STATES OF AMERICA

CONTENTS

PREDILECTIONS

FICTION

INTRODUCTION

Roger Burlingame begins his biography of Elmer Davis, *Don't Let Them Scare You* (J. B. Lippincott Company, 1961), by recalling the "scarcely credible" years of that sickness in American life called McCarthyism: "The rabble-rousing Senator held the Congress in the hollow of his hand, including many of those members who hated him most, intimidated one President and gained the temporary support of such otherwise intelligent statesmen as Robert Taft. That he was able to humiliate the Army, to cause the FBI to circumvent its rules, and to render inoperative portions of the Constitution itself was not because of his personal power, appealing as it was to the vulgar, but because he was the spokesman for an inarticulate fear. . . .

"In the most desperate days of the panic," he goes on, "when many dared not move or speak without looking over their shoulder for the fancied specter, a slow, even, Middle-Western voice brought reassurance into millions of American homes. It presented the extreme contrast with the reckless shouts that rose from the Senate floor. It appraised, it reasoned, it recalled to an America unafraid; its tone and cadence were those of an old Yankee . . . certainly; of the stubborn vision that made the impossible feasible through the tough march that once joined the oceans. And the words were the words of the Founding Fathers, infused with wise biblical advice but couched in the colloquial usage of the rural fireside.

"Again and again, in various words but never in any that obscured the basic meaning, the voice said:

The first and great commandment is, Don't let them scare you. For the men who are trying to do that to us are scared themselves. They are afraid that what they think will not stand critical examination; they are afraid that the principles on which this Republic was founded and has been conducted are wrong. They will tell you that there is a hazard in the freedom of the mind, and of course there is, as in any freedom. In trying to think right you run the risk of thinking wrong. But there is no hazard at all, no uncertainty, in letting somebody else tell you what to think; that is sheer damnation.

To former listeners and readers the country over Elmer Davis remains a symbol of the most effective resistance to McCarthyism. That part of his lifework is unfortunately still pertinent today. Superpatriots prescribing what we may say and think, power groups planning how to enforce such prescriptions, moves in the name of "Constitutionalism" to save the Constitution from itself by changing it beyond recognition: these and other examples show how the blight of ten years ago survived the end of what was called "McCarthyism."

The pressing relevance today of much of what he wrote is one good reason for this collection. If today there is at least a more resolute and articulate opposition than before to what he called the "antifreedom crusade," his example helped inspire it. This book provides an object lesson in candor and close reasoning repeatedly deployed in defense of freedom.

But old friends' also call for many of his nonpolemical works. Specially treasured essays, short stories, novels—the Godfrey Gloom stories, "Portrait of a Cleric," "On Being Kept by a Cat," "On Not Being Dead, As Reported," *Giant Killer*—these and certain others enjoy with their partisans the status of classics. Bringing them all under one cover to revive old friendships and inaugurate new ones is a second good reason for the book.

Finally, this collection may be technically informative. It covers nearly forty years in the development of a professional writer who attained success in three quite different careers. Analytical readers may here remark the underlying constants in all his work as well as the changes over the years in technique and content. Both what the man was and how he learned, by trying many different things, to bring it forth may be best studied by comparing his writing in different times and different genres.

I have selected what appears here, cutting some parts and adding explanations and editorial comment. I was chosen to do it because editing and writing are things I do, and I happen to be more familiar with the subject matter than anyone else. My being the author's son has obvious advantages and obvious disadvantages. Most of the latter, however, may be easily overcome: simply note the filial relationship here and now and prepare therewith to discount any unduly biased evaluations.

In a small group I would speak of him as "Dad," but to do so here would seem like folksy insistence on a prerogative I don't care to assert. To be constantly writing "My father," on the other hand, would surely soon come to sound pompous. This leaves the choice between "Davis" and "Elmer Davis"; since the latter costs an extra word per occurrence, with no real improvement in tone, I will risk appearing too phlegmatic and usually write just "Davis."

His colleagues almost always explained Davis's pre-eminence in terms first of unusual qualities of character, next insisting on the importance of learning and ability in transmitting these qualities.

"Character was the first word for Elmer Davis," said Louis M. Lyons, the distinguished Nieman Fellowship curator, in reviewing *Don't Let Them Scare You.* "But also he was a master craftsman. It was not an accident that he became the greatest reporter of his time. . . ."

Likewise Brooks Atkinson: "His greatness as a political commentator derived from his responsible personal character combined with his prodigious store of knowledge . . . [of which, furthermore] he had a remarkable capacity for making orderly use."

"Putting things into proper perspective was the special quality of genius that Elmer Davis brought to his profession," said John Crosby. "If you get just one master of common sense in a century you are lucky." In technique he compared him to Voltaire: "The two men— Voltaire and Davis—were very similar; they both got straight to the heart of the matter; they said it in few words; their utterances were a mixture of candor and courage which in any society quite properly passes as wit. . . ."

In this way his personal qualities were described in terms ranging from "character," "courage," "honesty," "integrity," "uprightness and candor," "wisdom and clarity," "salt and truth," to "common sense," "tough mind and tender heart," and "basic" or "100 per cent Americanism." (These last, sadly, not affirmed by all professed custodians of "Americanism.")

If personal character accounted for the special quality of much of his work, he was also widely admired for technical competence. Many writers ascribed this in part to his learning; I suppose they had in mind more his habit of making daily and unassuming use of learning than formal attainments. Oddly enough, in view of this reputation for learning (the reputation—not learning itself—seems overweighty for this) Davis had a great name for wit. "Witty," "merry," "gay," and "lighthearted" were terms often applied to his earlier writings. An old book jacket beside me quotes reviews of his first novel (*Times Have Changed,* 1923) : "The most amusing book we have read recently," said Heywood Broun; "Contains some of the funniest lines I have come across," said Fanny Butcher, and so on. In later years when his writing was generally more serious, if not indeed somber, he used the same wit for harsher or more genuinely satirical purposes.

He was not, on the other hand, a "literary" person. He was always more interested in content than in form and manner. But if he was no innovator he made himself master of certain standard forms in essays—polemical, critical, expository and familiar—short stories and novels. Frequently described left-handedly as a "master of the formula story" or "craftsman of the slicks," he used this mastery of form to gain freedom in choosing unconventional content for his fiction.

Some of his greatest technical successes were in two kinds of writing that are, strictly speaking, ephemeral, and therefore hardly appear in this volume. He was a newspaper reporter for the first ten years of his working life and he continued with occasional newspaper writing during the next fifteen years. Then again, having given a number of well-received radio broadcasts in the late 'twenties and the nineteen-thirties, he was a regular radio commentator from 1939 till the end of his working life (except for three and a half years during the war).

Much of his writing for these media was the very best of its kind. His radio writing was almost universally acclaimed for a compression that gave in less than five minutes not only the essential news, but a clear perspective and sharp comment with it. The pity is that he worked in the early days of radio news when monitoring records were not systematically preserved; since he himself never saved the written script (except on special request), there is no complete record of those broadcasts.

Good as it was of its kind, his newspaper and radio writing was for the day only. As a professional writer he did other kinds of writing—short stories turned out to pay bills, quick reviews, some kinds of magazine article—which might be said to be for the week or month only. Almost everything appearing here, on the other hand, has an imprimatur: it appeared in a book. That means either that it was written for the more lasting life of a book from the very first, or that having been written for a magazine, it was later judged by Davis himself to be worth including in a bound collection of his work.

It will simplify later comment to fix some sort of outline of Davis's life. Readers interested in detail may find it in Burlingame's biography quoted above.

All of his life was conditioned by his Middle-Western background. His father came from Mississippi of Anglo-Welsh-Celtic stock, was a devout Baptist, settled down as bank cashier in the small Ohio river town of Aurora in southern Indiana, lost to illness in a period of three years his first wife and two of their three children, then married late in life a young schoolteacher barely older than his surviving son. Elmer Davis, born in 1890, was the only child of the second marriage.

He lived sixteen years in Aurora and four more at Franklin College upstate. He got a Rhodes Scholarship on graduation at the age of twenty and with it he left Indiana for good. That scholarship paid for three years of term at Oxford alternating with long vacations on the continent and travel in the Near East. The rigorous classical training for his degree in "Greats" laid a foundation for many later references to Davis's "enormous learning," "classical scholarship," or "amazing erudition." (Examinations in Greats were then still written in Latin and Greek; most Americans at Oxford avoided this curriculum.)

He was always grateful for his Oxford training but he was not—as millions of radio listeners very well know—one of those Americans who try to bring Oxford back with them. He never went back to Indiana but the speech always stayed with him; and the speech, no doubt, was just the symbol of much more. (Not that I subscribe to popular exaggerations referring to his "gravelly" Indiana accent or, as one inspired geographer put it, "Hogan's Creek twang." Twenty years of Indiana—even if the formative years—were considerably modified by the next thirty of New York residence and world travel. But his speech was very much American.)

His father's death in 1913 left Davis with a dependent mother as he sought his first job, but even in that depression year he would not play it safe and go back to teach in Indiana. He brought his mother to New York, and a stopgap job in magazine editing pulled them through until he went to work for the *New York Times*.

His work may be best understood in relation to three distinct phases of his career. Rather than refer to "early," "middle" and "late" Davis, as if he were an Egyptian dynasty, I will speak of the newspaper, the free-lance, and the radio period. These periods are well defined, if by nothing else, simply by the dates 1914-1924 for the first, 1924-1939 for the second, 1939-1956 for the last. Of course, he wrote for newspapers in each of the first and second periods, he did some radio broadcasting in each of the second and third, and he was indeed an active free-lance writer (as much of this book goes to show) in all three. But the first and third were periods of regular employment, while in the second he was dependent on free-lance earnings.

His Ford Peace Ship stories of 1915 brought him a reputation, and the *Times* afterward used him in roving correspondence here and abroad throughout the war, as well as its aftermath in the Balkans. Even after he became an editor of the *Times* he often worked on special assignments; by then he was a married man and the spur of family cares may have prodded him to write for magazine and book publication too. The success of his first real novel (the 1923 bestseller *Times Have Changed*) encouraged him to try independence.

Accordingly he began 1924 by not only quitting his job but leaving his adopted home town to try the idyllic life of a self-employed man in a Palm Beach bungalow. Some months' trial (my personal recollection is that my mother's disaffection with the local insects was a clincher) left him grateful for special assignments from his ex-employers for the summer's National Conventions, and by fall he was back in New York to begin eighteen years of residence on Morningside Heights. He was surely one of the few to sell Palm Beach property that year and lose money, but he recouped with a serial about the Florida boom *(White Pants Willie)*. Another serial of that year, *Friends of Mr. Sweeney* (published in *Collier's*), was to become in book form the most popular of his lighthearted novels.

For fifteen years thereafter his main source of income was writing short stories for magazines. He sustained and extended his familiarity with national politics and foreign affairs by regularly investigating them for magazine articles, even though such serious articles could never be made to pay. (For example, he could barely clear expenses on a trip to Europe with daily stories for the *Times* and NANA, together with an article or two for *Harper's*.) Furthermore, he could hardly find time to think through and write a novel unless he got such a well-developed idea that he could sell serial rights in advance. In fact, he wrote just three more novels.

The depression threw an extra burden on his finances, when they could least stand it, in the form of aging relatives who had suddenly lost most or all of their life savings. Personal hardships, however, were only a small part of the depression's shock. His world outlook had been formed in a forward-looking America and refined in England at the apparent height of its benevolent well-being. If the first World War was a blow to this, he managed like many Americans to come through it with the hope that now and here we could do things better. The depression struck at the roots of his American faith. It was no longer possible after that to feel that people sooner or later got their just deserts, that anyone willing and able to work could always find work to support himself and his family, that close pursuit of the simple old American virtues guaranteed some portion of reward. He did not, like some, henceforth reject everything he had once accepted; nor did he gradually suppress memories until he could persuade himself it had all been exaggerated, things hadn't been so bad for responsible people, after all—only irresponsible knockers kept harping on it. Davis and his kind could only pull in their belts and go ahead working at whatever they could do. But on considerably revised data. I feel that Davis's outlook was shadowed by a growing pessimism from then on. (He has been compared for his combination of moral force and pessimism with Reinhold Niebuhr, though I imagine neither was entirely gratified thereby.) It speaks strongly for his spirit that he never let this pessimism slow him down in fighting for what he thought right.

The war in Europe changed him, literally overnight, from a freelance writer to a radio commentator. For two and a half years his nightly five-minute broadcasts provided a sort of lodestone for millions of listeners. He was then called to Washington to bury his talents for the presumed public good in administering the new Office of War Information. When he returned to radio in 1946, he insisted on staying in Washington even though all the big network news centers were still (for various administrative and technological reasons) in his old home town of New York. But Washington was where the news was, he argued, and he stayed in the world's greatest capital from then on. He went back on the air with a fifteen-minute program that gave time for deeper analysis and sharper comment on special issues. These were years of constant hard work: even more so—not only in broadcasting, but in conferences, speeches, personal meetings—during the McCarthy era. The strain of a particularly hard year's work in 1953 evidently brought on the first of several strokes; it curtailed his radio activity for the next three years. He retired completely in 1956 and died in 1958.

I have said very little about the radio period partly because it took place recently in a mass medium and so will be better remembered by many, many more people, and partly because his writing of that last period is well represented in this book. In addition more than half of Burlingame's *Don't Let Them Scare You* is devoted to the radio and OWI period.

The writing collected here is what I thought most deserving either (as in most cases) on its own account or (in some) for what it shows of how his ideas and methods developed. I have not wanted to impose a factitious organization, but have kept fiction and nonfiction apart and arranged the latter under subject-matter headings. Each piece is prefaced with some comment as to its provenance and its place in his work. Cuts are marked by ellipses within brackets, [...], which may serve to emphasize their presence and to distinguish them from ellipses within his work. Where necessary I have provided within brackets some explanation of what was cut.

Davis published fifteen books during his lifetime, as follows.

Nine novels. *The Princess Cecilia* (1915) was literally a schoolboy effort which he later preferred to forget. *Times Have Changed* (1923), the first of his five "lighthearted" novels to appear in book form, was a bestseller. *I'll Show You the Town* (1924; serial version 1920) was made into a very successful movie from which Davis never got a cent. (This must have lent spice to his strong fight later as president of the Author's League for clear definition in sale contracts of authors' movie and other re-use rights.) *Friends of Mr. Sweeney* (1925; serial version 1924), a widely remembered book, was also made into a movie, but this one was not a financial success (Davis had a percentage of the rights this time). Incidentally, the title phrase, used to imply an acquaintance with some important person, seems to have become part of our language. I have often heard it used by people who had never heard of the book, although the original juxtaposition of the name "Sweeney" and the allegation were apparently Davis's (at least he could recall no previous ones). *The Keys of the City* (1925) was the last to be written of his light novels. In *Strange Woman* (1927) he used a standard novel form and his customary wit to illuminate more serious aspects of contemporary life. The whole first section of *Giant Killer* (1928; reprinted in 1943 by The Readers Club) appears in this book, with further comment on the novel. *White Pants Willie* (1932; serial version 1924) was one of the merrier "lighthearted" novels but the book came out in an unpropitious year for light hearts. He wrote *Bare Living* (1933) in collaboration with his close friend Guy Holt in a still unpropitious attempt to recapture the lighthearted approach of the early 1920's.

Two volumes of short stories: *Morals for Moderns* (1930) and *Love Among the Ruins* (1935). Two volumes of variegated essays: *Show Window* (1927) and *Not To Mention the War* (1940). Finally, two volumes on national affairs. *But We Were Born Free* (1954) was an inspiring beacon in a dark year; it was a bestseller. Its sequel was *Two Minutes Till Midnight* (1955) which Roger Burlingame described as "the ultimate testimony of his gifts as a philosopher and writer: his last great effort."

Robert Lloyd Davis

PERSONAL

[Davis's personality shows best in glints and flashes throughout his writing. Only an unusual occasion could bring him to write about himself; there had to be some excuse for hanging it on an impersonal topic. These three pieces may, even so, give some background for understanding his personality so that the later glints and flashes are more easily recognized.]

ON NOT BEING DEAD, AS REPORTED

[*This article deals with two widely separated and clearly important events in Davis's life, but perhaps there is more to be learned in the way he doesn't discuss those events than in anything he says about them. The comic pose of diffidence, almost of frailty, was typical of his approach to certain personal subjects, and this piece is still a favorite with many readers. (The assumption of diffidence and aged frailty is specially ironic in the light of the fact that Davis would within months enter on a new career with seventeen more years of active public life.) This was in* Harper's *in 1939 and there are no cuts.*]

Twice it has been my fortune to be reported missing in a catastrophe, and probably dead. Each time I denied the story as soon as I heard it, and seem to have been more generally believed than is usually the case when people have to contradict something that the papers have said about them; but if it happens again I shall fall back on that favorite formula of those whose misdeeds are unexpectedly brought to light, and refuse to dignify the rumor with a denial. For a third denial might not be wholly convincing, even to me; where there is smoke there is generally some fire; such an occurrence is bound to set you wondering if there may not be some truth in the story after all. And beyond that, to turn up alive after you have been reported dead is an unwarrantable imposition on your friends.

The first time it happened I was only twenty-six, and my repudiation of the canard was accordingly convinced and vigorous. I happened to be crossing from Holland to England on a steamer that was submarined and sunk—one of the most placid submarine sinkings on record, for the British Navy had time to get not only all the passengers but all their baggage off before she went under. (Indeed, the ship herself was raised after the war and put back into service, and there she is to this day, all ready to be sunk again.) But cross-channel communication was slow and uncertain in 1916; all that was known at first was that the ship had been sunk. Nothing had been heard about the passengers, so the Dutch public leaped to the conclusion which in those days was usually correct; and some days passed before my friends, and enemies, in Holland learned that I had not gone to the bottom after all.

My friends, I am afraid, took it in their stride; even before America was in the war anybody with an international acquaintance had become hardened to hearing the unexpected news of some friend's violent death any morning. When so many good men were being killed at the front every day there was no reason to waste any particular grief on a neutral who had accidentally got in the way of the war and been run over. The effect on my enemies was, in the long run, more deplorable.

They were not my enemies really—only a group of high-minded people who held with great fervor ideals on whose practicability I had been compelled to throw some doubt, in print; they were in fact the leaders and delegates of the Ford Peace Party, and they looked on me as one unsaved, who had not seen the light. Very likely there was more in that view than I would admit at the time. I still think the Ford Peace Party was a crazy enterprise; but an endeavor, however visionary and inadequate, to stop a war that was wrecking Europe appears in retrospect a little less crazy than most of the other purposes that were prevalent in Europe in 1916.

However, I was unable to see eye to eye with the leaders of this Children's Crusade, so it had sometimes come to black looks and harsh words. But when I was reported dead those who had thought so poorly of me were engulfed in a wave of Christian charity. "What a pity!" they said. "He was a young man of great promise." It was some years before I realized how callously inconsiderate it had been for me to turn up after that, alive and well, and just as unsaved as ever. Nobody who has risen to a noble gesture of generosity and forgiveness likes to be made to look foolish a couple of days later.

II

My alleged decease got no newspaper publicity that time, at least not in any newspaper that found me worthy of extended mention; so there was no opportunity to enjoy what might seem to the unthinking the rare privilege of reading my own obituary. But I know men who have had that privilege, and they tell me it is anything but a pleasure.

You may be scandalized at the discovery that the papers thought you were worth no more than a paragraph or two when you would have supposed you rated at least half a column. Even if you get as much (or almost as much) space as you think you deserve, you are likely to find that the source material which the writer of the obituary discovered in the clippings in the newspaper morgue deals chiefly with what you had always regarded as trivial aspects of your career; or probably indeed with its scandalous aspects, if it has had any. This is natural; all the writer has found is some record of the occasions on which you said or did something that was news; and all of us expect the great are most likely to become news by being conspicuously wicked, conspicuously unfortunate, or conspicuously ridiculous. Long years of industry and success in the hardware business, a lifetime of zealous and fruitful service to the church or the lodge, will pass all but unnoticed by the press. Whereas there are likely to be columns and columns in the newspaper files about the unfortunate occasion when that unbalanced woman to whom you had foolishly lent money, for no reason at all except disinterested benevolence, sued you for breach of promise, claiming that she never knew you were married.

For when a man dies the newspaper is compelled to function, to the best of its ability, as the Voice of History. Conscious enough of its own inadequacy, it must nevertheless do the best it can to represent the man not as he seemed to himself or to those who loved him (nor to those who hated him either); but the man as he was objectively, against his background, in proportion to his universe. How often when I was a young reporter have I called up a bereaved family for information about the deceased, to be told that he was one of Nature's noblemen and the kindest husband and father that ever lived. It takes a certain amount of tact in such moments to get what you want without having to explain that what you want is something worth putting in the paper, something that will place the man in his frame of reference. For most of us such an examination is likely to be deflationary; a man who has read his own obituary will never be quite the same again.

Not even if he is a man of consequence, who gets a creditable amount of space in the paper. Almost certainly, to run over this sketch of his life as seen by a stranger will be a melancholy exercise; he will know that some of his achievements have been overestimated, he will be disgusted to find that the accomplishments in which he has taken most pride do not seem very important to an outsider; and here and there some phrase, set down in all innocence, will be a bitter reminder of some of the things he had always intended to do, and never got round to. Viewed objectively, compared with the history of the general run of men, it may be a respectable record; but its subject cannot view it objectively, he must compare it not with what other men have accomplished, but with what he intended to accomplish when he started out. Few men can make that comparison with any great satisfaction.

Of the length and nature of my obituary, now in type in certain

New York newspaper offices, I know nothing; all I can be sure of is that it is longer than I deserve, for it is a tradition of the trade that both newspapermen and ex-newspapermen always get more space than they are really worth on the obituary page. But whatever its length and implications, I have no regrets that I escaped reading it, by however narrow a margin, after the late New England hurricane.

III

It is not my purpose to tell you about the hurricane. No cataclysm of Nature, except possibly Noah's flood, ever afflicted a region populated by so many professional writers; and most of them were prompt to cash in on it, especially if they carried no wind insurance and had to compensate their losses somehow. Already I have read five magazine articles about it; an account of it will be the climactic chapter in two novels that are to be published before you read this, and God knows how many more in preparation. I can only hope that the novelists will remember from personal experience that the hurricane fell alike on the just and on the unjust, and will not use it as a *deus ex machina* which removes all the undesirable characters while the hero and heroine come through unscathed. For there have been novels in which hurricanes, earthquakes, volcanic eruptions, etc., displayed as sure a marksmanship and as careful a discrimination as the United States Marines.

Two gentlemen from upper New Hampshire have testified in *Harper's* that, in that remote region, people were slow to realize the extent and gravity of the catastrophe. So, it must be confessed, were some of us on the Connecticut shore, right in the middle of things. When a hurricane is over you know that you are not dead; you realize it so vividly—especially if there had been some doubt about your survival, for a while—that it may not occur to you that people at a distance do not share your knowledge. It happened that no one was killed in the small community where I was living, that no one I knew personally was among the casualties in the nearby towns that suffered far more serious damage; and while we knew things had been pretty bad in our neighborhood, it took time to grasp the dimensions of the disaster, to perceive that when hundreds had been killed over a wide area, most of the millions who had not been killed were going to be worried about till definitely reported safe.

The process by which one is reported dead is simple and logical enough. One's friends call up the papers, asking, "What do you hear about X?" The wires being down, they have naturally heard nothing about X. Thus X is unreported, therefore X is missing; and a reading public unfamiliar with hurricanes draws the natural analogy from local and minor disasters, fires and train wrecks and so on, in which those at first reported missing usually turn out to be dead. So it happened that on the Saturday morning after the hurricane, when the yard had been cleaned up and the roads were open and we were ready to go back to town, the New York papers at last got into the devastated area, and I learned that I was missing. But that was only the beginning.

It was due to the generosity of my friends in the trade that I was posted as missing on the front page, in a position and size of type about equivalent to that allotted, on the other side of the page, to the mobilization of the Czechoslovak army (nobody could have dreamed that day that the two pieces of news would turn out to be of equal inconsequence). But it is a thoroughly natural presumption that a man missing in large headlines must be more completely missing than somebody whose unreportedness is buried in the body of the story. So in that day's evening papers the possibility was verging on certainty; and one of the radio stations, I am told, went to the length of reporting that my corpse had been seen floating out to sea.

And that was the end of the story. Between the hurricane and Hitler, the papers and the broadcasting stations were overloaded that week; there was little time or space for the correction of misapprehensions. News is the unusual, the not-to-be-expected; so I suppose I have no right to complain if it was news that Davis was dead, but not news, not worth putting in the papers, that Davis was not dead after all. The implications, however, are by no means flattering; and it all entailed a good deal of inconvenience to my friends. My wife for some reason was not listed as missing—somewhat illogically, for a hurricane, like an air raid, is no respecter of women and children; my friends drew the natural conclusion that she was somewhere else and began to ask her about me by telephone and telegraph. But, believing that I was dead but not quite sure, they were driven to all sorts of circumlocutions; trying to find language that was neither callous enough to grieve her if she were a widow, nor ominous enough to alarm her if she did not yet know whether she was or not.

To the friends I met after I came back to town the inconvenience was of another and perhaps graver sort. On each man's face I could see a look of startled surprise, not altogether unmixed with resentment; for they had done their grieving for Davis, and it could not but be regarded as an imposition when they discovered that it was all a mistake, and that some day they would have it to do over again. My contemporaries are approaching the time of life when to hear of the unexpected death of a friend is as common as it was in war days; and if you have work to do you cannot spend too much time worrying about it. When you hear that good old X is dead you put in perhaps two minutes thinking hard about good old X, and hoping that he left enough for his widow to live on; after which you put him out of your mind and get down to business, so that you may leave enough for your widow to live on when your time comes. Now and then in later life of course you will think of X again—when you see some piece of news in the paper that he would have particularly appreciated or particularly detested; when your partner misses a slam that X would have made if he had been playing the hand; or when recurrently you have to try to find a job for his widow, in case he didn't leave enough for her to live on.

But that is about all, except in the rare instances of some personality so vivid that when it is gone the landscape never looks quite so bright again. (Such, in my experience, were Guy Holt, Don Marquis, and Max Swain; such, I gather, was Elinor Wylie to those who knew her well; so indeed, as a personality rather than an artist, William Shakespeare seems to have been chiefly remembered by his friends.) But most of us do not rate so much remembrance, except by those to whom our passing means a radical change in all the circumstances of life; this is the world of the living, and there would be no time to live if we spent too much time thinking about the dead. Two minutes when the news is heard and an occasional passing recollection thereafter is about as much mourning as the average man can reasonably expect from most of those who knew him; it is entirely intelligible if my friends feel that they have done their mourning for me and owe me no more grief at any later date, when the story can no longer be denied.

IV

It appears also that practically all of my friends have read Mark Twain, or at least heard him quoted; for they were few indeed who, on seeing me reappear in the flesh, did not remark that the report seemed to have been greatly exaggerated. Endeavoring to escape that cliché, I contented myself with saying when comment was called for that it was at least premature; but I begin to wonder if that is altogether true.

For if I remember correctly the science I once studied (and if it has not since then been turned upside down, as other sciences have been), from the biologist's point of view we start dying the moment we are born—which is only another way of saying that every organism exists in time as well as in space, that it is not quite the same at any moment as it was the moment before. So, if I have an actuarial expectation of another quarter century of life, about two-thirds of all that will ever have been Davis has gone past already; from the time angle, I am two-thirds dead.*

I do not pretend to have any clear idea of what Time is (or Space either); Sir Arthur Eddington's famous diagram of the Present as a moving point between the infinite cones of the Past and the Future may mean something to Eddington, but it does not help the layman much. H. G. Wells, lately correcting in the *Saturday Review of Literature* the too extensive inferences that some people drew from the concept of Time as the fourth dimension which he once presented in *The Time Machine,* remarks that Time differs from other dimensions in that you can travel along it in only one direction. (And, it might be added, you must travel in that direction, at ever-increasing speed, whether you like it or not. As Don Marquis said about being fifty, a couple of years later you are sixty, and ten minutes after that you are eighty-five.)

Wells adds that "we live in measurable bits of time," but very small bits apparently, and quotes a suggestion of Sir Edwin Ray Lankester that perhaps "our brain cells live for an instant as the blood and fresh oxygen pulse to them and then become inactive till the next heartbeat reawakens them." Maybe so; at any rate it is obviously an unwarranted simplification to speak of a personality. If the brain lives in each fresh heartbeat, a man who has lived seventy years is a sequence of something like two and a half billion transitory personalities, whose resemblance is sometimes close and sometimes remote. The conclusion is substantially true even if the premise be a little shaky, as almost anybody can testify when meeting an old friend after ten years' separation. He is not the man he used to be—maybe better, probably worse, but certainly not the same.

The photographer can abstract the outward appearance of a single one of these personalities from the rest, but only the outward appearance; we habitually talk as if we could manage a sort of psychic photography, grasping the personality as it is at the moment; but it will not look quite the same to any two observers, no outsider can penetrate very deep, and in any case what you are trying to photograph is changing under your eyes much more rapidly than its outward appearance. To take an obvious instance—a man may look pretty much

* Charlie Merrill tells me that Montaigne thought of this before I did. But I leave it in the text; it is true enough to be passed along, for the benefit of others who have not read Montaigne.

the same, changed in expression no doubt but not in feature, the moment after he has been fired from a job he had held twenty years and expected to hold for the rest of his life, as he looked the moment before. But he is not the same and will never be the same again; even if he gets a better job and keeps it, the shock, the reminder of insecurity, the loss of prestige will have left permanent scars on all of his successive personalities thereafter.

Because our psychic mechanism is such that we must live for the most part in the present, we cannot manage this concept of the individual as a moving and changing picture; as a working hypothesis we must abstract the average of a comparatively few of his personalities and say, "That is the man." We used to omit his childhood from the excerpt, but the psychologists have taught us that that is a mistake; we still omit as a rule his old age, or the years after his activity has slowed down, for whatever reason; when we think of Napoleon we think of the average of all the Napoleons, say from 1795 to 1815; but we leave the six years between Waterloo and his death out of account. Yet the fat and ailing gentleman who lived on St. Helena was Napoleon; not the Napoleon of 1796 or of 1807 (again one must simplify, for there were many Napoleons in each of those years), but certainly *a* Napoleon—and indeed a Napoleon who had considerable effect on the subsequent history of Europe. A good many of the second guesses by spinning which he whiled away his leisure on St. Helena were woven into the fabric—the ideal if not the real fabric—of the Second Empire.

A rough average of a period of months or years is likely to be not so very far wrong as a working hypothesis; but our craving for stability is apt to make us forget how soon even these provisional abstractions become outdated. Hitler has displayed an unusual continuity of purpose and fixity of ideas, but the post-Munich Hitler is not, cannot be, the pre-Munich Hitler; such a triumph as he won in September 1938 by the superior force of his personality must have its effect on what is loosely called the character of any man.* It is nonsense to speak of

* As it certainly did. Why should Hitler have seized what was left of Czechoslovakia six months after he had promised the world to leave it alone, when he could have dominated Central Europe by subtler means without disillusioning the appeasers? No rational explanation will hold water; the only plausible theory is that his unbroken triumphs had engendered in him that confident insolence that the Greeks called *hubris*. In Greek tragedy it was invariably punished, and usually in Greek history as well: from which optimists have drawn the conclusion that Hitler too, having gone too far, must meet with retribution. It would be unsafe to suppose that there is any *must* about it; the laws of art are not necessarily valid in the world of events, and the historical instances are too few for confident induction. Genghis Khan also went too far, and then kept right on going.

the Lincoln of 1864; even with the crudest of abstractions there were half a dozen successive Lincolns in 1864. To be sure in Lincoln, as in most other individuals, there were certain characteristics that changed much more slowly, so slowly that we may think of them as permanent features of character. But of the manifestations of these traits the most that can truly be said is that some things are a little less impermanent than others.

v

We do not like to think of these matters, as a rule, because it is unpleasant to be reminded that we seem to be subject, like the rest of the cosmos, to the Second Law of Thermodynamics; that we are steadily running down. For a while, in some respects, the trend of the curve may be upward; the Shakespeare (an abstraction from innumerable momentary Shakespeares) who wrote *Hamlet* was not the Shakespeare who wrote *Love's Labour's Lost;* we say he was a better and greater Shakespeare, but it may not have seemed so to the self-observing mechanisms of that personality; he must have known that he was older, that he tired more easily; he had learned a good many things in the intervening years that could have been no fun for him to find out, however they broadened and deepened his understanding. But sooner or later for every man the curve turns downward, unless he escapes the misfortune of living too long by what may be the almost equally serious misfortune of dying too soon. (To this fairly obvious truth more attention might be paid by the income tax laws, which permit deductions for "the exhaustion, wear and tear, including obsolescence, of property used in the trade or business," unless that property happens to be a man's own energies and own brain.)

Somewhere in each human being's life there must be an optimum point, a moment when the average of all his successive personalities is higher than it ever was before, or will ever be again. But he can never identify that point himself; whether things to date have been good or bad, he usually hopes and very often believes that they are going to be better. Nor can outsiders discern that optimum point except in retrospect, and then none too confidently. Lincoln, almost alone among great men, seems to have died exactly at his peak; the average of all the Lincolns was higher on April 14, 1865, than it had ever been before—or might ever have been again.

Most people no doubt live too long—yet you cannot always be sure that even the elderly have lived long enough. It might have seemed to John Quincy Adams, leaving the White House in his sixty-second

year—the first of Presidents, except his father, to be denied re-election—
that he had passed his peak, that the average of all the John Quincy
Adamses would never stand so high again; yet a good deal of the best
of John Quincy Adams was still to come. Julius Caesar's average might
be higher if he had died a year or two earlier, before he had been too
much infected by Cleopatra's ideas—or it might be higher if he had
lived another twenty years.

These examples from the great may seem remote from a discussion
of the average man, but they have their bearing. When we say that X
is dead we mean the average of all the X's—an average different for
each observer, and none of them perhaps very close to the average that
might be computed by Omniscience. But what the phrase really implies is that a moving picture has ended, that the succession of innumerable more or less different X's has stopped, there will never be
any more of them. Going into the movie theater you ask the usher
if the feature is over; no, he says, it is only half over. So when a middle-aged man says in a moment of weariness that he is half dead, he is
telling the literal truth.

To say then that the report of my death was premature was to speak
inexactly; it would have been more correct to say that it was two-
thirds true, or perhaps even more. For at least two-thirds of all the
Davises have passed on and are not coming back. (A good many men,
and women, have tried sometimes to resurrect one of those vanished
personalities, but without success; the best you can hope for is to find,
as did the hero of *Conrad in Quest of His Youth,* something roughly
similar, and approximately as satisfactory.) The young man who was
mistakenly reported to have been drowned in 1916, himself an average
impression created on the senses by the rapid succession of thousands
of bits of film, is dead, and I cannot regret him very much; he was a
good deal of an ass, he muffed some excellent opportunities—yet he
had possibilities that his successors might have realized, and did not.
Of those successors some few, I hope, were worth being remembered
a little, and missed a little; but more than I like to think of are well
buried, with no tears shed even by the current average who inherits
what is loosely termed their identity.

To go away, said some Frenchman, is to die a little; true enough,
but to stay where you are is also to die a little; in the midst of life we
are in death, and the fear of dying (for there are people who fear
dying in itself, aside from the pain and inconvenience of the final illness) ought to be mitigated by the reflection that we are dying all the
time, and that most of the job has already been done. Few of the peo-

ple I know are afraid of death, except as it might affect persons or institutions more or less dependent on them; which means that what they are afraid of is not death but the cessation of activity and usefulness. With regard to that not much can be said except that it is going to happen to us all some day, no matter how much we dislike the idea; and that to worry about it in advance is likely to make it happen all the sooner.

At any rate, the next time I am reported dead I shall not dignify the rumor with a denial. If it is not yet entirely true, people will find that out in due time.

ON THE EVE: REMINISCENCES OF 1913

[*This article first appeared in the* Forum *in 1931. The time of writ-ing—though more than halfway as far back in years, and equally out of the memory of more than half the human race—was very different from that being remembered. It was after the fall (two falls, in fact—World War and World Depression), while 1913 was prelapsarian. This arti-cle, however, tells not about the loss of innocence but about the quality of innocence; it tells something about the world of 1913, in particular about young American men and women at that time, and hence (some-where in there) about Davis himself then. In such a work, references to matters of otherwise long-dead interest are part of the whole picture, so once again I have cut nothing.*]

It was lately and casually remarked in public print that 1913 was the peak year of human felicity; to which opinion persons older than its author, and persons younger, have taken some excep-tion. Everybody, they object, thinks that the peak of human felicity was the year in which he first began to sit up and take notice. Why should a man who happened to leave college in 1913 erect an accident of chronology into a philosophy of history, to the discredit of all the years in which other men left college and went out to see if the uni-verse was as represented? . . . Well, I shall try to tell you.

Granted that I am prejudiced in favor of 1913 because it was the year in which I first came to the surface. Granted that the middle gen-eration to which I now belong finds the Golden Age always in the past—the good old days when you could get a dinner with wine for what the hors-d'oeuvres cost now, when traffic and livers were less con-gested, and everything was veiled with a glamor which seems beyond recapture. Granted too that for the young, except in times of direst cataclysm, the Golden Age is always here and now, so that Ovid spoke for all the Younger Generations of all time when he wrote:

Prisca juvent alios, ego me nunc denique natum
Gratulor; haec aetas moribus apta meis.

Still, I think that we of 1913 found a better here and now than any generation which will follow us for some decades to come. Every younger generation is the heir of all the ages; but in our time the assets of the estate had accumulated to a legacy beyond all imagining, and we had not yet discovered that they were offset by some appalling liabilities. In other words, we came up before the war—just before the war—in what seems to the retrospective eye an age of incredible innocence and security.

II

Security. . . . For forty years in Europe, for fifty years in America, there had been no great war to check material and intellectual progress. Wars were still fought, but only in remote and romantic regions such as Manchuria, South Africa, the Balkans, Mexico; and only outlandish nations engaged in them on any considerable scale. Never since the Pax Romana had the Western world had so long a breathing spell, and never had it been so well equipped to take advantage of it. Wealth piled up at a rate undreamed of; there was more ease, more leisure for thought as well as recreation. Problems still existed, but it was generally agreed that human ingenuity and good will would solve them in the course of time.

Even in Europe, where I was living when the year began, the average man had never felt so secure. There was an increasing tension in international relations, diplomats exchanged politely menacing notes, general staffs laid plans for invasions, military budgets grew ever larger, there were recurrent crises. But of all this the average man knew only what he read in the papers; whereas he had daily first-hand knowledge of the growing internationalism of business, travel, sport, amusement that promised to make frontiers in Europe no more than lines on the map. There had been internationalism before, but it was limited to the Church, the nobility, the educated classes. This new internationalism touched, in the cities at least, everyone.

So war seemed an outgrown bogyman of the childhood of the race. Was there a crisis? Well, there had been a crisis year before last and would be a crisis year after next; but the issue would be no more than a diplomatic triumph of one side or the other, the resignation of one Minister of Foreign Affairs, and the decoration of his rival. Mr. Normann Angell had lately demonstrated that war was no longer profitable even to the victors; so if the danger ever became real the international bankers would prevent war. Or the international Socialists; or, if all else failed, the German Emperor, whose quarter-century of peaceful rule we were just then celebrating, would interpose his unanswerable veto.

So most of Europe felt, outside the governing circles. But how much more secure was America! Europe, to us, was the storied Old World, whose cathedrals and castles we viewed on summer tours but whose problems lay outside our sphere. We had problems of our own, about which the muckrakers had for some years been making a loud disturbance; but in 1912 we had gone to Armageddon, and most of us had come home fairly well satisfied with the result. The moderates had elected Wilson, the radicals had got rid of Taft, and the conservatives could thank God that at any rate they had beaten Roosevelt. Now the obviously needed reforms could be enacted, without much danger that reform would run wild.

True, 1913 was a year of business depression, as anyone who was then hunting his first job must remember. But the depression was easily explained. Republicans blamed it on a Democratic administration, Democrats laid it to the machinations of Republican wielders of the Money Power who wanted to discredit the administration. In any case, the business cycle was as much a part of the order of nature as seedtime and harvest. No one dreamed that perhaps our whole system had some incurable defect. There would be ups and downs in business as in international politics; but nothing really disastrous could ever happen again.

In this confidence we who came into our inheritance in 1913 could feel free to give our attention to the normal concerns of young people— love, amusement, and ideas. It seems to me that never since then has amusement had quite the tang or ideas quite the confident assurance; that even love has never since been quite so delicately flavored a blend of reality and illusion. . . . Laugh, if you like; but let me tell you.

III

Innocence and security. . . . But it did not seem innocent at the time; that was part of its charm. Our moral mentors told us that it was an age of unprecedented license and corruption, and that we boys and girls who had just cracked our shells were a brood of vipers from the pit. Why? Well, a fundamental change in manners, first visible two or three years earlier, was now in full swing; and behind it lay an almost equally fundamental change in ideas. The resultant product was what we then called, and not altogether unjustly, the emancipation of women. It was at last being admitted that women were people, even if all the implications of that concession were not yet apparent. The intellectual double standard had broken down, and the clergy correctly foresaw that the breakdown of the physical double standard would be an early consequence.

This is old stuff now, but it was new stuff then, and what has happened in subsequent decades of the new era was less decisive than what happened in the first two years. The change was the fruit of half a century's fermenting ideas; but what touched it off, about 1911, was the accidental coincidence of the revival of dancing and a wave of moral reform. Everbody was dancing now. The slashed skirts invented to make dancing easier had disclosed the long-guarded secret that ladies had legs; respectable women in increasing numbers had begun to smoke, and to drink in public places. Worst of all, it was now permissible for men and women, together, to talk about sex, provided it was treated on a high plane, as a social problem that could never have any personal application. (I would not say it never did have a personal application, but that happened more rarely than young people of today might believe.) But sex talk first came in by a side door.

Past centuries had accepted prostitution as a necessary evil. The nineteenth century still accepted it, on condition that it was never mentioned. But about 1910 there began a successful agitation for the abolition of the red-light districts of American cities; and to abolish them you had to mention them. Suddenly nice women discovered that what they had always known but had never dared to talk about could be discussed with propriety, provided you called it the white slave problem and insisted on the need of wiping out this blot on civilization. It was assumed in those days that every prostitute was an unwilling victim, a white slave, and that the lords of this nefarious traffic daily prowled the streets in search of new prey.

Hence the story of the young matron from Glen Ridge, or Garden City, or New Rochelle—everybody who told it knew somebody who knew her personally, and it was as much as your life was worth not to believe it—who came to town for a day's shopping and sat down in a subway car beside a man who stealthily pricked her with a poisoned needle; whereupon she lost consciousness and was carried off—over his shoulder, presumably—to a life of shame. Hence the frequent arrest of unfortunate males who had happened to sit down in subway cars beside women with hives and active imaginations. Hence a flood of plays about virtuous girls trapped by white slavers—plays that were denounced by the clergy, endorsed by forward-looking social workers, raided by the police, and fierily defended in magazine articles on "Public Conscience and the Stage."

Naïve? Childish? Unreal? Yes, as a childish unreality hangs over all the doings of the Golden Age. But I think it was healthier than the bored indifference with which the public, in the days of prosperity and prohibition, regarded the doings of our racketeers; not to mention the scandalous disclosures about the doings of the New York vice squad and women's court some years ago. The public conscience of 1913 may have been adolescent and hysterical; still there was a public conscience. We may have misconceived our problems and have been largely mistaken in what we tried to do about them; still, we felt that when there was a problem something could be and ought to be done about it. Such a public conscience, municipal and national, did not reappear for nearly two decades. New York is a far more civilized city now than it was a few years ago; but it needed the double impact of hard times and some atrocious scandals to make us go back to the house-cleaning job that John Purroy Mitchel began in 1913.

At any rate, the white slavery uproar gave the women freedom of speech such as had not been known in centuries, just at the moment when they gained an unprecedented freedom of movement. Before 1911 Virtue had been segregated almost as closely as Vice. Young men might prowl about, but nice girls went out only under chaperonage, to selected places; and the middle-aged of both sexes resigned themselves to the somnolent fireside as a matter of course.

The new dances changed all that; anybody could dance them and everybody tried. Above all it was the age of dancing—and of rejuvenation. Father and mother, puffing away in the turkey trot, worked the fat off their bodies and their minds too; for the moment, all the world seemed young. The frontier of senescence had all at once been pushed back twenty years, so that we who were just beginning could count on a youth far longer than any generation before us had ever known.

IV

It ran all over the world, this dancing craze, the latest and most pervasive phase of the internationalism of culture and interest that had grown up in decades of peace. In London and Paris, Berlin and New York, the surface of society, the interests of the people one met, were the same; all the world over it was the age of tango teas. Not that many of us could dance the tango, though we all tried; nor did we drink much tea. In fact we did not drink much of anything; in a world so full of a number of things liquor was a subsidiary item; we used it as the spark, not as the fuel.

Smoking, for the girls, was a more important gesture. All young people want to kick up their heels and defy convention; most of them would prefer to do it at a not too heavy cost. As a play of Shaw's then current put it, they need to lose their respectability while retaining their self-respect. His heroine did that by going to jail for beating up on a cop, but for most girls of the day smoking met the need. It had till lately been a badge of infamy, it still aroused the fury of conservatives; yet no sensible person could believe it did any real harm. As a safety valve, the girls have never had anything like it.

But it was not only what the girls did that excited the conservatives, but where they did it. Now that Vice had been driven out of the restricted district and Virtue had been lured away from the fireside, institutions sprang up—mostly around Times Square—for the entertainment of both. We called them cabarets; they were much like the modern night club except that they were day clubs too, doing their biggest business at the tango tea. Before about 1912 it was generally true that the righteous could be seen in certain places, the wicked in certain others; now the two streams intermingled for the first time. . . . So nice girls went to tango teas at cabarets, and drank cocktails, and smoked cigarettes, and talked sex with boys; and of course there was a tremendous uproar.

The clergy trumpeted denunciations, and lay conservatives joined in. Indignant Senior takes his pen in hand to write to the *Times*: "Who is at home now? All are hasting and chasing after the Great God Amusement." So Indignant Senior was writing in Babylon, when he had to chop his complaint in a brick. A bishop, rarely liberal, advises his clergy to stop denouncing the slit skirt—which was going out of style anyway—and instead preach Jesus Christ and Him crucified; with the approving echo of an editorial writer who observes that holy men need not dwell in detail on unholy things, since "women who listen to sound religious and ethical teaching will not dress immodestly." The police order all cafés but John Dunston's to close at one A. M., Mayor Gaynor denouncing them as "places of all-night orgies, drunkenness, and shamelessness." Thomas Healy, locking his bar at the appointed hour, advises his guests that the law permits them to stay and finish their food; whereupon the police swarm in and throw the diners out by force. (As it happened, in their enthusiasm they also threw out the District Attorney, so that crusade was promptly stepped on.)

This Thomas Healy was renowned for his exorbitance; he charged a quarter for a cocktail or highball which at any other cabaret cost fifteen cents. But even Healy had never heard of the cover charge. It was, you perceive, a simple age; when the Stock Exchange table took up half a column in the newspaper, and a dinner with wine could be had for half a dollar. Not the best wine, or the best dinner, but good enough for youth. And orchestra seats at the theater were two dollars apiece; and after the theater you could take your girl to a cabaret, and dance and drink till closing time for two or three dollars more. . . .

But it was not mere cheapness that gave a tang to amusement; it was our conscious defiance of conventions we did not respect. There were conventions which most of us did respect, but they were not yet in question. (For a minor instance, you could take your girl to Maxim's or Bustanoby's; you might perhaps take your wife to Joel Rinaldo's, but never your fiancée.) We leaped defiantly over the molehills our elders had made into mountains; having thus proved our strength and spirit we felt no need to explore the real mountains that loomed ominous a little farther on. They called us vile and abandoned, but we knew we were nothing of the sort; we had merely looked over the conventions of the day and rejected those which seemed superannuated. From the purely hedonistic standpoint, I think we got more fun out of life than the young people of a later age when no conventions were any more than what Mr. Cabell calls "inefficient and outmoded monsters in the way."

v

We had ideas. Bernard Shaw had provided most of them, but a score of English writers were following the trail he blazed. It was in England, I think, that the pre-war generation was most promising— boys and girls who were keen and zestful, at once polished and enthusiastic. (Those lightfoot lads are dead now, or disheartened; and the rose-lipped girls grow old without husbands.) American writers still lagged behind. The big problem novel of 1913 was Mr. Winston Churchill's *The Inside of the Cup,* dealing with the agitations of an Episcopal clergyman who was not sure his church was right about divorce; and Mr. Henry Sydnor Harrison was the rising hope of American letters. Poetry made a better showing; a year or so before, it had broken out like a rash all over the corn belt, and now a poet sat on every fence post, caroling free verse. Pretty good verse, too; those blended carolings seemed only the prelude to a great national festival of song—but the prelude turned out to be all of the show. Where are those poets now? Some of them write good biographies of Lincoln and some write bad biographies of Lincoln; some of them write indifferent fiction, and the most have merely folded up in silence.

But though we still had to import most of our ideas, we had them; and each of us believed that his own idea would presently bring into being the all-but-perfect society. The march of civilization had freed man from his traditional worries—food and security. Ruinous wars, destructive social upheavals were as certainly outgrown as famine, pandemic diseases, religious bigotry. Man was free to think, he could think boldly, for the machinery of society was foolproof. If society still needed improvement, that could be accomplished by the direct primary, or the popular election of senators, or the initiative, referendum, and recall; or by giving the vote to women.

More and more woman suffrage became the most discussed of issues; but it was only an aspect of the profounder issue of feminism—perhaps the most widespread and certainly the most exciting of the millennial hopes of the time. Women wanted to be people—to step down from their Victorian pedestals and associate with men on the same level. We young men wanted no Victorian slave-goddesses, but comrades and companions, free and equal, who would be intelligently interested in our interests, and who of course would also feel for us, and inspire in us, that mysterious emotional intoxication that the nineteenth century called romantic love.

Well, the ladies came down—farther down, perhaps, than they expected, but few people would doubt that the world is on the whole a good deal better off. But you can't have everything, and we pre-war feminists expected it; most of us would have been shocked if we had foreseen that fifteen years later André Maurois would describe modern love as a sort of sensual friendship. We wanted friendship and we wanted sensuality; but we also wanted and expected more—more, perhaps, than there is.

But in 1913 we did not know it was more than there is. We wanted and got girls who were friends and comrades; but they had not yet left off being a little remote and mysterious. Physically, they were swathed from neck to instep, as women always had been; even when they bathed in the surf they wore knee-length skirts, and stockings. But their clothes looked all right at the time, as whatever girls are wearing at any time looks all right to boys of their own age. Chubbiness, in those days, was the feminine ideal; the boyish form was still unknown, and Bonwit Teller's advertisements pictured corsets for the normal woman such as Bonwit Teller still may sell, but only Lane Bryant would dare to advertise.

But these were mysteries, at least in theory, to the young men of 1913; and in such matters theory counts for more than practice. Mentally, too, the girl of 1913, emancipated though she tried to be, had her reticences which would have seemed stuffily prudish a little later, after we had heard of Freud. We stood just on the threshold of revelation, and had not learned that there too we expected more, perhaps, than there is. . . .

Yes, love in those days was a delicately flavored blend of reality and illusion, of candor and mystery. You took a girl to a tango tea; she drank with you and smoked with you, like a man and a brother. As a person, a free and equal comrade, intelligently interested in the world you and she were going to live in, she talked to you—about everything. "Everything" generally meant sex; it startled you to realize that this creature whom your early training and the books you read had taught you to consider as something strange, mysterious, and apart was a human being like yourself, with a body and a mind—two attributes which nineteenth-century doctrine had generally denied her. But just as you felt that this matter-of-fact impersonal discussion might be dimming an ancient glamor she did something, or said something, or looked something that made you realize that after all she was a creature of another and an incalculable sort. She was at once the seeker and the sought, a comrade and a mystery.

So we played our romantic comedy, and never dreamed that other actors, with other lines to speak, were about to burst in from the wings.

VI

Well, there is no use now in crying over spilt milk; especially as there was never so much milk in the pitcher as we thought. Our aspirations were fantastic and our doings absurd, considering the tremendous irony of what was coming; we look back at our unsuspecting selves as a Greek audience must have looked at the pride of unsuspecting Oedipus. What we did and what we hoped for alike seem naïve, childish, unreal.

Any tendency to humility that we of 1913 may possess has been abetted by our juniors. They tell us, truly, that we were a foolish and visionary lot, misled by all sorts of illusions. I understand that all that has been changed. "Post-war minds," writes the possessor of one of those minds in the *Outlook,* "have been disciplined and disillusioned." To the middle-aged observer the disillusion is more apparent than the discipline—except in the case of those unfortunates who, to buy release from the painful necessity of thinking, have sold their souls to the Party Line. Even the disillusion is selective; the post-war mind sees through the illusions of 1913, but I am not so confident as some of its possessors that it has attained to intuitive perception of eternal truth. But that may be just as well. Illusion is the most powerful of motive forces. Even our illusions of 1913 might have carried us a long way, though probably not where we expected.

Like all younger generations, we knew a great many things that are not so; but we meant well. I am old-fashioned enough to believe that, other things being equal, good intentions are more useful than bad intentions, or no intentions at all; but we, the last generation for some decades to live in a world of innocence and security, shall probably also remain for some decades the last that could have much faith in good intentions as such. The lesson of August 1914 was reënforced in October 1929; we live in a world of peril and uncertainty, paved with the good intentions of our ancestors—paving stones which have too often turned into stumbling blocks.

With an irrational optimism befitting an alumnus of the absurd age in which I came to the surface, I still believe that higher peaks of human felicity may be ahead; that our race, if it keeps on trying, might make a quite habitable place of the planet on which it resides. But it will be some time before anybody can expect the millennial dawn as confidently as young people expected it in the age of tango teas.

GRANDEURS AND MISERIES OF OLD AGE

[*This represents a forty-year jump from the time of the tango teas, almost the whole span of his career. When he wrote this for* Harper's *there were still to be a few fairly good years for him, though he was in fact recovering from the first of his "hypertensive accidents." He was therefore "on warning," but he did not let that show in the article. Minor cuts.*]

I am almost sixty-four years old. That is not very old by modern standards, especially in a country whose benevolent government urges on me the advantages of being older still. When I am sixty-five, the Bureau of Internal Revenue assures me, I shall be able to deduct another $600 from my taxable income; and if I have the additional felicity to become blind, I can deduct some more.

I have no ambition to go blind at any age, despite this allurement; for that matter I am not anxious to be sixty-five, though I shall be unless I die pretty soon. My fan mail includes a good many gleeful predictions that I am going to be lynched; but barring that misfortune, I ought to be good for another ten or fifteen years if there is anything in the doctrine of hereditary longevity. But no matter how long I may last I am not persuaded that the best is yet to be, even by Catherine Drinker Bowen's eloquent disquisition in *Harper's* on the magnificence of age. I recognize and applaud her endeavor to reassure us that what is going to happen to all of us, whether we like it or not, is really something pretty good; but I cannot feel that the general public can draw much encouragement from the truly magnificent old age of the various worthies she mentions, notably Mr. Justice Oliver Wendell Holmes.

It is no doubt true, as she says, that "luck being equal, whether a man at eighty finds himself reaping the harvest or the whirlwind depends on how he has spent his forties and thirties and twenties." But luck is not equal; and it may be that to be an Oliver Wendell Holmes or a John Dewey at ninety you had to be a Holmes or a Dewey from the start, both in physical constitution and in potential mental capacity.

I once asked John Dewey how he maintained such intellectual and physical activity at an advanced age, and he said that when you have survived a childhood in Vermont you can take just about anything that happens to you afterward. I have no statistics on the juvenile mortality in Vermont in the eighteen-sixties; no doubt all those who survived were tough, but they were not all Deweys. I have a friend aged eighty-four who is better than I am; but to judge from the record she always was, at any age.

To feel that Mrs. Bowen has been overly optimistic is not to accept the dark view of old age held by the author of Ecclesiastes; but that is partly because medical science has made considerable advances since his day. Considerable, but not yet enough. When the grinders cease because they are few, the dentist can replace them; when eyes that look out of the windows be darkened, the oculist can take effective measures. But who can give us back those elastic arteries? (Since writing the foregoing, I have happily discovered that bourbon retards their ossification.)

[· · ·]

Perhaps in this matter there is no such thing as the average man. It is common knowledge that some people grow old faster than others, and not till lately has there been official demarcation of the frontier between youth and age. In the fall of 1953 the President said that one reason he appointed Earl Warren as Chief Justice was "his relative youth"—sixty-two. On the same day the Governor of Puerto Rico pardoned a prisoner on account of "his advanced age"—sixty-three. Between those two years, then, must lie the Great Divide, though I seem to have been working so hard that I never noticed it when I passed over it.

But in their relation to old age men differ vastly not only in their abilities and their physical strength, but economically and occupationally. If the insurance companies can be believed, I cannot say much about the average man either; for they tell us, or used to tell us, that 99 per cent of all men of my age are dependent on their children, or pensions, or charity. And even among the one per cent of us who can still make a living there are differences—for instance, whether we are responsible only for ourselves or for organizations and institutions. Most of us in my business, the news business, are responsible only for ourselves; in my particular branch of it there are three men who are ten years older than I am and still going strong; and one of the greatest of editorial writers, the late E. M. Kingsbury, was still at it when he was ninety. But if one of us should go haywire, he could be bounced out with no loss to anybody but himself. The danger that men in responsible executive positions might go haywire is the most serious hazard of old age.

The steady physical deterioration that afflicts most of us is deplorable, but so long as it remains merely physical it is not disastrous. Far worse is the danger that in advanced years a man's mind might go back on him at some unpredictable moment and drive him to make mistakes that would have been unthinkable a year or two earlier. That is why some of our aged statesmen, to all appearance as good as ever, nevertheless find it advisable to retire before that unforeseeable day when all at once they will not be as good as ever, or good at all. Some of them do not retire; Gladstone was beginning to slip, physically at least, in his ministry, though he saw it and left office before the consequences became too serious. Hindenburg, elected president of the German Reich at seventy-seven, hoped (so Walter Goerlitz tells us) that he would not be left in office till he became senile; "for one never knows one's self when that is happening." He was left in office; it happened, but he did not know it was happening; and that was one of the reasons for the downfall of the German Republic.

The older a man grows, the greater the danger that this will happen to him. Against this and minor miseries of age, what are the offsets? Not all, I am afraid, that have sometimes been recommended. Much has been written about the joys of calm contemplation, in old age, of a long and honorable life. But it is a rare man, unless he has great skill at self-deception, who can review a career, however bespangled with good deeds and glory, without his eye's lighting on something that could have been done otherwise and better, and might have made a considerable difference if it had been done better; but it is too late to do anything about it now. The pleasure in such retrospection seems to me by no means unalloyed.

[He then discusses two other oft-proposed compensations of old age: the "joy of seeing long endeavor come to ultimate fruition," and the consolation that "most of your troubles are behind you." But, he argues, the endeavors very often fail to bear fruit, or bear fruit only very exiguously, or one may simply not be able to enjoy the fruit any more. (Here he tells of vaudeville trouper Frank Bacon, who waited a lifetime for a "great idea" to pan out; finally rewarded with a Broadway hit in his old age, he said: "Well, I can still use the money.") As

*for the second, he holds it just as likely that most of your troubles are
ahead of you, no matter how bad you think things have been.*]

There is also mere curiosity. I hope to keep on living for a while to
see what happens, but I realize that I may not like it at all. Abraham
Lincoln, if he had lived another ten years, would have had a very poor
opinion of what the United States had become; but it is always possible that with his tremendous personal prestige and his unequaled
political skill he might have prevented it from becoming what it was
by 1875. Lesser men can have no such expectation.

There is, however, one offset to the inevitable infirmities, at least for
us of the one per cent who have been lucky enough to be able to keep
our noses above water; and that is freedom—freedom from the passions of youth. I don't mean what you mean; from that particular passion, I should imagine, few men or women are ever happy to be set
free. We read in the pages of history that Sophocles the tragic poet, at
the age of eighty-nine, was asked by some impertinent young squirt if
he were still able to enjoy the pleasures of love. "My friend," said
Sophocles solemnly, "I give thanks to the gods every day that I have
been freed from that tyrannous desire." It is, however, the general
opinion of men old enough to have an opinion that Sophocles was
merely making the best of a bad job—whistling in the graveyard of
his capacities.

The dominant passion of most young men—and middle-aged men,
for that matter—is a lust for Success; they bend most of their efforts
toward making a name, or a fortune, or both. But the time comes
when they have either made it or not, and it is too late to do much
more about it. Accordingly—always provided you have done well
enough to keep afloat—ambition fades away; you no longer give a
damn, or at any rate not much of a damn.

This too needs qualification, in both directions. A senator who in
his eighties is defeated—as several senators have been—for re-election to
a seat that he has held for thirty years probably feels even worse about
it than he would have felt thirty years earlier; and those unfortunate
novelists who under some obscure compulsion still push out a book a
year, long after they have nothing left to say, probably hate unfavorable reviews just as much as they did in their youth.

Nor can you ever be quite sure when a man is through. Winston
Churchill, at sixty-two, was a failure. He had been, at times, a considerable figure in each party, but now he was out of both parties; he

had just tried to organize a King's party to support Edward VIII in the abdication crisis and had failed not only immediately but rather ludicrously; he told his friends that he was done for. Three years later he was called on to save his country, and he did it.

But not many of us are Churchills, any more than we are Lincolns. Nevertheless we of the one per cent can savor the sense of freedom that comes from the disappearance of ambition. When we were younger, getting and spending we laid waste our powers—and sometimes, in the headlong drive for success, some of us were in danger of laying waste something still more important, our conscience. A good many young men have sometimes been confronted with something that they know they ought to do; but if they did it, it might have an unfavorable if not disastrous effect on their future. They should have done it anyway, no doubt; but it is a good deal easier not to worry about the effect on your future when your future is behind you.

It is quite true that 'tis man's perdition to be safe when for the truth he ought to die—or, as the phrase is more likely to translate itself in these times, when for the truth he ought to lose his job, with small chance of getting another. But it is, emotionally if not ethically, a somewhat different matter to tell a young man with a wife and children whom he is barely able to support on his salary that for the truth, his wife and children ought to starve too. And that is a situation that increasingly comes up in the present drive, Congressional and local, against freedom of thought—particularly in the schools and colleges where above all freedom of thought must be preserved.

Professors and teachers in schools and colleges are tempted to pull in their horns, to say nothing at all; otherwise their students, or their students' parents, might report them to the American Legion—as has happened—and any deviation from the norm of reactionary thinking will be regarded as subversion. With the result also, as Mrs. Roosevelt reported after her nation-wide travels in the winter of 1953, that the young people who are just coming up and see what is happening begin to be afraid to think and afraid to act, for fear that something they may say or do now will be dug up and thrown at them twenty years later and ruin their careers. (Senator McCarthy has several times damned, or tried to damn, middle-aged men for what they did or said in college and have long since repudiated.) A despotism might be able to stand this loss of heart, though I doubt it; but a republic whose young people are in that state of mind is on its way downhill.

We have got to defeat this attack on the freedom of the mind; and I think we can defeat it if enough of us stand up against it—enough of all kinds of people, rich and poor, young and old. But it takes courage for a young man with a family to stand up to it; all the more obligation on those of us who have nothing left to lose. At any age it is better to be a dead lion than a living dog—though better still, of course, to be a living and victorious lion; but it is easier to run the risk of being killed (or fired) in action if before long you are going to be dead anyway. This freedom seems to me the chief consolation of old age.

POLITICS

[Politics always fascinated Davis. Partly, no doubt, as the living embodiment of American principles: the way our system actually is made to work. Partly, of course, because in his newspaper and radio periods it was a central part of his work. But partly just because he was a Hoosier. After all, as he wrote in 1926, "The essence of Indiana is literature and politics." (In 1926 he could still say this; even then, of course, the word "literature" had to be taken in the wide sense in which, for instance, George Ade and James Whitcomb Riley might be exemplars.) Readers of the first two pieces below will be convinced as to the "politics."

[Much as he dealt with everyday raw politics, very little of his enduring work is directly concerned with it. Typically he treats the issues being decided rather than means of securing public consent to the decisions. Plain politics comes into his writing as background—supplying texture and a practical interpretation to discussions of principle, or providing the realistic surroundings for fictional writings.

[Thus of the three "pieces" below only one originally appeared as an article on politics. The first is a small collection of bits from newspaper stories about national conventions over a period of sixteen years; the second is extracted from a longer article whose subject was really Indiana, not just its conventions. The third is selected from a long profile of Big Bill Thompson. In another part of this book the short stories "Amateur" and "Home Grounds" have political settings, and a great deal of the section on National Affairs has more or less continuous reference to national politics.]

GODFREY GLOOM

[*Everything else in this book was written to endure longer than what a reporter writes today for tomorrow's paper. Even reporting "classics" are usually interesting, outside of possible historical interest in the events they report, only to journalism students. But no editor would feel happy overlooking the warm reminiscences from many old convention followers of the famous Godfrey Gloom. Invented to while away the tedious hours between filing regular news stories on the Democratic Convention at San Francisco in 1920, Gloom quickly became a fixture; he was so well established by 1936 that his "death" after the Philadelphia convention was page-one news. Another reason to include the Gloom stories is that they are practically the only representatives of the genre "dialect humor" in Davis's work, and every Hoosier writer should show what he can do with dialect. The dialect here is suggested with diction and idiom, not with outlandish spellings or its few grammatical errors. But many readers say that after reading some of Mr. Gloom they begin to hear the tone of his voice. It must take them back to a time long dead. In any event, most admirers valued the stories for their re-creation of the excitements and disappointments of our once-greatest shows: the National Conventions of the major parties.*

[*I have picked out a few passages I liked; I hope they are typical and, incidentally, that they capture something of that tone of voice.*]

[*The Democratic Convention in 1920.*]

SAN FRANCISCO, June 26.—Among the oldest of the old-timers who will attend the Democratic Convention is Godfrey G. Gloom, a prominent pawpaw grower of Amity, Ind., who has been a convention addict for fifty years. [. . .] A Times correspondent today found him in the Palace Hotel lobby, looking as if he expected the worst.

"No, I'm not a delegate this year," he said. "I always run for the job and generally get beat, and then I come to the convention to have the satisfaction of seeing what a mess they make out of it. If the Democratic Party had taken my advice—— Why, I says to some of the boys in '96, says I, 'You don't want to fall for that fellow Bryan: he thinks Bacon wrote Shakespeare.' " [. . .]

"I was an original Wilson man in '04, but they laughed at me. Well, the fellows that laughed at me are all postmasters now, and you see what's happened to the original Wilson men like me and Harvey. When I seconded the nomination of Blue Jeans Williams for Governor in '76 some of them told me that a pair of lungs like mine ought to go a long way in the Democratic Party, but lungs was plentiful in those days and brains was unpopular, so I never got very far in politics. Nothing like these prohibition times, when you can't even raise a good breath."

[*The story two days later illustrated one of the delights of the Gloom stories: The sudden revelation that the wit had all along been cutting both ways. He had been comparing this convention with that which had just previously nominated Harding at Chicago.*]

SAN FRANCISCO, June 28.—Whatever other distinctions this present Democratic convention may or may not attain, there is no doubt about its being the scaredest convention that ever convened, in the opinion of Godfrey G. Gloom of Amity, Ind. [. . .]

"There is a great difference between this convention and the gathering of our Republican friends at Chicago," Mr. Gloom observed. "That convention, so far as the rank and file were concerned, seemed to be kind of lacking in conviction. It seemed to me that there was a lamentable air of expediency about it. Nothing like that could be said of this crowd. If I were in a sportive mood I might say that those who haven't the convictions at least have indictments, like Charles F. Murphy; but I am deadly serious. So far as I can learn, every Democratic delegate came here with a heart bulging with convictions, but all the tortures of the Inquisition wouldn't pry out of him what his convictions are."

[*One Democratic hopeful was Attorney General A. Mitchell Palmer, of "Palmer raids" fame during the "Red Scare" of 1919. In a not unhallowed ritual Palmer staffed the convention with Justice Department employees, then rounded them all up with what vagrant hirelings he could find to hold a "demonstration."*]

"Yes, sir," said Godfrey G. Gloom, the oldest living conventioneer, "I witnessed that awe-inspiring manifestation of the people's will, that universal shout of vox populi calling for the name of A. Mitchell Palmer. Seldom have I seen anything that was more imposing, or more of an imposition if you like.

"What this convention will do, I can't say nor what the people want, though from long observation I have come to expect the worst. I don't know who is the people's choice, but if you ask me who is the choice of the United States District Attorneys, the trustees of alien enemy property, the ushers, the assistant Sergeants-at-arms, the convention officers, the street corner bands, and the college students who want to pick up a little money in vacation—I answer that they are unanimously for A. Mitchell Palmer."

[*The convention took 44 ballots to decide on the ticket of Cox and Roosevelt. Gloom's explanation of this choice appeared on Sunday, July 4th.*]

"It's all the fault of this false idea of fair play. The Republicans went and picked out a man nobody wanted and few had ever heard of, and some people here seem to feel it would be unsportsmanlike to take advantage of them."

* * * * *

[*If that was a long and unprofitable convention, it was as nothing to the one four years later in New York. Davis had by this time quit the* Times *to free-lance, but after his Florida disappointment he was glad to find congenial work on special assignment back up North. The convention showed its form from the start.*]

June 25.—Godfrey G. Gloom, the unterrified Hoosier Democrat, was discovered yesterday afternoon by a Times reporter lounging in the basement of the Garden and pensively chewing his gold-mounted quill toothpick.

"What do you think of the opening session?" the reporter asked.

"Well," said Mr. Gloom reflectively, "it has reconciled me to declining years and the inexorable approach of the grim reaper. If there was one thing that this session made clear it was that it pays a Democrat to be dead. If you're alive, it seems that you've got no chance to be nominated for President, at least if you're anybody that's ever been heard of, but the minute you're dead you become the choice of the party.

"Four years ago Woodrow Wilson was alive and in the White House. The unterrified Democracy assembled at San Francisco took forty-four ballots and Wilson never got over two votes on any of them. His strength was precisely as great as that of the three leading comedians of the convention, Bryan and Ring Lardner and Irvin Cobb. But today, Wilson being in his tomb, the convention was willing to nominate him by acclamation.

"[. . .] Yes, sir, Wilson could have had this nomination, and failing Wilson, the evident choice of the convention was Grover Cleveland."

[*The Democrats might have made something of the Teapot Dome
and other scandals revealed during the past winter in investigations
under Senator Tom Walsh of Montana, but Godfrey Gloom was doubtful. On June 26th he quoted Davis's colleague, Arthur Brisbane.*]

"While the Democrats are still making up their minds whether or
not they want Doheny's lawyer [Harry Doheny was the Teapot Dome
lessor] to head up the ticket, the Republicans are trying to make
Standard Oil put down the price of gas, and that, says Brisbane very
truly, is a winning issue.

"If the Democrats nominated George Washington and the Republicans nominated Judas Iscariot and the Republicans cut the price of
gas to ten cents a gallon before election, Judas Iscariot would be the
next president of the United States. Politics is a harmless indoor
sport, but gasoline is what makes the world go round."

[*Former Treasury Secretary William Gibbs McAdoo, supported by
the Drys and the Ku Klux Klan, and Governor Al Smith, wet and
Catholic, were the only strong candidates. They were irreconcilable,
but neither could win against the other. In this classic situation the
next day's papers were busy scouting the form of dark horses.*]

"Do you think it looks like a dark horse for the nomination?" the
reporter asked Mr. Gloom.

"It certainly don't look like any of these here pale horses that have
been trotted out and demonstrated so copiously."

[*The day after that Gloom had replied, when asked why McAdoo
wouldn't take a stand on the Ku Klux Klan, that McAdoo was basically
a Republican.*]

"We Democrats have the curious idea that if we regard something—
like the Klan, for instance—as disgraceful and outrageous then we
ought to say so. You never catch the Republicans doing that if it will
offend any noticeable block of voters.

"The Democrats would rather be right than win and the Republicans would rather win than be right, and it looks as if both sides would
get what they want . . .

"After all, when the Republicans did such a good business selling
gold bricks in 1920 they'd be nothing but fools to try to improve the
grade of their goods before the customers demand it."

[*The next day, on the other hand, the headline said* PARTY DISSEN-
SION PAINS MR. GLOOM.]

"I just heard Newton D. Baker say, 'Four years ago the Republican party abandoned its ideals: where is it now?'

"The answer is, it's in office and intends to stay in office . . ."

[*But in the fight between an outspoken and a weasel-worded plank on the Klan the chairman ruled that the inoffensive version had passed, much to the surprise of some observers. The next day:*]

"What did you think of the fight over the Klan plank?" the reporter asked.

"Well, at least it showed this convention ain't ruled by a machine, not even an adding machine . . ."

[*The next day . . .*]

"How do you think the prospects of the leading candidates look?" the reporter asked.

"Oh, they look right bad, right bad," said Mr. Gloom. "This is a dark night for the nation, in fact, if you believe what was said at the McAdoo consecration service on Sunday.

"The corrupt subsidized press and the liquor interests and the Bolsheviks of Soviet Russia are all bearin' down on us and McAdoo has got to be nominated to save the country. So McAdoo tells us, anyway, and it looks to me very much as if the country ain't goin' to be saved at that price. Looks as if the Bolsheviks are goin' to get full control of this convention and maybe nominate some wild revolutionary like [the ultimate nominee, conservative John W.] Davis or Underwood or Carter Glass.

"The curious thing is that all the Republicans I've talked to seem to think the Democrats should nominate McAdoo too—to save the country from a Democratic administration . . ."

[*Two days later McAdoo's strength had reached its height on the 42nd ballot without pulling enough votes to win; the convention settled down in its deadlock.*]

"What do you think of the continuing deadlock?" the reporter asked.

"It's good and dead," said Mr. Gloom, "one of the most deceased deadlocks I ever did see in my life. Just verifies the suspicion I expressed some days ago that the one fatal handicap on a Democratic candidate in this convention is to have been heard of. Them as hadn't been unfavorably heard of before this convention are being unfavorably heard of now."

[*As the situation continued the same through the next day—the Fourth of July—the reporter had a suggestion.*]

"You remember," the reporter suggested, "that the man who nominated David Franklin Houston asked the delegates not to vote for him?"

"Yes sir," said Mr. Gloom, "and they took his advice by acclamation."

"But perhaps the time has come when Houston might have some chance to break the deadlock."

"Don't you believe it," said Mr. Gloom firmly. "There's nothing in Houston's favor but the fact that a lot of people believe he's more fit to be President than anybody that's been voted for. What of that? There's probably a million people in the United States, male and female, that's more fit to be President than anybody so far mentioned in this convention, or Cal Coolidge or Bob LaFollette either."

[*Two days later a page-one by-line straight news story of Davis's expressed in its brief lead after Saturday's adjournment the way everyone had begun to feel: "Nothing the Democrats did in the Garden yesterday became them like their leaving it." But reconvening after the weekend found them still in much the same stasis, so that on Tuesday Godfrey Gloom had another suggestion as he talked to the reporter.*]

"Curious thing this afternoon when they got that there telegram from President Coolidge thanking them for their condolences—his name got a terrific round of applause—more than they give to any Democratic candidate . . . Thinks I to myself, well now, why wouldn't it be a good idea to nominate Coolidge? We might get in on the distribution of paying jobs then [. . .]

"You may say we wouldn't get our fair half of the public offices since the Republicans got Coolidge's ear first, but on the other hand this convention would be nominating him of its own free will, which is more than could be said of that well steam-rolled action at Cleveland."

[*On Wednesday, July 9th, the* Times *headline read* MR. GLOOM FIGURES ON SETTLING HERE.]

"You're going to be a permanent New Yorker?" the reporter asked.

"Depends on the Democrats. My curiosity having been aroused, I am determined to stay till the end of the convention."

[*Which came after the 103rd ballot.*]

* * * * *

[*In 1928 the Democrats finally nominated Smith, but that wasn't the year to stand up against the promise of a car in every garage and a chicken in every pot. In 1932, though, the Fourth Year of the Abolition of Poverty, to use a phrase coined by Davis in other writings, Godfrey Gloom went to both conventions.*]

CHICAGO, June 13.—[. . .] "What are you doing at a Republican convention, Mr. Gloom?"

"Enjoying myself [. . .] It'll be an unusual and diverting experience, thinks I, to see these fellows trying to explain away hard times and frantically searching the record of the last four years for something they can point to with pride . . ."

[*The headline the next day read* CHICAGO RETICENCE PUZZLES MR. GLOOM.]

"Have you heard anything about who these Republicans are going to nominate for President?" he inquired anxiously.

"Why," said the reporter in some surprise, "they are going to renominate President Hoover, of course."

"Hoover, eh," said Mr. Gloom. "Yes, I would have thought so. But I been in Chicago thirty-six hours and he is the one prominent Republican whose name I haven't heard mentioned yet, in any connection. I hear a lot about Abraham Lincoln and Theodore Roosevelt, and Mellon and Coolidge, and even Frank Smith and Len Small; but not a word about Hoover has come to my ears [. . .]

"I wouldn't be a bit surprised if when the roll-call for nominations comes the spokesman for the California delegation gets up and says, 'I propose the name of a man who—well, you all know who I mean.'

"And everybody will know who is meant, sure enough . . . the man who promised the abolition of poverty."

[*The next day Mr. Gloom was explaining to the reporter his experience in listening to the keynote speech.*]

"I had stepped out in the lobby to get a stogey when Senator Dickinson started his speech, so when I got back I was a little confused. I sat down and listened to this bell-mouthed orator from Iowa describing the happy situation of some country or other, under the guidance of a great Executive, whom, as it happened, he didn't name [. . .]

"Believe me, my young friend, it was a beautiful and beguiling pic-

ture he painted. I shut my eyes and feasted my ears while Senator
Dickinson went on telling about this great Executive who had prevented a catastrophe, averted a financial panic, put millions of men
back to work, and headed off a drop in agricultural prices [. . .] Well,
[a "literary critic"] tells me the hard times are going to create a revival of popular demand for romantic and imaginative literature,
something that bears no relation to the sorrows of the present day."

[*The next day the reporter met Mr. Gloom, who had been looking
for the delegates but found them all out on the Lake Front.*]
"What are they doing out on the Lake Front?" the reporter asked.
"Sinking their convictions in the interest of harmony. [. . .]
"Dr. Butler said the other day, 'There is no place anywhere for
a pussyfooter,' and he was almost exactly right. No place at all but the
White House. And if you think that remark is dictated by partisan
animosity, I invite you to take a look at the behavior of the leading
candidate [Franklin Roosevelt] for the Democratic nomination."
[*Roosevelt's pre-convention twisting had led Davis to say elsewhere
that he was "a man who thinks that the shortest distance between two
points is not a straight line but a corkscrew."*]

[*There were other Democratic candidates, of course, and it took
some jockeying. On June 26th at the Democratic convention—also in
Chicago—the reporter canvassed some of the possibilities with Mr.
Gloom, winding up with a comment that many of them were not
known nationally.*]
"That's one advantage for Al Smith," the reporter ventured. "He
has a name that people remember."
"Yes," said Mr. Gloom, "but so does Roosevelt."

[*The next day Mr. Gloom at first "found secession rife" in the words
of the headline among what he called "the unterrified but frequently
disgruntled Democrats."*]
"I spent a large part of the day lookin' for delegates who would admit they would still vote the Democratic ticket even if they didn't get
just what they wanted, and they were as hard to find as optimists in
Wall Street.
"But Jim Ham Lewis's withdrawal changed all that." [Senator
James Hamilton Lewis had been a favorite son candidate from Illinois; when he released his delegates they swarmed to Roosevelt.] "A
fellow shoved up against me in the corridor of the candidates' floor in

the Congress Hotel and I asked him why he was in such a hurry. 'To get aboard,' he says. 'I hear the Paris embassy is gone, but maybe I can still climb on in time to qualify for the postoffice back in Bingville.' "

[*After that it was a shoo-in.*]

* * * * *

[*The Republican convention for 1936 was in Cleveland. After the shellacking of 1932 it was clear that Republicans would have to woo some Democratic votes. It seemed for a while as if they liked all Democrats but one. In a story datelined* CLEVELAND, *June 13, Mr. Gloom gave an excuse for later going to the Democratic convention, which he expected to be a bore.*]

"These Republicans have said so many kind words about the Democratic party during this convention that I think I'd better make a personal inspection."

[*But Philadelphia was just as he expected. On June 23rd things were so quiet he had trouble finding the convention. On June 24th:*]

"So, Mr. Gloom," said the reporter, "you were successful in finding the convention after all."

"I was," said the veteran, "but for a long time I was in doubt as to just what convention I had found. Readin' the public prints this morning I learn that this is either a Fascist or a Communist convention, according to which Republican newspaper you happen to prefer [Philadelphia was a town then of many Republican papers] but by the time I got myself set down in the gallery I'd begun to think maybe it was a Republican convention."

"What led you to that conclusion?" asked the reporter in surprise.

"The way they were going about it," said Mr. Gloom, "all for harmony and no nonsense about principle."

[*In some doubt, Mr. Gloom finally came on June 27 to reluctant support of the candidate.*]

"What, Mr. Gloom," said the reporter. "After all your political hesitations, have you decided to pledge your allegiance to the Democrats after all?"

"Well, on the whole, and by a slight majority, yes," said Mr. Gloom. "I can't say I've been much impressed by the arguments in Roosevelt's favor [. . .] but after reading the arguments advanced against him I conclude that he must have a good deal of merit after all."

[*On Sunday, June 28, 1936, a page-one headline read* LAST JEFFER-
SONIAN EXPIRES WITH CONVENTION; GODFREY GLOOM A VICTIM OF MODERN
DEVICES.]

Godfrey G. Gloom, the aged Jeffersonian from Amity, Ind., died this
evening as a result of injuries sustained when he was crossing a street
in West Philadelphia on his way to Franklin Field.

Mr. Gloom had leaped, with an agility hardly to be expected in one
of his years, out of the way of a car carrying a radio commentator,
only to be knocked headlong by a motorcycle bearing the plates of a
newspaper photographer [. . .] [In the old tradition of Opera, Mr.
Gloom raised himself on his elbow and delivered himself of a few last
words.]

"It is entirely fitting," Mr. Gloom pursued, "that I should meet
my end through the agency of those gadgets of modern progress, the
radio and newspaper photography. It is these more than anything else
that have ruined what was the most cherished pastime of my declining
years, attendance at national conventions." [He complained of how
in recent years photographers had always been getting between the
speakers and the hearers, shooting off flash bulbs, while . . .] "As for
the radio, its demoralizing effect on convention oratory is well known.
If it had taken the roaring out of oratory it could well be commended,
but it has merely taken out the spontaneity [. . .]

"And in any case," said the oldster, his voice growing stronger now,
"there seems no more place in American politics for a genuine old-
fashioned Jeffersonian. Jefferson has now been endorsed by both parties, and there seems as little prospect that the endorsement will ever
be repudiated as that either party will ever put Jeffersonian doctrines
into practice.

"And maybe," added Mr. Gloom to the astonishment of his hearers,
"that is just as well. For the principles of Thomas Jefferson I have
unshaken respect; but when he translated those principles into concrete policies he did so according to the peculiar conditions of his time,
as any man of sense would have done.

"And surely it is not inexact to characterize his time as the horse-
and-buggy days; to return to it, and to return to the possibility of
literal application of Mr. Jefferson's theories, we should have to cut
the power lines, tear up the railroad tracks, shut down the factories,
and in general return to the economy of 1800.

"I am convinced that if Mr. Jefferson were alive today he would
stick to his principles of standing up for the rights of ordinary people
by whatever means seems most advantageously adapted to that end."

STATE CONVENTION

[*In 1926 Indiana was widely believed to be in sad decline. The Ku Klux Klan controlled the Republican Party with the help of the Anti-Saloon League, and the Republicans had ridden Coolidge's coattails in 1924 to control the state. One of their first enactments was a state prohibition law (the so-called "smell law") more all-embracing in definition of violations and more vindictive in punishment than the national Volstead Act. Of its results Davis wrote the following.*]

No Hoosier who has a treasured bottle anywhere around the house dares to fire his cook, or get into a dispute with the plumber. Plumbers, and carpenters, and readers of gas and electric meters, are said to look for liquor with great diligence when they enter a house; if they can reach it they take some of it; if not they reserve their information in case there is any argument about the bill. In so far as the moral leaders of the United States are laboring to make this a country of spies, of sneaks, of snoopers, and informers (which is pretty far) Indiana undoubtedly has a good running start.

[*But, he pointed out, "As usual, things are not as bad as they sound." In the first place, the Grand Dragon of the Klan had recently been sentenced to twenty years for rape and murder; and although "he managed to run the state government from jail during his trial," he seemed "to be less successful in running it from the remote penitentiary near the Michigan line." Next a Grand Titan was convicted of rape, and Davis thought there was by 1926 a "dislocation of Klan leadership" with "two discordant parties among the sheeted paladins themselves, doubtless the pro-rape and the anti-rape factions."*]

[*As for the Anti-Saloon League, its state superintendent had got so self-important as to rebuke the state Supreme Court for "wet tendencies," and had consequently been cited for contempt. His lawyers offered "the defense that he was only exercising the inalienable right of every citizen to free thought and free speech," but, as Davis said, "when the Anti-Saloon League has to come out for free speech it has lost its Hindenburg Line."*]

[*So, he argued, things were not really so bad; in fact, the Klan had
even had one good effect.*]

. . . the political solidification of most of the intelligent people of the
state. For the Klan in Indiana is essentially a proletarian dictatorship.
Like all proletarian movements, it includes a few astute individuals,
themselves anything but proletarian, who control it and direct it in
their own interests; but its membership is almost exclusively composed
of the hillbillies, the Great Unteachables. And because the state is
controlled by organized ignorance and malice, most of the intellectuals
have been forced together for self-defense.

[*This was in an article called "Have Faith in Indiana," which he
described in a footnote as a "pious effort to defend the old Fatherland
against unjust aspersions," though perhaps it is hardly surprising that
not all Hoosiers appreciated his attentions. The text for his defense
was that "The essence of Indiana is literature and politics"; in these
he claimed "The Hoosier essence is still there." His evidence on the
score of literature was halfhearted, even taking the term in its widest
sense. As to politics, he told about a state convention.*]

After literature, politics—after it only in the temporal sense, before
it in metaphysical pre-existence; for politics in Indiana is alpha and
omega, the beginning and the end. I went to a Democratic State Convention, and any doubts that might have survived as to the still-there-
ness of Indiana were straightway dissipated. It didn't look like the
state conventions I remembered from twenty years ago; among thirteen
hundred delegates there were not half a dozen black frock coats and
string ties, and women were as frequent on the floor as in the gallery.
But they were the same old sort of people; what is more, they behaved
in the same old way.

The business of the convention was the adoption of a platform, and
the selection of a Senatorial candidate to oppose the Honorable and
perennial James Eli Watson. There was a prospect of a fight on the
floor over the platform; a belligerent faction wanted to demand the
repeal of this famous state prohibition law. Now anybody knows what
a Democratic national convention would have done in a situation like
that—it would have fought all day and all night and gone home to vote
for Coolidge. Not so in Indiana. Probably most of the delegates
thought the prohibition law was outrageous, but they were not quite
sure that most of the voters did; the movement to demand repeal, instead of dying with its boots on in full convention, was quietly as-
phyxiated in committee; and the convention unanimously adopted a

platform which referred to prohibition only in opposing unlawful and unconstitutional searches and seizures. (When a Republican convention stands by the Constitution it means it is for prohibition; when a Democratic convention stands by the Constitution it means it is against prohibition.)

Then came the fight for the Senatorial nomination. There were half a dozen candidates between most of whom the differences were merely regional. There was to be sure one wet candidate; he stood for an issue, the paramount issue of the moment; he took his stand firmly and unequivocally on one side of that issue; he represented a Principle. Therefore, he ran sixth in a field of six on the first ballot and practically disappeared off the map on the second. Indiana knows that principles and politics don't mix.

For the rest, there was in the first place Mr. John E. Fredrick, who was supposed to have the favor of Mr. Thomas Taggart. One hears that Mr. Taggart had no favorite, but much of the old organization backed Fredrick. There was also the veteran William A. Cullop, strong in the southwestern part of the state but not much favored elsewhere; and there were three or four others, including a Mr. Stump.

Nobody knew much about this young Mr. Stump, except that he had a good war record and was much in demand as a speaker at high-school commencements. He had no strong political backing, and it did not occur to anybody (until the first ballot showed him running surprisingly well) that a high-school commencement orator makes a wide acquaintance which he can cash in on if he knows how. Mr. Stump knew how; on the second ballot he was second only to Fredrick; but on the third ballot Fredrick threw in his strength, he rose to within a few dozen votes of the six hundred and sixty necessary to a choice, it was perfectly plain that on the fourth ballot Fredrick would go over.

Then something happened. Fredrick had attacked Cullop on the ground that he was too old. Well, thought Cullop, Mr. Stump is young and looks younger; if they want a young man, let them have him. Before the result of the third ballot was announced one county after another began to change its vote, from Cullop to Stump. Cullop had only a hundred or two of votes left, but they were scattered in many counties. County by county, he threw them in—five votes here and seven there, a spoonful at a time but impressive in their cumulative effect. Well-instructed delegates began to shout; the band in the gallery began to play; a score of chairmen of county delegations clamored for the chair's attention to get a chance to change their votes.

Hasty and belated, the Fredrick managers tried to set a backfire; what little undercover strength they had left was thrown in by the same method, the changing of county votes before the result of the ballot was announced. But already they had used almost everything they had, counting on natural momentum to put them over on the next ballot; and in politics as in war the last unbroken reserve turns the tide. Cullop had it—twenty-three votes in his home county which he threw to Stump when the Fredrick managers were just beginning to get up steam. That upset the equilibrium and from that time on it was only a question of who could get on the Stump bandwagon first. In ten minutes Mr. Fredrick had been pulled off the very steps of the throne and tumbled into the junk room.

I have seen a good many conventions, state and national, but I never saw anything so smoothly done as that. Military historians tell us that the Germans won the war of 1870 because while the French were figuring out what was the right thing to do the Germans were doing the right thing by pure reflex action. So is it in Indiana politics; in a crisis their muscles and their adrenal glands do most of their thinking for them. They have made a lifework of it; they know how. But the end of a perfect day was still to come. There appeared on the speakers' stand Captain Albert Stump, the nominee of his convention, who forthwith addressed those who had become his constituents.

It was a trying moment for a young and inexperienced man; but evidently Mr. Stump also knew how. Not a word that could inflame aching wounds; not a word that did not make for peace, harmony, and optimism. What he said I do not remember; but I have a general impression that he spoke favorably of God and the flag, and he certainly said something agreeable about home and mother. When he had finished, thirteen hundred Democrats went out with the comfortable feeling that they had picked the best possible candidate; a man who was every Democrat's friend and no Democrat's enemy, who would come as near as any man could to enabling every county leader to carry his county ticket. Of course he did not actually beat Jim Watson, though he gave him a scare. But that only proves my thesis; Indiana without Jim Watson to represent it at Washington would not be the Indiana of song and story; he is as essential and characteristic a feature of the landscape as the sycamore or the shikepoke.

Only one thought saddened us unterrified Democrats as we left that convention hall—the memory of the glorious opportunity that had been booted away at Madison Square Garden two years before. If only the national party could acquire something of the guile of Cullop and the tact of Stump— But nobody could who was not born and raised in Indiana.

So I came home feeling that despite kleagles and smell laws and hard times, the decline and fall of Hoosier culture was a myth unsupported by the evidence. Stands Indiana where she did? She does!

PORTRAIT OF AN ELECTED PERSON

[*Living in New York must have helped him to find Chicago's mayor Big Bill Thompson more amusing than disturbing, but the almost friendly tone of this profile of a demagogue seems to me to reflect a special quality of much writing of the nineteen-twenties. The artless verve with which the era's best writers handled vice and corruption showed a naïve sort of sophistication bordering on cynicism. Partly postwar disillusion, this must have been even more due to the ubiquitous public demoralization of prohibition and its concomitants. And there, no doubt, is the true source of Davis's indulgence. Whatever his other faults, Thompson was on the right side in the great issue of the times. I have cut a large amount of amusing detail from the long original to keep this piece within bounds.*]

One morning in April of 1927 the whither-are-we-drifting boys had the time of their lives. A dreadful thing had happened: the Honorable William E. Dever, regarded by Serious Persons as the best mayor Chicago ever had, had tried for re-election and gone down in disastrous defeat. What was worse, he had been beaten by the ex-Honorable William Hale Thompson, who in times past had proven himself (to Serious Persons) the worst mayor Chicago had ever had.

Thompson is best known to the outer world for his famous description of Chicago, just after America declared war on Germany, as "the sixth German city in the world," and for a wartime administration so anti-war that Chicago narrowly escaped being put under martial law. But at home they know more about him than that, for they had him as mayor for eight years; and if you ask Serious Persons in Chicago about him they begin to groan. Some of them have become sufficiently toughened to laugh instead, but most of them groan even yet. If they can stop groaning long enough they will tell you that he is a political accident, an ignoramus, a buffoon. His campaign of 1927 set a record, even in American municipal politics, for irrelevance and bad taste. His cardinal issue had been settled a hundred years before he was born —freedom from the British yoke. He called his Irish-Catholic opponent a tool of the King of England, and from the platform he bellowed promises to "hand King George one on the snoot" if the royal nose were ever unveiled in Chicago.

And, as observed above, he beat the best mayor Chicago had ever had by some eighty-three thousand votes; which occasioned much despairing of the Republic. There were pained inquiries as to what is the matter with Chicago, doleful analyses of the collapse of democracy. About the only positive note in the melancholy chorus was offered by an earnest young man in New York, who wrote a newspaper editorial declaring that Thompson should be exposed.

This article is not a response to that appeal; I am not going to try to expose William Hale Thompson. For one reason, the Chicago papers have been exposing him as hard as they could for a dozen years; but more powerfully still, he has been exposing himself. He is no shrinking violet who seeks the shade; exposure is what he lives on, and he feeds himself a good dose of it every day. Considering what he has done in that direction, I might as well try to expose the Washington Monument.

Nor shall I endeavor to expose Chicago. It seems to me that Chicago has come in for a good deal of unjust derision in connection with Big Bill Thompson. I believe he would go just as big in any other large city of the United States. Certainly New York can point no finger of scorn; New York would probably have gone on re-electing Hylan as long as Tammany had gone on nominating him; and Thompson seems to me ten times as clever as Hylan.

Hylan and Thompson have often been bracketed together—the Great Twin Brethren our ablest political satirist once called them. Both are professional patriots of the anti-British type, both enjoy the favor of Hearst; and they used to foregather now and then for reciprocal back-scratching, admitting in loud tones that they were the best mayors New York and Chicago had ever had. But it was an unequal partnership; Hylan had none of Thompson's originality, none of his instinctive perception of immediate advantage; moreover, Hylan believed everything he said, even if other men wrote it for him and he didn't quite know what it was all about.

Thompson impresses me as far too shrewd to swallow his own bunk; and this opinion is corroborated by men of insight, who have known him thirty years. Serious Persons in Chicago call him an ignoramus. If he is, he is an ignoramus of the type of Henry Ford. Ford is densely ignorant about ninety-eight per cent of the field of human knowledge, but about the other two per cent he knows more than any other man who ever lived. Thompson may be ignorant of the art of government, but he is an expert of the first rank in the art of getting elected; and in a democracy no man is going to have much chance to practice the art of government unless he has mastered the art of getting elected first.

Why do I waste good white paper on the statement of this obvious truth? Because, obvious as it may be, it commonly escapes the notice of city clubs, reform associations, and good-government leagues.

The simple and all-sufficient explanation of Thompson is the explanation of Ford as well: they are artists. The artist is not required to possess the general education that is looked for in other men; he may have it or he may not; nobody cares—if he can do one thing surpassingly well, that is enough. Thompson knows what he has to know, and knows it better than anybody else in Chicago. Will Rogers commented on the late election with his usual insight: "They was trying to beat Bill with the better-element vote. The trouble with Chicago is that there ain't much better element." That is no news to William Hale Thompson; he knows what other elements want, and he knows how to convince them that he will give it to them.

So, if this article turns out to be an exposure of anybody, it will be an exposure of the Better Element, of the Serious Persons. The trouble with the Better Element is that it habitually regards politics in the optative instead of the indicative mood; it thinks in such phrases as "the voters should," "the people ought." Not till the Serious Persons realize that their major premise is "the voters do," "the people won't," are we going to get a grade of municipal government that is anything to brag about. Last April the Better Element of Chicago made enough mistakes to ruin a better candidate than Dever; with all the experience of recent decades behind them, they still tried to jam virtue, or what was called virtue, down the public throat. Not, of course, that all of Dever's supporters were Serious Persons; they included some very practical politicians, notably one George Brennan. But Mr. Brennan, during the campaign, seems to have been under some evil spell; he behaved almost like a Better Element himself.

An astute observer who has known him for many years remarked to me that Thompson has a tabloid mind. You might go farther and say that he is a tabloid, in his own person. Chicago has no tabloid newspaper, but the tabloid state of mind is endemic among the population, and Big Bill has filled a long-felt want.

The essence of a tabloid is that anybody can understand it; even people who cannot read ninety-six-point type can look at pictures.

So with Thompson; whatever else he may not do, he never fails to make himself clear. Of late years the Irish and Germans have stirred up much agitation in the larger cities about alleged pro-British school histories. How much there is in their argument is a matter of contention, but one thing is sure—to find out whether they are right or not you must read the histories, and you must have some knowledge of the events they deal with. Not many people, in Chicago or elsewhere, care enough about the truth to do that. So Thompson simplified the issue with a stroke of genuis; he denounced William McAndrew, superintendent of the Chicago schools, as "King George's stool pigeon." That is as plain as the picture on the front cover of a tabloid; like the picture, it may be faked, but few of the customers are going to be curious enough to inquire into that.

This matter of schools, which played a considerable part in the late campaign, might have been supposed to be a delicate topic for Thompson. Toward the close of his second administration two dozen of his henchmen were indicted for stealing school money. One of them was Fred Lundin, the Columbus who had discovered Thompson years before (like Columbus, Lundin never dreamed what an expansive continent he was discovering, or what it was destined to do to him). None of these gentlemen was convicted; but their indictment put the capstone on a pretty general condemnation of the Thompson administration of the schools.

Under Dever, who followed Thompson, there were new men in the Board of Education; McAndrew was brought from New York as superintendent, and the schools improved perceptibly. None of Dever's school men was indicted; but Thompson had an easy explanation for that. "The King of England wouldn't let them be indicted." Who, you may ask, would believe that? Well, a lot of Chicago voters.

[· · ·]

Like a tabloid, too, the Mayor lives from day to day, fresh every morning. What if his pet issue falls by the wayside, rejected by an obtuse Federal government, by a hostile legislature, or even—this has happened—by a referendum of the Chicago voters? That was yesterday's issue, as dead as yesterday's newspaper. Tomorrow morning Big Bill will have another, and whatever you may think about its merits, you can be sure that his side of it will be as clear as plate glass. In the twelve years since his public career began he has been on both sides of practically every question—consecutively, as a rule, but in one notable instance he was on both sides simultaneously. Even his cardinal issue, the great guiding principle of his life, "America First," suffered a brief eclipse; while America was at war with Germany he was for America second. But this has done him no harm.

For he understands his people as well as Sophocles understood the Athenians. Like Sophocles, he gives them a periodic catharsis of pity and terror, and like Sophocles he finishes off with slapstick stuff that sends them home laughing. The Athenians thought so well of Sophocles' plays that they elected him admiral, and from all accounts he was about as good an admiral as Big Bill is a mayor. The art of politics has a lot to learn from the show business, and William Hale Thompson has learned it.

[· · ·]

Thompson is a millionaire and the son of a millionaire, the grandson of Chicago's first fire chief; in short, as aristocracy goes in Chicago, he is a patrician; and if, when he went into politics, he divested himself of his patriciate and applied for membership in the common people, he was only following the example of such excellent practical politicians as Julius Cæsar and Theodore Roosevelt.

[· · ·]

I surmise that he feels himself a sportsman much more than a politician; and he certainly looks it. You will not find many men of his type in the city halls of the country; but you will find plenty of them in the clubhouse at Saratoga or Churchill Downs, at the ringside at heavyweight championship fights, in the field boxes at world series games. See him in the street, and you might not know who he was; but you could be pretty sure he was not president of the Civil Service Reform Association or the Anti-Saloon League. I believe that Thompson's appearance alone is worth thousands of votes.

[Follows a description of his early political career and how he was taken up and promoted for mayor by one Fred Lundin.]

This Lundin had first come to Chicago, years back, as a medicine man, peddling the old Indian remedy from the tail of the wagon under the gasoline flare; and in that calling he had learned the great truth which no politician and no artist should ever forget—that it does not make any difference how good an article you are selling unless you can get them to stop and listen. He had managed to put together the disjected fragments of William Lorimer's old Republican machine; and, poking around the bulrushes in search of a candidate, he had stumbled on William Hale Thompson.

For Lundin, Thompson must have seemed made to order. A million-aire sportsman, able to finance his own campaign if other sources of income failed; with a wide acquaintance, an attractive appearance, a popular personality; and (so it may have been reasoned) not so heavy in the cerebrum as to endanger Lundin's intentions of being the power behind the throne. So Thompson put on the traditional Stetson hat of the cattleman, took the name of Cowboy Bill, and started campaigning for the nomination.

Nobody but Lundin took him seriously.

[*His opponent in the Republican primary was Judge Harry Olson, who was so confident of victory he didn't even bother to campaign.*]

Worse still, Olson's financial backers were asleep at the switch; on the eve of the primaries the money to pay the local workers was lacking; one by one precinct captains turned up at the Olson headquarters, found the cupboard bare, and went home to do their bit for Thompson. On primary day the bulk of the Republicans marked the Democratic ballot and helped Sweitzer beat Carter Harrison; while the regulars turned out and gave Thompson the Republican nomination, and the support of the better-element reformers which went with it.

Carter Harrison was down but he was not out; he whetted his knife, after the Chicago fashion, and set to work to help Thompson beat Sweitzer. (Even yet, after twelve years, Thompson's conglomerate retinue includes a group which calls itself the "Carter Harrison Democracy.") Other people were also out to beat Sweitzer; he was a Catholic, and the sentiment which was later to flower in the Ku Klux Klan appeared toward the end of the campaign and drove all the fanatical Protestants to vote for Thompson. Sweitzer was of German ancestry; a few days before the election leading Germans, Austrians, Magyars of Chicago got out a handbill adorned with portraits of Kaiser Wilhelm and the Emperor-King Franz Josef, urging all citizens of Central European origin to vote for Sweitzer and the Fatherland. So all the pro-Ally vote—which included the Czech vote, powerful in Chicago—went for Thompson.

And in the meantime Big Bill was getting other votes by his own endeavors. The great Negro influx was not yet at its height, but already the Negroes dominated Thompson's own ward, and he was shrewd enough to recognize their rising power and play up to them. In that day the Sunday closing of saloons was a hardy annual issue in every American city; Thompson promised the reformers he would close the saloons, and secretly promised the saloon-keepers he would not. So on the 6th of April, 1915, the Honorable William Hale

Thompson, the wet-dry-Nordic-Negro-Protestant-pro-Ally-Better-Ele-
ment-Carter-Harrison candidate, beat the unhappy Sweitzer by a
margin of 148,000 votes—the most sweeping victory recorded up to
that time, in any municipal election ever held in the United States.

Chickens come home to roost, but they never roost long on Big
Bill Thompson; he moves right out from under them. Before he had
been in office three months the reformers came down on him, and demanded the closing of saloons on Sunday. Thereupon the saloon-
keepers produced his secret pre-election promise (he had even put it
in writing) not to close the saloons on Sunday. Thompson closed them
all the same and became immediately the hero of the Anti-Saloon
League. True, it appeared before long that a good many saloons were
open on Sunday, these being saloons that had the right political con-
nections; but that happened in every American city in those days, and
Big Bill had no difficulty in being a wet-dry till something else attracted public attention.

[*Even the massive support of the German and Negro minorities he
had so well cultivated left Thompson 150,000 short of a majority in
the 1919 elections, but his four opponents competed with each other so
strenuously that he won out (over Sweitzer again) by a plurality of
18,000. Continuing nonperformance might have been a handicap too.*]
But in 1921 he began to slip.

It would be a pleasure to report that he slipped because of the inadequacy of the government which he and Lundin had given the city,
which he and Lundin and Len Small were giving the state, but he did
not; he slipped because of factional quarrels.

[*These factional quarrels were too much for him, so . . .*]
A month before the primaries he withdrew from the campaign,
"overcome," he said, "by the forces of grasping wealth and aggrandize-
ment." A little later he offered another explanation, "My friends have
crucified me."

The friend who is said to have been busiest in crucifying Big Bill
was State's Attorney Robert E. Crowe.

[· · ·]

Arthur C. Lueder got the Republican nomination for mayor, while
the Democrats put up Judge William E. Dever.

Where was William Hale Thompson while the battle of that year's
election was being fought out? Don't worry, friends; he was there. In

the three Negro wards Thompson's lieutenants kept the Negro voters at home on election day, and the scattering white residents who went to the polls carried those wards for Dever. It was a warning that in Chicago it is easier to nail a man to the cross than to keep him there.

Dever was elected, and straightway engaged in the hazardous occupation of being the best mayor Chicago ever had. I take that designation on the word of the Better Element; to the foreign eye there appear some flaws in this perfection. But Dever undoubtedly had some tough problems to handle, one of them being the transit situation. [*Dever's transit plan was voted down.*]

But worse was to come. If you want to see the man who more than anyone else is responsible for Thompson's return to power, gaze on the austere countenance of the Honorable Andrew J. Volstead. Dever essayed to enforce the prohibition laws, and while that optimistic enterprise was still in its infancy Judge Gary introduced him, at a dinner of prohibitionists in New York, as "the man who showed Chicago that the law was going to be enforced."

This was about as accurate as most of Judge Gary's pronouncements outside of his own special field. Dever, in fact, was the man who showed Chicago that if you entrust the police with the enforcement or non-enforcement of the prohibition laws, the police will waste little time on anything else, least of all on the onerous, perilous, and unprofitable business of suppressing crime. Chicago was never a notably peaceable or law-abiding city, but the great outburst of robbery, homicide, and machine-gunning came after Thompson went out of office. It came under the best mayor Chicago ever had.

Homicide, of course, is not much of a crime in the eyes of the professional prohibitionist; but many Chicago homicides are only incidental to what the prohibitionist regards as graver offenses. For while the ladies who kill their husbands, or their lovers, may get most of the newspaper space, most of the killing done in Chicago results from private feuds in the underworld. And most underworld feuds of late years have sprung from disputes over bootlegging privileges, in the city whose standard of law enforcement aroused the admiration of Judge Gary.

I have never heard of a time, since the Volstead Act and the state-search-and-seizure went into effect, when it was very hard to get a drink in Chicago. One hears that in the early days the privilege of violating the liquor laws was in the hands of ward and precinct politicians, who passed it around where they thought it would do the most good. When Dever transferred it to the police (for as the power to tax is the power to destroy, so the power to suppress is the power to tolerate) he simultaneously demoralized the police and alienated the politicians. Which is one reason why reform mayors are not re-elected.

Mr. Dever, being an intelligent as well as an honest man, was not long blind to this; in 1926 he told the American Bar Association that "the liquor question is not yet settled," and intimated a belief that it never could be settled, in the cities, on the present line of attack. Immediately the drys damned him as a traitor; the wets, of course, were against him already. Yet he went stubbornly and dutifully on, trying to enforce a law which he had virtually admitted was unenforceable. Which is another reason why reform mayors are not re-elected.

Meanwhile, where was Big Bill the Builder? He was coming back from Elba, preceded by several brass bands.

It will be recalled that when a well-known politician retired from office some twenty years ago, leaving his successor well supplied with rope to hang himself, he whiled away the requisite interval by going to Africa to hunt big game. Thompson got a somewhat similar idea in the spring of 1924.

Somebody had told him—and, as before stated, Big Bill usually listens to people who tell him something—that in Borneo there was a fish that climbed trees; and straightway the ex-Mayor reverted to the status of a sportsman-scientist and set out to find it. He bet a friend twenty-five thousand dollars that he would bring back that fish, or at least motion pictures of its tree-climbing; he organized the South Seas Research Association for scientific inquiry; and he constructed a vessel which was duly christened the *Big Bill* and ornamented with a wooden statue of the Builder by way of figurehead. In that ship he was going to sail to Borneo and bring back the tree-climbing fish; and on the way he would go down the river to New Orleans, spreading propaganda for the Illinois Lakes-to-Gulf Waterway, which is one of the enterprises that he takes up and boosts whenever there is no other immediate material for boosting.

Of course the scoffers, the knockers—Big Bill despises knockers—got to work at once. They alleged that his tree-climbing fish was no novelty; that it had been described and depicted in magazines sixty years ago; that an American scientific expedition had lately brought back the motion pictures which Thompson was about to seek; that, in fact, several mounted specimens could be seen in Chicago, at the Field Museum.

None of which worried Big Bill; he went right on with his well-advertised expedition, and seventy-five thousand people saw his ship start out on her voyage to Borneo via the Chicago Drainage Canal.

Something happened every day—something that got into the papers; one day, even, a newspaperman from Zion City (the village that voted the earth was flat) fell overboard and was properly rescued, by none other than William Hale Thompson.

So the *Big Bill* proceeded on its watery way—not all water, at that— as far as New Orleans. There Thompson was compelled to leave it; business recalled him to Chicago. His friends left, too, or so many of them as had not fallen away on the trip down the river; and the unhappy captain, who apparently had supposed all the time that they were really going to Borneo, was left with his schooner on his hands and was last heard of hiring her out to fishing parties in the Bay of Panama. As for the twenty-five-thousand-dollar bet, what happened to that is not recorded.

They laugh at Big Bill even yet for that enterprise, but I fail to see why. At a time when he was out of politics it got him about a kilometer of newspaper space; it kept him in the public eye, no matter how; it reminded the public that here was a man who Did Things, or at any rate started to do them. And how many people notice what happens to any high adventure after it leaves the front page?

Our hero's tower of refuge in those days was the Fish Fans Club, that ornate and bedizened galley, resembling the Bucentaur in which the Doges of Venice used to fare forth for the symbolic marriage with the Adriatic, which is familiar to all visitors to Chicago who have ridden up into Lincoln Park and seen it anchored just off the shore. (Possibly this aquatic stronghold was intended as a reminder that Chicago's future lies on the water, as well as on land and in the air.) The Fish Fans Club itself has a history, of which only the high points can be touched here. The hull of this stately craft was originally only a humble barge; it was purchased and reconstructed by the club members, but malicious persons allege that all the work of preparing the anchorage was done by Park employees on the taxpayers' time.

However this may be, the Fish Fans Club has the name of being a pleasant retreat for persons wearied by the cares of state. Two or three years ago, while Thompson was in private life, Federal prohibition officers raided the gallant craft and found an immense quantity of liquor; but it turned out that this was the private property of a caretaker resident aboard so no harm was done to any person of consequence. But on election night of 1927 the club was almost the scene of an appalling catastrophe.

Thompson was receiving returns there that night and naturally all his friends were eager to crowd in and congratulate him. As many as the galley was built to accommodate were soon aboard, and then as

many more; and still they came. Now the barge which was the sub-
structure of this brave vessel had been caulked up to a few feet above
the normal water line, able to take care of any load that was reasonably to be expected; but such a crowd had swarmed aboard this night
that it was borne down until the water rose high on its sides, rose to
a level where the seams were open. At once the vessel sprang a hundred leaks; and presently the engineer rushed up to the president of
the club and whispered hoarsely—"Captain, the ship is sinking! All
hands ashore!"

Well, by that time the boys and girls were all busy celebrating the
famous victory; no mere president of a club could have made himself
heard. To get this mob ashore along a narrow gangplank would be
difficult enough; but harder yet would it be to get them started. In this
perilous crisis only one man could impose silence, only one voice would
be heard with respect; the president of the club hastily informed the
chosen favorite of the people and the Honorable William Hale
Thompson essayed to deliver the warning in time.

Thompson got a hearing; he told his guests that the Fish Fans Club
had sprung a leak; he advised all present to walk (not run) to the
nearest exit. Whereupon they all looked at each other mirthfully and
said, "Ha, ha! Bill will have his little joke." So they stayed aboard,
and the ship went on sinking; but happily when it had sunk about
two feet it struck the bottom of the lake, and rested there, somewhat
precariously, until the visitors had gone and it could be pumped out
the next day.

* * * * *

He was out of favor, for a time, with the dominant group in the
national Republican organization; but on one issue he guessed right
when they guessed wrong. When the Republican National platform
of 1924 spoke favorably of the World Court, Thompson exploded that
"our foreign policy has been dictated by the King of England." Where
is that World Court now? Smothered in its sleep, like Desdemona, and
Big Bill made some slight contribution toward smothering it, incidentally and simultaneously making a larger contribution toward the
return of Big Bill.

In 1926 that missionary bishop of the mavericks, William E. Borah,
was going the rounds making speeches against senators who had voted
for the World Court. When he came to Chicago Big Bill took charge
of the meeting and ran away with it; Borah and George Washington
were only secondary figures. Last fall Thompson put an anti-World

Court candidate, Colonel Frank Smith, into the Senate. Smith had been chairman of the Utilities Commission, and his campaign fund had received heavy contributions from Samuel Insull, who owns most of the utilities around Chicago. A senatorial committee, you will remember, asked about this; among other people, they asked Big Bill Thompson. What was his explanation of this curious behavior of his candidate? Why, that "I have tried to carry out the policies of George Washington and the twenty-six presidents who followed him." America First.

[· · ·]

Before Thompson could get back in the City Hall he must get the Republican nomination; and he got it with the help of the man who had crucified him four years earlier, the Honorable Robert E. Crowe.

Mr. Crowe, they say, had had delusions of grandeur, but by this time he had got over them; he had discovered that he and Big Bill might be reciprocally useful. There was room for a great ally in Thompson's camp, for by this time he had broken with his friend and discoverer, Lundin. He had said harsh words about Crowe four years earlier, had said that if he ever shook Crowe's hand again you could set him down as a crook. But remarks like that are rarely taken too seriously by working politicians. Righteousness and peace kissed each other, Crowe and Thompson came together, with three cheers for George Washington; Thompson helped Crowe elect his county ticket last fall, having first pledged them to America First and no World Court; then Crowe helped Thompson to the mayoralty nomination, and they set out to beat the best mayor Chicago had ever had.

Say what you like about the taste of that campaign, it was a theatrical masterpiece. Lundin, for instance, had set up an independent candidate, Dr. John Dill Robertson. Thompson proclaimed that Lundin was a rat and Robertson was a rat, and he brought two caged rats up on the platform as visual reminder. Tabloid stuff—picture on the front cover, story inside, if you care to look for it. And I surmise that King George, whose involuntary appearance in the campaign aroused so much ridicule and disgust, played just about the same part as these caged rats. He was a tabloid picture too.

For every time Thompson said "King George" every German in Chicago had his whole 1917 complex recalled to his attention; the Germans might have remembered anyway who had been their friend when they needed a friend, but Thompson took no chances. But King George was worth more than that. The great offense of King George's stool pigeon McAndrew (that is, the great ostensible offense; I suspect a competent administration of the schools was one of the real counts against him) dealt with certain textbooks. These were not school books; they were used only in teachers' training courses which McAndrew had recommended; but they were a good talking point. For these books, it appears, shamefully distort Revolutionary history, as follows:

(1) They speak of the Scotch-Irish in Washington's army, when as every Irishman knows these were South Irish. (There are a good many thousand Irish voters in Chicago.)

(2) They pay insufficient attention to the deeds of the Polish Revolutionary heroes, Pulaski and Kosciuszko. (There are a hundred thousand Polish voters in Chicago.)

(3) They fail to mention the exploits of Steuben and the immense number of German soldiers in Washington's army. (There are two hundred thousand German voters in Chicago.)

Why no protest was made against the undoubted belittling of the achievements of the Negro soldiers in Washington's army I do not know. Probably Thompson was sure of the Negroes without that.

So much for King George. But, as observed above, it was not King George but Volstead, and the downstate legislators who had passed the search-and-seizure law, that really ruined Dever. Thompson could count on the Germans and the Negroes, but most of the hundred thousand Polish voters in Chicago are normally Democratic. They are also normally wet, or abnormally wet, if you like. Anyhow, when Thompson strode up and down the platform promising to send the police back to their old job of fighting the crooks, and declaring that "I'll fire any cop who walks into a man's house without a warrant and fans the mattress for a pint flask," he got most of the Polish vote, and he got a good many other votes too. Chicago, brethren of the dry cause, is joined to its idols; it still contains a good many people who regard murder as a more serious matter than taking a drink.

If you doubt the accuracy of this diagnosis, consider this: In November George Brennan, running for senator as a wet against the dry Frank Smith, carried Chicago by 83,000. Five months later Brennan's candidate Dever, running as a dry against the wet Thompson, lost Chicago by 83,000.

[· · ·]

The culminating blunder was committed by no less a person than George Brennan himself, when in a peevish moment he remarked that "all the hoodlums are for Thompson." Big Bill seized on that with a whoop of joy; he stigmatized the Democrats as aristocrats; he paraded the platform bellowing a merry appeal—"Hoodlums, come out and vote, and bring another hoodlum with you." (Al Jolson, just after the election, gave Big Bill a bulldog which the donor had named "Big Boy," but Thompson had a better inspiration than that; he gave the dog a new name and put it on his collar for all the world to see— "Hoodlum—Mayor's Office—Chicago.") Showman stuff? Yes, and good showman stuff; it made votes. And behind that he had the solid support of the Germans and Negroes, he had the scattering—but considerable—support of the people who thought that the police might better be trying to prevent homicide than fanning mattresses for pint flasks.

Is there any mystery, now, about that election? Well, one mystery, perhaps—in spite of everything, 430,000 people voted for Dever.

[· · ·]

Thompson, at this writing, has been in office two months and a half, and already some things have happened, while some other things may be predicted with reasonable confidence. In spite of all temptations to belong to other nations, he will be for America First (unless there is another war with Germany; or with **Poland, or Czechoslovakia, or** Africa). And he will have plenty of issues; they may not last long, but he will let go of them before they die on his hands. For like most artists he lives by inspiration, not by reason, and he seldom rides an inspiration till it gives out. He can always get another one, just as good.

[· · ·]

Whatever else happens in the next four years, you can be sure there will always be a good show at the City Hall, always a fresh picture on the front cover of the tabloid every morning. Big Bill learned from Lundin, if he did not already know it by instinct, that you have to make them stop and listen, in the light of the gasoline flare, before you can sell them the old Indian remedy.

NATIONAL AFFAIRS

[*He was best known for his searching and often cutting commentary on national and international affairs. Here his basic equipment of character, competence and learning as refined by nearly forty years' experience was brought to focus by a deep-felt belief in our form of government. The effect this commentary could have on others was described by E. B. White in a* New Yorker *review of* But We Were Born Free. *"Mr. Davis is a devout man," White wrote. "His religion is the secular religion that unifies America—faith in freedom, in self-government, in democracy. . . . He has the edge on many of freedom's admirers because he is well acquainted with politics and politicians and has always been found lounging in the center of an argument or the middle of a convention hall. Being a scholar and a moderate man, he is not easily swept off balance."*

[*At the end of the same review White answered Davis's expressed doubts that his words had much effect. Davis had noted that when he spoke it was usually to audiences full of people who already knew these things, who already agreed with him. What use is there in preaching to the converted? he asked. White answered with one use: "The courage and the knack to keep freedom alive are handed along from one generation to the next," he argued. "In every audience, however sympathetic it may be to the speaker, are a few youthful listeners who may be hearing about the mysteries [of keeping freedom alive] for the first time . . . Something of Elmer Davis's wisdom and courage will rub off from this book onto someone who didn't even know he was born free, someone who assumed that the rights we cherish bloom naturally, like Johnny-jump-ups. These are the ears that make it all worth while." He concluded the review: "To the man from Aurora, Indiana (a name that means 'light of morning'), the Founding Fathers are alive today. And he in turn, with his salt and truth, makes them live for others." The first four pieces in this section are from the book White was reviewing.*]

THROUGH THE PERILOUS NIGHT

[The first chapter of But We Were Born Free *was more than 100 pages of careful exposition and documentation of the then-raging antifreedom crusade. All of it is still interesting today, both as history and for its resemblance to events of the counterpart campaign being waged now. But space allocations require that I cut more than half.]*

More than eighteen hundred years ago a great historian wrote that "rare is the felicity of the times when you can think what you like and say what you think." That felicity has indeed been rare throughout human history. Tacitus himself had lived through times when it was suicidal to say what you thought, and hazardous to let it be suspected that you were thinking at all; he survived into a more tolerant age, but that lasted for only a few generations till the lid closed down again. Since then the lid has been on and off—mostly on. In the false dawn of the eighteenth century it was lifted once more; and the men who made our government thought they could guarantee that the lid would stay off by almost immediately writing into the Constitution as its very first amendment the guarantee of freedom of religion, of speech, of the press—all corollaries of the basic right to think what you like. That seemed to have settled that; with a great price our ancestors obtained this freedom, but we were born free.

So we were; but that freedom can be retained only by the eternal vigilance which has always been its price. In 1943 the Supreme Court declared that "if there is any fixed star in our constitutional constellation, it is that no official, high or petty, can prescribe what shall be orthodox in politics, nationalism, religion, or other matters of opinion; or force citizens to confess by word or act their faith therein." Since then, however, that fixed star has become somewhat obscured by clouds; and in 1953 the Ford Foundation found it advisable to allocate $15,000,000 to one of its subsidiaries, whose function was frankly stated as the restoring of respectability to the individual freedoms guaranteed by the Constitution.

Since the most conspicuous of recent encroachments on these freedoms had been the work of Congressional committees, Congress might have been expected to respond to this gesture; and it did. The Honorable Brazilla Carroll Reece of East Tennessee proposed, and the House of Representatives adopted (though not without a fight), a resolution to appoint a committee to investigate the tax-exempt foundations to see if they are using their money for un-American or subversive purposes. They had already been investigated on that point a few months earlier, and all the big ones had been acquitted; but in Congressional jurisprudence no man (or institution) is ever acquitted. If a committee is weak enough to find him not guilty, you merely get another committee to try him again.

And while Mr. Reece, in his speech proposing the resolution, attacked all the big foundations, it was evidently the Ford Foundation that chiefly aroused his ire. Its endeavor to remove restrictions on freedom of thought, inquiry and expression was in his opinion subversion of our institutions (so now the Constitution itself is subversive): he said it would aid the Communist conspiracy, that the leaders of the Ford Foundation have a conception of civil liberty similar to that of the Communists—a comment he might more pertinently have applied to himself. But in spite of the observation of two Republican members, Mr. Fulton and Mr. Javits, that the resolution seemed aimed not at Communists but at people whose political and economic opinions differed from those of Mr. Reece, the House voted him his committee.

By coincidence, a Congressional committee that same day approved a bill to erect a monument to the freedoms guaranteed by the Constitution—the very freedoms that the Ford Foundation is trying to defend. The monument was to be erected right outside Arlington Cemetery. If Mr. Reece and those like him have their way, it had better be put up inside the cemetery, along with the monuments to all the other distinguished dead.

This is of course only one incident in the attack now going on against these freedoms—an attack on various levels, federal, state and municipal, with the co-operation of many unofficial but zealous vigilantes—which, while it is nothing novel in our history, is worse than any other such crusade in my recollection. How far it is organized I do not know. Some people think they see evidence of what Senator McCarthy would call a pattern—a nation-wide conspiracy; I cannot discern it, though many of the crusaders certainly co-operate locally. (As they conspicuously do in Los Angeles, and as they did in Washington in the attack on Assistant Secretary of Defense Anna Rosenberg in December 1950; but respectable conservatives rallied to her support, and that venture soon proved to be a sinking ship; the rats jumped overboard, biting one another as they went.) But even if it is not nationally organized it is nationally dangerous; just as in a great air raid a hundred local fires may coalesce into a fire storm, in which the whole is greater than the sum of its parts, so local movements around the country add up into what seems to be a general attack not only on schools and colleges and libraries, on teachers and textbooks, but on all people who think and write (except reactionaries), an attack on freedom of inquiry, freedom of teaching, freedom of dissent—in short, on the freedom of the mind, the basic freedom from which all other freedoms spring.

Who is doing all this? Well, various kinds of people; it is hard to include them under one name. Reactionaries? But there are men who are reactionary in political and economic opinions and still do not approve of the suppression of thought. Fascists? But there are not very many real Fascists in this country; there are some—particularly conspicuous in the attacks on the schools and colleges—but it is hard to tell how many of them are Fascists on principle and how many are Fascists for revenue only, as the easiest way to shake down the rich for support of their committees and their magazines. They are no great danger anyway, for there is no longer a formidable and hostile foreign power, as there was fifteen years ago, to which they can give their allegiance; Peron's Argentina and Franco's Spain are hardly big enough to count. (Franco may prove, like Stalin, to be more dangerous when he is our ally than when we were barely on speaking terms with him.)

But if real Fascists are few, there is a dangerously large number of people—many but by no means all of them rich—who could be called Fascistoid. Fascism has to have at least a pretense of doctrine; in Italy the doctrine was ignored, in Germany it was never more than a thing of shreds and patches; but there is one cardinal principle that was not ignored in either country and seems to be sympathetically regarded by many people here—the principle that our side has a right to put your side down and keep you down, regardless.

[*He lists some groups that had been identified with the antifreedom crusade in those days: extreme isolationists; politically ignorant economic conservatives (who honestly don't know the difference between partial Socialism and Communism); Machiavellian economic conservatives (who find it profitable to pretend they don't know the difference);*

extreme economic conservatives; the Asia-First China-Lobby crowd; all those who want to make use of such a crusade to attack labor groups, minority groups, ministerial groups, liberal Democrats, liberal Republicans, liberal journalists, writers, educators and other professional people. But it would be wrong, he argued, to suppose these are all.]

[These elements] might be called (God help us) an elite; they have a good deal of influence, a great deal of money, and even some ideas, twisted and erroneous as those ideas may be. But they are backed up by a popular support—people who have little money, no influence except as they derive it from numbers, and nothing that could be called ideas; but plenty of emotion. The kind of people who a generation ago made up the mass membership of the Ku Klux Klan, which a few smart men at the top manipulated in their own interest; and I am afraid there are more of them now than there were then. I have guessed that people like that may amount to fifteen or twenty per cent of the population of the country, and hope that estimate is not too low—as some of my friends think whose material for a guess is as good as mine. People, they are, whose dominant surface emotion is hatred; but underlying that, besides an appalling ignorance, is fear. They are afraid to think because it is hard work, afraid to let other people think because it might turn out that what they themselves have always thought is wrong. It hurts more to have a belief pulled than to have a tooth pulled, and no intellectual novocain is available.

In so far as their fear has any logical basis, it implies that the principles of freedom on which this republic was founded will not stand examination.

[· · ·]

Fear of intelligence, fear of thinking, fear to trust your own opinions in the give and take of discussion—this in the strongest nation in the world—a nation which only a decade ago put forth the greatest military effort in all history (nothing the Germans or the Russians ever did equaled the simultaneous achievements of Eisenhower's invasion of Normandy and Spruance's conquest of the Marianas), a nation that could do the same again if it had to—provided we had the guts, provided we had not let our bowels turn to water. How many of our fellow citizens have become afraid of their own shadows I do not know; but there are far too many—"morticians of the mind," ex-President Truman has called them—and there are plenty of ambitious politicians

who find, in making them afraid of their own shadows, the road to
power.

[· · ·]

But, they tell us, there is something to be afraid of—something terrible—Communism. Well, Communism is dangerous, but they are not
afraid of it where it exists, where it is powerful and dangerous, in Russia; these antifreedom crusaders show no interest in Russia at all. They
are unable to distinguish, as Philip Rahv once wrote, between Communism as a danger *to* America and Communism as a danger *in* America; or, as George Kennan put it, they think Communism is something
invented in this country about 1945. (This view, once confined to the
unlettered, seems to be spreading into the more influential circles.
There are some just-below-the-top-level members of the administration
who, if asked to name the two most important and dangerous Communists of recent years, would give you not Stalin and Malenkov, but
Alger Hiss and Harry Dexter White.) I have no doubt that many of
the crusaders—especially the unofficial vigilantes—really believe that
Communism is a purely American phenomenon, but they have a
strange conception of Communism. It is merely opinions different
from their own. Some of the most active crusaders, however, are not
after Communism at all. It is hard to know what to call the people
they really are attacking, since "liberals" and "progressives" are both
terms that have been discredited by some of the people who have used
them; but we know what they used to mean, and they describe the
targets of this crusade. They are after people who think for themselves
and whose thinking does not agree with theirs—in so far as what they
do can be called thinking.

McCarthy has made this evident enough. In the winter of 1953,
when there promised to be great competition between Congressional
committees for the privilege of investigating Communists in the schools
(finally settled by letting two of them do it at once while the third
went on to even juicier fields), McCarthy, shrewder than his competitors, said he was going after not merely Communists but Communist
thinkers. The distinction was prudent: whether a man is a Communist
is a matter of fact, though the fact may sometimes be hard to determine; but a Communist thinker is anybody whose thinking you choose
to regard as Communist. McCarthy presently gave us his definition;
his examination of Jim Wechsler made it clear that in his opinion a
Communist is anybody who criticizes McCarthy. He had already

called the Milwaukee *Journal* and the Washington *Post* local editions of the *Daily Worker;* some sense of prudence has up to this time prevented him from calling the weekly *America,* which has also criticized him, the Jesuit edition of the *Daily Worker;* but give him time. Indeed his line of thinking had become apparent during the presidential campaign, with his attack on the "Communist" influences around Stevenson. In his usual manner, when he is not protected by the immunity of the Senate floor, he didn't quite call these men Communists, but the innuendo was clear. Wilson Wyatt, Arthur Schlesinger, Jr., Jim Wechsler, Archie MacLeish, "Richard" De Voto—men who were fighting Communism long before McCarthy ever discovered it as a paying issue; when he was beating Bob La Follette out of the senatorial nomination with the aid of Communist votes, and later when he was using propaganda from German Communists to save the lives of Nazi officers who had murdered American prisoners at Malmédy.

So a Communist is anybody you don't agree with. (Even Robert Alphonso Taft was once called a follower of the Communist line by a real-estate lobbyist because he was in favor of public housing.) And a good many of our citizens, in the name of anti-Communism, would suppress the freedoms guaranteed by the Constitution which are one of the principal differences between a free and a totalitarian society.

It has been argued that the Founding Fathers could not foresee the international Communist conspiracy; if they had, they would never have adopted the Bill of Rights. This has a certain superficial plausibility; only a few years after our government got started it was faced with a comparable movement—Jacobinism, which, starting as a worldwide crusade for liberty, soon became an agency of French imperialism. Accordingly, some of the Founding Fathers—by no means all—supported the Sedition Act of 1798, which made it a crime to write or say anything false, scandalous or malicious against the President or Congress with intent to bring them into disrepute. (As Federalist judges interpreted it the word "false" was apt to be ignored.) Then as now the pretext was fear that some of our citizens were loyal to a dangerous foreign power rather than to their own country; then as now, many honest but thickheaded citizens were convinced that any disagreement with their own opinions was disloyalty; then as now, this sentiment was skillfully used by reactionary politicians to try to ruin men and suppress opinions that they didn't like, even though there was no taint of disloyalty about them.

That, however, was a very different matter from the present attack on freedom; it was a duly enacted law, designed to keep in power an administration and a party which had lost the confidence of the people; and being a law, it could be repealed. It was repealed, though too late to save the Federalist party. The men who enacted it had forgotten that there was a practical as well as a philosophical justification for the Bill of Rights, at least in a country which still had free elections, so that the government could change hands; legalized repression could be exercised by whichever party was in power; and the logical end of that would have been such proscriptions and counterproscriptions as distinguished the last days of the Roman Republic.

If false, scandalous and malicious attacks on the President and Congress had still been a crime in the first fifteen years of the nineteenth century, a good many eminent Federalists would have gone to jail—some of them with good reason, for they were actually meditating and plotting treason. But Jefferson believed and said that error of opinion may be tolerated so long as truth is free to combat it; and on that principle (with occasional lapses) we have operated ever since. We are still operating on it, in theory; recent statutory restrictions on the freedom of speech have not been very serious; but there has been terrific extralegal pressure from those who feel that truth cannot be tolerated, even when error is free to combat it. Men do not now go to jail, unless they are imprudent enough to perjure themselves before Congressional committees; they merely lose their jobs and their reputations—sometimes with reason but more often not; for the procedures of some Congressional committees I have seen in action—notably the Internal Security Committee under Senator McCarran's chairmanship—would have shocked even such a Federalist fanatic as Mr. Justice Samuel Chase.

All this has created what has correctly been called a climate of fear; to call it a reign of terror is certainly a very considerable exaggeration on a national basis, though locally a good many people have been terrorized. This exaggeration has been particularly prevalent abroad; some of it, particularly in a small section of the English press, is due if not to malice at least to *Schadenfreude*. But there is some excuse for it among foreigners whose knowledge of the United States is limited, particularly if they happen to have seen what could be called a reign of terror among American officials in Germany, created by the performances of Cohn and Schine. As Joseph C. Harsch reported to the *Christian Science Monitor*:

A European looks around him and sees actual evidence of an American police power operating in Europe which owes its allegiance not to the American government but to Senator McCarthy. He has personal agents in many European countries. They interview Europeans about American government officials. There is in fact a private secret police force working for Senator McCarthy; and to any and every European a private police force means just one thing, an instrument of power outside the existing and regular government. This condition has always, in European experience, led to an extra-constitutional seizure of power.

No wonder the Europeans are worried; no wonder Americans who see that sort of thing at first hand are worried too.

Reactionary writers who approve the results of this crusade, though they are a little too respectable to take part in it themselves, are fond of saying, "Who's getting hurt? Whose freedom is restricted?" People say to me, "You can still talk, can't you, and nobody stops you?" No, nobody has stopped me yet, because my employers are men of courage; about once a week somebody tries it. As to who's getting hurt, plenty of schoolteachers, college professors, and librarians could give you the answer. The National Educational Association reported recently, after studying five hundred school systems, that there is less academic freedom in the country than there was in 1940; that teachers are reluctant to discuss controversial subjects for fear of local reprisals.

Arthur Sulzberger, publisher of the *New York Times,* said not long ago that there has been dropped upon utterance and ideas a smoke screen of intimidation that dims essential thought and essential speech; if the publisher of the best and perhaps the strongest newspaper in the country feels that way, how much more must lesser men feel it? The *Times,* conspicuously, has not been intimidated, though I have no doubt it has been tried; neither have the publications that McCarthy has directly attacked—the Milwaukee *Journal,* the Washington *Post,* the New York *Post, Time* magazine. Nor have other newspapers— notably the Denver *Post* and the St. Louis *Post-Dispatch.* But a good many editors seem to feel that if you pretend you don't see it, it isn't there.

This was made evident by the fiasco of the action of the Society of Newspaper Editors when Jim Wechsler of the New York *Post* asked them if McCarthy's attack on him was not an infringement on the freedom of the press. A committee of eleven men was appointed—its chairman, Russ Wiggins of the Washington *Post.* It deliberated solemnly and finally came to the conclusion—at least seven of its eleven members did—that if it were an infringement on the freedom of the press that would be a bad thing, but they couldn't decide whether it was or not.

Ask one of these seven for whom the bell tolls, and he won't know till it is ringing right beside his desk.

Four others—Chairman Wiggins, Herbert Brucker, William Tugman and Eugene Pulliam, Jr.—said it *was* an attack on the freedom of the press and they didn't like it; whereupon McCarthy demanded that the Society of Newspaper Editors investigate Wiggins and his paper. The editors, displaying a courage with which few would have credited them, ignored this demand. But meanwhile a number of highly reputable journalists had argued that, since McCarthy's attack had in fact failed to intimidate Wechsler, it was no attack on the freedom of the press at all. This amounts to saying that attempted rape is no crime if the girl is lucky enough to fight off her assailant.

Newspapermen are supposed to be better able than most people to see and to understand what is happening. For the mass supporters of this obscurantist crusade an excuse is offered—that the international situation is on their nerves; it causes apprehension, and the fact that the average citizen can do nothing about it creates frustration. The excuse would be more impressive if these people showed any interest in the Russian danger (even the reactionaries in Congress show little interest when it comes to appropriations for defense); but it is undeniably true that we live in a world of danger and tension, a tension which is likely to continue a good many years longer. We face a very powerful and dangerous foreign enemy—two enemies indeed, Russia and China—whose rulers are animated by a creed that makes truly peaceful coexistence impossible so long as they take that creed seriously; yet nobody in this country wants to solve that situation by war if it can prudently be avoided. So what should a mature and intelligent nation do in such a crisis? Why, we ought to keep our heads, keep our nerves steady, refuse to be upset by trivial provocations but be alert to really serious dangers; we ought to distinguish between our real friends and our real enemies, make an accurate identification of the direction of the peril and a correct appreciation of its magnitude. In short, we ought to think—a right denied in totalitarian countries to anybody but a few men at the top, whose thinking is warped by dogma; but guaranteed to us by the Constitution. The right to think is the real difference between us and the enemy; it is likely to give us ultimate victory in the cold war—or in a hot war, if that should break out.

That is what a mature and intelligent nation ought to do and what many of our citizens are doing. But many others, unable to find a better outlet for their frustration, take it out on their less influential neighbors, in the mood of a man who, being afraid to stand up to his wife in a domestic argument, relieves his feelings by kicking the cat.

[*He cites the cases of the couple jailed overnight in Houston for allegedly "talking Communist" in a restaurant, it being asserted that one of them had said Chiang Kai-shek was fighting a losing battle; and of the Lincoln, Nebraska, Legion post's decision to publicize a membership campaign by attacking a University textbook.*]

There had indeed been two or three phone calls to the Legion from students who objected to the book; two of them also objected that the professor was a Democrat. One of them said the book was presented as gospel truth which could not be contradicted, and this, if true, would have been a grave indictment of the professor; but many students came forward to declare that it was not true. The book—which had been selected by the professor on the basis of reviews in scholarly publications as the best he could get—was used as a basis for discussion and was freely criticized by students and the professor himself.

One gratifying consequence of this attack was that people stood up on their hind legs and roared in protest against it—the faculty, the student body, many people in the town. The Legion soon showed signs of wanting to let go of the hot potato and presently passed it to the regents of the university, who, so far as I have heard up to this time, have done nothing about it.

But there was a still more interesting aspect to this episode—it was an example of the new theory of literary and artistic criticism. The book was published by one of the best commercial publishers, but under the auspices—whatever that means—of the Institute of Pacific Relations, which was then being kicked around by the McCarran committee; it was edited by Lawrence Rosinger, and one chapter was by Owen Lattimore. Now I have not read this book; disinterested persons who have read it could find nothing subversive in it. But apparently nobody in the Legion ever read it either. If they did, they did not find the fact worth mentioning, either in their original protest or in their letter to the regents some weeks later; nor did they offer any specific criticisms of its content. All they know is who wrote it. As they said, "The sponsorship of the Institute of Pacific Relations makes the book suspect. The contribution of Owen Lattimore makes the book suspect. The editorship of Lawrence Rosinger makes the book suspect."

Suspect—a historic word; the favorite word of Robespierre in the Reign of Terror when he was marking off somebody for the guillotine.

"He is suspect"; that was enough. And many people seem to hold that it is still enough, to damn not only a man but his works, no matter what is in them. In the winter of 1952-53 the American Legion all over the country was picketing the theaters showing Charlie Chaplin's latest picture. I have not seen this picture—not because I am afraid to go through picket lines but because I seldom have time to see pictures; but I read many reviews of it, none of which found anything subversive in it. So far as I know, the Legion never claimed there was anything subversive in it; all they know is who made it—a man whose associations and alleged political opinions they don't like; one of their leaders around Washington said that if you buy a ticket to a Chaplin picture you are trading with the enemy. Among the musical compositions that were to have been played in President Eisenhower's inaugural festivities was Aaron Copland's "Lincoln Portrait." On the protest of a Chicago congressman it was thrown out—not because it is not good music, not because it was an inadequate representation of Lincoln, but because the congressman disapproved of Copland's associations and alleged opinions.

Till that happened, I thought the United States was growing up. In 1917-18 Wagner's operas could not be played in this country because he was a German. In the late war there would have been far more reason for banning Wagner; he was one of the spiritual ancestors of Nazism; indeed the first Nazi ever portrayed on the stage was Siegfried. But in 1941 everybody decided that if it is good music the political opinions of the composer do not make it suspect, and we all went to see *The Ring* with as much enjoyment as ever. This sensible rule, applied to Fascist sympathizers, apparently does not apply—like some other rules—to people suspected of Communist sympathies. In the spring of 1953 the Veterans of Foreign Wars extracted a promise from the Voice of America that it would not put on its programs any of the music of Roy Harris, who in 1943 had composed a symphony which he dedicated to the Soviet Union. Maybe you remember 1943—a year when we were engaged in a great war in which the Russians (through no fault of their own) were our allies, a war whose outcome was then still undecided. The Russian victory at Stalingrad was one of the battles that decided it. At that time the most important thing in the world was to kill Germans, and the Russians were killing more of them than anybody else; there was reason for dedicating a symphony, in 1943, to the Soviet Union. Why Harris did not later withdraw his dedication (on demand) as Beethoven, without demand, had withdrawn his dedication of the "Eroica" to Napoleon, I do not know. I am not acquainted with Mr. Harris; maybe he still likes the Soviet Union, or maybe he just didn't like the demand. Maybe he doesn't like to be pushed around; and if this country ever runs out of people who don't like to be pushed around, we are done for.

This now seems to be the primary criterion of modern literary and artistic criticism: never mind what is in it—all you need to know is who did it; if he is suspect, it doesn't matter what is in it. It may seem surprising that people who feel that way have not picketed the numerous art galleries where Picasso's pictures are hung; but they probably never heard of Picasso.

2

These extralegal pressures could be discouraged, though not stopped, if high officials spoke up against them; but officials who did so might alienate voters; the candidate who defended the freedom of the mind before the American Legion convention lost the election (probably not for that reason, but politicians hate to take chances); and up to this writing (November) the executive branch of the government has done little to defend even its own officials against the antifreedom campaign. Meanwhile, Congressional committees—some of them—have been running wild; and I mean wild.

The work of Congressional investigating committees, if not essential to good government—some well-governed countries manage to get along without anything of the sort—can at least under our system be a great contribution to good government when the committees are decently conducted, as the majority of them are. But some of them have so behaved that even members of Congress have questioned what they are doing no less than the way they are doing it. The theory of Congressional investigation is that it is to provide information which might be the basis for action by Congress—that is, passing a law. But it is a serious question whether Congress has a right to investigate in fields where the Constitution forbids it to legislate, as some committees did last year.

Even where that constitutional uncertainty does not intrude, there may be doubt as to the pertinence, if not the authority, of the investigation.

[*For instance, there was the simultaneous decision in 1953 of three Congressional committees to investigate American schools and colleges. The committees were McCarthy's Senate Government Operations Committee, Jenner's Senate Internal Security Committee, and Velde's House Un-American Activities Committee.*]

American schools and colleges, already under many local attacks, were further threatened in the winter of 1953 when all three of these committees announced an intention to investigate them. They all promised to keep out of one another's way, but it was evident that they would have to go over pretty much the same material and the same people. The constitutional prohibition of double jeopardy couldn't stop them; that applies only to the courts. One committee after another can bring the same man before them and compel him to tell the same story over again—which offers the hopeful possibility that there may be discrepancies in his testimony so that you can indict him for perjury. Unless, of course, he happens to be one of the professional ex-Communist informers who seem to constitute a pool on which any Congressional committee can draw. In that case discrepancies in his testimony are disregarded.

Education had reason to tremble at the prospect of investigation by Jenner, Velde and McCarthy; all of them, in advance, were breathing out threatenings and slaughter, with McCarthy gleefully predicting that there would be "an awful lot of screaming about academic freedom." Beyond that, what were the qualifications of the investigators? Jenner's I have discussed; Velde was chiefly known, before he came to his chairmanship, for the introduction of a bill in the previous session—for a wonder, nothing was done about it—requiring the Librarian of Congress to go through the books in his library, all nine million of them, and mark any and all subversive passages. And suppose that Librarian Luther Evans, after completing this fairly extensive course of required reading, had failed to mark as subversive certain material that looked subversive to Velde—assuming that Velde had ever read it? Then, presumably, we should have to get a new Librarian. Conceivably, this might have been one of the reasons that led Luther Evans to resign his job and become head of UNESCO—a fairly hot spot itself, but farther away from Capitol Hill.

As for McCarthy——Archbishop Richard J. Cushing of Boston has said that "despite any extremes, or mistakes that might have been made, I don't believe anything has brought the evils and methods of Communism more to the attention of the American people than his investigations." This amounts to saying that nothing brings the danger of fire more to the attention of the public than turning in false alarms all over town. I cannot recall that all his "exposures," before he became a committee chairman, had ever got a single Communist; since then he seems to have caught a few minnows, but no big fish. No wonder. He was not after Communist fish; he was after people, including a few ex-Communists who are now active and effective anti-

Communists, whose opinions disagree with his; and whom he has smeared by all sorts of distortions and misrepresentations. The Archbishop's praise of him would seem to imply that the end justifies the means. I do not at all suppose that that was intended, but if it had been it would still be wrong, for McCarthy has not attained his professed end, of bringing the evils and methods of Communism to the attention of the people, though he *has* attained what seems to have been his real end, of persuading many people that all liberals are Communists.

[• • •]

3

These were the men who announced, in the winter of 1953, that they were going to investigate American education. What right they had to investigate it is open to some doubt; schools and state universities are under the jurisdiction of state authorities, and the authority of Congress over private institutions is not clear to me—in spite of a memorandum a year ago from the staff of the Internal Security Committee, quoted with approval by Senator Ferguson, which declared that it is the duty of Congress to see that educational institutions implant only sound ideas in the minds of students. This is not among the powers granted to Congress by the Constitution. The First Amendment says that Congress shall make no law abridging the freedom of speech; it does not say "except in schools and colleges." It also forbids abridgment of the freedom of the press, or the making of any law prohibiting the free exercise of religion. Yet the colleges, the churches and the press all came under Congressional inquisition in the year 1953.

The excuse is that these freedoms were not being abridged, that Congress was only going after individual teachers, clergymen or editors who happened to be Communists. But the only editor attacked, most clergymen who were attacked, and some of the teachers, were not Communists. The colleges admitted the legitimacy of these investigations, but whether as a matter of law or of public relations is unknown to me; it was obvious that any one which refused to co-operate would be smeared as a nest of Communism. It is true that some of them recognized limits; as Dr. Conant said in his farewell report at Harvard, "the independence of each college and university would be threatened if governmental agencies of any sort started inquiries into the nature of the instruction that was given." But you can get the same effect, without specifically going into the nature of the instruction, by putting the heat on every teacher who gives a certain kind of instruction—as every reactionary school board knows, and every reactionary college trustee. Since, however, these are the legal controllers of the schools and colleges, this is perhaps not an interference with their independence, even if it plays hell with academic freedom and ultimately with the standing of the school or college.

Academic freedom. I have heard and read many arguments this past year on its definition, and even participated in one or two. I have heard it claimed by Communists on the witness stand; but if they are genuine blown-in-the-glass Communists (and I doubt if there are any others left in this country any more), the claim was phony. They have no such freedom; they must obey the orders of their party when it gives orders. There is certainly no academic freedom in Russia, where history is rewritten to suit the changing party line, as in Orwell's *1984;* and even geneticists must accept and teach the doctrines of Lysenko because the Central Committee of the Communist party says they are true.

We are a long way from that, even though some of our fellow citizens are trying to bring us around to it, even though I do not doubt that there are college teachers who find it advisable not to teach what the chairman of the board of trustees regards as untrue. Academic freedom, I should think, is the right of any man professionally qualified by study and experience to teach anything that honestly seems to him to be true, without reprisal. Sidney Hook, whose anti-Communism I do not suppose even McCarthy would question, holds that we should protect the academic freedom of any man who as a result of his own study and experiments concludes that the doctrines of Lysenko are true, though not if he accepts them because the Communist party tells him to. I should think that the professional qualifications of such a man might be regarded with some skepticism; but as Hook reminds us, so much that used to be scientific heresy is now regarded as scientific truth that we cannot afford to shut the door on any honest speculator.

This conception of academic freedom does not seem to be widely held in Congress. Nevertheless, not much of the damage that was anticipated from these investigations has occurred. It cannot be said that it was prevented by the effective defense of the educators, which was very spotty; some of them stood up, some caved in. It did not occur because McCarthy has not yet got around to education, finding government a more profitable field; because Jenner, whatever his other qualities, lacks the relentless vindictiveness of McCarran; and because Velde turned out to be so inept that the friends of freedom may reasonably regard him as their secret weapon.

[*Velde's ineptitude is illustrated with two anecdotes, and then Davis turns to Jenner. His committee failed to find the "many hundreds" of Communists he had promised to identify among the nation's more than a million teachers; "but he did turn up several dozen of whom some fifty or so refused to answer questions, taking refuge in the Fifth Amendment." This led to a discussion of that amendment.*]

"There may be many different sets of circumstances," says Dean Andrews, "under which a man, knowing himself to be innocent of any wrong, might nevertheless wish to invoke the Fifth Amendment. Perhaps he cannot afford the heavy cost of defending himself, nor afford the time" (in case of a conflict of testimony which led to his indictment for perjury); "perhaps he dreads the strain of a possible prosecution, the humiliation, the black mark against him in the eyes of his friends even though he should be acquitted, the risk of being unjustly found guilty."

These considerations, of course, apply particularly to sensitive men. The lesson would seem to be that, during the present prevalence of Congressional investigations, no citizen can afford to be sensitive. "Why in the world," Dean Andrews goes on, "should an innocent man be presumed to be guilty of something, just because he uses, to protect himself, a right guaranteed by the United States Constitution?" Well, maybe he shouldn't be, but most people will so presume him. To fall back on the Fifth Amendment is any citizen's right, innocent or guilty; but in either case it is bad public relations.

There is another reason why some people I have heard of who never were Communists have sought this refuge: they were afraid that if they said they were not Communists some of these professional ex-Communist witnesses who play the circuit of the Congressional committees, as horse players go from one track to another, would denounce them as Communists, and then they would get indicted for perjury.

The fear seems plausible but is, I think, exaggerated. These wandering minstrels, as one target of the Jenner committee called them—I have no doubt that he was a Communist but that seems no reason to deprive him of credit for a pointed phrase—these people's testimony is generally accepted at face value by Congressional committees; but not always.

[*Follows an examination of some of the "wandering minstrels'" work for the Jenner committee. One of them was reported at the time to have tried to implicate the then Foreign Minister of Canada, Lester Pearson.*]

It was widely believed in Canada that this information had been leaked to the speaker by the committee—something which the history of Congressional committees investigating Communism made plausible enough. Of course, among Americans who knew Mike Pearson, the universal reaction was "Who on earth would believe that he would do anything to help Communism?" Well, one man could—the man who called George Marshall a living lie and an eager front for traitors— Senator Jenner. One newspaper could—the Chicago *Tribune,* which three days before Pearl Harbor published to the world (including Hitler, who luckily didn't believe it) the plans by which we would fight a war if we had to fight a war. Men who themselves were so indifferent to national interests could easily believe that other men are as indifferent as they are.

And once again the national interest of the United States was gravely harmed by this attack on the Foreign Minister of our closest and most necessary ally—the national interest, and the international interest of the Atlantic alliance. For this coincided with Senator McCarthy's proposal to get American prisoners out of China by cutting off all aid to England, our next closest and most necessary ally. Stirring up suspicion and ill feeling among the three nations which are the core of the Atlantic alliance can tend only to the isolation and weakening of the United States. That happens also to be the principal objective of the Soviet government; but they have an obvious motive, and a reasonable one from the Soviet point of view. Jenner and McCarthy seem to have helped out the objective of the Soviet government, in the name of anti-Communism, from no motive except their own publicity and their own power.

4

In due course the churches came in for attention—though all the chairmen loudly declared that they were not attacking the churches, still less religion as such, but only exposing individual clergymen who were Communists. To no one's surprise, it appeared that as usual their definition of a Communist is a man who wants reforms; a minister who believes that Christianity implies some endeavor to improve conditions here below instead of a single-minded concentration on preparation for the next world must be a Communist. That is, if he is a Protestant, or in some cases a Jew. There are many Catholic priests who labor earnestly for social reforms; it is probably a tribute to the power of their Church that no Congressional committee has attacked them, for the record of the committees would indicate that it is due to no hesitations on principle.

The Jews, so far, have been hit with only a few sideswipes; but the Protestants have taken a terrific beating. A wandering minstrel named Joseph Zack Kornfeder, who has testified before many committees on many subjects, told the Un-American Activities Committee that six hundred Protestant ministers were Communists and several thousand more were fellow travelers. He named a few names, whose bearers are now under investigation by ecclesiastical authorities. Mr. Kornfeder's qualifications as an authority on Protestantism today appear to consist in the fact that he was a Communist twenty years ago. A still more horrendous story however was told by J. B. Matthews—an ex-wandering minstrel, among many other things, who now appears to have a-job with the Hearst papers and was for about a minute staff director of McCarthy's committee. Matthews used to be a Methodist missionary; I trust that the heathen derived benefit from his ministrations, since it is not clear that anybody else ever has. Twenty years ago he was attacking the Protestant churches because they were liberal and thus (according to Matthews) backing the leadership of business reaction; some clergymen even spoke favorably of that (according to Matthews) reactionary big-business outfit, the Roosevelt administration. Last summer he published a magazine article attacking the Protestant clergy because they are liberal and thus backing Communism. "The largest single group supporting the Communist apparatus in the United States today is composed of Protestant clergymen," the article began. Ten pages later it said that "the vast majority of American Protestant clergymen are loyal to the free institutions of this country," but seven thousand of them have been "drawn into the network of the Communist conspiracy." Matthews named ninety-five; quite a number of them turned out to be dead, most of the others were known as liberal reformers. But to the all-or-nothing mind the liberal reformer is the worst man in the world. You may attack him from the Communistoid or the Fascistoid standpoint or—as many have done—from both in succession; but to this type of mind the liberal reformer is wrong—and the more successful the wronger.

It appears that a good many clergymen had signed petitions in favor of liberal social reforms which they favored, reforms which the Communists professed to favor too. The reverend gentlemen would certainly have been wiser to look more closely into the origins of some of these petitions; but all this falls somewhat short of Matthews' sweeping assertions.

That magazine article cost him his job with the McCarthy committee—through no fault of McCarthy's. Later, in a broadcast, Matthews
admitted that he could not personally under oath name fifteen Protestant clergymen who are Communists, or any who is a Communist
spy; but he believed on information from others that there were at
least a handful, and he stuck to his story that there are seven thousand
or more who have bowed the knee to Baal and are serving Communism. The Methodist Bishop Lord has suggested that these are
probably men who support public housing, fight for civil rights and
believe in world peace. It would certainly be rash to assert that there
are no Protestant ministers who are Communists, but, over all, Matthews seems to be as wrong now as he was twenty years ago when he
was on the other side of the argument.

[· · ·]

But to your impassioned patriot a sense of proportion is as subversive as a dispassionate weighing of the evidence. Some years ago, when
McCarthy was making his first attacks on the State Department, I
ventured to suggest in a broadcast that these were merely accusations,
so far; we had better wait and see if the evidence justified convictions.
Whereupon an infuriated citizen, apparently a man of standing in his
community, wrote me, "We cannot wait for convictions; what we want
is confessions." But suppose there is nothing to confess? That is no
problem in Russia or any other totalitarian country; they get the confessions anyway. But this republic has not been operated on that
principle, so far.

Some people apparently would have it so operated; when you are
fighting Communism, they think, anything goes. Whether civil liberties should apply to people who, if they got into power, would destroy
civil liberties is an old problem, which was raised in many countries,
and by Hitler's activities as well as Stalin's. The conclusion usually
reached has been that they ought to apply to everybody; subversion
should be kept down, but by other means.

The President seemingly thinks otherwise—or did, at least, when he
made his campaign speech at Milwaukee in October 1952. "The Bill
of Rights contains no grant of privilege for a group of people to join
together to destroy the Bill of Rights. A group like the Communist
conspiracy, dedicated to the ultimate destruction of all civil liberties,
cannot be allowed to claim civil liberties as its privileged sanctuary."
In other words, the Bill of Rights not only should not apply to Communists, which is a matter of opinion, but does not, which is a matter

of fact. Has the President read it? I can find nothing in its language
that says, or even implies, that any citizen or group of citizens is ex-
cepted from its guarantees. If the Constitution is to apply to everybody but Communists, pretty soon it might apply to everybody but
Socialists, or Jehovah's Witnesses, or Episcopalians, or Democrats—
anybody whom the majority didn't like and chose to regard as subversive. To prevent the majority from doing anything that may suit
its whim of the moment is precisely the reason why we have a Constitution.

But is not Communism a deadly danger? Certainly it is, in Russia,
and as operated from Russia; certainly the Communist party in this
country is dedicated to the service of Russian imperialism. But such
danger as it presents is a matter of espionage and sabotage, and if the
FBI is half as good as we hope it is, it ought to be able to take care of
that. In 1932 Communism was a more serious danger; the economic
system of the United States had broken down, the governmental system sometimes seemed on the verge of breakdown. People used to ask
helplessly, "Do you think there is going to be a revolution?"—not as
if they either wanted a revolution or were resolutely determined not
to have one, but as if there was nothing they could do about it. I do
not think there was any serious danger of a revolution then (though
greater men disagreed with me); if there had been one the Communists could not have started it, nor do I think they could have got
control of it. Still their alternative to collapse had some plausibility—
till it began to fade before a new administration, new policies, the beginnings of recovery.

[· · ·]

I am not unmindful of the fact that Mr. J. Edgar Hoover tells us
each year that Communism is a greater danger than it ever was before—which, if true, is a serious reflection on Mr. Hoover and his
organization, whose business it is to root it out. But I am not too much
alarmed; these statements are usually made before the Appropriations
Committee, when he is asking for (and always getting) more money
for his agency. I have had some experience in government, and much
observation of it, and I cannot recall that the head of any agency, appearing before the Appropriations Committee, ever underestimated
the need for his services.

Yet the Communist party, tiny and dwindling as it is, serves one useful purpose in the minds of many of our public men: it provides them
with a cover for attacks on liberalism and progressive reforms—attacks

which might have less hope of success if they had to be made honestly, out in the open; and, quite as important, it enables them in denouncing Communism to find the road to publicity and power. It has been quite a meal ticket for some of our statesmen whose natural gifts might not otherwise have carried them very far; and not merely for statesmen. There are a good many little organizations around the country—most of them fly-by-night but one or two fairly influential—which have made of fighting Communism (or rather what they choose to call Communism) a lucrative business; I sometimes suspect that the people engaged in that business are more numerous than the Communists. From the standpoint of all these gentlemen, in office or out, if Communism did not exist, it would be necessary to invent it. (A few of those organizations are sincere and effective; but far from all.)

All these investigations have certain characteristics in common—the elastic inference, the doctrine of guilt by association, the reliance on the testimony of the touring company of ex-Communists that makes the rounds of the committees—"people," as the Washington *Star* once described them, "whose only claim to credibility is that they used to belong to a society of liars." Sometimes certainly they have told the truth; sometimes, just as certainly, they have indulged in the inventive imagination.

This is an old story; with McCarthy, something new has been added. His vindictiveness, if not less than McCarran's, is certainly of a different type. McCarran used to grab his victim by the throat and shake him till he had got everything out of him; McCarthy seems to lose interest after he has got all out of him that would do any good to McCarthy. But he is a master of the obscene innuendo, and he has more effrontery in direct attack than any of his fellow saviors of the nation. None of them, when Jim Wechsler had optimistically supposed he could show evidence of his anti-Communism by producing an attack on him by the *Daily Worker,* would have thought of suggesting, as McCarthy did, that he probably wrote it himself as a cover for his nefarious activities.

[· · ·]

It was proved in the senatorial elections of 1950, and some of those of 1952, that it pays better to call your opponents Communists, or soft on Communism, than to discuss the issues. Nineteen fifty-four also may be that kind of year; Senator Ferguson seems to think so. He is up for re-election and his prospects are uncertain; his denunciation of "radical eggheads" suggests that he feels that his best hope of victory lies in an attack on intelligence. Mr. Ferguson, of course, is a man of principle, but I doubt if his hostility to intelligence on principle is strong enough to lead him to attack it, or attack anything else, unless he felt that by so doing he would get votes. There will be plenty of other men running for office in the fall of 1954 who feel that way.

[· · ·]

Nor is there much the ordinary citizen can do about Congressional committees if he is haled before them. There may be limits on their investigative rights, but those rights can be delimited only by litigation which would be too long and costly for the average man. None of them has recently gone so far as the late J. Parnell Thomas, who once told a witness, "You have no rights except what this committee chooses to give you"; but the committee controls the procedure and has a dozen ways to oppress the witness, if it chooses. And even if he stands up well, and seems to have made a good showing in his testimony, it is the committee which writes the eventual report and can slant it so as to give a very different impression.

But we can all do something to resist this general drive against the freedom of the mind. The first thing to remember is, Don't let them scare you. Arthur Sulzberger said recently that what bothered him was not the superzealot attackers so much as the lack of plain old-fashioned guts on the part of the people who give in to them. And it has been shown in a dozen places that if you stand up to them you can often stop them.

Not always and not finally, for it will be a very long time indeed before we are rid—if ever—of the kind of people who want to make other people think their way, or else stop thinking at all. But we can hold them in check, push them back—always remembering to keep an eye on them, always remembering that eternal vigilance is the price of liberty. Particularly the attacks on the schools can be checked, as they have been checked in many places. You are not going to cure the genuine Fascists who spearhead these attacks, but they get their support largely from the people who are ignorant and afraid; get rid of the ignorance and you get rid of a good deal of the fear. It is usually possible to educate a school board; indeed it is possible to educate a Legion post, and it has been done. There seems no logical necessity for local veterans' organizations to fall into the hands of reactionaries, even though the major national organizations have done so; if local posts do so too, it is because the reactionaries work at it and most people don't.

In Hagerstown, Maryland, the few local believers in world government brought to town a play that advocated it. Some leading members of the Legion burst out with attacks on the play and some of the
participants, but they had their facts wrong and were talked down.
But even before that happened the local chapter of the Veterans of
Foreign Wars had announced that they were just as much opposed to
world government as the Legion (so am I, if that makes any difference) but that they were also opposed to "scare tactics"; they urged all
citizens to go and see the play and make up their minds about it.
Which is all that anyone could ask.

In Oregon, all the veterans got educated. There had been the usual
sort of attacks on the schools; but the state commander of the American Legion, speaking for practically all the veterans' organizations,
came to their support. If there is complaint about the schools, he said,
the educational authorities should have the opportunity to clean house,
or determine whether it was necessary to clean house, without being
harassed by outside organizations. There, the veterans' societies had
taken the trouble to find out what it was all about, and somebody had
taken the trouble to help them. That could happen elsewhere, if somebody would only take the trouble.

Such education, of course, could be a two-way process. It was the
opposite direction which the President [Eisenhower] emphasized in his
talk to the United Churchwomen at Atlantic City in the fall of 1953. A
small group, he said, had come to him to complain about certain things
in our public-school system. "And I asked this group one question
only. . . . Have you taken the trouble to find out what is the philosophy
of these people to whom you are entrusting the most precious possession you have—your children? If you join the ranks of the critics and
say that these teachers are not doing a good job, then why haven't you
done your part of the job?—brought them in, talked to them, to see
whether you can either straighten them out, or get ones of whom you
can approve."

The value of such a straightening-out process would seem to depend
on two things—whether the parents have an informed and intelligent
opinion as to what the schools ought to accomplish, so that they can
competently evaluate the philosophy of the teachers; and whether, if
they fail to straighten the teachers out, they would leave any action to
the school board or other duly constituted authority after public discussion, or would use whatever extraofficial political or economic
power the parents might possess to "get ones of which they approve."
That the teachers might conceivably straighten the parents out was

apparently unthinkable to the President. No doubt his intention was to promote a more general citizen interest in education, but his language could be misinterpreted as a license to every pressure group to put the heat on.

The colleges are in a tougher spot. Some of their organizations displayed a visionary optimism about the educative possibilities of Congressional investigations; and what happens in an individual college usually depends on the courage of its president and the intelligence of its trustees and alumni. (It is one of the facts of life, painful though it may be, that courage comes easier the bigger the endowment. Harvard, Columbia and Chicago would probably have stood up anyway, in view of their traditions; but they needed less propping than some others.) Yet none of the things that Jenner and Velde actually did lived up to their thundering in the index; indeed the investigations, and the big talk that preceded them, may have done some good in compelling the colleges to do some hard thinking about what they had that was worth fighting for.

As for the general attack on freedom of thought, it comes in such manifold form that it requires more kinds of defense than can be listed here; and sometimes the defense will be in vain. When a magazine fiction editor is fired because another editor, unknown to him, bought a nonfiction article which evoked some protest; when an actress is dropped from a radio program because a couple of dozen telephone calls, probably stimulated, scared the sponsor—why, in such cases there is nothing much you can do about it except to regret that there are so many cowards in the world. But sometimes the defense is successful; and you never get anywhere unless you stand up and fight.

This was stated in the fall of 1953, at the dinner of the Four Freedoms Foundation, in language so much to the point that I shall not venture to try to improve on it:

> The good life is not possible without freedom. But only the people, by their will and by their dedication to freedom, can make the good life come to pass. We cannot leave it to the courts alone, because many of the invasions of these freedoms are so devious and so subtle that they cannot be brought before the courts.
>
> The responsibility for these freedoms falls on free men. And free men can preserve them only if they are militant about freedom. We ought to get angry when these rights are violated, and make ourselves heard until the wrong is righted. . . . There are times when the defense of freedom calls for vigorous action. This action may lead to trouble, and frequently does. Effective effort to preserve freedom may involve discomfort and risk. It takes faith, unselfish-

ness and courage to stand up to a bully; or to stand up for a whole community when it has been frightened into subjection. But it has to be done, if
we are to remain free.

We have to start wherever we can—in the family, the lodge, the business
community, the union, our local government, party, church—and work outward; asserting, demanding, insisting that the most unpopular persons are
entitled to all the freedoms, to fundamental fairness. Almost always, the
issues are raised over unpopular people or unpopular causes. In the cause of
freedom, we have to battle for the rights of people with whom we do not
agree, and whom, in many cases, we may not like. These people test the
strength of the freedoms which protect all of us. If we do not defend their
rights, we endanger our own.

Since the foregoing was said by Harry S. Truman, I suppose many
people will disregard it. But is the defense of the liberties whose
guarantees the Founding Fathers wrote into the Constitution a partisan
issue? Not even McCarthy has explicitly said so, yet. I hope it never
will become a partisan issue, for that would mean a schism in the
nation as deep, and perhaps as irreparable, as we had in 1860. And
then at least there was principle on both sides; this time all the principle would be on one side, and it might not be the winning side, unless we stood up and fought for freedom.

The first and great commandment is, Don't let them scare you. For
the men who are trying to do this to us are scared themselves. They
are afraid that what they think will not stand critical examination;
they are afraid that the principles on which this republic was founded
and has been conducted are wrong. They will tell you that there is a
hazard in the freedom of the mind, and of course there is, as in any
freedom. In trying to think right you run the risk of thinking wrong.
But there is no hazard at all, no uncertainty, in letting somebody else
tell you what to think; that is sheer damnation. Judge Learned Hand,
in that famous speech to the Board of Regents of the State of New
York which has become practically the breviary of the friends of freedom, acknowledges the hazard and has the answer to it. "God knows
there is a risk in refusing to act until the facts are all in; but is there
not greater risk in abandoning the conditions of all rational inquiry?
Risk for risk, for myself I had rather take my chance that some traitors
will escape detection than spread abroad a spirit of general suspicion
and distrust, which accepts rumor and gossip in place of undismayed
and intimidated inquiry. . . . The mutual conflict on which all else
depends can be maintained only by an open mind and a brave reliance
on free discussion. I do not say that these will suffice. Who knows

but we are on a slope which leads down to aboriginal savagery? But of this I *am* sure—if we are to escape, we must not yield a foot upon demanding a fair field, and an honest race, to all ideas." This nation was conceived in liberty and dedicated to the principle—among others—that honest men may honestly disagree; that if they all say what they think, a majority of the people will be able to distinguish truth from error; that in the competition in the market place of ideas, the sounder ideas will in the long run win out. For almost four years past we have been engaged in a cold civil war—it is nothing less—testing whether any nation so conceived and so dedicated can long endure.

I believe it will endure, but only if we stand up for it. The frightened men who are trying to frighten us, because they have no faith in their country, are wrong; and even wronger are the smart men who are trying to use the frightened men for their own ends. The United States has worked; the principles of freedom on which it was founded—free thought as well as political liberty—have worked. This is the faith once delivered to the fathers—the faith for which they were willing to fight and, if necessary, die, but for which they fought and won. Those men, whose heirs and beneficiaries we are, risked, and knew they were risking, their lives, their fortunes and their sacred honor. We shall have no heirs and beneficiaries, and shall deserve to have none, if we lack the courage to preserve the heritage they won for us. The national board of Americans for Democratic Action reminds us that this will remain the land of the free only so long as it is the home of the brave.

IMPROVING ON THE FOUNDING FATHERS

[*At this writing there are serious campaigns afoot to complete ratification of three crippling amendments to the Constitution. The men behind them have different, sometimes even conflicting, motives; but the chief goal for these new amendments, as it was for those discussed in the article below, is to restrict the power to govern of the federal government.*

[*This is commonly represented as being praiseworthy in itself. Such is, in fact, the principal premise in the avowed philosophy of many office seekers; though when worsening domestic and international problems call more and more for careful, expert and rapid decision this seems a philosophy for ostriches.*

[*But in fact most such amendments are not really designed to reduce government's impact on individual people at all. What they would indeed accomplish is to transfer power from the federal government—with its well-publicized operation and manifold forms of susceptibility to public influence—to more sympathetic, or more easily controlled, organs. Thus the same people who argue for "liberty" from federal government frequently advocate denying to individuals the civil liberties that protect them from unwarranted governmental intrusions. As a matter of fact, the purpose of some proposed amendments has been explicitly to prevent the federal government from protecting individuals against unconstitutional invasions of their rights by state governments.*

[*Ten years ago the same heady sort of ferment was already aboil. The subject of this next piece is that same campaign as it looked then. The major effort of the government-limiting forces in those days was an attack on the power of the United States government to make treaties. This was the Bricker amendment. There were others, too, from various attempts to banish or emasculate the income tax to the boldest and simplest measure of all—simply change the means of amending the Constitution so that your side can amend it any way it likes. Most of these would designate state legislatures as the ultimate safe repository for powers taken from the federal government even when those powers were meant to protect individuals from, among others, state legislatures.*

[*The best answer is given in unremitting pains to publicize exactly
what these amendments propose and to show who ultimately gets the
power.*]

        In these days when there is so much argument over what
school children learn, if anything, it would be hazardous to say that
every schoolboy knows—or indeed that any schoolboy knows—that
William E. Gladstone once described our Constitution as the most
wonderful work ever struck off at one time by the brain and purpose
of man. And if some few schoolboys do know it, I wonder how many of
them are aware that the author of this fulsome praise, when he was
engaged in diplomatic negotiations with the United States, took a very
dim view (as have other men before and since) of the constitutional
requirement that treaties must be approved by two thirds of the Senate. Likewise many of our own citizens, who would regard criticism
of the Constitution in general as no better than blasphemy, get greatly
annoyed with anything in it that happens to interfere with something
they want to do.

    For all that it is a good Constitution—a Constitution that fits us; or
perhaps, rather, after a hundred and sixty-four years, we have come to
fit it. Yet good as it is, we have found it necessary to make twenty-two
alterations in it. The first ten were virtually a part of the original
document; of the rest, one merely canceled out another. Still there
have been quite a number of changes, and people are trying to tinker
with it still.

    I do not say that some tinkering would not improve it; the provi-
sions for the presidential election could still let us in for trouble.

[*He here analyzes several imperfections in our present electoral machinery and a number of others in the provisions for succession to the
presidency in various contingencies. Some of these could be cured by
legislation, he suggests, but what seem like the best cures for others
would require amendments.*]

    Even if our Constitution has these loopholes in it, it is a pretty good
Constitution none the less. It does not establish a very efficient government, but it was not intended to. As Mr. Justice Brandeis once
said, "The doctrine of the separation of powers was adopted, not to
promote efficiency but to preclude the exercise of arbitrary power. The
purpose was not to avoid friction, but by means of the inevitable friction to save the people from autocracy." The government of England,

in which an executive with a large majority in the House of Commons can do pretty nearly anything it wants to do, works well for the English, who are a calm and equable nation; if we had such a system we might tear ourselves to pieces.

But if our government was deliberately made not very efficient, it has always proved efficient enough to do what it had to do, even though President Lincoln had to subject the Constitution to some interpretations which must have rattled the bones of the Founding Fathers. This was not the idea, at first. The men who had won the Revolutionary War seem to have thought, for a brief period, that they could get along with the Articles of Confederation—a government which was about as near no government as any civilized nation ever tried to operate. "The decentralizing democrats," says Herbert Agar, "had written the constitution they wanted, and it was a good constitution for their purposes; but their purposes were not adequate in a world of power and cruelty and greed."

Yes, but it was not only the decentralizing democrats. I suspect that one strong reason why conservatives as well as liberals accepted the Articles of Confederation without much argument was the same emotion that displayed itself in 1919 and in 1945—the feeling of a nation which has just won a great war that now it has won all its wars, solved all its problems, and can live happily ever after.

[· · ·]

Even on this favored continent such sentiments were not universal. They were not shared, for instance, by the United Empire Loyalists, chopping new homes for themselves out of the Canadian wilderness; in their eyes, the nation that had chased them out was hardly a *gens pia*. And it did not take long to prove that the Articles of Confederation were based on a much too optimistic view of human nature, both abroad and at home; they had not only failed to abolish original sin, but had not much constricted its operations. All credit to our ancestors (or most of them) for seeing very soon that the Articles would not do (and perhaps almost as much credit for not doing anything about it till the Congress under the Confederation had accomplished its one great act of statesmanship, the ordinance for the government of the Northwest Territory). When the Constitutional Convention met, its members were zealous to take precautions against executive, and still more against legislative, tyranny; but they knew that for all their precautions they must still make a government that would work.

In these times perhaps more than ever, except in the crisis of civil war, we need a government that can do what it has to do. It may be that, as optimists hope, the leaders of world Communism may some-day abate their zeal and give up their hopes of world conquest—settle down to a more or less peaceful coexistence, as did Islam with Christendom (though only after a thousand years, and only when the military superiority of Christendom had been definitely established). But till that happy day comes we shall need a government that can do what has to be done.

It would seem that such a situation calls for as high a degree of national unity as is possible in a democracy, short of a shooting war. Instead of which, as I was saying earlier, we have a good many citizens who seem to think that the enemy is their fellow citizens who disagree with them, rather than somebody abroad; and many others—some of them eminent, more of them rich—think that the enemy is not the government of the Soviet Union or of the Chinese People's Republic, but the government of the United States. During the Roosevelt and Truman administrations it could be supposed that their enemy was only a liberal government; but since January of 1953 it has been evident that their enemy is no particular administration but government itself, and they are continually trying to weaken its power—not only by less forthright methods but by the frontal attack of constitutional amendment.

The only one of these endeavors that has so far succeeded is probably the one that will do least harm, but it could do some harm at that; indeed it has done some harm already by imbedding its underlying assumptions in the structure of our government. The Eightieth Congress proposed, and a sufficient number of state legislatures ratified, the Twenty-second Amendment to the Constitution, limiting any man's tenure of the Presidential office hereafter to two terms. The question of Presidential re-eligibility (once or oftener) had been thoroughly debated in the Constitutional Convention, by men possibly as able and patriotic as the members of the Eightieth Congress; and they chose to impose no limit. The argument against limitation was classically stated by Alexander Hamilton in the *Federalist.* There are times when a nation absolutely needs a particular man in a particular situation; don't call him indispensable if you don't want to, but there are crises—the outbreak of war, for instance—when it would be foolish to substitute inexperience for experience. There is a further argument that would not have appealed much to Hamilton but that has some pertinence in contemporary American political theory; to say that you can't select what Washington once called the man most capable of serving the public in some great emergency means that you don't trust the people. If in some crisis now beyond foreseeing they should feel that they need a particular man, the wisdom of the Eightieth Congress has decreed that they can't have him if he has served two terms already.

I heard the entire debate in the House of Representatives on the resolution proposing this amendment. No attempt was made to refute Hamilton's argument (I doubt if many members had ever heard of it); indeed until the last two minutes of a long afternoon there was no reasoned attempt to support the change at all. Then Mr. Michener of Michigan came up with an argument that would have been pertinent if true—that a President long in office could fill up the public service, in low positions as well as high, with his appointees, who would always vote for him in order to keep their jobs. Unfortunately for this thesis the heaviest concentration of federal employees in any area where they can vote is in the suburban counties around Washington in Maryland and Virginia; and during the Roosevelt and Truman administrations those counties had the habit of going Republican. Many of their inhabitants have since been fired; if those who have not been fired have a proper gratitude to the administration that spared them, while a thousand fell at their side and ten thousand at their right hand, they may provide belated support for Mr. Michener's argument.

But all the rest of that House debate was one long hymn of hate against Roosevelt; men who couldn't lick him when he was living relieved their feelings by dancing on his grave. The psychiatric value of such an emotional release was no doubt considerable; but it might have been accomplished with less injury to the nation by the process which the Roman Senate, after the death of an Emperor whom they hadn't liked, used to call *damnatio memoriae*—repealing his enactments, smashing his statues and chiseling his name off the public buildings erected during his administration.

That Congress, particularly the Senate, distrusts any President is an old story; it began when President Washington had been in office only three months. That Congress distrusts the Supreme Court, unless it happens to agree with the Congressional majority, also is not news. What I had never expected to see, till it happened, was the Senate distrusting the Senate. Yet that is the meaning of the famous Bricker amendment, in whose introduction Mr. Bricker persuaded no less than sixty-three of his colleagues to join him, limiting the treaty-making power. Mr. Bricker proposed it in an impassioned speech in which he painted a horrendous picture of a revolutionary President, sup-

ported by corrupt senators, putting over a treaty that would sell the
United States down the river into God knows what abyss of tyranny
and atheism. This argument had been anticipated by John Jay in
the *Federalist;* a man must have been very unfortunate in his inter-
course with the world, he said, or possess a heart very susceptible of
such impressions, who would believe that the President and two thirds
of the Senate would ever be capable of such unworthy conduct. But
it must be admitted that this was written before our present form of
government was in operation. John Jay had not known any senators. John Bricker has known a lot of them. He knows more of them
than I do, and knows them better; it is not for me to question his estimate of his colleagues.

The Bricker amendment is of course aimed at that clause in Article
VI of the Constitution which provides that laws made in pursuance of
the Constitution, and all treaties made under the authority of the
United States, shall be the supreme law of the land, anything in the
Constitution or the laws of any of the states notwithstanding. From
what is this "authority of the United States" derived? Obviously from
the Constitution itself; the Tenth Amendment spells it out that that is
all the authority the federal government has got. So the clause of the
Bricker amendment, in its latest and much modified form, declaring
that a provision of a treaty which conflicts with the Constitution shall
be of no force and effect, merely insists that the Constitution means
what it says. (To quiet the fears of the timorous, must we thereafter
have still another amendment declaring that the Bricker amendment
means what it says?)

[· · ·]

That the Bricker amendment, even in its modified version, would
have hobbled if not crippled the treaty-making power is evident; that
is what it is for. It does not go quite so far as a proposal advanced
during the argument over the adoption of the Constitution, that treaties
—all treaties, whether or not they involved any internal rearrangements—should be repealable by act of Congress. John Jay had something to say about that too: "A treaty is only another name for a bargain,
and it would be impossible to find a nation who would make any bargain with us which should be binding on them absolutely, but on us
only so long and so far as we may think proper to be bound by it."
And there might be almost as much reluctance to make a treaty which,
after two thirds of the Senate had approved it, would still be no good
until both Houses of Congress had given further approval by passing
a law.

Of course some treaties fall into that class already—those whose exe-
cution requires an appropriation. As early as 1796 the House of Representatives had fought for and established its right to act on appropriations, even if a treaty clearly called for them. And the Constitutional Convention had considered, and rejected, an alternative method
for approving treaties—by a majority of both Houses of Congress. The
provision that two thirds of the Senate must approve was adopted instead to guarantee that neither Northern nor Southern states could
put over a treaty disastrous to the interests of the other section; we
might have had no Constitution without it. If it was a mistake, it
was a mistake unavoidable at the time; the Founding Fathers did not
foresee the rise of parties, but it is hard to see how they could have
done any better with the immediate problem they had to deal with.

But the two-thirds rule has made so much trouble that there has
been increasing support in recent years for the other method—approval
by a majority in both Houses. That support, naturally, has been most
evident in that body which furiously insists that it is not the lower
House of Congress but a legislative organ coeval and coequal with the
Senate. But the makers of the Constitution had other objections to
that, besides the decisive one of the conflict of sectional interests. Those
objections were summed up by Hamilton in the *Federalist;* the "fluctu-
ating and multitudinous" composition of the House would make it
unsuitable for such responsibility. This has less force now that the
Senate is fifty per cent more multitudinous than was the House in 1789,
but the argument that we should change that provision of the Constitution is only sounding brass and tinkling cymbal; a change would
require the consent of two thirds of the Senate, which would never give
up such a cherished prerogative.

[· · ·]

But to many citizens all these arguments are outweighed by fear.
Ostensibly the fear that motivates them is fear of the United Nations,
but their real motive is fear of the government of the United States.
As a *New York Times* editorial put it, it is "fear of ourselves, of our
traditional processes of government, and of the ability of our properly
constituted representatives to look after our own interests. It represents an effort to erect a sort of voodoo wall of rigid constitutional and
statutory safeguards to protect us from the realities of political life."

For documentation of that you can read the speeches of my old college friend Frank Holman, past president of the American Bar Association, who seems to have played Svengali to Bricker's Trilby in this
whole affair and whose vision of the future is even more hagridden

than Bricker's. "Who can say that such precious rights as jury trial and the writ of habeas corpus may not, in the opinion of the Supreme Court, have to yield to the common denominator of basic rights as understood by fifty-seven other nations?" (Arthur H. Dean writes in *Foreign Affairs* that the Supreme Court is about as likely to do that as to reverse its decision in *Marbury v. Madison* and deprive itself of the right to nullify laws that conflict with the Constitution.) But Holman sees another frightful prospect; a treaty might "accord to the nationals of all countries the privilege to aspire to the office of President of the United States." So, if we don't adopt the Bricker amendment, we are likely to get a Russian or a Chinese President—and not Chiang Kai-shek, who is apparently the favorite candidate of some of our statesmen. Holman did stop short of the ultimate absurdities offered as serious arguments by some people on his side—that the Genocide Convention, which there is little chance that the United States will ever adopt, would permit foreigners (Russians, no doubt) to invade this country to punish lynching, and would forbid the practice of contraception, now illegal only in Connecticut.

Well, when people say they see flying saucers it is not much use telling them that it is only an optical illusion; let's see if there is anything we can hold onto. On the Bricker-Holman theory we can't trust the President, or the Senate, or the Supreme Court (or even the House of Representatives, much); where then is our hope? Ah, here is where the famous "which clause" comes in. "A treaty shall become effective as internal law only through legislation which would be valid in absence of a treaty." This is the one which knocks out the constitutional provision that treaties made under the authority of the United States shall be the supreme law of the land, "anything in the constitution or the laws of any state to the contrary notwithstanding." The United States as a sovereign power could not make arrangements in dealing with other powers unless they covered matters ordinarily within Congressional authority. That is to say, if that very able lawyer the Secretary of State has correctly analyzed this proposal (on his second try), many treaties would require the approval of all forty-eight states to become effective.

That this would cause a certain reluctance on the part of foreign powers to enter into treaties with us is obvious; but the main point about it is that here at last we discover the only officials whom these scared bunnies supporting the Bricker amendment really trust—the members of the state legislatures, the very men whom the Founding Fathers distrusted above all others.

If we feel that way we had better repeal the whole Constitution and go back to the Articles of Confederation, with no executive, no judiciary, no taxing power in Congress, and no state compelled to do anything it didn't want to do. And we face just that possibility, though I do not expect that it will be realized, in another proposal for amendment.

The Constitution provides an alternative process of amendment which has never been used—application to Congress by the legislatures of two thirds of the states to call a convention for the proposing of amendments, which thereafter would not have to run the gantlet of Congress but would become part of the Constitution when ratified by three fourths of the states. Congress on such application must call the convention; nobody knows how its members would be chosen, whether by popular vote or by state legislatures (or even by appointment, since Congress could apparently enact any method that it might prefer). Application has been made by some twenty-odd legislatures, not far short of the necessary two thirds, in the interest of one particular amendment. But the Constitution says that the purpose of this convention shall be the proposing of amendments, plural; many eminent lawyers hold that it could propose as many as it wanted to—could, if it wished, propose to throw the entire Constitution aside. It wouldn't do that, of course; but I am sure that if such a convention ever met, there would be some very determined attacks on the Bill of Rights—the Fifth Amendment particularly, and very likely the First one too.

These attacks might or might not succeed; the amendment most likely to be approved by such a convention would be the one in whose interest it was proposed—that Congress be forbidden to impose income estate taxes above twenty-five per cent, except in case of a major war. In this form it was too raw to gain much support, as soon as people began talking about it, so it was materially modified by Senator Dirksen and Representative Chauncey Reed; but no matter how thin you slice it, it tastes the same. It is a program for transferring as much as possible of the tax burden from the rich to the poor—about sixteen billion dollars, according to an estimate by the New Council for American Business. I have read elaborate arguments that it is nothing of the sort, which are not at all convincing. In these times, and in such times as we are likely to have to live through for several decades, the government will need a great deal of money; it is going to have to get it out of somebody, painful as this will be to all of us. And the argument that the twenty-five-per-cent limit would give relief to the lower brackets is not impressive; it could mean that people who now pay twenty-two per cent would have to pay twenty-five. Or else—and this of course is what the twenty-five-per-centers are shooting at—a sales tax, which would fall most heavily on the people who have to spend their incomes, with no surplus for investment.

Ironically, it looks at this writing as if these gentlemen might get their sales tax, if it can be jammed through Congress; but they will still be stuck with their income tax too. For the government still needs money, and the idea of reducing that need by disarming our defenses does not seem to have taken hold very widely, especially in the Northern cities exposed to enemy attack.

This twenty-five-per-cent proposal, however, it not the only competitor for the honor of being the Twenty-third Amendment. There is another—that the government be forbidden to engage in any kind of business whatsoever. Probably most of the men behind this have their eyes on atomic-energy and public-power developments—which they may get their hooks on anyway, under present policies—but they have singularly neglected their best talking point: that if this amendment were adopted, the government would have to sell the Post Office Department to private industry.

There would be no bidders on this insolvent institution unless all lids on the rates were taken off. With rates boosted to a point that would show a profit, the flood of publicity and promotional material that now overloads the desk of everybody in the news business would shrink to the vanishing point; and if first-class mail cost a quarter instead of three cents, fewer letters would be written, and fewer people would get into trouble. Also it is possible that private industry might be able to solve the problem of putting gum on our postage stamps that would stick, which seems to be beyond the capacity of Postmaster General Summerfield, as it was of his Democratic predecessors.

A more modest amendment, proposed by Senator McCarran, went through the Senate in the spring of 1953 without difficulty, as might have been expected, but died in the House, as might also have been expected. It simply provided that the President could not take possession of private property except in a manner prescribed by act of Congress. The general public may have supposed that the Supreme Court had said just that, in dealing with the President's seizure of the steel mills in 1952; but the eagle eye of McCarran saw deeper. What the Supreme Court said was that the President could not do it *in those circumstances;* it did not say that he could never do it in any circumstances. Even some of those who concurred in the opinion that slapped him down suggested that in time of insurrection or invasion (and a general atomic-bombing attack might be as serious as invasion) he might have more authority.

"In the absence of action by Congress," said Mr. Justice Clark, "the President's independent power to act depends on the gravity of the situation confronting the nation." The McCarran amendment clearly calls for action by Congress; but can Congress predict, and provide against, every emergency in which quick action might be essential? What the McCarran amendment means is that no unforeseen contingency shall ever occur; and I doubt if to guarantee that is within the power of Congress, even if the Constitution should grant it such authority.

All these proposed amendments—as well as the Twenty-second, which was actually adopted—have one thing in common: they would weaken a government which their proponents evidently regard as too strong. Fear of a too strong federal government is nothing new; it was widely and eloquently expressed in the debate over the adoption of the Constitution. There is, however, one difference: in 1788 those who feared a strong government were mostly the poor and the champions of the poor; now it is the champions of the rich—who are richer and more powerful than could have been foreseen when this government was established and who, if the government were weakened, would be more powerful still.

Whether this country would be better off, in a time of placid international relations, if the rich were more powerful than they have been in the twenty years before January 1953 is a legitimately debatable question. But those were not years—at least the last dozen—of placid international relations; nor will the next twenty years be so either. In this "businessman's administration" the rich will certainly be more influential than they have been in the twenty years preceding it, but it looks as if they may avoid the grosser errors of the period from 1921 to 1933; and in any case the structure of government still stands, with little damage, and is in the hands of men who seem to realize that the international situation is and will continue to be of overriding importance. We should buy an increase in the power of any class in the community at too high a price if it meant weakening the government of the United States in a time when it may have to be able to act firmly, and to act fast.

HISTORY IN DOUBLETHINK

[*The deference often shown in Congressional hearings ten years ago to the political pronouncements of certain ex-Communists might have been funny if it hadn't sometimes been nearly tragic. These men had changed sides completely but retained in full their certainty of superiority to the unsaved, that "their dogmas, whatever they may be, are complete, perfect and infallible." This Davis saw as the mark of the totalitarian mind.*

[*The first aim of this piece was to set forth the irony of official deference to men whose chief claim to be believed was that they had been completely wrong some years before. A second but equally important point was its rejection of the "generation on trial" theme. It is not true, Davis said, that great numbers of American intellectuals were taken in by Communists in the nineteen-thirties. The ones who were taken in were noisy about it, to be sure; and it is easy to see why they would like to believe today that their past perversion was simply part of some mass phenomenon—or, if not "mass," one which caught all those of high intellect and refined sensibility. Here an American intellectual who had been sharply and publicly opposed to Communism throughout his working life refutes their claim. The newspapers, magazines and books of the thirties are still available; it is easy to find out for ourselves that most intellectuals were not taken in.*]

How long will these ex-Communists and ex-sympathizers abuse the patience of the vast majority which had sense enough never to be Communists or sympathizers at all? They have a constitutional right, of course, to tell us what we must do to be saved—as they have always done. Twenty years ago they were telling us the direct opposite of what they tell us now; but they were just as sure then as now that they had the sole and sufficient key to salvation and that those who did not accept it were forever damned. One becomes bored.

The arrogance of the ex-Communists is the most irritating thing about them, but not the most dangerous; and for that arrogance they have, in this country, official countenance. Congressional committees always seem willing to take the word of an ex-Communist—provided he has become a reactionary—against that of a man who never was a Communist. This preference may seem in contradiction to the stringent provisions of the McCarran Internal Security Act against the admission into this country of ex-Communists from abroad; but those provisions are only a phase of the protective tariff. The lucrative home market for exposures and revelations must be protected for domestic industry against the pauper labor of Europe. With this Congressional benediction there is some excuse for the ex-Communists to think they are a superior species.

But they thought that when they were Communists too; through a hundred-and-eighty-degree turn in their opinions they have clung to this certainty of their superiority to the unsaved—and to the concomitant certainty that their dogmas, whatever they may be, are complete, perfect and infallible. This is the mark of the *anima naturaliter totalitariana;* for I suspect it is not so much that Communism is an ineradicable taint, its aftereffects lingering in the system after the patient appears to be completely cured, as that it is people of this habit of mind who are most likely to become Communists. It is no accident that so many ex-Communists have become extreme reactionaries; it is remakable only that some few of them have escaped into sanity. Aside from these saving few, Communist and ex-Communist are only species of the same genus; and I do not see why we should pay any more attention to them now than we did then.

For it is worth remembering, and worth reminding the young—before the ex-Communists pervert history any further—that not very many people did pay attention to them, even twenty years ago when what was then the American way of life (many people thought it was the only way) had come pretty close to breakdown. Some few thought they had found the answer in Technocracy, a somewhat more numerous few in Communism; but most people preferred to try another of the American ways of life; in the presidential election of 1932 the Communists got a hundred thousand votes out of forty million. In the "intellectual" world the infection was stronger than elsewhere, yet even this turned out to be no more than a temporary nuisance. It spoiled some potentially good writers, it made considerable noise for a while; but it passed like any other fad, leaving as perhaps its principal legacy the angry writings of ex-Communists turned reactionary, who are still telling us what we must do to be saved. Where is their claim to authority? Not in their record.

But they seem able to persuade some people who were not there that their aberration was an all but universal aberration. Whittaker

Chambers tells us that "from 1930 on a small intellectual army passed over to the Communist party." So it did, and a small army can look like a large army to a man who is in the midst of it; marching in step with his comrades, he might never notice the far larger army on the next road that is headed in the other direction. Alistair Cooke, who was not among us in those days, thought that in Alger Hiss a generation was on trial. That was not true even of his generation of "intellectuals"—not even of young intellectuals who graduated from college, looked around them and could see no jobs. Some of them fell for Communism; most did not. I suspect that Cooke's friends include some ex-Communists who cannot bring themselves to admit that their error was at all unusual; who must persuade others, as they have already persuaded themselves, that if minds of their quality were deluded, all other minds must have been deluded too.

Deceiving others is not yet too easy; men may write books and editorials and magazine articles, but evidence to the contrary is still available in the libraries. The first essential is to deceive one's self; and that, to the totalitarian mind (whether Communist or ex-Communist), offers little difficulty.

Control of the past depends above all on the training of memory. To make sure that all written records agree with the orthodoxy of the moment is merely a mechanical act. But it is also necessary to remember that events happened in the desired manner. And if it is necessary to rearrange one's memories or to tamper with written records, then it is necessary to forget that one has done so.

So wrote Emmanuel Goldstein in *The Theory and Practice of Oligarchical Collectivism* (quoted by George Orwell in *1984*). This, of course, is the well-known art of Doublethink; Communists have to learn it, and ex-Communists find it hard to forget. And those of them who have bounced back all the way from one extreme to the other find it easier to keep practicing Doublethink because there is one cardinal principle that they have carried with them. They used to tell us that black was white, and damn us for doubting them. Now they admit it is black; but then and now they insist that there is no such thing as gray. If this requires a man to misread history, that is a small matter, so long as it enables him to retain confidence in his own intellectual integrity. And it would be unfair to say that he tries to persuade others to misread history; he remembers that events happened in the desired manner.

These reflections are obviously evoked by the great hullabaloo over

Witness and will, I presume, be denounced as part of the "moral lynch-ing" of Whittaker Chambers. Well, on the evidence as known, I think Chambers told the truth about his relations with Hiss; I incline to be-lieve him (with some reservations) about most of the other people with whom he claims to have been involved in subversive activities; and he writes with cogency and authority about the strange and turbid inner world of Whittaker Chambers. But he seems to have understood very little of what was going on around him, as is amply proved by his mis-interpretations of history. A man who felt that he was returning in 1938 to the same world he had left in 1925, and who seems seriously to have accepted the suggestion that the Roosevelt administration might have him shot, had little awareness of objective reality.

The reason of course is obvious: Communism and the reaction from Communism had been the great fact in Chambers's life; it was incon-ceivable to him that it was not the great fact, if not in the life of all other individuals, at least in that of the society in which he existed. He quotes, and accepts, Krivitzky's remark that "there are only revo-lutionists and counter-revolutionists"—which Chambers underlines by adding that "in action, there is no middle ground." Yet one of the most protuberant facts of the history of the past twenty years is that there is a middle ground, and that in America and Western Europe the people who hold that middle ground have defeated both extremes. This is a matter of record; but since it doesn't fit in with the divinely handed-down interpretation of history it is necessary to remember that events happened in the desired manner, regardless of the facts.

Greater men than Chambers share this habit of mind. I do not sup-pose that John Dos Passos was ever a Communist; but certainly his sympathies, twenty or thirty years ago, were as near to the red end of the spectrum as they are now to the ultraviolet. At each end, he looked at the world through the appropriately colored glasses—which accounts for his seeing many things so clearly and not seeing many other things at all. He now feels that "we live in a society dedicated to its own de-struction. How can it be," he asks, "that in a few short years we have sunk so low?" The answer is easy: we haven't—except in the opinion of a man who, instead of contrasting 1952 with 1932, merely contrasts his own ideologies of those years.

[· · ·]

I can venture these criticisms of Dos Passos, for some of whose gifts I have much admiration, in the confidence that they will not disturb him at all; he has discounted all criticism beforehand. He is pretty sure that "the 'liberals' who control communications in the press and the radio and the schools and the colleges in this country have already crawled under the yoke of the Communist party"; we are not dues-paying members (maybe he thinks we are too parsimonious) but we are the dupes of a sinister hoax. Thus lightly to dismiss all contrary opinion no doubt helps a man to feel comfortable inside himself; but I do not think it makes him a very useful guide to the people—a vast majority—who are not blind to the realities under their noses.

A curious thing about these ex-Communists is that they seem to derive a melancholy satisfaction from the conviction that they are on the losing side. A non-Communist Chinese, just at present, might be excused for thinking so; but there is no evidence for it in American history, except as rewritten by Doublethink. I suspect the answer is that they are naturally religious, temperamentally inclined to view the world in terms of catastrophe and apocalypse; someday the heavens will be rolled up like a scroll; *Dies irae, dies illa, solvit saeclum in favilla;* and they can view this with equanimity, since their personal salvation is secure. But once again, this makes them undependable guides for the vast majority which believes—as the vast majority of Americans has believed throughout our history, and has repeatedly proved—that something can be done about it, even if not so much as could be wished.

And the essential damage that could be done by these totalitarian thinkers—totalitarian no matter which end of the spectrum they may be on—would be to convince other people that there is no use trying to do anything about it; that those who are trying are only crypto-Communists even if they may not know it. A notable example is Chambers's comments on the New Deal revolution—which, as he and Senator Taft agreed, was a Socialist revolution in the name of liberalism. It has been amply pointed out that people who call it that do not know what Socialism means; but Chambers does indeed hit its essential point when he calls it "a shift of power from business to Government." It was that, and I happen to believe that was a good idea—always provided that you do not give excessive power to Government, as we have not. (Even Chambers has to acknowledge that it was Government, after all, which convicted Hiss.)

Chambers apparently does not approve of that shift, and thinks we were better off when business had the power. It is the privilege of any citizen to think so; but when he says "it was a struggle for revolutionary power, which in our age is always a struggle for control of the masses," he confuses, or is likely to make his readers confuse, two kinds of revolutions carried out by two different methods. The Roosevelt revolution was the sixth we have had; and like all the others, it was stopped before it went too far. There was a revolution in the early days of independence, a counter-revolution in 1787, a counter-counter-revolution in 1800; none of them found it necessary to resort to the guns of a cruiser, the dispersal of an elected assembly by bayonets, or the mechanisms of the police state. We had another partial revolution in Jackson's day; still another, begun by the Congressional elections of 1866 and consummated twenty years later by the Supreme Court's decision that the Fourteenth Amendment protects corporations, transferred power from Government to business. The Roosevelt revolution merely reversed that. Chambers has a right to dislike the reversal, but when he implies that the Roosevelt revolution and Communist revolution differed only in degree, whosoever is deceived thereby is not wise.

All these are matters of record and will remain so unless—which I do not expect—the Doublethinkers get control of the country and "make sure that all written records agree with the orthodoxy of the moment." Until then, they are more of a nuisance than a menace—as they were in the days when they thought that salvation was to be found in Moscow. They are religious people; as Arthur Schlesinger, Jr., has pointed out, a man may be religious without feeling certain that he has the complete and unalterable final truth and that those who disagree with him are damned in time and in eternity. But these people must feel that. Some of them, finding that final truth is not in Moscow, have sought and found it in Rome; hardier characters become their own Popes and are just as sure of their own infallibility as they were in the days when they parroted the resolutions of the Comintern.

There is another kind of thinking, which some religious people find not inconsonant with their view of the relations between man and God. I described it in the *Saturday Review* twenty years ago and it seems pertinent to quote that description now:

> To admit that there are questions which even our so impressive intelligence is unable to answer, and at the same time not to despair of the ability of the human race to find, eventually, better answers than we can reach as yet—to recognize that there is nothing to do but keep on trying as well as we can, and to be as content as we can with the small gains that in the course of ages amount to something—that requires some courage and some balance.

That kind of thinking has played a great part in American history, from Benjamin Franklin down to John Dewey; and it has worked.

But the Communists against whom I was writing then had no use for it, nor have most of them now that they are ex-Communists. There must be a final truth and they must have it; experimental thinking is only a groping in the dark. And if its successes are written in the record of American history from Jefferson (yes, and Hamilton) through Lincoln down to Franklin Roosevelt, that fact can be obliterated by remembering that events happened in the desired manner—by knowing that press and radio and schools and colleges are all controlled by the Communists and that the Roosevelt administration had its critics shot.

I repeat—one becomes bored.

ARE WE WORTH SAVING? AND IF SO, WHY?

[*This 1953 Phi Beta Kappa oration at Harvard was later printed in* Harper's *as well as the* Harvard Alumni Bulletin *and then used for the last chapter in* But We Were Born Free. *Our civilization had put forth two great missionary efforts, he, began, the Catholic effort of the sixteenth century and the Protestant effort of the nineteenth. These were both expressions of a strong and vigorous culture. In fact, "By the nineteenth century the West had no doubt that it was the culmination of all human progress to date." This led him to examine the values in our civilization.*]

In the middle of the twentieth century the principal questions in dispute among Western intellectuals seem to be whether the West can be saved, and if it is worth saving. The two most popular of recent historical philosophers both think the Western world is going downhill, and one of them seems to feel that it won't be much loss. Spengler appreciated the loss more than Toynbee; if he felt that it was inevitable, that was perhaps because he was an artist rather than a philosopher. Yet, though it may be only a coincidence, it is certainly a disquieting one that he and Toynbee, starting from very different premises, come out to about the same conclusion as to the phase of development that our civilization has reached; and still more disquieting, as to what lies ahead—what Spengler called Caesarism, and Toynbee the universal state.

There are optimists, of course, who think that a really universal state—a world-wide state—could be created by some other means than military force; Spengler and Toynbee are not among them nor, to compare small things with great, am I. So long as Communists remain Communists any world coalition government would be subject to the same dangers, and likely to meet the same fate, as the coalition governments of Poland and Czechoslovakia; and there is still wisdom enough in the West not to run that risk.

[· · ·]

Spengler is dead and can write no more; he has said his say; within his artistic scheme, the progressive deterioration of any culture seemed inevitable. Any man who keeps on writing and talking is likely to contradict himself; Toynbee has written so much that he has involved himself in about as many contradictions as Dr. John H. Watson, when he set down the history of Sherlock Holmes. A few years ago Toynbee seemed to have some hope that the creative minority of our civilization had not yet lost its creativity, not yet become a merely dominant minority, for the inadequacy of whose rule the internal proletariat would have to compensate by creating or adopting a universal religion; now he seems to think we have passed the point of no return. We passed it, apparently—or at least so he thought when he delivered the Reith Lectures last year; he may since have changed his mind again—we passed it toward the end of the seventeenth century, when men became disgusted with the endless religious wars which neither side ever decisively won, and turned to secular interests—turned from preoccupation with preparation for the next world to consideration of what could be done with this one; and, increasingly, to what could be done with it through technology.

And for this apostasy, thinks Toynbee, God has punished us—punished the West by the loss of the East; not only our territorial possessions and our commerce there but our moral influence in an East which increasingly turns toward our Communist enemy. The East rejected our religion, and our technology with it, when they were parts of an indivisible way of life; it accepted our technology when it was divorced from our religion (and incidentally had become far more efficient; that is to say, far more worth accepting) with consequences which became apparent at Pearl Harbor in 1941 and more recently in Korea. "The fortunes," he says, "of Western civilization in the mission field veered right around from conspicuous failures to conspicuous successes as soon as its attitude toward its own ancestral religion had veered around from a warm devotion to a cool skepticism." Which appears to mean, when the mission field had become the field of a new kind of missionary, offering no longer the lamp of life but oil for the lamps of China, and all that went with it.

History does not support this interpretation. It has been subjected to a number of searching criticisms—notably by Professor Michael Karpovitch in the *New Leader* and by G. F. Hudson in *Commentary*. Karpovitch, after pointing out that Toynbee is wrong on all the things that Karpovitch knows most about, suavely admits that no doubt he is right in other fields. Hudson makes a more general attack on the entire doctrine, to which a layman can offer only a couple of corroborative footnotes. The great success of Protestant missions—not to mention a vigorous revival of Catholic missions and the beginnings of the penetration of the East by Western technology as well—came at a time when

the cool skepticism of the eighteenth century had been buried under a
new wave of evangelical fervor, when Protestantism was not only as
vigorous but as dogmatic as the Catholicism of the Counter-Reformation.
(I do not know whether Toynbee regards Modernist Protestantism as a
religion at all; but he can hardly deny that title to Fundamentalist
Protestantism.)

What at present appears to be the failure of Protestantism in China
seems to be due less to divine wrath at apostasy than to an intensified
form of the thing that caused the eventual failure of Catholicism in
Japan, when it had lost little if any of its energy and fervor in Europe—
the fear of a suspicious and despotic government that religion had been
merely the cover for imperialistic political intrigues. In either case there
was little evidence on which to base that fear; but despots need little
evidence—especially despots newly come to power, who still feel insecure.

It might indeed be argued that the West, in its relation with the East,
is being punished for its sins. But the sin is not apostasy; it is too great
faith. We have all observed that the sin that is most surely and sharply
punished is a mistake—however well intended, however it may have
seemed at the time the thing to do. The punishment is often delayed,
and falls on the descendants of those who made the mistake—often on
innocent bystanders. "Those eighteen upon whom the tower of Siloam
fell, and slew them—think ye that they were sinners above all men that
dwelt in Jerusalem?" We are authoritatively assured that they were not.
The sin was that of the architect or the contractor; the punishment fell
on people who only happened to be around. Many Europeans and
Americans have suffered in Asia, and may presently suffer in Africa, for
mistakes for which they were in no way responsible—mistakes made
from the highest motives, as a result of faith.

For alongside the theological religion of the West, which in the past
two and a half centuries has had its ups as well as its downs, there was
growing up in Western Europe and America a secular religion, held as
fervently by devout Christians as by rationalists—the faith in freedom,
in self-government, in democracy. (Indeed, the only living ex-president
of Columbia University* has more than once implied that only believers
in a theological religion can believe in this secular religion too. The
evidence for this cannot be found in history.) The Westerners who
interpenetrated the East in the nineteenth century, whether missionaries, engineers, businessmen or administrators, mostly carried this
religion with them. They made many mistakes; but it was devotion to

*Dwight D. Eisenhower

this secular religion that led them to make what, from the standpoint of practical consequences, was the worst mistake the West ever made in dealing with the East. They educated the natives.

Not merely in the operation of modern weapons, though they did that first, for the greater convenience of Western powers warring among themselves; these were men of faith, faith in the whole Western culture of which this secular religion was becoming steadily a more important part. Many of those whom they educated sprang from cultures far older than ours and in some respects more distinguished. But it was the Western culture that seemed to work, so it did not have to be forced on them; in this case they really did call us to deliver their minds, at least, from error's chain. We educated them in Western medicine and engineering, in Western government and law. And in the course of that education the pupils were exposed to the fact that there were such things as freedom and self-government and democracy—things which the educators obviously regarded as good for themselves; it was only a question of time till the pupils began to suspect that they might be good for everybody. Educate any man, of whatever race or color, in what he didn't know before and you are taking a chance; how he will turn out will depend somewhat on the education but more on his background and environment and on what was in him to start with; you may get a Nehru and you may get a Jomo Kenyatta. The one thing they have in common is a conviction that those who educated them, having fulfilled that function, ought to get out.

I have enough faith in that secular religion to believe that in the long run the consequences of this will be beneficial—as they seem to be already in the successor states of the Indian Empire. But that is no consolation to those on whom various towers of Siloam have fallen elsewhere.

This digression was necessitated by the fact that the most popular of contemporary historians has offered an explanation not only for our unsatisfactory relations with Asia and Africa but for the general dilemma of our times—an explanation which not only to me but to many of my betters seems no explanation at all. But what then is the matter with us? What have we left, if anything, that is worth saving?

This first and obvious answer, of course, is "If we aren't worth saving, who is?" Faulty as we are, we seem infinitely preferable—by our standards—to the moral nihilism and intellectual rigidity of the Soviet system which is competing with us for the allegiance of the East; competing indeed, though with little success outside of France and Italy, for the allegiance of our own citizens. Unfortunately, we do not always seem preferable to those among whom our missionaries, and those of the opposition, are working; and if through force or deception they have once accepted the opposition's gospel, they find that the choice is irrevocable.

[· · ·]

Granted, however, that from anything that could be called an ethical viewpoint we are better worth saving than our adversaries, this is no proof that we are going to be saved unless we have the qualities that enable us to save ourselves. The western Roman Empire was far more worth saving than the barbarian tribal dominions that surrounded it and eventually overran it; but its own faults brought it down. This is worth mentioning since not only Spengler and Toynbee but lesser men have dealt with our predicament in terms of what befell civilizations of the past; and these analyses, however embellished with facts, or conjectures, from Chinese and Mayan and Sumerian history, all rest pretty much on the one case about which we have tolerably complete information—the decline and fall of the Roman Empire. Many historians have attempted to explain it; almost all of them, even Gibbon —even Rostovtzeff—seem to me to explain it largely in terms of their own experience, and observation of their own times.

I shall not add to that confusion, but shall only point out one or two details in which our situation is different. We know now that the happiness and prosperity of the age of the Antonines, which so impressed Gibbon, was only relative—considerable no doubt compared to what had gone before and what was to come afterward, but behind the spendid front there was a dry rot inside. Economically the Empire was deteriorating; and intellectually, too.

Economically the Western world is doing pretty well nowadays; and in the English-speaking and Scandinavian countries (Switzerland and the Low Countries as well) the problem that Rome never solved and that finally did more than anything else to bring Rome down has been solved with a fair degree of success—the problem of passing prosperity around, of seeing that everybody gets some of it. If France and Italy solved that problem too, the Communist parties in those countries would soon shrink to the hard core. Our civilization, said Rostovtzeff thirty years ago—lately echoed and emphasized by Professor Robinson of Brown—our civilization will not last unless it be a civilization not of one class but of the masses. This is a warning that might more pertinently be directed toward the Soviet Union than the United States, in so far as what exists in the Soviet Union can be called a civilization. As for Rostovtzeff's last despairing question, "Is not every civilization bound to decay as soon as it penetrates the masses?" we can only say that we shall in due course find out. We have started in that direction and we can't turn back.

The Romans, outside of the cities, never got started; and even there civilization was a narrowing pyramid, with a hollow top. The most notable thing about the age of the Antonines was its intellectual sterility, in a period of rest between calamities when the Western world might have made vast advances and fortified itself against the calamities that were to come—the classic case of what Toynbee calls the loss of creativity in the dominant minority. Are we losing it? Dr. J. G. de Beus of the Netherlands Embassy in Washington, who has lately analyzed these forecasts of the future, thinks the Western world is still vigorously creative—not only in science and technology but in politics, domestic and foreign, and in art and letters as well.

[· · ·]

The first condition of the survival of any civilization is that it should win its wars. Rome did, till its armies wore themselves out fighting one another.

[· · ·]

What a civilization like ours, which is not a universal state but a coalition of independent powers, can do to insure its own continuance depends quite as much on how each state manages its own internal affairs. Here the Romans met the proximate cause of their disaster. When they had a good man at the head of the state all went well—unless he was a good man like Antoninus Pius, perhaps the most virtuous of all rulers of a great realm and certainly pre-eminent in manly beauty, but he appears to have been only a glorified Calvin Coolidge, who sat there and went through the motions while the problems piled up for his unhappy successor. But when the Romans got a bad man in, there was no way to get him out except by assassination or revolution. Over a period of ninety years almost every Emperor—and they were many—was got out by one or the other of those methods—good men as well as bad.

The nations which embody Western civilization are no longer subject to that danger, but their political systems have other defects. Mr. Walter Lippmann remarks that if the free world is in peril, it is not because our enemies are so strong but because the free nations are so badly governed; and they are badly governed because of the usurpation of power by the national legislatures. . . . Well—we must discriminate. In the nations of the British Commonwealth the supremacy of the legislature is the essence of their constitutions, and they have learned how to make it work. In the French Republic it is also the essence of the constitution; in the three quarters of a century of the Third and Fourth Republics they have not learned how to make it work. In our own republic it is in flat conflict with the Constitution, and no wonder it doesn't work. It is an old story; long before the recent publicized attacks on the State Department, and on the President's control of foreign policy, the principal problem of our government was Congressional usurpation, usually through committees, of executive functions. Congress not only tells administrators what they must do, which is its right, but how to do it, which is not its right and is wholly outside Congress's field of practical competence as well as of authority.

A Congress which ate raw meat during the last few years of a Democratic administration has shown that it is not going back to a milk diet just because the Republicans are in power. Nor would it do so even in wartime unless compelled, as it has been compelled by every strong President. Until the question whether it would be so compelled again may arise, we might reflect that all the periods of Congressional government in our history have been periods either of bad government or of do-nothing government. There have been times when we could afford a do-nothing government; we can afford it no longer. Still less a bad government.

But to return from this digression into the factors that will make it practically possible—or practically impossible—to save us; back to the original question, Why should we be saved? What have we got that our adversaries have not that makes us worth saving? Our faults, God knows, are numerous and glaring enough; recognition of those faults is the chief cause of the loss of confidence that has afflicted so many people of the Western world. But we do recognize them; we do not pretend that our failures were decreed by ineluctable historical necessity; nor do we rewrite history according to the precepts of Doublethink, to prove that they never happened at all.

What we have to offer, to the contemporary world and to the future, is a method—and the freedom of the mind that makes that method possible. Not an infallible method, but the best yet discovered for reaching increasingly closer approximations to the truth. It will never offer its conclusions with such assurance as does dialectical materialism—which, by a singular coincidence, always seems to produce the conclusions that are convenient for the men in power. It can only say, We have kept the door open for exploration of all possibilities, consideration of all objections, application of all possible tests; and this is what seems to be true. Maybe something else will seem more probable later on, but this is the best we can do now. Or, as the method was summarized long ago—Prove all things; hold fast that which is good.

This method has been responsible for almost all human progress. Outside the Western world it does not exist, except in those parts of the East which have been influenced by Western thought; if it died here, it would die there too. Ex-President Conant of Harvard has remarked that the right to think and question and investigate is the basic difference between the free world and the world of totalitarianism. It might well be the basic difference that would save us, if it came to a shooting war; and whether it does that or not, this one thing—the scientific method, and above all the freedom of the mind that makes it possible—is what makes us worth saving. As G. F. Hudson has observed, "To repudiate faith in freedom is to abandon Western civilization."

The founders of this republic held that faith so firmly that its guarantee was embedded in the very first amendment to the Constitution, almost as soon as the Constitution was adopted. Yet lately that faith has been repudiated by many of our fellow citizens, if indeed they ever held it, and in that repudiation lies our greatest danger; it is this, rather than any external attack, that might bring us down. That repudiation takes various forms and appears on various levels. One phase of it was the recent attack on the Bureau of Standards and particularly the manner in which the Secretary of Commerce questioned its objectivity. As Eugene Rabinowitch commented in the *Bulletin of the Atomic Scientists,* the government has the right, if it should so choose, to subordinate the findings of science to the demands of business; but it has no right to attempt to coerce the scientists into adjusting their findings to those demands. That is Lysenkoism; it is something we had better leave to the enemy. Happily, the Secretary of Commerce now seems to have come around to that point of view.

But far more widespread and more dangerous is the general attack on the freedom of the mind. George Kennan said at Notre Dame that it springs from forces too diffuse to be described by their association with the name of any one man or any one political concept—forces which perhaps were summarized by John Duncan Miller of the London *Times,* in the early days of McCarthyism, as a revolt of the primitives against intelligence. Unfortunately, it cannot be denied that after centuries of education we still have plenty of primitives—some of them white-collar or even top-hat primitives; a sediment, a sludge, at the bottom of American society—and I am afraid a fairly deep layer at that; people who seem actuated only by hatred and fear and envy. All the products of ignorance, for their fear is not a rational fear of a very formidable and unfriendly foreign power. I have received thousands of letters from people like that in recent years and they do not seem interested in Russia at all: what they hate and fear is their own neighbors who try to think. In the name of anti-Communism they try to strike down the freedom of the mind, which above all things differentiates us from the Communists; in the name of Americanism they try to suppress the right to think what you like and say what you think, in the evident conviction—in so far as they have reasoned conviction at all—that the principles on which this Republic was founded and has been operated will not bear examination. People like that are not merely un-American; they are anti-American.

We have now reached the point where, if agents of the FBI appear in the home town of a prominent man and begin asking questions about him, his neighbors know that he is either on his way to jail or to high public office. I doubt if such confusion is healthy. Judge Learned Hand, in a speech so often quoted that perhaps everybody now knows it by heart, has said that he believes that that community is already in process of dissolution where each man begins to eye his neighbor as a possible enemy, where nonconformity with the accepted creed is a mark of disaffection, where denunciation takes the place of evidence and orthodoxy chokes freedom of dissent.

If we are not to become such a community, the friends of freedom will have to stand up and fight.

In saying all this I am talking not about Western civilization but about the United States. And without apology, for we are the principal component of Western civilization, at least in the material sense. If we go down it all goes down—and when we confront a totalitarian dictatorship, whatever goes down stays down; it doesn't get up again. And we shall go down, unless we recognize what we have to fight for and have the courage to fight for it. What makes Western civilization worth saving is the freedom of the mind, now under heavy attack from the primitives—including some university graduates—who have persisted among us. If we have not the courage to defend that faith, it won't matter much whether we are saved or not.

I do not think Stalin could have licked us; I do not think that whoever now may be running Russia can lick us. But McCarthy and the spirit of McCarthyism could lick us—no doubt without intention, but they could—by getting us to fighting among ourselves like the Romans, by persuading every man that he must keep on looking over his shoulder, to make sure that the man beside him doesn't stab him in the back. There is still enough vitality in Western civilization to save us, unless we insist on disemboweling ourselves.

I should perhaps have begun this sermon with a text, a text taken from the fourth chapter of the first book of Samuel, the eighth and ninth verses—the mutual exhortations of the Philistines before the battle of Ebenezer. "Woe unto us!" they said when they realized that the Israelites had brought the Ark of God with them to battle. "Woe unto us! Who shall deliver us out of the hands of these mighty gods?" But then, realizing that nobody else was going to deliver them, they said to one another, "Be strong, and quit yourselves like men; and fight." And they did fight, and delivered themselves. So may we; but only if we quit ourselves like men. This republic was not established by cowards; and cowards will not preserve it.

ISN'T GOD GOING TO SAVE US?

[Parts of this article appeared in Harper's *before it was rewritten to appear as Chapter V in* Two Minutes Till Midnight. *I have cut about half, most of it devoted to developing a number of examples.]*

Many pious persons—religiously pious or politically pious—are sure we should win the next war no matter what weapons or what allies we may or may not have. Dr. Syngman Rhee, both religious and political, said at his Methodist Church in Washington, "We have God with us leading us by the hand, so I am not afraid." President Eisenhower, who thinks nobody can be a believer in democracy without "religious fervor," on the Fourth of July sent a message to the Philadelphia celebration that totalitarian doctrines "are certain to go, because in the long run nothing can stand before man's intense desire for personal liberty and his determination to worship in his own way." And the Vice-President has said that we shall win because we are on the right side.

So it seems that some contribution to this discussion could be made by some things I wrote before Dwight D. Eisenhower was President of the United States, but which are still pertinent, even in an administration which has merchandised God more energetically than any other in my recollection.

The Ethiopian thinks God is black; the mathematician thinks He is a mathematician. Caliban thought that He made things weak, that He might weakness vex; and Bruce Barton thinks He must be at least as good as Bruce Barton. These diverse images of various facets of deity as reflected in its creatures might usefully be borne in mind by the worthy persons who say that the sort of thing that is going on nowadays (this was written early in 1940) must be contrary to the will of God.

They may not put it that way but that is what they mean. They said that the Russian victory over Finland in the Winter War was contrary to the order of Nature—an argument hard to maintain, since in the natural order odds of fifty to one are likely to outweigh even the most superhuman courage, patriotism and endurance. They contended that Hitler would not win the big war then going on, because if he did History would have no meaning.

[· · ·]

What people mean when they say that the current trend of events is contrary to the order of Nature, or a denial of the meaning of History, is simply that this is the sort of thing that would not be allowed to happen if they were God. They would ruthlessly interfere with the order of Nature if their sense of the fitness of things required it; they would, if they had the power, deflect the current of History and make it come out to the answer they like to believe is written in the back of the book. But they can't do it; God has not seen fit to do it; and so these earnest persons confront the oldest of human dilemmas. Either God is not so good as Bruce Barton, who would never have tolerated much that has happened in recent years if he knew how to stop it, or else the Almighty is less powerful than those who invoke Him would like to think.

Impale yourself on whichever horn of this dilemma you prefer; but like many dilemmas, it is an artificial construct which fails to exhaust the possibilities. God may not be like that at all; it implies an anthropomorphic view of deity which may be wrong. (I should say, Which is almost certainly wrong, if I were not reluctant to join the innumerable caravan of those who know exactly what God is and wants.) It is worth noting that the most powerful of human beings, at the time this was first written, did not share the view of my friends; Hitler did not think that God was like Hitler. (Stalin, of course, had his own deity, revealed to him by dialectical materialism.) Hitler's theology, like most of his doctrine, was not wholly consistent; with an unfailing instinct he used whatever premise might be most suitable at the moment, even if it conflicted with something he said at some other moment. But the general outline was clear enough. God and Nature are different aspects of the same thing (Hitler perhaps never heard that this doctrine was first set forth in a Jewish document, the Book of Job, or that its principal proponent in more recent centuries was the Jew Spinoza). In Nature's rule book are laid down immutable laws, violation of which brings inescapable penalties; and God is simply the Official Scorer, who keeps the record of what happens to people who obey the rules and to those who break them.

With this basic determinism, however, free will was ingeniously intertwined in Hitler's theory.

[· · ·]

This was a highly effective working theology, with just about enough determinism to convince its adherents that they were sure to win, and not so much that they would be tempted to think that they could coast in without exerting themselves. Superficially the theory of God as the Scorekeeper resembled that once set down by a distinguished American sports writer:

> But when the One Great Scorer comes
> To write beside your name,
> He writes, not that you won or lost,
> But how you played the game.

So wrote Grantland Rice; but no scorekeeper he may ever have professionally encountered would have been so slipshod. The principal point in the scorekeeper's record is who won and who lost, a report of a result to which the details of the box score are subsidiary. What Mr. Rice really meant is that God is not a scorekeeper but a sports writer; but even Mr. Rice, reporting the brilliant and sportsmanlike playing of the losers, had to tell us pretty well up in the lead of the story that they lost none the less. So with historical reporters.

Hitler's doctrine seems better borne out by the evidence. The races of men, he held, struggle against one another for survival and dominance, each striving to outfight and outbreed all the rest; and the One Great Scorer watches the game with an objective and disinterested eye. He bestows no unearned favors on even so intrinsically superior a race as the Germans; He only keeps score, setting down Bismarck's hits and Hitler's runs and Bethmann-Hollweg's errors—concerned only with writing down results in the Book of Life and Death from whose record there is no appeal. And this doctrine reached its most brilliant flowering in Hitler's philosophy of rebellion.

[? · ·]

Most people find it hard to throw their full strength into a struggle unless they have the conviction, in whatever euphemisms they may prefer to phrase it, that God is on their side. No wonder. Through the century that ended in 1914 our side was winning; and all of us

now in our sixties, who grew up in a world where democracy and liberty and enlightenment and humanitarianism had been pretty steadily
increasing ever since our great-grandparents' day, took that sort of
thing as the order of Nature, the unfolding meaning of History, the
evident will of God. What has happened since does not seem to have
shattered that faith, at least in this relatively favored nation.

Again, no wonder. It comes hard to admit that this apparently pre-
destined triumph of the sort of thing we believe in may have been no
end product of history but a mere passing phase, that we may be enter-
ing a long new age of cruelty and violence and superstition. That
God has not stacked the deck in our favor; that what we believe makes
life worth living may presently be only another half-forgotten error of
the ancients unless we get out and do something about it; that we are
facing a desperate struggle, and there is no certainty at all that we are
going to win: these are conclusions that few people will accept if they
can find any other way out. For if we lose, we lose everything. The
One Great Scorer will not care how well or how badly we played; all
He will put down is that we lost, and the values that we call civilized
will be replaced, in life and in history, by values as abhorrent to ours
as ours would be to a Renaissance despot or a Soviet commissar.

[· · ·]

It is, I hope and believe, improbable, but in the light of past history
it is quite conceivable, that our grandchildren may take totalitarian
doctrines as gospel truth and may regard our faith in democracy, liberty, objective truth and objective justice with as much horror as we
regard the views of our ancestors on infant damnation.

My friends would never permit that to happen, nor would they
permit many other things that go on happening, if they were God;
but their bewilderment is at least a healthier frame of mind than any
attempt to fit recent history—or, for that matter, past history—into a
moral framework. To recognize that—if there be such a thing as punishment for sin—bad luck and honest mistakes appear to be offenses
far more heinous than the slaughter of the innocents or grinding down
the faces of the poor seems preferable to any attempt to explain history
within a moral framework—an attempt which is likely to issue only in
an insult to both divine and human intelligence.

I trust that no scared patriot will assume from the foregoing that I
suppose God is or will be on the side of the Russians. I want to make
it clear that I do not—first to keep from being lynched when the next
war comes, if the enemy should have some early successes; and second

because, if I may say so without assuming that, like a theologian, I
know exactly what God is and wants, I should like to encourage what
seems to me a sounder view of Man's relation to his Creator, now
more obscured than usual in Washington, where our governmental
theology shows an increasing resemblance to some of the more deplorable techniques of advertising.

The President of the National Council of Churches of Christ has
warned us that unless this nation is brought more fully under God,
both the nation and world peace will be in peril; but it is hard to see
how that can be done, more than it has already been done by this administration, without getting rid of the First Amendment of the Constitution. However, our peculiar brand of official religion works in
both directions; a Washington clergyman said last summer that God's
last hope is Eisenhower—a limitation on the power of the Deity which
at least some of the devout would not admit. In a recent issue of the
Reporter, the Reverend William Lee Miller had some comments on
our "official piety." The Vice-President has said that "free worship is
our greatest defense against enemies from without" (it is an excellent
thing, but its chief value is against enemies from within); the President
himself has said that faith is "our surest strength, our greatest resource."

Mr. Miller has his doubts as to whether it is either correct or wise to
hold that religion is a national resource (like the oil of Texas, the iron
of Minnesota) "especially useful for anti-Communist purposes," even
though our most eminent theologian, J. Edgar Hoover, says so. It is
certainly true that religion historically has been found useful in war,
but usually in the promotion of activities repugnant to Christian
ethics, such as the Crusaders' massacre of the entire population of
Jerusalem when they took the city.

And Mr. Miller has other and graver objections to these "general,
inoffensive and externalized religious affirmations" which we get from
our betters almost every day. "The God they mention," he says, "cannot be the God Whose ways are not our ways, Whose thoughts are not
our thoughts, and Whose purposes are larger than and different from
those of the Republican administration, America, the free world or
mankind." And Who may (I wouldn't pretend to know) conceivably
regard the present Russo-American antagonism with indifference.

CAN CIVILIZATION SURVIVE?

[*One of the commonest arguments against preparation for a nuclear war says "There can be no winner in nuclear war." An unspoken link here is supposed to equate that perhaps acceptable premise with "Winner and loser will be equally unfortunate." From there you see that preparation is useless.*

[*This is an equivocation. "Winner" in the first, and very likely acceptable, statement means someone who is better off after the war. "Winner" in the second means the fellow better off than the loser. Many people will refuse to accept this second statement though believing the first.*

[*That the argument is fallacious does not prove its proponents are wrong in their conclusions, but it does show they should get a better argument. Davis evidently felt this ten years ago. The first chapter of* Two Minutes Till Midnight *treated various possibilities inherent in thermonuclear war, as he perceived these in 1955. If most of that discussion has become somewhat dated, his answer to the "no winner" argument is still relevant.*]

There would not be much left after such a war, as Churchill has pointed out; but there would be more left for the winners than for the losers. It has often been said that there would be no victors, but that is not true. Nobody would have much left, but if we were the winners we should have the most essential and most valuable thing left: our freedom, and the opportunity to go on. It would be harder to go on, morally and intellectually as well as materially, but we should have to learn how to do it.

Ever since Hiroshima (Nagasaki, for some reason, gets very little sympathy) it has been fashionable to say that another war would destroy civilization. Even Mr. Malenkov fell into that phrasing once, though usually he makes it clear to his flock that only capitalist civilization would be destroyed. But both the expressions of concern and the sometimes fantastic remedies that have been proposed to avert the danger have usually had a materialistic emphasis—as if civilization consisted of improved real estate, which would be flattened by hydrogen or atomic bombs. But civilization is not buildings, however beautiful or historic or whatever they contain. Civilization is something inside the people, or some of the people, who live and work in those buildings—the way they feel, the way they think, their capacity for thinking. Certainly it needs some economic foundation—more now than it used to, since now there must be some technological foundation too. But all that is only the background, not the thing itself.

Civilization is not what your ancestors have built, but your capacity to build—intellectually and spiritually as well as architecturally. The French forgot that in 1940; they refused to defend Paris, which their ancestors had built, for fear that it might be destroyed. Given four years to think it over, under the stimulus of totalitarian occupation, they fought to liberate the essence of Paris at the risk of the destruction of its physical plant. They had remembered, by that time, what Paris is.

Which we might remember, too, when we consider how to save what is left of civilization. Let us by all means save, if we can, the improved real estate; but it would do no good to save the physical plant at the cost of what goes on inside it and which it exists to sustain.

[· · ·]

There are optimists who hold that even if the Communists conquered the world they would eventually soften up, like the barbarians who overran the Roman Empire, and a new civilization would evolve. But it could evolve only out of what is in Communist culture now. The barbarians who overran Rome were backwoodsmen who knew they had much to learn from the Romans; the men who rule in Moscow have made it a matter of dogma that they have nothing to learn from anybody.

The essence of their system is not an economic or a political doctrine, or practice; it is a technique—the technique of seizing and retaining power. And despite what used to be heard about the state withering away, experience has proved—as George Orwell discerned—that the objective is not any purpose for which power might be exercised, but power itself. The present association of the technique with Marxism is a historical accident—the accident that the political genius who invented it happened to call himself a Marxist, however he reinterpreted Marxian dogma to suit his own convenience. David Shub's biography of Lenin ought to have ended forever the theory that Lenin's pure and noble doctrines were perverted by his successor. Lenin invented the whole thing; Stalin merely added a few embellishments. And his method could be used in the service of any totalitarian system—or, as the case of the Nazis proved, of no coherent system at all. An evil knowledge has been let loose on the world; and it could cause as much trouble, and for as long, as the atomic bomb.

This technique is one to which the democracies have not yet found any satisfactory answer. It used to be thought that if a nation was internally sound—free, democratic, educated, with a reasonable prosperity reasonably well distributed—it was immune to infection. But Czechoslovakia was such a nation, and the Leninist jujitsu upset it in a week. Incidentally, the mere existence of this technique is a conclusive argument against the notion, still held here and there though not so widely as formerly, that we could prevent the destruction of civilization by setting up a world government. In such a government Russia and its satellites would have to have a considerable part; and a world government in which Communists sat on every committee and had places in every administrative office would be far more permeable to the Leninist technique than any national government.

The ethical values of a "civilization" growing out of that system would be the ethical values that it has now. Lenin may have thought he was a Marxist, but according to Shub he derives far more from early Russian revolutionaries who held that whatever promotes the success of the revolution is moral, what hinders it immoral. Lenin Marxized the formula a little; morality is what unites the workers around the proletariat. But what is the proletariat? Lenin invented the professional revolutionary as trustee for the proletariat, and ever since then Communist morality has been whatever promoted the interest of the faction of professional revolutionaries that had the upper hand. The cruder Nazis blurted it out: right is what serves the interest of the state; wrong is what harms it. But whether they called it the state, the revolution or the proletariat they all meant the same thing: all power to Our Side, and anything goes to get it or keep it. The ethics of capitalist democracy leave much to be desired, but they are certainly an improvement on that.

But there is an even stronger reason for believing that nothing we call civilization could grow out of the Communist system. There was at least this to be said for the Nazis: their doctrinal system was so absurd that they often did not take it seriously themselves. Russian totalitarianism is tied to a doctrine which, if it does not claim to have discovered yet the complete final truth—and sometimes it seems to come pretty close to claiming that—at least professes to possess the infallible method by which truth is ascertainable. Dialectical materialism may seem in theory a promising tool for progressive discovery of the truth; but as it operates in practice discoverers are permitted to explore only in certain directions, as Russian historians, musicians and even scientists have found out. (Unfortunately not atomic scientists, who seem to be free to find out what will work.)

There too Lenin brought Marx and Engels up to date: Truth is what helps Our Side. The naïve Nazis said so outright; Communists swathe it in Marxian dialectic, but it comes to the same thing. I shall not attempt to define the nature of truth; a definition that identifies it with what is convenient to men in power seems inadequate. But if Russia defeated the West in war, if totalitarianism attained world-wide power—as the Marxian gospel insists it must—this is the definition that everybody would have to accept, under penalty of torture and the firing squad. I do not see how anything that could be called a civilization could grow out of that.

We can no doubt learn to live in the same world with men like that, but only by the exercise of eternal vigilance. We could not live under them. The life that is lived under them is of course to their notion the highest form of civilization, but it is about as different from what we call civilization as the life of the dinosaurs. Ours, God knows, has plenty of shortcomings, but so long as thinking is free the door is open and we can move on. The next war, calamitous as it would be to everybody, would not destroy civilization unless we lost it.

[*He reverted to this theme at the very end of the book. Here is the last paragraph of* Two Minutes Till Midnight.]

Whatever happens—whatever may drop on us, and whatever it does to us—we must remember that there is no exit in what a few people have suggested already and more might suggest in that great and terrible day. We must not quit, we must not surrender. The people who are on the various ground zeros that day will probably be the most fortunate; but as for those who are not, let them remember that their behavior will in all truth nobly save, or meanly lose, the last best hope of earth.

WHAT ARE WARS FOR? OR, HOW NOT
TO DO IT THE NEXT TIME

[Part of this article about another aspect of the central question of our times appeared in Harper's *before it was made into Chapter IV of* Two Minutes Till Midnight. *Its discursive treatment of various mistakes of past wartime policy does not admit of ready summary. But points raised here have as much interest today as ten years ago, and I wanted to preserve as many of these as possible. I have tried to separate them from the rest of the original by frequent cuts, usually with no explanation of the connecting material.]*

[• • •]

What are wars for? Clausewitz, a soldier, said that they are only an instrument—the continuation of national policy by other means, the endeavor to enforce by arms the acquiescence of another nation in your national objective, an acquiescence you have been unable to obtain by milder pressures. But to do that you must have a national objective in the first place. You must know what you want; you must see clearly the end you are fighting for—the end to which military victory, whether limited or total, is only a means. We have not done that in our greatest wars. In 1918 we helped our allies win complete military victory, and then refused to help them consolidate the political objectives which might have made victory lasting; and in the last war we seemed to regard military victory as a sufficient end in itself.

[• • •]

Pearl Harbor in a sense united the nation; but even after that there were many people in the United States who were willing to fight for victory but wanted it understood that they were not fighting for any principles. Some of them merely wanted it understood that they were not fighting for Roosevelt's principles; others seemed to take pride in not fighting for any principles at all. They would fight for victory, but not for any ends that victory, after all its cost in human suffering, might achieve.

I have sometimes suspected that people like that did not constitute so large a percentage of the population of the United States as they

did of a membership of the Seventy-eighth Congress—a body elected
in a mood of impatience and frustration, four days before the land-
ings in North Africa and ten days before the naval victories off Guadal-
canal. It is possible that if Mr. Roosevelt had neglected the direction
of the war to exercise all his powers of leadership on the home front,
he might have got the great majority of the people united in a fight
for principles. But he apparently thought otherwise, and he knew
more about public sentiment than I do. He knew that unless we won
the war it wouldn't matter much what we had fought for; so he called
it the War for Survival—which it was—without much emphasis, in
public, on what we were to do after we had succeeded in surviving.

Nevertheless he did have one major political objective; and, learning from Wilson's mistakes, he succeeded in carrying the nation with
him in supporting it: the creation of a world organization which, after
the aggressors of the moment had been overthrown, might keep the
peace thereafter. That organization is now in difficulties because one
of our allies, in the course of the war, became so strong and remained
so voracious that it is now a danger to everybody else, especially us.
I do not see how that could have been prevented without risking the
survival of German power, which would have been just as dangerous
if not more so. If that happy contingency anticipated by so many
conservatives before the war, and by so many (if not quite the same
ones) now—a struggle to the death between Germany and Russia—
had appeared in 1945, on which side would the Western powers have
been? A totalitarian dictatorship can change sides in the middle of a
war; the feat is somewhat more difficult for a democracy. Mr. Roosevelt undoubtedly trusted the Russians too much (though he was beginning to get over it before he died) and bet too much on a single
card—the United Nations. But this major decision, when there were
dangers in any course he might have chosen, can validly be criticized
only by someone (there was only one) of equal stature and equal
responsibility.

Churchill's criticisms appear, *passim,* in the later volumes of his
history, especially the last one. It has lately and glowingly been re-
viewed by Hanson Baldwin in the *Atlantic* under the title "Churchill
Was Right."

[· · ·]

Baldwin is one of those who feel that we made military victory needlessly difficult, and needlessly destructive to western Europe, by in-

sistence on unconditional surrender. So did many American military commanders, who over and over again asked Mr. Roosevelt to soften, or at least to define, unconditional surrender, in the belief that that would make victory easier.

[· · ·]

But the unquestionably good effect of unconditional surrender—an effect which was its primary purpose—was on the Germans. It forever prevented them from telling again the story they told after 1918, so incessantly that they finally came to believe it themselves, that they had never been defeated but had capitulated on terms and had been betrayed. This time they were licked, and they know it.

[· · ·]

The military effects of unconditional surrender have been vastly overestimated, and so have the political effects. There is little evidence from German sources that unconditional surrender prolonged the war or was responsible for the stubborn resistance of the Germans even in that final winter. The citation in support of that view of a quotation from Dr. Goebbels is not convincing, for Goebbels had no very good reputation for veracity. Unconditional surrender, says Baldwin, meant "the creation of vacuums of power—the complete destruction of two nations—Germany and Japan—which in modern history had been the traditional counterpoise to Soviet Russia." Well, we couldn't destroy all three of them; and Germany and Japan happened to be the ones that had attacked us, even though we are trying to rebuild them now.

Who, on this alternative theory, would have surrendered on terms? Not Hitler; not Göring or Himmler or Goebbels or Bormann. It would have had to be somebody else—somebody not too deeply involved in the Nazi crimes, at home and abroad. The generals? The men involved in the plot of July 1944? Well, there were some relatively respectable generals in that affair, as well as respectable civilians; but there would have been no enthusiasm in the United States, and probably not much in England, for making peace with German generals. Maybe there should have been, but there would not. (I shall get around presently to the part of public opinion in such matters.) Surrender on terms doubtless seems an excellent idea to people who have seen what happened after (but not necessarily because of) unconditional surrender, but who would have surrendered? And on what terms? We finally made a concession to the Japanese—mild for us, considerable for them—and accepted a surrender from a cabinet which had succeeded the one that made the war (or rather from the Emperor himself, operating through that cabinet); but in Germany there was no Emperor and no machinery for getting a successor administration. It was Hitler or nobody.

I find it as difficult to believe that Churchill was right on strategy as that unconditional surrender was a mistake. Baldwin says that "the British plans, a twentieth-century outgrowth of the time-tested strategy of the past," were explained in general terms as early as the Newfoundland conference of 1941. No vast armies, but raids on the Continent by armored divisions, whose operations would be supplemented by risings of the local patriots. Well, they told me that, as I suppose they told all American correspondents whom they could trust, several months before the Newfoundland conference, not because this was an outgrowth of the time-tested strategy of the past but because that was the only way they could fight, then. Raids on the Continent, supported by the risings of the Resistance—something like that happened once or twice, and the result was the hanging of some useful Resistance fighters. If we had depended on those tactics to liberate the Continent, it would still be German.

Beyond that, of course, was Churchill's idea of a Balkan campaign. From the military point of view it made no sense to Eisenhower, and if Churchill wanted it (as he did) for political reasons, that was the President's business.

[· · ·]

I do not know the distribution of the Axis forces in Yugoslavia in August 1944; but that invasion would have had to go, if it were in force, through the mountainous frontier that had stopped the entire Italian army for two years in the old war. The ten American and French divisions which invaded southern France might have had some trouble there; and afterward—well, ask the men who fought in Italy how soft was the soft underbelly of the Axis. All these ruminations about the wonderful results that might have been achieved by a Balkan campaign instead of what we did sound a little like a man's daydreaming about how happy he could have been with Betty if he hadn't married Sylvia instead and got into those quarrels.

Churchill's rightness is much more apparent in central Europe, at a time when President Roosevelt was about to die (though no one knew it yet) without having brought his successor up to date. It is obvious now that it would have been better if the Western armies had taken Berlin, and also if Patton had been permitted to go on and occupy Prague, which would probably have cost no casualties at all. But American strategy was still obsessed by the fear of the creation of a "national redoubt" where the tough die-hard Germans would make their last stand—a fear which was the last great achievement of Dr. Goebbels. Whether American occupation of Prague would have been enough to save Czechoslovakia, after Benes's unfortunate agreement with the Russians at Kosice, may be doubtful; but it was worth trying. Not long before the end of the war Churchill emphasized the importance of Berlin and Prague and further said that a settlement must be reached between the West and the East in Europe "before the armies of democracy melted" or gave up any of the German territory they had conquered.

But our leaders, civilian and military both, receded from their furthermost conquests in conformity with earlier agreements (some of which, Baldwin notes, Russia had already violated); and American armies rapidly melted away. This last, however, cannot be blamed on our military leaders, who had made only a minor redeployment to the Pacific, nor on the new administration. The cry of "Bring the boys home," which rang from end to end of the Capitol, reflected a general popular sentiment; if it had been put to a vote in a plebiscite it would have carried better than 99 to 1. On that point Churchill was certainly right, but it was the entire American people who were wrong and are still paying for it. Let us hope we do not have to pay too much more.

I have given considerable space to Churchill's analysis of our mistakes in the last war, since it is the most authoritative even if it does not seem to be faultless. Not many of the points on which he was right are likely to be pertinent next time; nor, as I have said, would unconditional surrender be useful even if it were attainable. It is none of my business how our Joint Chiefs of Staff would propose to fight a war against Russia and/or China, and if I did know I could not tell. But one thing they certainly would not do—attempt an overland march to Moscow.

[*He then turns to the gradual change in the conduct of diplomacy during this century: how once-secret diplomatic processes are now often conducted in the full glare of international publicity. This constant democratic observation has often hampered our diplomacy in modern times.*]

Yet it is under this diplomatic system that the democratic world has operated for thirty-odd years past; and in view of the history of those years it is not surprising that some people have wondered if all this was not a terrible mistake. International relations, it is argued, are beyond the comprehension of the average man who has no time to study their complexities. We were better off, so the argument runs, when foreign policy was conducted by educated and leisured gentlemen who understood all the factors involved and could arrive at sound decisions based on the national interest, without having to worry about making them palatable to the ill-informed and emotional masses. And the argument is usually pointed up by contrasting the Treaty of Versailles with the Congress of Vienna, which made a settlement that averted a general war for a century.

If there is a case for aristocratic diplomacy, that instance does not prove it. The pattern in which the Congress of Vienna tried to freeze both the map and the political philosophy of Europe was maintained, almost from the first, only by force; it was badly shaken in 1830, worse shaken in 1848, and almost nothing was left of it after 1866. Meanwhile there had been plenty of wars, several of which narrowly escaped being general—and escaped, it would seem in retrospect, pretty largely by luck. It is true that the period from 1871 to 1914 was the most peaceful Europe had known since the days of Antoninus Pius; but that stability, by no means perfect, was attained only after most of the errors of the Congress of Vienna had been corrected.

Yet the noblemen who met at Vienna had one great achievement to their credit which would have been impossible to democratic diplomats: the early alignment of two of the victorious powers, England and Austria, with the defeated power, France, to resist the aggressive demands of Russia and its Prussian satellite. That may have prevented another and calamitous war; certainly it prevented some undesirable readjustments of the map of Europe—or, more exactly, postponed them, since readjustments not dissimilar, in substance if not in form, were made a hundred and thirty years later. No such clear evidence of Russian ambitions was available at Potsdam in 1945 as at Vienna in 1814; nor were there diplomats in the Western delegations comparable in skill and experience to some of the men of Vienna. But even if Jimmy Byrnes had been a Metternich and Ernest Bevin a Castlereagh, American and British public opinion would never have tolerated, in the summer of 1945, the attempt to arrange an alliance with Germany against Russia which we actually got to work on five years later. Men who had dared to propose it, in the first flush of a common victory and the afterglow of a common hatred, would have been howled out of office. Proof of that is the uproar caused, nine years later, by Churchill's disclosure that he would have given arms back to the Germans if the Russians had kept on coming.

[· · ·]

But what is public opinion? G. P. Baker, in his biography of a man who understood public opinion as well, and used it as effectively, as any politician in history—Augustus Caesar—unkindly calls it "a crazy labyrinth of hopes, fears, prejudices, ignorances, passions, and fantasies." Yet the public opinion of Italy and the Caesarian army did come to the right decision between Augustus and Marc Antony, as public opinion has often done since. I suppose that public opinion, in the Almost Perfect State, could be defined as the judgment of the majority of the people, after they have had ample imformation and time to sort it out (if they can) from the misinformation that accompanies it. But how is that judgment to be ascertained? How be sure that it is the will of the people and not merely of the small segment of the people that makes the most noise or has the greatest nuisance value? No certain method has yet been found.

Practically, Presidents and Secretaries of State usually have to determine it by rule of thumb—a combination of newspaper editorials (with the necessary deductions for partisanship), reports from party leaders and trusted personal informants, letters to the White House and members of Congress (again with deductions, since people who don't like something are more likely to write or telegraph than those who do), and any other evidence that seems valuable. This is far from satisfactory and no wonder there have been some rather desperate efforts to find something better.

There are to be sure five hundred and thirty-one selected citizens —selected by the people themselves—who constitutionally have considerable authority (mostly negative) over foreign policy, and may be supposed to represent the will of the people. It is said that the members of Congress are an average of the nation. I am not too sure of that. Some of them are much above the average; too many are merely the lowest common denominator of the pressures in their district. And what they do on foreign policy is apt to be determined by domestic exigencies, or supposed exigencies, of their party. When one Republican congressman demands the annexation of Canada, whether the Canadians like it or not, he can be laughed off, though the Canadians did not seem to think he was very funny. When two hundred of them demand the dismissal of an excellent Secretary of State on the eve of an important international conference, it is more serious.

[· · ·]

The classic instance of extraconstitutional pressure by Congress was the heat put on President Truman in 1951 by most of the Republicans and some few Democrats to try to make him adopt General MacArthur's policy of a (he hoped) limited extension of the war. This was no formal action. Members of Congress have the same right as any other citizens to speak their minds; but their position gives their views more publicity, if not more weight, than those of the man on the street corner. And when they attempt to force the administration into a policy in which it does not believe by noise, uproar, propaganda, talk of impeachment, it becomes a form of extraconstitutional pressure approximating mob rule. For all the while there was at hand an unquestioned constitutional authority which Congress could have exercised if it had chosen. Only Senator Harry Cain of Washington proposed that they exercise it. He offered alternative resolutions—one calling for withdrawal from Korea, which in form was only advisory, but could easily have been implemented by Congressional refusal of appropriations. The other was mandatory—a declaration of war on China. Mr. Cain's colleagues wanted the President to make war on China; he proposed to make him do it, for a President who refused to fight a war that Congress had declared could certainly be impeached.

But if Congress thus exerted its authority, there was an unspoken corollary—that Congress must accept responsibility for what happened. Senator Cain's resolution got no support whatever. Many men wanted to make the President do it, but they lacked the guts to do it themselves.

[· · ·]

War, for a despotism, may be what Clausewitz called it; but for a democracy it is less the continuation of a policy than failure of a policy, a last resort to what diplomacy has been unable to avert. American public opinion has risen adequately to the challenge of both of our great wars, though belatedly in both cases and stirred up by incidentals—the German submarine campaign in 1917, the surprise of Pearl Harbor in 1941—rather than by the real issues, the dangers to vital American interests. But in tensions short of war, in those crucial intervals when war has been postponed, public opinion has usually been less realistic. The catastrophe of the forties might have come anyway, but the isolationism of the thirties helped to bring it on; and the chief source of our present troubles is the headlong demobilization in 1945, demanded by a public opinion as nearly unanimous as this country has ever seen.

If we do that next time, we may win the next war but we shall again lose it afterward. We won't even win it if we keep kicking our friends around and if we listen to the isolationists who are talking again about going it alone. We might not win it anyway, even if we behave sensibly. But we have got to fight it if it is started, or else give in; and no man who would give in is fit to be a citizen of the United States.

Whether we fight it—or, more exactly whether we fight it in time—is likely to depend on how it begins. Adolf Hitler, who made many mistakes but also had some remarkable political insights, once observed that "a shrewd victor will, if possible, keep imposing his demands on the conquered by degrees. He can then, in dealing with a nation that has lost its character—and this means everyone that submits voluntarily —count on its never finding in any particular act of oppression a sufficient excuse for taking up arms once once. On the contrary—the more the exactions that have been willingly endured, the less justifiable does it seem to resist at last on account of a new and apparently isolated (though to be sure constantly recurring) imposition."

[. . .]

The classic instance of the procedure which Hitler described—until the performance he gave himself in the 1930s—was the Roman treatment of Carthage before the third and last Punic War. The treaty of peace after the second war had not left much to Carthage. Most of the colonies were gone, a ruinous indemnity had been imposed, and there was in Africa a king, Masinissa, of great ability and greater ambitions, who seems to have provided for the Romans the agent who could be disavowed if he went too far, while they could take advantage of everything he gained. Carthage was forbidden to declare war; Masinissa took one bit of Carthaginian territory and then another and the Carthaginians could do nothing about it but appeal to Rome—which always decided against them. Finally Masinissa went too far and the Carthaginians put themselves legally in the wrong by going to war with him. They lost the war and then had to square themselves with the Romans, if they could.

The Romans imposed their demands by degrees. First they demanded three hundred noble hostages; the Carthaginians gave them those. Then they demanded the surrender of all Carthaginian war material; the Carthaginians gave them that. Then they demanded that Carthage itself, the great and rich seaport, be abandoned and that the inhabitants who lived on its business move inland. That was too much. The Carthaginians said no, and even with improvised weapons they conducted a long successful defense. But finally the Romans got a good general (as they usually did, in the end); Carthage burned for seventeen days, and the surviving inhabitants were sold into slavery.

Not much has been heard in the past two years—except in the Vice-President's broadcast of March 1954—of that myth of 1952: that the aim of Russian strategy was to get us to spend ourselves into bankruptcy for armaments. But it will probably pop up again in 1956; the mid-term platform of the Republican National Committee says that "we are getting more defense for less money." Symington and Finletter question the first half of that statement; but we are certainly spending less money.

I don't suppose the men who make that boast have ever heard of Carthage, but it was once the most important nation in the world. Its history is that of a nation which found it more pleasant to save its money than to save its liberty, and in the end lost both.

MORES

[The rest of his nonfiction seems to me to fall naturally under two headings. Much of it offers and seeks to justify judgment concerning questions of public behavior—mores. Other articles, perhaps more of them in his total output, deal with divers questions of personal taste. Each heading covers a variegated output, but the distinction seems to me to be reflected in Davis's manner of approaching his subjects.]

PORTRAIT OF A CLERIC

[*If the facts in this profile were beyond question, and impartial ob-*
servers thought the portrait a fair one, it still showed some courage
for Harper's *to print such a deflation of boosterism in 1926. But this*
piece soon was accepted as a classic in its genre. John Rice's opinion
that it is "the best piece of satirical writing ever done in America" (re-
affirmed in 1942 in his autobiography) was only more explicit than
many others. Roger Burlingame described it at length in Don't Let
Them Scare You, *concluding that it was "the most thoroughly Davis*
piece of all his articles."]

On Morningside Heights in the city of New York a great
Gothic church is rising, the Cathedral of St. John the Divine. It was
begun as long ago as 1892; but in a whole generation the exertions of
the pious—the prosperous and pious, for this is an Episcopalian cathedral—sufficed only to complete the choir and crossing. For years this
fragment towered magnificent but incomplete, the product of an effort
that seemed to have spent itself.

But now the nave is building, the transepts are in prospect, there
is more than a hope that before long the whole immense edifice will
be completed, clear up to the cross that tops the spire—five hundred
feet above the pavement, the cathedral boosters will tell you, six hundred and fifty feet above tidewater—one of the three largest cathedrals
in the world. Inevitably, it will be a monument, a monument to the
bishop who achieved in a few weeks of driving effort what three previous bishops had failed to accomplish in three decades. And he
achieved it in accordance with the best of precedent—the twelfth-
century precedent of the great age of cathedral building, when the
whole community was united in one grand endeavor; the Scriptural
precedent of the man who, when his invited guests failed to arrive,
sent out into the byways and hedges and dragged everybody in.

This was the great inspiration of the Right Reverend William
Thomas Manning, Episcopal Bishop of New York—to sweep the whole
twentieth-century community of New York, Catholic, Protestant, Jewish, and about one per cent Episcopalian, into a great twelfth-century

crusade for the building of "a house of prayer for all people." It was —or is so far—the crowning achievement of a brilliant career. Bishop Manning, after all, is more than a cathedral builder. He is the champion of orthodoxy, defender of the faith, doughty upholder of the Virgin Birth, supporter of the Volstead Act, corrector of dogma and morals, extirpator of heresy; and withal an ecclesiastical statesman, if not in the thirteenth-century tradition, at least in that of the seventeenth. Bishop of the most opulent diocese in the most elegant of churches, he is still young as bishops go, and brighter glories may lie beyond. Enthusiastic after-dinner speakers have called him the First Citizen of New York, the First Churchman of America; without eliciting his visible disapproval, they have suggested him for the as yet nonexistent office of Archbishop of the American Episcopal Church.

Upon what meat doth this our Bishop feed, that he hath grown so great? I reveal no guarded secrets, nor am I a psychographer to uncover the hidden springs of action; I merely study the public record open to all. But from this record one or two rather curious conclusions emerge. Notoriously the right reverend bishop owes his episcopal rank to that right irreverend layman, Mr. William Randolph Hearst. Moreover, Doctor Manning regards his church (when it is politic so to regard it) as "part of the ancient historic Catholic Church"; and certainly it was in a Catholic spirit that he drew all New York into the building of a cathedral which is alleged to embody the community's spiritual aspiration. But for the method which made the cathedral possible he is indebted to that notable Protestant sectary, the Reverend Doctor Billy Sunday.

Doctor Manning is presumably cognizant and approving of his biography as it appears in *Who's Who*. In the American version of that volume the place of his birth is not mentioned; in the English *Who's Who* it is set down that he was born in Northampton, England. Tradition says that he came to this country with his parents in boyhood and lived in Nebraska and California before going for his secular and theological education to the University of the South at Sewanee, Tennessee. Hagiography has neglected those early years, though there is a legend that the future bishop once sold groceries. But it seems curious and ungrateful that the English birthplace should have been omitted from the American *Who's Who;* curious, since Doctor Manning has never made any secret of his Anglophile sympathies; ungrateful, since if he had not been born in England he would not now be Bishop of New York.

In 1903 he came from Nashville to New York, as vicar of one of the chapels of Trinity Parish, a small, slight man, with no particularly impressive pulpit eloquence to overcome the handicap of his stature, but a man with a good record, sound in theology from the conservative point of view, endowed by marriage with the modest wealth which a metropolitan clergyman always finds useful. Within a year he was made assistant rector of Trinity Parish, whose burdens lay heavy on the aged Dr. Morgan Dix; in 1908, upon Doctor Dix's death, he succeeded in due course to the rectorate.

Now Trinity is the wealthiest and most important parish in the country; its rector is the most powerful vassal of the Bishop of New York; with the vicars of his nine chapels bound to him by subinfeudation, he is a bigger man than many provincial bishops.

[· · ·]

He became a leader of the Anglo-Catholic party which wanted to change the name of the Protestant Episcopal Church to the American Catholic Church. His defense of the "historical and unbroken continuity" of Catholic tradition made the Low Churchmen his enemies; and they beat him, at the diocesan convention of 1915, for delegate to the next year's General Convention—the first time in all history that a rector of Trinity had been defeated for an elective office. It was predicted, then, that the defeat would make him a bishop. But as matters turned out it took a good deal more than that to make him a bishop.

For in the next few years there rose the question of the Congregational Concordat—an arrangement by which Congregational preachers, having received Episcopal ordination, might minister to Episcopalians. To the Protestant mind there seems nothing so very terrible about this, since the Congregationalists had to become a sort of sub-caliber Episcopalians before they could be trusted with these ministrations; but it roused the ire of Anglo-Catholics—all but Manning. He was beginning to be deeply interested in ecclesiastical unity, and to his Catholic brethren it seemed that he was forgetting the ancient principle that ecclesiastical unity could be attained only by everybody becoming Catholic. When Manning came out for the Concordat, his Anglo-Catholic friends whetted their knives for the lost leader.

In 1919 Bishop Greer died and the rector of Trinity was nominated for his seat. So was Doctor Stires of St. Thomas's, the Low-Church candidate; so also was Suffragan Bishop Burch. Burch was the long shot, for all that he had been Greer's assistant; he had come late to the priesthood, having spent his early life in the godless occupation of editing a newspaper. None the less Burch was elected—partly by the votes of the rural clergy who rather distrusted that urban potentate, the rector of Trinity, but partly by the votes of High Churchmen, who deserted Manning because they felt that his Catholicity was not to be trusted whenever a visible advantage appeared to lie in flirting with Protestantism.

Also, by this time Manning had many enemies, within and without the Church. Some of them, outside especially, were highly to his credit. From the beginning of the war he had been outspokenly pro-Ally and pro-English.

[· · ·]

Now granted the fact, whether you like it or not, that foreign-born Americans are apt to retain some fondness for the Old Country, it does not appear why a privilege conceded to an American born in Italy or Ireland or Germany should be withheld from an American born in England. But New York is a peculiar city with peculiar institutions. Every New Yorker has, if he is wise, two fatherlands, his own and Ireland. Manning, the most prominent Anglo-American, inevitably incurred the hatred of the Irish and the abuse of the Hearst newspapers; but it took a grotesque episode just after the war to seal and ratify the enmity that was to be the making of his fortune.

The war had ended in integral victory, and in that month before the Peace Conference met integral victory seemed to promise an integrated world. The one far-off divine event toward which the whole creation moved seemed visibly at hand; in that millennial dawn our returning army, victors at Armageddon, must be welcomed as triumphant crusaders. Accordingly Mayor Hylan appointed a Committee of Welcome which included about all the prominent citizens of New York; which included among others, and in no obscure position, Mr. William Randolph Hearst.

If it had been meant as a joke it would have marked Hylan as a greater man than Aristophanes; but, like all Hylan's humor, it was unintentional. He saw no reason why Hearst who had made Hylan did not deserve a chief place on any of Hylan's committees. But other citizens saw much reason why Hearst, with his familiar war record, was out of place on this particular committee. They resigned, one after another, with roars of disapproval; Doctor Manning resigned, roaring if anything louder than the rest. Those who resigned got up a rival organization, the Citizens' Committee of Welcome, on which

Manning was in the foreground; and they proclaimed a mass meeting in Madison Square Garden to speak out the public reprobation of the iniquitous Hearst appointment.

That meeting turned out to be a grander jest than the appointment itself, the first forewarning of the great political discovery of 1919, that the millennium had been indefinitely postponed. Three or four thousand indignant patriots rattled around in the great open spaces of the Garden, their fiery fulminations interrupted by raucous shouts of "Hurrah for Hoist, de woikingman's friend." For Mr. Hearst's astute lieutenants had not only brought in several hundred deep-lunged civilians to offer a minority report; they even had on hand a detachment of the returning heroes who had caused all the hullabaloo, soldiers and sailors in uniform. And when an exasperated chairman demanded that all who sympathized with Hearst leave the hall, the heroes in uniform led the recessional. They may have come only from nearby training camps, they may have marched out to be fed at Hearst's expense; none the less they marched out, the meeting fell flat, and the Citizens' Committee of Welcome fell with it, never to rise again.

But from its ruins there was to spring, in the fullness of time, a Bishop of New York.

Bishop Burch died suddenly, little more than a year after his elevation. Again the diocesan delegates must elect a bishop, and again Manning was a candidate. Having failed through too much Protestanism, he had lately been very Catholic. Dr. Percy Stickney Grant of the Church of the Ascension—a radical, a pacifist, a Low Churchman, everything that Manning hated—had preached a sermon on divorce; and Manning had replied with a denunciation of Grant's views as no better than approval of free love. Grant was more or less of a maverick; but among Low Churchmen there was an uneasy feeling that Manning was already a little too episcopal in his pronouncements for one who was still a mere rector (if the rector of Trinity can be called a mere rector). On the other hand, High Churchmen welcomed the returning prodigal. Doctor Carstensen, very high, observed that the diocese needed a bishop who would ride some of the straying brethren "with a curb bit." Everybody knew he meant Grant as the wild horse and Manning as the bronco buster.

At this moment some malignant spirit inspired the unhappy Grant, who knew well enough what was in store for him if Manning were made bishop, to warn the diocese against electing any but a native American. There may have been some echo of that feeling but, coming from Grant, the suggestion would probably have been laughed off.

Fortunately for the Man of Destiny, on the day of election it was no longer a suggestion from Grant but an order from Hearst.

That day the Hearst papers carried a huge black editorial headed: "Is An English Bishop Necessary? Why? Is There No Fit American?" It was illustrated with a picture of benighted African heathen rolling over and slapping their thighs to welcome a British explorer, and the Episcopalians of New York were asked if they meant to roll over and slap their thighs before Manning. In all solemnity, they were warned that this election would decide whether they were an American Church "or only an institution for pro-British propaganda." To make sure that the message reached the delegates, it had been telegraphed to every one of them; for good measure, newsboys were stationed at the door of the Synod House to give papers to all who entered. It was Hearst's reply to the Garden meeting, and a reply in kind; the meeting had been a flop, and so was the editorial.

This was a heated election; Catholic and Protestant factions in the church were ready for a fight. Chief among the Protestants was Dr. Leighton Parks of St. Bartholomew's, who denounced Catholicism of all sorts and asked if America was to remain America or become "a Roman Catholic Irish republic." The question had some point in those days, but it is rather hard to follow the line of thought that connected Ireland and Manning. At any rate, one of Manning's supporters countered by reading the Hearst pastoral from the platform, and from that time on the only question was whether the Low Churchmen feared Manning more than they hated Hearst.

The Protestant vote was divided between Slattery of Grace Church and Stires of St. Thomas's; on the second ballot Manning, supported by the High Churchmen, had a long lead. To unify the Protestant forces Stires withdrew, and then came the break. That Hearst editorial still rankled; some of Stires's supporters felt that it was not that they hated Catholicism less, but Hearst more; on the third ballot, Manning was elected. As surely as any Ghibelline nominee of a medieval emperor, he owed his see to a secular potentate. But one doubts if Mr. Hearst got much satisfaction out of it.

Once a Bishop, Doctor Manning began to behave very episcopally. He had opinions, and though he has never pretended to such omniscience as Dr. S. Parkes Cadman, he has this advantage over Cadman, that his opinions can be enforced by acts—when it seems expedient. The qualification is important.

For while our Bishop can be strict, he knows how to temper justice with mercy, or at least with caution. Perhaps, indeed, he is not by nature authoritarian at all. A psychographer might explain his tendencies toward autocracy in terms of his small physical stature, the compensating gesture of a man who has to stand on a box in a group photograph to look sufficiently impressive. If Napoleon had been six feet tall, Europe might have enjoyed unbroken peace after the treaty of Amiens. But I am no psychographer; I can only report what our Bishop has done and said.

He supports the Volstead Act as zealously as any Methodist, but with the un-Methodist qualification that he does not regard temperate drinking as a sin. He is against it, but for social reasons. But go back a decade, and one finds evidence that he is a prohibitionist for other reasons as well.

In the diocesan convention of 1916, when Doctor Manning was still rector of Trinity, there appeared a resolution pledging the clergy to personal abstinence, support of existing excise laws, and work for local option in New York. (The Eighteenth Amendment, then, was only a millennial dream.) This proposal was the work of the Reverend James V. Chalmers, rector of a poor parish on the upper East Side, the most active of the few prohibitionists in the diocese. Chalmers was used to introducing his resolution, vainly, at every convention. Once more he introduced it, and supported it with a speech about the evils of drink among the poor; but obviously without much hope of its adoption.

Then up rose the powerful rector of Trinity, unknown as yet to the public as an outspoken dry, pleading for the resolution as a stroke of ecclesiastical statesmanship, to put the church in line with a moral movement. (Yes, the dry cause was still so regarded, in 1916.) "We have been asked," he said, "to do this for the poor; but I say we must do it for the Church and the power of the Church."

They did it. One recusant who dared to mention the miracle at Cana of Galilee was literally howled down. These Episcopalians had no such convenient dogma as comforts the evangelical sects, that the wine made at Cana was unfermented grape juice of the kind Mr. Bryan used to serve at diplomatic dinners; for all they knew on authority it was real wine. Nevertheless, the man who mentioned it was howled down and the resolution adopted by acclamation. It was Chalmers's resolution but Manning's victory; they had done it, not for the poor, but for the power of the Church. Manning had had the foresight to recognize that the water wagon was a band wagon, and he had swung the Church aboard.

On divorce, he has always held the Catholic position—that there is no such thing. A few years ago he appealed to Congress for a Federal divorce law, with a pretty strong intimation that his idea of the proper law was no divorce at all. But a little later he was urging the churches to unite against divorce, and recently he has so far weakened as to advocate love and forbearance in the home as the best remedy. One cannot help wondering if our Bishop, reflecting on the history of prohibition, is beginning to lose his faith in the efficacy of the secular arm.

But where his own arm can enforce obedience that arm is powerful, as none learned better than his old enemy, the luckless Grant. In 1921 Doctor Grant's engagement was announced to a lady who had two ex-husbands living. The Episcopal canon permits remarriage to the innocent party in a divorce for adultery, but Doctor Grant's fiancée had secured her second divorce on the unhallowed ground of desertion. Naturally, Bishop Manning forbade the clergy of his diocese to perform the marriage. There was much sympathy for the pair held apart by sacerdotal authority, especially as they were not so forgetful of the proprieties as to go on and get married by a city clerk or a Presbyterian. After years of vain waiting for the Bishop to relent, the engagement was broken.

Meanwhile the martyred Grant was in more trouble. He preached a sermon which seemed to cast doubt on the divinity of Christ. Bishop Manning promptly ordered him to recant, resign, or be tried for heresy. Liberals of all faiths and of no faith at all rallied around the menaced Grant, champion of religious freedom against dogmatic intolerance and episcopal tyranny; they were all set for a fight but their hero ran out on them. He replied to the Bishop in a long letter which sounded as if it had been written by a highly competent lawyer. Expert theologians read it through and remained in doubt whether Grant had recanted. The one thing sure was that he had not resigned.

Well, then—a heresy trial? In that excited period, men said it would split the Church. Would the Bishop risk it? The Bishop announced that he would—against any clergyman whose denial of the divinity of Christ was "clear, courageous, and unambiguous." This was hint enough for the prudent Grant, whose further utterances could not possibly be described by these adjectives; and the equally prudent Bishop, having enforced what Mayor Gaynor used to call outward order and decency, did not see fit to search the underbrush for latent heresy. In due time Grant resigned on the plea of ill health, and Doctor Manning was left in the serenity of one who has seen four-and-twenty leaders of revolts.

The iron hand in the velvet glove caressed, about this same time, Dr. William Norman Guthrie, of St. Mark's in the Bouwerie, who had taken to adorning his services with eurhythmic dances and picturesque bits of assorted symbolism. One Sunday, when barefoot girls danced in his edifice, the police reserves had to be called out to handle the crowd. The Bishop ordered him to desist from these pagan practices, and when he was stubborn, withdrew episcopal ministration from his parish. St. Mark's threatened to secede from the Church; once more excited liberals rallied round the persecuted victim; but once more they had picked a poor hero. Guthrie's dances, however satisfactory to the religious sense of Aztecs and Hindus, seemed a little inappropriate, even to Unitarians, in a Christian church. Presently the vestry of St. Mark's came down like Davy Crockett's coon, and the offending Guthrie came down with them.

Meantime another issue had been met with Christian tolerance and diplomacy. Doctor Manning has always been a Fundamentalist and frank about it. Proclaiming that there is no conflict between faith and science, no harm in evolution, he has still declared that "Christianity stands or falls with the facts about Jesus Christ, His supernatural birth, His bodily resurrection, His ascension into Heaven. If these things did not happen, the Christian gospel ceases to have reality or meaning; the whole truth of the New Testament disappears."

In 1923 the bishops uttered a pastoral letter laying down these basic dogmas, and pointed the declaration by threatening to try for heresy an obscure Texas rector who was suspect on the Virgin Birth. Thereupon Manning's ancient foe, Dr. Leighton Parks, told his flock of St. Bartholomew's that the bishops had no authority to fix dogmas, that there was Scriptural justification for denial of the Virgin Birth, and (most unkindest cut of all) that if he wanted to know about this much-talked-of Catholic tradition he would ask no Episcopal bishop, but Cardinal Hayes.

Was Doctor Parks tried for heresy? He was not. He had frankly told his flock one reason why he would not be tried—that Bishop Manning's delicacy would restrain him from proceeding against an old antagonist. Perhaps this explains the immunity which Doctor Parks actually enjoyed, but bishops were stayed by no such personal scruples in the great age of the Church. St. Bartholomew's is a great and rich parish, where heresy might be supposed to be more dangerous than in Texas. But Doctor Parks had not personally and explicitly denied the Virgin Birth; and Doctor Manning was getting ready to build a cathedral.

Through the war years it had been understood that whoever was bishop after the war would have to do something about the cathedral. But great and good men had been trying to do something about it for thirty years, with no noteworthy result. There was plenty of Episcopalian money in New York but most of it was still *in situ;* it was not flowing into the cathedral. What was to be done? Well, there was Scriptural precedent, when the chosen people had shown themselves unworthy of everlasting life, for turning unto the Gentiles.

How was it to be done? The Reverend Doctor Billy Sunday had shown the way. When that powerful vessel of the Spirit preached in New York in 1917 he had had only partial support from the Episcopalians. Doctor Manning was one of many who had held aloof—quite reasonably, for he did not believe in that kind of religion; quite honorably, for he merely remained silent, offering no obstacle to the good work, if any. But no thoughtful man could overlook the lessons of the Sunday campaign as it actually worked out.

It was known that many evangelical clergymen held about the same opinion of Doctor Sunday's kind of religion as did the rector of Trinity but, not being the rector of Trinity, they did not dare stand aside. They had to go with the crowd, and shout louder than anybody to avert suspicion. In other words, the evangelical clergy could be stampeded; they dared not stay off any band wagon which proclaimed itself the vehicle of the Good Cause.

Quite as important, the newspapers could be stampeded. Few New York editors and publishers felt any sympathy, temperamental or intellectual, with the Sunday evangel; but they knew that many of their readers did, so the newspapers ran before the great wind of that revival. What was possible to Billy Sunday ought to be easy for the Bishop of New York; and it was.

It remained to find a formula, and the Bishop found it in a phrase in the constitution of his cathedral—"a house of prayer for all people." What did that mean? In the twelfth century, the great age of cathedral building, it could be taken literally; for all people, then, were loyal to the One Church; a whole community could be united in a great common endeavor to build a Gothic cathedral, because a Gothic cathedral in those days expressed the highest aspirations of all men.

But twentieth-century New York is not Gothic; twentieth-century New York is split up among a hundred religions, and only about one per cent of its inhabitants belong to Doctor Manning's church. The other ninety-nine per cent had to be dragged in somehow. The Catholics could not be counted on for much more than benevolent neutrality, but then Catholics as a rule are not wealthy. There is much Protestant money in New York and more Jewish money; and Jews could be flattered, Protestants could be coerced—if it could be made tò appear that it was not Manning's cathedral, not an Episcopalian cathedral, but everybody's cathedral, "a house of prayer for all people."

It was an act of faith to believe that a twelfth-century campaign was possible in twentieth-century New York; but it was an act of genius to put it over, and put it over by sheer assertion.

No one could doubt our Bishop's Americanism after observing his truly American approach to this problem. He began to talk about the size of his cathedral, five hundred feet above the street, six hundred and fifty feet above tidewater, one of the two or three biggest cathedrals in the world. "New York," he said, "needs and must have a building to represent religion on a scale equal to the structures which represent the other great interests of our life, business, educational, social."

After Bigness, Organization. The job of raising the money was entrusted to a firm of professionals, willing to raise money for any good cause for a fair fee, plus expenses. The whole town was organized, committees in every parish, in every sect, in every industry, rival committees which were to meet and report each day at a pep luncheon while the drive went on. The evangelical clergy lined up for the good cause; the newspapers took it all at face value. Non-Episcopalians, unfellowshipped in "the ancient historic Catholic church," were allowed to take the lead; Elihu Root, a Presbyterian, headed the general committee. For this is not our cathedral, it is your cathedral, everybody's cathedral, a house of prayer for all people.

In the enthusiasm of getting started, nobody asked what that meant. It would have been indelicate and at times hazardous. For while Episcopalians are not numerous, even in New York, they are rich and powerful, not to be lightly offended; and the example of Billy Sunday had been followed with such success that everybody was climbing on the bandwagon. This time, at last, it was Manning's own bandwagon.

The drive started with a great mass meeting in Madison Square Garden. The lesson of that anti-Hearst meeting had been taken to heart; no danger, this time, of an empty house; thirteen thousand tickets had been distributed among the Episcopal parishes (another idea borrowed from Billy Sunday). The theme announced by the brazen trumpet of episcopal declaration was taken up by the muted strings of a hundred minor pulpits and the dulcet woodwind of sob stories contributed by an able press agent; it thundered in the battery of every newspaper editorial page—"a home for the spiritually home-less," "a great common church expressing the aspiration of all New York."

It went over with a whoop, a community crusade in the best twelfth-century manner. There were even—take it on the authority of New York's most sober newspaper—miracles, two or three of them. Whether they too were provided by the press service of the drive, or appeared to the pious eye of the feature writer, I do not know; but if you believe what you see in the papers, miracles there certainly were.[1] Whether everybody swallowed the miracles may be doubted, but everybody who counted swallowed the cathedral.

Nothing in the way of a donation, said Doctor Manning, would be declined; and with one exception, to be noted presently, nothing ever was. But each could contribute his tithe in kind. For the cathedral, comedians capered on the stage and hockey players performed in the Garden; Paavo Nurmi and Willie Ritola broke records *ad majorem Dei gloriam;* and President Coolidge contributed good wishes, framed in these well-chosen words: "I trust that the efforts being made for this purpose will meet with the success its importance warrants."

From each his own offering, to each his own reward. The funds raised by hockey games and track meets, for instance, were attributed to the Sports Bay, a great pictorial window expressing the joyful la-bors of amateur athletes. Humanitarian protests have forced a change in the design, the excision of a picture of a sportsman shooting a live pigeon; but it does not appear that the money, if any, contributed by pigeon shooters has been declined.

Then there is a Journalism Bay, to be honored with the name of the late Frank A. Munsey. Considering the esteem in which Mr. Munsey was and is generally held by newspapermen, this is about as tactful as dedicating a hypothetical Bill of Rights Bay to Wayne B. Wheeler, or the actual Women's Transept to Bluebeard. But Mr. Munsey left a heavy contribution to the Journalism Bay.

Money was being raised by the million; not much from Catholics, though there were well-advertised contributions from Catholics hold-ing elective office, but Jews and evangelical Protestants fell over one another to reach the table which waited in vain for most of the invited guests. Indeed, some three weeks after the drive started, George W. Wickersham, Vice Chairman of the Citizens' Committee, himself an Episcopalian and addressing other Episcopalians, saw fit to observe,

---

[1] The man who got these miracles into the newspapers—a most competent man he is, too—is now working for the firm of money raisers who put over the campaign. Whether his miracles are repeaters I do not know.

"I have been wondering sometimes of late if we are going to let our Presbyterian and Methodist friends build the cathedral."

Other people had been wondering that too, as the campaign went on, but this was the first time it had ever been said by a member of the organization. The first time, and the last; for whatever reason, Mr. Wickersham made no further public appearance in the cathedral drive.

But where was the *advocatus diaboli?* He was there, but for a long time his discordant squawk was drowned in the chorus of praise.

The first protests dealt with an apparent triviality. Gothic architecture was the natural flowering of the twelfth-century, the great cathedral age; it expressed, then, the highest ideal, an ideal actually common to all. But captious persons complained that in twentieth-century New York, with a diversity of religions and an adequately significant native architecture, a Gothic cathedral was at best an anachronism.[2]

And at worst it was something very dubious indeed. For Gothic architecture expressed twelfth-century religion, the religion of that "ancient historic Catholic Church" that Bishop Manning used to talk about. That kind of religion was meaningless or abhorrent to the Jews and evangelical Protestants who were contributing so heavily to the Cathedral of St. John the Divine; it was alien, even, to Low-Church Episcopalians. If this was really our great common church, its form ought to express such ideals as our time holds with measurable approach to unanimity; if it meant what it seemed to mean, how could it be a house of prayer for all people? (Especially as the architect in charge was that belligerent synthetic Goth, Mr. Ralph Adams Cram, himself so twelfth-century-Catholic that he makes even Manning look like a Baptist.)

These observations were made, however, by unchurched infidels, echoed by the lately chastised Guthrie of St. Mark's in the Bouwerie, who put in a feeble plea for "American architecture." But there was on record Doctor Manning's denunciation of a proposal for a skyscraper cathedral in Chicago ("a poor imitation of the Woolworth Building with a cathedral concealed somewhere inside"); and, more powerfully, there was the fact that the Cathedral of St. John the Divine, a quarter finished, was already Gothic. Once, painfully, it had been altered from Romanesque; it could hardly be altered again. And meanwhile another issue had come up.

2 These objections, of course, apply *a fortiori* to the Gothic church now being built in Riverside Drive for Dr. Fosdick's congregation of Modernist Baptists. So far as architectural relevance goes, that church might as well be a replica of the Parthenon or the Temple of Karnak.

A fortnight after the campaign started Bishop Manning published the news of the princely gift of half a million dollars from John D. Rockefeller, Jr., a Baptist. The next day Mr. Rockefeller published something the Bishop had forgotten, the correspondence preceding the gift. It is amazingly interesting; its most interesting passage, however, escaped public comment, though without doubt certain Anglo-Catholic clergymen kept it, and pondered it in their hearts. Doctor Manning, once the apostle of Anglo-Catholicism, had called his cathedral "the common center and rallying point of Protestant Christianity."

Protestant Christianity! This is the Manning who had said, "The word Protestant reflects the controversial spirit of a bygone age; we have progressed beyond it." But evidently we can retrogress back to it when it is a question of half a million Baptist dollars. Is there not high authority for making friends with the Mammon of Unrighteousness?

Concession to Mammon, however, has its limits, as the correspondence disclosed. Mr. Rockefeller had been "deeply impressed" by what the Bishop had said and written to him (Doctor Manning, evidently, had worked for that donation) "about the broad purpose of the cathedral." In furtherance of that catholic (with a small c) purpose, Mr. Rockefeller suggested: "Since a large minority of the funds which have already gone into the cathedral has come from members of other churches, it would seem but fitting that this large outside friendly interest should be represented by the election of a small number of laymen of sister churches to the Board of Trustees." Mr. Rockefeller desired to express the hope that this might be done, "if not now, in the near future." But he did not make that a condition of his gift.

Bishop Manning, replying, said that "we may certainly hope, and we should also pray and believe," for church unity; but "the time has not yet arrived," and "any attempt prematurely to force such an arrangement would retard the cause of unity rather than aid it." Now Rockefeller had said nothing about church unity; he had talked only about minority representation of other churches among the trustees of the cathedral. But Manning, after knocking down the straw man, came back to the point. "The clause" (expressing Rockefeller's pious hope) "that you add to your gift imposes no obligation, legal or moral, on the trustees. This being the case, we accept the more gratefully your generous pledge of $500,000."

If that formula of acceptance is not law-proof, then there are no good lawyers in the Episcopal Church.   .

None the less, Rockefeller had taken off the lid. The newspapers, which hitherto had refused to print criticisms of the cathedral, had to admit them now; especially as just after accepting Rockefeller's five hundred thousand Doctor Manning sent back a modest contribution of five hundred from the offending Guthrie—the only contribution, so far as recorded, that he ever refused. The contrast was a little too pointed; and Rockefeller had given respectability to those who were beginning to wonder just what was meant by his sonorous phrase, "a house of prayer for all people."

Low-Church clergymen and magazines supported his argument; they cited the fact that the Episcopal Cathedral in Washington had actually had trustees of other faiths. One of their organs, asking what a house of prayer for all people really meant, pointed out that if it meant only that anyone who felt the need could go in and pray, that function was performed by every church of every faith in the country. In vain did Bishop Manning declare that "the true and fine meaning of the phrase is understood by all." The inveterate Parks, disclosing the fact that he was not whooping up the cathedral drive in his parish, declared flatly that "this is not a house of prayer for all people." As the discussion became acrimonious, the forthright Carstensen—he who had once demanded the curb bit for Percy Grant, and not in vain —was goaded into blurting out, "It is not for all kinds of prayer or all kinds of people." In other words, it was for all people who were willing to pray like Episcopalians.

Now no one could have objected if the Episcopalians had said, "We want to build ourselves a cathedral and should gratefully receive any contributions that brethren of other faiths might care to offer." But when they said, "It is not our cathedral, it is your cathedral," when in fact it was and remained their cathedral—why, if the merchandiser had been any but a Bishop, offering holy wares, this would have seemed perilously like misrepresentation of the quality of the goods.

But what of the secular press, that informed guide of public opinion? The secular press, with one exception, ducked the argument, aside from a few pious platitudes about sympathy and understanding. The exception was the *World*, New York's great moral newspaper, so pathetically eager to support all worthy causes, and so recklessly precipitate in picking them out. Just as the *World* later recanted its support of the turpitudinous Vera Cathcart, in whose behalf it had printed chapters from the New Testament as editorials, so now it came out valorously with the editorial second thought, "Bishop Manning Should Reconsider."

In response, presumably, to this warning (the etiology can doubtless be verified in the *World Almanac*) the Bishop did indeed unbend. Not to the point of admitting trustees of other faiths; gently he asked

if anyone would wish to see the cathedral change its statutes "of im-
memorial standing" (fifty years) in connection with the acceptance of a
large sum of money. To which obviously the answer was, Not if it can
get the money otherwise. But he preached at the Fifth Avenue Presbyterian Church, declaring that "the time has come for a new synthe-
sis of the deep religious values represented by all Christian com-
munions" (though not for minority representation on the cathedral
board). In May, when the intensive campaign was over, when ten million dollars had been raised and more was in sight, new trustees were
to be chosen. Low Churchmen proposed that Rockefeller, a Baptist,
and Root and Arthur Curtiss James, Presbyterians, should be elected.
But all the vacancies were filled by Episcopalians. Rockefeller had
the best of the argument and Manning had the money; presumably,
each was content.

It must not be supposed, however, that the contributory evangelicals
got nothing. Doctor Manning actually held three interdenominational
services, inviting evangelical clergymen, mere godly laymen according
to Episcopal doctrine, to preach in the house of prayer for all people.
By pure accident of ritual, it chanced that their unordained feet did
not tread the holy ground of the sanctuary; but they preached from the
pulpit. After that who could doubt that it was everybody's cathedral,
even if the Episcopalians did continue to own and operate it? "The
discussion," said the Bishop, "has cleared the air; let us hope it will
stay clear." By way of further clarification a *Times* editorial added,
"Those who do not wish to contribute may with propriety keep quiet."

So the cathedral is rising, expressing the common ideals of our great
city (though now that the intensive campaign is over, nobody seems
to know just what they are). There have been no interdenominational
services lately, but it is a safe bet that there will be, if, as, and when
required. For money is still needed for the cathedral, and Jews and
evangelical Protestants still have it.

Meanwhile our Bishop (now that Grant is dead and Guthrie in
eclipse) beams with brotherly love. Whether, in the view of a High-
Church bishop, Jews can be saved, is a question I am not competent
to consider; but at least they have their reward here below. The
gloomy Dean Inge, when in New York lately, asked why the Jews
should want to rebuild Zion; let them rather, he suggested, build a
new Temple of Solomon in New York. With laudable promptitude
Doctor Manning came to the defense of the persecuted people; "the
broadmindedness and public spirit of the Jews of this city have been
conspicuously shown"—how? You have guessed it. "By their generous

gifts to the Cathedral of St. John the Divine." Doctor Manning even went so far as to risk the charge of platitudinarianism; "many," he added, "of my best friends are Jews."

And for a compliment on the other side, one may refer to the Reverend Doctor Billy Sunday, who has spoken with approval of the cathedral—"a big church"—and of its builder. "Bishop Manning is one of the finest fellows going. He is true blue, foursquare on God and the Bible."

One pious hope has not been realized; before the drive started Doctor Manning declared that "the building of the cathedral will not in any way lessen the support given to other good causes, but will have the opposite effect." In fact, the cathedral campaign practically sank, for months, the ten-million-dollar drive for the Presbyterian Hospital, since salvaged from the depths by great effort; and most ironically that campaign was in the hands of the same firm of money raisers who got their due profit out of the Cathedral of St. John the Divine. But the cathedral is the house of God; the hospital, serving only man, could well be compelled to wait. Man, indeed, does not seem to count for much in the Bishop's view of the universe. There are wide green lawns in the cathedral close, and in the old days, before Doctor Manning was in charge, babies from the nearby apartment houses were allowed to play there. Now they are kept out—put out by the caretakers, if by some mischance they get in anyway; which might seem a little hard to reconcile with a well-known utterance of Jesus. But Jesus, of course, was not a Bishop.

Meanwhile the cathedral rises, a monument to the man of vision who got contributions from all people for a house of prayer owned by only one per cent of the people, who put religion over in a big way. It will be a beautiful building, if you like Gothic architecture; an impressive building, if you do not require architecture that expresses something of the life around it. Beyond doubt, the hopes and prayers and sacrifices of thousands of humble Christians, the true salt of the earth, have gone into it; people who know what their cathedral means to them and have never read the legal tortuosities of the Bishop's reply to Rockefeller. And beyond doubt some spiritual uplift has been felt by evangelical clergymen who hug to their bosoms the condescension of those three interdenominational services, by Jews who reflect that the Bishop counts them among his best friends.

In the fullness of time our Bishop (he may be an Archbishop by then) will be gathered to his reward; but the cathedral will remain. Perhaps his monument may be more enduring than his brass.

THE COMSTOCK LOAD

[*This article started from the concurrence in 1927 of publication of a biography of Anthony Comstock and the most virulent campaign of theater censorship New York had seen in a generation. Although much of the original article was devoted to this campaign, its main topics were two of more lasting interest suggested by the original events. One was psychological: what kind of man is the innate moralist, the born censor? The other was historical: what have been the sources, and in particular the religious sources, of public support of censorship of the arts?*

[*The true-born censor is a man who knows he is right regardless of the evidence: as Davis puts it, that one with God is a majority. Anthony Comstock of the old Vice Society was, if nearly an extreme, the perfect type of the crusading censor. His diary description of a croquet game, "I insisted on fair play and some thought different," sums him up: there was always the right side and those who thought different. This is the type that Shaw hit off in the lines of Johnny in* Misalliance: *"You can draw a line and make the other chaps toe it. That's what I call morality."*

[*Comstock's biographers, perhaps in the leniency of the sophisticated twenties, seem to have given him a good deal of credit for good intentions. This is an argument we have heard more recently about other bullies. It is probably very questionable whether the intentions are sincerely good in these cases. But in any case there was good precedent for Davis's argument (long before Existentialism became popular) that "not what a man meant, but what he did" should be taken as grounds for judgment.*

[*The other topic was historical; so much of its discussion dealt with events of vanishing interest that I have cut most of it. The historical fact itself, though, is an interesting one. The support of nineteenth-century censorship organizations was almost all from Protestant groups. Today we still live with the stereotype of the narrow-minded Puritan wielding his flail with prurient glee. It was traditionally always a* WASP *(white Anglo-Saxon Protestant) in the censor's post. But the most casual thought reveals that the powerful censorship groups of our day are no longer* WASP. *Change any one of the three epithets—W, A-S or*

P—and you'll get one or more powerful pressure groups. But the WASP
*has long since lost its sting, except for mild local eruptions. This article
identifies 1927 as the year when leadership in censoring the arts passed
over from Protestant groups to Catholic ones.*

[I have cut it to about half its original length.]

      The agitation for a censorship of the arts recurs as irregu-
larly but as inevitably as Florida hurricanes, and any prudent artist
will build his house accordingly. 1927 was another year of the Big
Wind, and this time the hurricane was the most destructive of a generation.

There were two consequences which may presently bring immense
injury to all the arts. One was a tightening of the New York obscenity
laws, which, though at first sight it may seem little more than ridiculous, opens the way for about all that the wildest fanatics have been
howling for in recent years; and the other was the bringing of a new
and enormous re-enforcement to the champions of censorship. The
recent excitement resurrected all the old war cries on both sides; among
them, on the side which may be provisionally if not quite accurately
described as the friends of the arts, much indignant protest against
"Comstockery." But this year's censorship wave, in New York and
Boston, was not Comstockery. It was something much older and more
formidable; it was the result of the entry into the argument of a force
which had been rather quiescent of late years, and might have remained quiescent still if it had not been provoked by the criminal folly
of a few theatrical producers. The cardinal distinction of the censorship movement of 1927 was that for the first time in American history
the decisive forces behind it were not Protestant but Catholic, even
though in New York the Protestants were still allowed to appear in
their traditional posts of leadership. That is a much more serious
matter than the sporadic and derisory activity of vice societies, as all
the arts may presently discover.

      It happened that the biography of Anthony Comstock, by Heywood
Broun and Margaret Leech, appeared, most felicitously for the authors,
while this excitement was at its height. As the first publication of the
Literary Guild, this book provoked so much excitement and debate
over trade ethics, trade customs, and what not, that actually to read
the *corpus delicti* in so notable a test case seemed as irrelevant as
poking into the private life of Dred Scott. But a great many people

read it none the less and found it instructive and amusing; I found it
so, but found something else rather disquieting. This book came near
converting me to the principle, so beloved of patriotic societies, that
the business of biography is moral edification. A study which treats
Anthony Comstock almost with admiration, which makes him out at
worst as a human being in whose defense extenuating circumstances
might be urged, comes near deserving suppression by the Vice Society
as pernicious to the morals of American youth.

For all of us may appeal to extenuating circumstances; the argument
that in the course of justice none of us should see salvation has been
perverted into the genial contention that in the course of charitable
good-fellowship all of us might as well see salvation. But such salvation
as there is or ever will be (one may in reason hope for at least some
temporary amelioration for the race, however cheerless the prospects of
the individual) must be achieved by hard work; and the criterion of
a man's goodness or badness is whether he has helped or hindered.
(If you don't believe this, read no farther; you won't believe the rest
of it either.) Comstock, on the whole, seems to have hindered, even if
you allow for the service he rendered by making his ideas ridiculous.
He was unquestionably sincere, as the saying goes; but one would have
supposed that after six thousand years of civilization the human race
might have outgrown the practice of regarding sincerity as a virtue in
itself.

Possibly Miss Leech and Mr. Broun would not go that far; but they
appear to regard life from the standpoint of motive and intention,
which is natural enough, for they are novelists. But it seems to some
of us (and with the concurrence of so good a novelist as Samuel Butler) that life may more properly and usefully be regarded from the
standpoint of results. Not what a man meant, but what he did—and if
you say that what he did was not his own fault, but that of his environment or his ancestors, you are saying what may be true, but is
irrelevant to the more urgent question of what all of us, together, are
going to be able to do. Once begin making exculpatory allowances
and you had better scamper back to the shelter of an atonement theory
as quickly as you can, for that is the only place where you will find
safety.

This biography, of course, must have been finished before the outburst of censorious zeal that marked the early months of 1927; and the
authors may owe some of their excess of Christian charity to a conviction that the devil was already bound in the bottomless pit and that
there was no use kicking a fiend who was down. If St. Michael, vic-

torious, had sat down to write an obituary of the dragon, he might have felt a sportsmanlike impulse to deal generously with the record of that old serpent; which he would no doubt have regretted if the dragon had come out of his coma and started to fight all over again after the paper had gone to press. A year earlier it might have seemed safe to dance Comstock's scalp; but he is not dead so long as our statute books are weighted with the oppressive and unreasonable laws that he devised and lobbied through Congress and Legislature. There will probably never be another Comstock; he was a unique and peculiar embodiment of a spirit which existed before him, and still persists, and would persist if he had never lived at all. But thanks to him that spirit is armed with a weapon of unholy power; because of his fanatical singlemindedness, his irresistible energy, his genuine conviction of what most people, even in his time, believed only perfunctorily, that one with God is a majority, each of his successors is armed for offense and defense almost as invincibly as Siegfried and Perseus. This is the burden of Anthony, the Comstock load.

The customary defense of Comstock is that all his blunders are nullified by his service in suppressing the smut pamphlets which seem to have been pretty generally on sale sixty years ago. How much harm this printed filth actually did may be open to question, but it does not appear that it ever did any good except to the people who got the money for it. Mr. Broun indeed argues that such works as *Only a Boy* vaccinate impressionable youth against the undesirable glamor of sex, which may be true. But they are quite as likely to vaccinate against the desirable glamor, if one admits that there may be such a thing. No tears need be shed over this first stage of Comstock's activity, but it is going pretty far to treat it as complete justification for the later Comstock, who attacked *Mrs. Warren's Profession* and the wax figures in department store show windows with equal zeal; or to treat it, as some worthy persons did, as full justification for the prosecution of *Jurgen* by Mr. Comstock's successor.

Indeed, one finishes the biography with the impression that there was a deeper irrelevance in Comstock's crusades against pornography and what he thought was pornography. His abnormal fear and hatred of sex or anything that suggested it to his superheated mind was, after all, not his dominant characteristic. Essentially he was a bully; if the human race were asexual, reproducing by fission, Comstock would still have been a nuisance. Courage he certainly had and plenty of it— but he was a large and powerful man who could reasonably count on getting the best of any physical encounter; and behind him, after the first few years, he had the Law, which in that less sophisticated day was still some protection against the knife and the gun.

Possibly the most significant sentence in the book is a quotation from Comstock's diary, occasioned by no more flagitious an occurrence than a game of croquet with his wife and a few friends: "I insisted on fair play and some thought different." There, in a line, is the biography of Anthony Comstock. Whatever he insisted on was fair play, and God help those who "thought different."

[· · ·]

From the beginning he had much success, but the courts had an inconvenient habit of occasionally acquitting people whose guilt was clear enough to Comstock. More law was needed, then, and Comstock got it; got it by a persistent and indefatigable effort which certainly compels admiration, whatever you think of his creed and his methods. Not that there was any grave danger that legislators of the early seventies would offer open opposition to his demands; they agreed with his doctrines in theory at least, even if few of them cared enough about purity to give their time to its preservation. But they were too busy to pay much attention to Anthony's crusade until, like the unjust judge in Holy Writ, they were wearied by his continual coming and gave in.

This was in the Gilded Age, the low water mark of American public morals; lower even than the new benediction of understanding between public officials and private interests which took place in the golden prime of Harding. Of the members of the Congress which wrote Comstock's views on obscenity into the statutes of the United States where they remain in force to this day, it is hardly an exaggeration to say that half of them had already been caught stealing, and the others were wondering how soon they too would be detected. But of all this the holy Anthony was oblivious.

[· · ·]

There does not seem to be much evidence that the sexual morality of the American people was materially higher in the late seventies than in the earlier seventies; but whatever the boys and girls might be doing, Comstock certainly purified the newsstands. Armed with the sword he himself had forged, he was irresistible. In a decade or so his victory over his first enemy was complete; the obscene pamphlets which had provoked him into an activity that had made him famous had been driven into a furtive obscurity from which they have never since emerged. And here was Comstock, renowned and powerful, with the laws of his own writing behind him, his own hand-made fighting machine, the Vice Society, at his command—and his occupation gone. Not unnaturally he made himself more occupations, and some of them were grotesque enough.

Some of them were worse than that. He appointed himself the champion of orthodoxy and found the free-love doctrines of earnest atheists an excuse for persecuting them less as free lovers than as atheists. He drove to suicide an unbalanced woman guilty of writing a book which endeavored, however clumsily, to make marriage more decent and beautiful—but this was only one of fifteen suicides which he was proud of having inspired, and the last one. As time passed people stopped committing suicide to gratify him; sex appeared less a peril, contributions to the Vice Society decreased, the world seemed moving away from Comstock. Desperately he tried to catch up with it, tried this and that. He spent much time attacking lotteries, and local gambling houses which were by-products of political corruption. But a short-sightedness that sprang inevitably from his temperament and upbringing confined him to accidentals; he was unable to diagnose the disease of which protected gambling and protected prostitution were symptoms, and so he missed the chance of his lifetime. The more intelligent Parkhurst grasped political corruption as a whole; on that issue he got the spotlight, and thrust Comstock into a shadow from which he never really emerged.

He descended to raiding art stores, trying to suppress the catalogue of the Art Students' League, turning "September Morn" from an unimportant painting into a valuable commercial property; he essayed to abolish Bernarr MacFadden and Bernard Shaw; but he seldom got anywhere.

[· · ·]

Yet still the soldier of the Lord went on fighting, and not the Lord's battles only. More quarrelsome and ill-tempered as the years went by, he kept getting into fights, not with agents of Satan selling implements of sin, but with lawyers who dared to cross-examine him, with pedestrians who resented being knocked down because they brushed against him on crowded sidewalks. He had pampered his overbearing and bellicose disposition because he had been big enough and strong enough to get away with it; when he grew too old to win his fights, he still could not help provoking them. Here, plainly, was the ruling passion of his life; his pathological sex phobia merely happened to give it a picturesque direction.

Well, what did he accomplish? Comstock is gone but Shaw and MacFadden are still with us; and between Comstock and MacFadden it would be uncharitable to express a preference. Sex is still with us, for all Comstock's efforts; rather noticeably with us, one might say. But certainly the deliberate obscenity of our time—and without going into the question of what is and is not obscene, one may remark that obviously there is a good deal on the stage and the newsstands today which at least tries to be obscene—is more suave, less repulsive than the obscenity which Comstock drove underground. Unless you hold with Comstock that sex is sin, that improvement in taste—much room as is left for further improvement—is something gained.

But not all of that credit can be given to Comstock; it is a change in the popular temper, the popular taste; it might have happened without him.

[*Here he devotes twelve pages to the events that led to Catholics replacing Protestants and coming forward as leaders of the censorship campaign in 1927.*]

Comstock himself may seem to have been thrust into obscurity by this new movement, but he has played his part. We owe to him the laws which made dissemination of contraceptive information obscene by definition; we owe to him the all-embracing phraseology of the present statutes, which enables a judge to interpret them according to his own taste. An indecent play, by the New York law as it stood before amendment (and this part of course still stands), is one which "would tend to the corruption of the morals of youth, or others." And so a judge before whom *The Captive* was finally brought, indirectly, happened to be inclined to follow the strict letter of the law (another judge might as reasonably have given the opposite decision, and with as sound recent precedent); he admitted that this play was not likely to harm an intelligent and normal adult, but he refused to authorize its production for fear it might do injury to those whom previous court decisions have described as "the young, the immature, the ignorant, or the sensually inclined." In other words, the diet of all of us must be that prescribed for the weakest stomach; for fear that the wicked may be still further depraved, the pervert still further perverted, the clean and intelligent must be treated as of no account.

We owe that to Comstock. He was a psychopathic case; and if you say that we all are, more or less, it must be observed that in his instance it was considerably more. In his chosen field, this foul-minded man ruled the nation for a couple of decades. It would be inexact to say that his soul goes marching on; it was a peculiar soul, hardly to be duplicated. But the weapons he invented and manufactured still arm the forces of repression; his laws are still on the books, and laws which profess to effect the moral improvement of the citizenry are rarely repealed in this virtuous nation. For a century to come, all the forces of obscurantism will have reason to be grateful to him.

BEDS OF IVORY

[Of the varying kinds of anti-Semitism in this world, one is just a magnified form of xenophobia: the redneck's hatred for the cosmopolite. In the 1926 piece in Show Window *Davis identified this kind of anti-Semitism with what he called "anti-New-Yorkism" and amused himself by discrediting it with anti-Semites by tracing it back to the prophetic tradition. I have made extensive cuts, trying to give just enough to preserve the flavor of this piece.]*

American anti-Semitism is peculiarly a problem for New Yorkers, and not merely because half the Jews of the country live in New York. A good deal that takes the form of anti-Semitism is really anti-New-Yorkism. Which is the most cogent of arguments for the demobilization of antagonism between Jews and Gentiles in New York.

[· · ·]

New Yorkers are born, not made; but they may be born anywhere. A natural New Yorker born in North Carolina and a natural New Yorker born in the Russian Pale have more in common than the Carolina New Yorker and the folks back home in North Carolina, when he returns for a visit after ten years in Manhattan. And when it comes to New Yorkers, whether Jew or Christian, of western European ancestry and culture, there are no vital differences beyond individual variations.

[· · ·]

Hillbillies may then obscurely feel that they are standing up for the primitive Aryan culture of the countryside against that abominable Jewish institution, the city. But they are not. They are following the lead of the Jew quite as much as is the urban businessman. Or even more; they are following a Jewish tradition which the Jews themselves have outgrown.

For where did this peculiarly religious antipathy of the back country against the city originate, this conviction that God made the country and man made the town; that the horny-handed agriculturist, despite his addiction to roadside amours and wholesale ax murders, is none the less the guardian of all the virtues, while the scoundrelly desk man is skating along the primrose path from which he must be forcibly diverted, for the good of his own soul, by the embattled farmer? Well, that question may take us a long way back. I suspect that it originated ten or fifteen thousand years ago, when some Neolithic hunter, going into the thatched village to trade a bearskin for a new stone hatchet, ran up for the first time against the law of supply and demand. But its first appearance in history—Western history, at any rate—is plainly visible; and from that first appearance the filiation of ideas and reasoning and even vocabulary can be traced down clearly to the fire-breathing rural evangelists and country politicians of our own time. As a religious and moral issue—or, if you prefer to be candid about it, a social-economic issue presented in religious and moral language—it began with the words of Amos, who was among the herdsmen of Tekoa, which he saw concerning Israel in the days of Uzziah king of Judah, and in the days of Jeroboam the son of Joash king of Israel, two years before the earthquake.

This Amos looked around him and gathered the impression that things were going wrong in a variety of ways, as possibly they were. Amos thereupon concluded that the evils of the time could be cured only by a return to the old-time religion; by which he meant, as every prophet in every age has meant, to his personally revised concept of the old-time religion, and no other. The Jewish prophetic tradition has been the source of much of the spiritual vitality of the Western world, Jewish or Christian, but its sociology can hardly be regarded as very sound.

For consider some of the words of Amos the herdsman of Tekoa. "Woe to them that are at ease in Zion, and trust in the mountain of Samaria . . . that lie upon beds of ivory, and stretch themselves upon their couches . . . that chant to the sound of the viol, and invent to themselves instruments of music, like David; that drink wine in bowls, and anoint themselves with the chief ointments; but they are not grieved for the affliction of Joseph."

There were no beds of ivory in Tekoa. Back there in the hills they were not guilty of the moral turpitude of inventing to themselves instruments of music, and chanting to the sound of the viol. No doubt they drank wine, but they drank it from a goatskin, *more majorum*, and not from bowls. And because the abandoned denizens of the city, or some of them, had beds of ivory and liked music with their meals, Amos concluded that they were not grieved for the affliction of Joseph.

All sacred tradition agrees with him. But if you turn to profane history you must conclude that they who seemed to be at ease in Zion, and trusting in the mountain of Samaria, were just as grieved as Amos for the affliction of Joseph. Only, they were not so ready with cocksure remedies, for they knew more about it.

What was the affliction of Joseph? Well, it seems there had been some bad crop seasons. People still pray for rain in some parts of this extensive country, but even in Kansas they are no longer inclined to blame local dry spells on divine wrath inspired by the wetness of New York. Aside from this temporary hardship the affliction of Joseph consisted·simply in this, that Israel was a small buffer state, occupying strategically important territory between two great powers.

[· · ·]

Amos, too, did the best he could; he blamed what seemed blameworthy by the standards of Tekoa, the only standards he knew; and two years afterward came the earthquake, and Amos stood justified before the Lord and before the people. Never since then has there failed some inspired gatherer of sycamore fruit who hears the compelling inward voice, and goes forth to preach judgment and damnation against those who lie on beds of ivory and chant to the sound of the viol, and drink wine in bowls when the goatskin is good enough for Tekoa.

The social sciences were not highly developed in the eighth century B.C.; a rustic Hebrew zealot cannot be blamed very harshly for thinking that there was some connection between military-economic power and correctness in theology. But when one finds the same line of reasoning in statesmen of this enlightened republic one cannot help wondering just what is meant by the concept of human progress.

[· · ·]

These gentlemen are following the oldest and most respectable Hebrew tradition. If there is any anti-Semitism, in the most fundamental sense, in this present controversy, it is practiced by the Jews and Gentiles of New York, who claim no more than the privilege of living according to their own notions without submitting to the cultural dictation of the farmer. Amos's theories about the debilitating influence of urban luxury no longer seem to have much influence among his co-religionists. If the Jews have learned that he was mistaken, it seems not beyond hope that some day the generality of Christians may perceive it too.

ON THE GENTILITY OF GENTILES

[Seven years later he turned to a different type of anti-Semitism. This mild real-estate-conditioned conformity is very different from the anti-cityism discussed earlier, or the city page of anti-Semitism he mentioned briefly in hoping for a "demobilization of antagonism." If Davis's response now is more condemnatory, that is surely due to Hitler; for this article appeared in 1933, in Harper's. *Hitler's actions and German acquiescence showed the dangers in acquiescing to any kind of anti-Semitism.*

[I have made many cuts, excising about half of the original. Most of the material so removed gave examples, or historical comment.]

Each spring there arises in my family the problem of where we are to spend the summer; and among the countless summer colonies within two or three hours of New York whose prices are within the reach of a middle-class professional man the choice somehow narrows down in the end to the three or four settlements where we have spent previous summers. They offer plenty of variety; some are in the mountains, some beside the sea; some are addicted to golf, some to tennis; at one or two you have to do a good deal of dressing up, at the others you can wear anything you like; here the nucleus of New Yorkers is diluted by Brooklynites, there by Bostonians or Philadelphians. But in one respect all these resorts are alike; wherever we go, wherever we can afford to go, we can't ask the Rosenblatts down for a week-end.

Nor the Ecksteins, nor the Blaufarbs. The Ecksteins and the Blaufarbs would feel that they were slumming if they visited any of the summer colonies I could afford; at their country places they have Gentile neighbors, Gentile friends—Gentiles who are rich enough and prominent enough to be able to afford to associate with anybody they happen to like. But no place within reach of my purse will admit Ecksteins or Blaufarbs, even as guests. The rich seem able to endure their company without defilement, but not the middle class.

The Rosenblatts have little contact with the rich; they differ in no way from the typical family at any of our moderate-priced colonies—except of course that they have more brains, and perhaps a little more money. Like the rest of us, they are solid and settled persons; their interests, social and intellectual, are our interests; their manners are our manners—or perhaps a little better; like the rest of us, they entertain a somewhat tepid respect for religion in the abstract, but seldom enter a house of worship. Yet it is enough to damn them that they are Jews.

[· · ·]

The same feeling shows itself in other places than summer colonies. Once I lived in a suburb—a typical suburb, chiefly inhabited by Aryan Protestants who were desperately clinging to the ragged edge by tooth and toenail, trying to meet the mortgage payments and keep up a front at the same time. A neighbor of mine had a bitter grievance against the real estate company, or the club committee, or somebody else in authority; and getting no satisfaction, he was driven to the awful threat, "I'll sell my house to Jews!" He could not have done it; the sort of Jews who cared to live in that suburb would not have bought his modest cottage. We had several Jewish residents, and the least opulent of them lived in a house far better than his.

[· · ·]

Now any group of people may reasonably prefer to live, if they can, in the company of people of their own sort, especially when they live in the isolated intimacy of a summer colony, or even the semi-isolation and semi-intimacy of a residential suburb. To say that we want in our colony only families of the same general background as our own, families who are (or were, in the days before everybody went broke) adequately but not offensively prosperous, and sufficiently but not inconveniently intellectual—that is no more than good sense, and could give legitimate offense to nobody. But when families which meet the test in all other respects are excluded merely because they are what is called Jews, that is rather disquieting; and less disquieting to the Jew (who can always find some place to spend the summer) than to the reflective Gentile.

For what is a Jew? Wherein lies the difference that debars the Rosenblatts and their like from our summer colonies? Not in religion, surely. There may be an occasional Catholic family in these settlements, but the overwhelming majority is Protestant, in the sense that we are of Protestant background and habit of mind. But few of us go to church; and those who have any interest in organized religion give their somewhat Laodicean allegiance to Modernist Protestantism, whose differences from Reformed Judaism are infinitesimal. The religious differences would be sound reason for excluding orthodox Jews (who would not want to fellowship with us anyway), but none of the Jewish families we know is orthodox.

Nor is it a matter of race. If the evidence of history and of eyewitness observation is worth anything, the Jews are no more a race than the Germans; like every nation in modern Europe (to say nothing of America), they are a mixture of races unified by a culture in so far as they are unified at all. Even that culture is chiefly of alien and largely of Christian imposition; what people think of as traditional Jewish characteristics cannot be discerned in the Jews who appear in the first trustworthy historical passages of the Old Testament. The Jews of David's day were ignorant and bigoted farmers, exactly like the hillbillies who made up the strength of the Ku Klux Klan. The Phoenicians were the smart businessmen of that period, and while Hiram King of Tyre complained that Solomon had gypped him in a real estate deal, that seems to have been a distinct exception. Then and for centuries after the bulk of the Jews had the hillbilly's distrust of the city slicker who appreciates the amenities of life; the roars of Amos of Tekoa against those who lie on beds of ivory, and chant to the sound of viols, and drink wine in bowls (they used goatskin bags, back in Tekoa) set the keynote to which rural fanatics have faithfully attuned their vituperations for twenty-seven hundred years.

Judaism as we know it began with the Exile, and some think that Hebrew business ability was learned by the rivers of Babylon; but as late as New Testament days the typical Palestine Jew was an ignorant and bigoted farmer. The Jews scattered about the Roman Empire were artisans more often than businessmen; the Syrian was the shrewd trader of those times. Probably many "Jews" of today are the descendants of converted Carthaginians, and I believe that there is a theory that Jewish business ability dates from the annexation of that gifted commercial race. But the most authentic Carthaginians in the United States, the Minorcans of St. Augustine, seem to have lost those ancestral impulses; like Fafner, they lie quiet and possess; and I do not see why traits that died out of Christianized Carthaginians should have survived in Hebraeized Carthaginians but for Christian compulsion.

All of this, perhaps, is irrelevant to the feeling of my summer neighbors; they are concerned with the manifestations of Jewish shrewdness and solidarity, not with its origins. The point is that these manifestations have all but disappeared from the Jews we know.

[· · ·]

Now the culture that is molding all middle-class Manhattan today is the local culture of an island metropolis, little understood and still less liked by the hinterland. Where a man came from, and which of the countless races represented in New York supplied his ancestry, is a matter of less importance to most of us than our common interests and our common habits of mind. This is true of almost all New Yorkers of Protestant background, of almost all Jews who have escaped from the ghetto tradition; of most of the Catholics who do not carry their Catholicism to the point of making a religion of it. The dominant influences that shape the Rosenblatts are the same that shape the Smiths and the O'Gradys; and it seems irrational that a summer colony which admits the Smiths and the O'Gradys should keep the Rosenblatts out.

And, finally, my summer neighbors cannot be accused of anti-Semitism in the ordinary sense of that word; they are as indignant as anybody at the behavior of the Hitlerites; they abhor the idea of persecution of Jews, of discrimination against Jews in business, professions, public life. But they will not have Jewish neighbors, even if the Jews are in all perceptible respects like themselves.

The one imperceptible but decisive difference is that Jews are Jews, whatever that means, and we are Aryan Protestants, even though our Aryanism is theoretical and our Protestantism vestigial. Ask any of us, and we would admit that Aryan Protestants are the salt of the earth; though we should not say so without being asked.

[· · ·]

It is a healthy way to feel—so long as you are really convinced of your superiority and do not try to prove it by the offensive arrogance which is the symptom of the inferiority complex.

As arrogance goes, the exclusion of Jews, agreeable as well as disagreeable, from summer colonies is a not very offensive variety; but I am afraid it is an unmistakable symptom none the less.

Being an Aryan Protestant, I am as firmly convinced of the high merit of Aryan Protestants as anybody; indeed rather more confident of the merit of Aryanism than are the Nazis. I am so sure of it that I feel no need to prove it by breaking the windows of Jewish stores, or to insist that I must not be exposed to the competition of Jews in my profession.

[· · ·]

That is why I hate Adolf Hitler and his followers as no Jew can ever hate them; they have made Aryan virtues ridiculous.

The Germans profess to be the most Aryan of Aryans. "Nordic blood represents that Mystery which has replaced and vanquished the ancient sacrifice," says a gentleman now high in the German government, named (somewhat surprisingly) Rosenberg. But since there are Gentile Cohans and Leavys in Ireland, there may well be Aryan Rosenbergs in Germany. You would suppose that sixty-odd million Aryans endowed with this invincible holiness would not need to be afraid of six hundred thousand Jews, but they are. When, before the Nazis had captured the government, their strong-arm men swept down the Kurfürstendamm in Berlin one Passover, beating up all Jews or suspected Jews, you would expect that each of these Aryan heroes, strong in his self-conscious superiority, would attack twenty Semites. Not so; twenty Aryans ganged on a single Jew.

[· · ·]

And it seems that the Jews have an even worse vice. They are eternal aliens, unassimilable—the tapeworm in the organism, as the well-remembered Count Reventlow delicately puts it. Their racial-religious culture has such vitality that no surrounding culture can dissolve or even dilute it.

If this is so, the Jews do not know it and never have known it. All Jewish history, down to the triumph of Christianity, resounds with complaints that Jews would not be Jews if they had a chance to be anything else. King Solomon married some goy wives, and immediately began to be what would nowadays be called an assimilationist. So did King Ahab, a hundred and fifty years later. Those were early and simple days; but presently the prophets developed the concept of a peculiar and chosen people, the favorite of the one God of all the earth. It followed that this people's culture, rooted in true religion, was superior to all other cultures; and it was a source of bitter annoyance to the prophets that Jews exposed to any other culture usually wanted to try it.

Even after the Exile and the Return had confirmed the Chosen Remnant in its conviction that it was the salt of the earth, Jewish boys took to marrying goy girls from Ashdod, Ammon, Moab; and Jewish culture was apparently as much imperiled by these Gentile influences as German culture is alleged to be imperiled by Jewish influences. The pious Nehemiah had to use Nazi methods to get his people back on the right track. "I contended with them, and cursed them, and smote certain of them, and plucked off their hair. And one of the sons of Joiada, the son of Eliashib the high priest, was son-in-law to Sanballat the Horonite; therefore I chased him from me. Remember them, O my God, because they have denied the priesthood. Remember me, O my God, for good."

But the tendency seemed ineradicable. Jewish culture had managed to escape engulfment in Phoenician culture, Babylonian culture, Philistine culture; but it pretty nearly succumbed to Greek culture. A high priest of the Seleucid period "built a place of exercise, and brought the chief young men under his subjection, and made them wear a hat. Now such was the height of Greek fashions that the priests had no courage to serve any more at the altar; but despising the temple, and neglecting the sacrifices, hastened to be partakers of the unlawful allowance in the place of exercise, after the game of discus called them forth." What is the self-conscious superiority of God's chosen people, compared to the Gentile joys of throwing the discus and wearing a hat? Luckily there was raised up Judas Maccabaeus, the Hitler of his day, who rallied the hillbillies and saved the old-time religion.

It is one of the great achievements of Christianity that it managed to stamp out this inclination of the Jews not to be Jews if they could help it. For more than a thousand years before the Christians got control of the secular arm assimilation had repeatedly menaced the very existence of Judaism; but when Jews had no choice but to remain Jews or turn Christian they preferred to go on being Jews, even at the risk of expropriation, torture, and the stake. For fifteen hundred years they remained steadfast in their allegiance to their own culture; but when Christianity began to weaken, the old assimilationist tendencies revived. Many Jews even turned Christian when they were no longer in danger of being burned alive for not turning Christian. They were still God's chosen people, the salt of the earth; but when at last they could exercise freedom of choice without sacrificing their self-respect, many of them chose to discard their unique privileges, and do what was being done by the best people around them. And this is what German philosophers call "the eternal Jew."

[• • •]

It is an abrupt descent, perhaps, from the megalomaniac enthusiasms and noble rages of the German Nazis and their Jewish similars to the somewhat pallid preferences and antipathies of my summer neighbors.

[• • •]

This middle-class Protestant exclusiveness is hampering and delaying—though I do not believe it can permanently prevent—an assimilation which is important for the well-being of American society, and vitally important for the well-being of the metropolitan society of New York. But quite as unfortunate is the light it throws on the mentality of Aryan Protestants. If we were so sure of our superiority should we be afraid to expose it to comparison?

[• • •]

But my friends and summer neighbors are not the rich and great. They are good people—kindly, pleasant, useful; but it would be rather hard for them to claim any special superiority on visible and tangible evidence. If they must be superior, as apparently they must, they can be so only through setting up by implication—of course they would never put it so crudely—the doctrine that middle-class Aryan Protestants are automatically gentlefolk, and Jews of the same class are not. The definition of a gentleman is a debatable matter, which need not be gone into here; it need only be said that I know of no definition which would include all my Gentile friends and exclude all my Jewish friends unless you set up this unarguable delimitation by creed and race.

I think better of Aryan Protestantism than that; we have our peculiar virtues and we need not be afraid of comparisons.

[• • •]

As for the fading of our faith, Modernist Protestantism and Reformed Judaism are both half-way houses—wayside tourist camps for those who are on the way out from orthodoxy to complete freedom of thought, but do not feel strong enough to make the whole trip all at once. It would seem not only more intelligent but more fraternal, even more Christian, to make friends with our fellow travelers; they may have come from a different starting point but their destination is the same as our own. The Modernist clergy do this, of course, but few of their parishioners seem willing to follow them. Yet Jewish orthodoxy is disappearing more rapidly than Christian orthodoxy; and the Jews we meet in the half-way house may some day be useful and needed allies, if the present tribulation continues and begins to drive the weaker brethren back to the Everlasting Arms.

I do not suppose my summer neighbors perceive all these far-reaching implications of their insistence that the Rosenblatts must not be asked down for the week-end; but the implications are inescapable once you set any criterion but that of personal congeniality.

[· · ·]

In the cities where they live in the winter they are not perceptibly superior persons; they live where they can and as they can, and they are likely to be outshone by their Jewish neighbors. (Unintentionally outshone, quite often; but that makes it all the worse.) But they must demonstrate their superiority in some way, and summer gives them their chance. They flock by themselves in aboriginal reservations, Aryan ghettos, to which any decently presentable Gentile who looks as if he could pay his rent can gain admission—provided he understands that he may have no Jewish guests.

Some of my Jewish friends are rather hurt by all this; which, after all, is more flattering than if they merely laughed.

NEWS AND THE WHOLE TRUTH

[*Two of the greatest assets of American journalism are its standard of objectivity and the spirit of competition that keeps reporters working to find more news. This* Atlantic *article, revised as Chapter II of* But We Were Born Free, *points out that neither one is an unmixed blessing. Competition has led to various kinds of excesses. "Objective reporting" has even more often in late years led to the promotion of completely false pictures of the facts. Davis was careful to emphasize the importance of attempting true objectivity; but this piece reports the frequent failure of such attempts and the need for a more "many-dimensional" approach to news.*

[*I have cut a number of examples concerning people who are no longer newsworthy.*]

Each spring the members of the American Newspaper Publishers Association assemble in convention and spend a good deal of their time eulogizing themselves. Conventions of editors and reporters, whether for newspapers or radio news, are more practical and less complacent. The American news business, press and radio, certainly deserves some eulogies; it is the most copious in the world, and I think its average quality is at least as good as any other's. But it is not yet good enough. Too often we tell the customers not what is really going on, but what seems to be going on. And I am not referring to the small minority of newspapers, and the smaller minority of newspapermen, who don't want to tell the truth, but to the great majority who do want to tell the truth but often fall short.

Too much of our news is one-dimensional, when truth has three dimensions (or maybe more); we still have inadequate defenses against men who try to load the news with propaganda; and in some fields the vast and increasing complexity of the news makes it continually more difficult—especially for us Washington reporters—to tell the public what really happened. Some of these failings are due to encrusted habits of the news business, which can be changed only slowly, but which many men are now trying to change; some of them will be harder to cure because they are only the reverse side of some of our greatest merits, and it is difficult to see how to get rid of them without endangering the merits too.

The merits which entail the worst drawbacks are competition and the striving for objectivity, and we should be much worse off without either. But objectivity often leans over backward so far that it makes the news business merely a transmission belt for pretentious phonies. As for competition, there is no doubt that the nation is much better served by three wire services—the Associated Press, the United Press and the International News Service, sometimes supplemented by the English Reuters—and by several radio networks than it would be by monopoly in either field. But competition means an overemphasis on speed, as has been noted by the Associated Press Managing Editors (not the editors of the AP but the men who use its service); and sometimes it leads to an exaggerated build-up.

Like most radio newsmen, I am heavily dependent on the wire services. I am supposed to be aware of all the world's news and to report what seems to me most important or that to which I can add something in the way of interpretation. But I can't cover it all my-self—not even all that happens in Washington; usually I cover about one story a day on foot, get angles or elucidations on half a dozen others by telephone, and must depend on the wire services for the rest. Experience has taught me, when the versions of the same story given by two wire services differ materially, to prefer the less exciting; the other might have been souped up to beat the competition.

[· · ·]

The United Nations Commission on Freedom of Information has been trying to work out an international code of ethics for newsmen—not an easy task in view of the different concepts of news (and of ethics) on the two sides of the Iron Curtain. The first and I believe the only one so far adopted (by a vote of six to nothing with five abstaining) says only that reporters, editors and commentators shall do their best to make sure that the information the public receives is factually accurate, with no fact willfully distorted and no essential fact deliberately suppressed.

I don't know why the American delegate abstained from voting for that innocuous declaration, unless for the reason that it doesn't go far enough. What is factual accuracy? Not merely what a man says, for sometimes he has said the contradictory thing in times past; and some-times, indeed, what he says is known to be false. Truth has three di-mensions; but the practices of the American news business—practices adopted in a praiseworthy ambition to be objective—too often give us only one-dimensional news—factually accurate so far as it goes, but very far indeed from the whole truth.

There was not much objectivity in the American press through most of the nineteenth century; if a story touched on the political or economic interest of the editor or owner, it was usually written so as to make his side look good. Some papers still follow that practice; but most of them, for some decades past, have accepted the principle that they ought to try to be objective in the news columns, leaving argument to the editorial page. Publish everything that is said on both sides of a controversial issue and let the reader make up his mind. A noble theory; but suppose that men who talk on one side (or on both) are known to be lying to serve their own personal interest, or suppose they don't know what they are talking about. To call attention to these facts, except on the editorial page, would not, according to most newspaper practice, be objective. Yet in the complex news of today how many readers have enough personal knowledge to distinguish fact from fiction, ignorance from knowledge, interest from impartiality?

This practice is perhaps not quite so prevalent now as it was twenty-five years or so ago—in the golden age of Calvin Coolidge, when it was the general opinion that things are what they seem. In those days, if the Honorable John P. Hoozis was an important person, you were likely to see him quoted at length in the newspapers on almost any subject, with no indication that he knew nothing at all about it, or no indication that he had a strong personal interest in getting people to believe what he said—even if the editor who printed the story happened to know it. He was an important man; he had made a statement; and it would not have been objective not to print it.

[· · ·]

It was the realization that objectivity had leaned so far over backward that it had become unobjective which led to the rise of the syndicated newspaper column, and a little later of the radio news commentary. These are both news and interpretation; our listeners, or readers, understand that we are saying, "This is the news and this is what I think it means." But even for us, with much more latitude than the ordinary reporter, it is becoming harder and harder to get at the three-dimensional truth in Washington—partly because the news becomes more and more complex, partly because so much of it is coming to consist of never-ending serial melodramas, like soap operas on the radio, or those newspaper cartoon strips that used to be comic.

Especially is this true of Congressional committee hearings, where

the same witnesses appear and reappear. Adequate coverage of such
stories entails reporting not only what a man says now, but the very
different thing he may have said last year—or last week.

[· · ·]

I am not here concerned with the ethics of this sort of thing—though
that is a topic on which much might be said—but with its effect on a
reporter's endeavor to give the public a reasonably accurate story. Reporters covering the McCarran hearings were continually in danger of
giving the public a false report, not of what was actually said in their
presence but of the three-dimensional truth of which what they hear
is only one dimension. But who can read all the books or documents
from which "pertinent excerpts" may be drawn? Who could remember them all, if he did?

[· · ·]

But to analyze and find the truth requires not only a good memory
but time. How does the average reporter get at the truth in cases like
this if he has to sit all day in a committee hearing and then come back
and write his story, with no time to check up on the witness's past
testimony or on the validity of the pertinent excerpts? How do I do it,
compelled as I am to keep an eye on all the world's news, pouring in
at the end of the day, besides the story that is right in front of me?
Yet, unless we try it, we give the public only one dimension of the
truth—a mere surface, under which something very different may lie
concealed.

[· · ·]

What to do? More and more, from inside as well as outside the
trade, there is a demand for interpretive reporting, which puts into
the one-dimensional story the other dimensions that will make it ap-
proximate the truth. But this entails serious dangers. I have seen some
undeniably well-intentioned endeavors to put in those other dimensions, but the dimensions were derived not from the evidence but from
the opinions or prejudices of the reporter; and if the practice were to
become general they might in some cases be derived from the opinions
and prejudices of the publisher, as they so often used to be. One Chicago *Tribune* is enough. And even if a man's conscience is as rigorous,
his mind as relentlessly objective, as the weights and measures in the
Bureau of Standards, he may still fall short of doing as accurate a job
as he means to do because he doesn't know all the angles, or hasn't

time to get around to them under the pressure of covering what is in front of him and writing a story about it.

[· · ·]

The good newspaper, the good news broadcaster, must walk a tight-rope between two great gulfs—on one side the false objectivity that takes everything at face value and lets the public be imposed on by the charlatan with the most brazen front; on the other, the "interpretive" reporting which fails to draw the line between objective and subjec-tive, between a reasonably well-established fact and what the reporter or editor wishes were the fact. To say that is easy; to do it is hard. No wonder that too many fall back on the incontrovertible objective fact that the Honorable John P. Hoozis said, colon quote—and never mind whether he was lying or not.

Yet more and more newsmen, in press and radio both, are coming to realize that we ought to do better than we are doing; and some of them are doing something about it. Dean Gordon Sabine of the Uni-versity of Oregon School of Journalism has observed that the rise of McCarthy has compelled newspapers of integrity to develop a form of reporting which puts into context what men like McCarthy have to say. "Reporting all the dimensions of the news," he said, "we used to think of as dangerous. Today the lack of it creates the danger. And if this new approach brings the editorial page to the front page, if it mixes interpretation with naked fact, then we must realize simply that today we recognize the complexity of the news much more clearly than we did thirty or forty years ago, and we recognize the need for more capable newsgatherers and writers, and even more intelligent deskmen and editors."

We do indeed. A man who can be trusted with interpretive report-ing must have both integrity and intelligence; even the *New York Times* seems to allow few if any of its reporters (except in the Sunday think-piece section) the freedom of interpretation that it accords to Bill White. Palmer Hoyt, publisher of the Denver *Post,* has issued to his staff a memorandum on how to treat the news about McCarthy so that the customers will not be deceived. "Many charges made by reck-less or impulsive public officials," he says, "can not and should not be ignored; but news stories and headlines can be presented in such a manner that the reading public will be able to measure the real worth or value and the true meaning of the stories." A principle which he works out in some detail; "we are anxious," he says, "to take every possible step to protect the innocent."

And not merely the innocent victim of McCarthy, but the innocent consumer, who has little or no means of evaluating what he sees in print. All of us in the news business ought to remember that our primary responsibility is to the man who buys his newspaper, or turns on his radio, expecting us to give him in so far as is humanly possible not only the truth and nothing but the truth, but the whole truth.

PREDILECTIONS

[In this mixed group the only unity may be that I see in each piece a predominant concern with matters of personal taste.]

ON BEING KEPT BY A CAT

[*Cat lovers have been practically unanimous in their praise for this piece from a 1938* Harper's *ever since its first appearance. The collection would be incomplete without reproducing this in full. Cat haters, if such there be reading here, should probably go on past this at once. Of the agnostic, some have liked it.*]

The lamented Freddie Mortimer of the *New York Times* was once moved to scorn by an item among the Lost and Found notices—an advertisement for a lost cat whose collar bore the inscription, "This is So-and-so's cat." Nothing, Mortimer contended, could be less accurate; the only identification that could truthfully be inscribed on any cat's collar would be, "This is this cat's cat."

For the gentleman who thought he owned the cat, not quite so much could be said. Madame Michelet (quoted by the learned Van Vechten, whose *The Tiger in the House* is practically the *Golden Bough* of cat lore) once computed that she had owned a hundred cats. "Say rather," her husband corrected, "that a hundred cats have owned you." Possibly he was jealous of the creatures who had usurped his rightful place as the domestic pet, but anybody with much feline experience knows he was right—especially people who do not keep servants, and must refuse invitations for week-ends because somebody has to stay at home to take care of the member of the family who cannot open ice-box doors. To the question often asked by the inexpert, "Do you keep a cat?" the proper answer is "No, a cat keeps me."

It is true that the courts have held that a cat is property, an opinion not concurred in by certain resort hotels which will take a cat for a dollar a day European plan; they make no such charge for your trunk. This seems to be one of the many instances in which business is more realistic than the law; the theory that a cat is property must be set down as one of those splendid flights of wishful thinking in which judges occasionally indulge. It would be pleasant to believe that somebody who is broke and looking for a job has equal power in contracting for wages with a prospective employer, so the courts have often held that this is so; it would be agreeable to a judge who is not used to having his injunctions disregarded to believe that the most inde-

pendent of all creatures is subject to human control. But the doctrine
breaks down under analysis.

Scholarly and subtle men have written much of late about the distinctions between various kinds of property. There are consumption
goods—clothes, for instance—which we all possess; and there the means
of production which are owned by capitalists, but owned in different
ways. I am, in economic terminology, a handicraft artisan owning my
own means of production—a typewriter, with which I earn my living;
I am also on an infinitesimal scale a capitalist. But my "ownership"
of, say, 1/435,000th part of the General Motors Corporation does not
enable me to do anything with that tiny fraction of a great institution
except to sell it if I choose. Henry Ford owns and uses the Ford Motor
Company as I own and use my typewriter; but all I "own" in General
Motors is a claim on a little of its profits, if men over whose actions I
have no control manage it well enough to make a profit.

Obviously, the cat who for some years has made his home with my
family falls into none of what I must apologize for calling these cate-
gories of property. He is not consumption goods but a consumer, and
a fairly heavy consumer at that; nor does he produce anything except
an intense satisfaction in those who associate with him. Nothing else
of utility to human beings, at least; he makes what a cat doubtless
regards as profits, and seems to think I have a claim on a share of
them. Whenever he kills a mouse in the apartment, or a snake at his
summer home in the country, he proudly brings it back to the family,
perhaps supposing that we might like to eat some of it. But even then
I stand in much the same economic relation to him as to Mr. Alfred P.
Sloan.

Reverse the situation, and the true property relation becomes apparent. I am to the cat what my typewriter is to me, or the Ford Motor
Company to Henry Ford—his means of production; in the course of
time he will eat up all the money I get for these observations.* If he
is not my sole proprietor, at least he owns enough stock in me to make
his wishes influential; and as for the members of the family who do
most of the work of caring for him, he seems to regard them as his
employees. If they do not work for him as and when he wants them to
work he expresses his opinion—though more politely than Mr. Tom
Girdler expresses his opinion in a similar situation.

* So he will—but not that particular money, only its equivalent. As it turned out
the entire family ate for a couple of months on the proceeds of this commentary,
at a time when no other income was coming in. That summer, we undeniably were
kept by a cat. Thus proving, as will be set forth later, that any cat can be a pro-
ducer when the situation requires.

This economic analysis of course does not apply to the alley cat, the free-lance cat who earns his living by his own exertions without exploiting the labor of others. But the house cat, the pet cat, so far from being property, is a capitalist, a member of the owner class, even if he catches a mouse now and then for sport. His mousing is comparable to the farming practiced by retired gentlemen of wealth, who do for amusement what their ancestors did because they had to. And when so many people are asking what the capitalist gives in return for what he gets, the cat too must stand examination.

II

"Probably the least useful of domestic animals," was the verdict of C. E. Browne and the late G. Stanley Hall, writing in the *Pedagogical Seminary;* which implies a very narrow concept of utility. The cat does not produce material wealth, nor acquire it unless he has to; and even then no more than he needs. But was Rembrandt the least useful of Dutchmen, or Bach of Germans? What Bach and Rembrandt produced (from the point of view of the sociologist, if not of the economist) was pleasure in others, and pleasure of a high order. That is what the cat produces too—the pleasure that comes from observing in many cats an astonishing beauty, and in practically all cats the perfection of grace; the still higher pleasure derived from contemplation of the most dignified and independent of living creatures. Tiberius Gracchus so admired the cat's independence that he put an image of a cat in the Temple of Liberty at Rome, as freedom's best symbol; at least so say Hall and Browne—Plutarch does not mention it. I do not know the explanation of Lenin's well-known fondness for cats; but perhaps he got an ironic satisfaction from the companionship of the only beings in Russia whom he could not boss.

The independence of course is far more conspicuous in alley cats, the most vigorous of all practitioners, in a civilized environment, of private initiative and rugged individualism. This ought to make the alley cat the favorite animal of the conservative rich; yet I suspect that if you took a census of these gentry you would find that most of them prefer the docile dog; their definition of individualism is usually "individualism for me." The cat, on the other hand, seems to be widely preferred by artists and writers—a tribe which with rare exceptions is almost fanatically individualistic, and values individualism and independence in its friends, human or animal.

But any cat is a potential alley cat; the most pampered of domestic pets could get along on his own if he had to. My cat (the possessive is used, here and hereinafter, purely for identification) is a silver Persian, who in his urban apartment leads a placid and sedentary life for nine months of the year. But when he goes to the country in June he is perfectly at home in woods and fields, and fights everything in sight. The cat's high sense of enlightened self-interest leads him to live on his income if he can—but because it is pleasanter, not because he must. The tendency is not unknown among human beings.

Besides the free-lance alley cat and the capitalistic house cat there is a third economic group—the salaried cats, in public or private employ. Mostly they are maintained to keep down rats and mice, though in wartime many served in the trenches or in submarines, to give gas alarms. In this class there are economic gradations, just as among human salaried employees; I suppose that from the feline point of view cats employed in meat markets rank highest—the movie stars or corporation presidents of the cat world. They experience all the vicissitudes of salaried employees too; lately the Mayor of Boston, in a drive for economy, slashed the salaries of the cats employed in the Public Library from $10 a year apiece to $9.85, for which relief Boston taxpayers were presumably grateful.

The cat makes the best of any situation in which he finds himself, but he is shrewd enough as a rule to prefer the pleasanter modes of life; I have known alley cats so jealous of their independence that they refused employment in groceries, but such resolution is rare. An illustration is the history of my friend Amos, a big brindle tom who used to live with an elderly couple in New York. The husband died; the wife decided to give up housekeeping and go live with her children, who for some reason had no room for Amos; so she put him in the Bide-a-Wee Home pending adoption. It happened that about that time a certain club discovered to its horror that there were rats in the basement, and the Board of Governors empowered the management to add a cat to the payroll. He went to the Bide-a-Wee Home, saw Amos and admired him (as who would not?) and employed him—after an exchange of references; for the lady who had been associated with Amos wanted to be sure that he joined the right club. Amos came, looked around, and evidently decided that this was not the club for him. The next day he vanished; but six weeks later he reappeared, looking somewhat bedraggled, and has been there ever since.

So far as the history of that interlude can be reconstructed, Amos went back home and discovered that home was not there any more; whereupon he decided to become an alley cat. He evidently succeeded in supporting himself by free-lancing; but like many a human being in the same situation, he finally concluded that it was too much of a strain and he had better go back to a salaried job; the job at the club might not be just what he wanted, but if it was the best proposition in sight he might as well take it. By now Amos enjoys club life; he knows the most comfortable chairs, and any of his fellow-members who dared to turn him out of his seat would hear from the House Committee. And he certainly earns his salary. Soon he had killed the last rat in the basement; then he began visiting the club across the street and killing their rats, proudly bringing them back to his own club to show that he was on the job. And now that both clubs are thoroughly deratted he has added the bank round the corner to his territory—appearing every morning as soon as it opens, with a face that asks the clearly legible question, "Any rats today? Anything a cat can do around here?"

Amos, it is obvious, has the instinct of workmanship, the delight in doing a job for its own sake; but he preferred the ease of the old home so long as he could get it. The American dream of the workman turning capitalist, and living in comfort without working any more, was familiar to every cat before America was ever heard of.

III

For the house cat has known better days, which may still linger in his racial memory; in Egypt he was once a god. Not that by any means all domestic cats of today are of Egyptian ancestry, any more than all Southerners are descended from the great ante-bellum plantation owners. But every Southerner literate enough to know the tradition cherishes the memory of the old white-pillared mansion that was burned by Sherman's army; and so it may be that every cat, even if all his ancestors came from Central Europe, likes to think that once his people were gods in Egypt.

The cat race, with its Manx and Siamese and Persian and all the other varieties, plainly has as many different kinds of ancestors as the German "race." The long-haired cats, the experts are inclined to think, are descended from the manul of Central Asia. I know this creature only from photographs, but he seems to have a formidable, even menacing dignity that would have made him a good playmate for Genghis Khan. As for short-haired cats, they come down from various wild species, European, Asiatic, African, and even American; there were domesticated cats in Mexico and Central America before the first Europeans came.

But the cat as a domestic institution of Western Culture first arose in Egypt, where there was a temple to the cat-goddess at Bubastis as early as 1500 B.C. Long before that Egyptian mythology told of the Great Cat, the celestial cat who kills the snake that sometimes tries to swallow the sun. (Those who remember one of the late Bert Williams's most famous stories will suspect that his name was Martin.) It is fairly certain that the first house cats in Europe were imported from Egypt—probably smuggled out, since the Egyptians did not like to let the sacred animals go. (Diodorus reports that in the days of Egyptian imperialism, armies campaigning abroad used to gather up all the cats they met and send them back to Egypt, where they would be treated with the proper respect.) It was in Egypt that the Greeks first encountered the cat—the *ailouros* they called him, the tail waver; and it is as an Egyptian animal, though apparently not unknown to Greek readers, that he is first mentioned in European literature, by Herodotus.

Soon after Herodotus's day cats appeared in both Greece and Italy. Richard Engelmann, in the annual of the Imperial German Archaeological Institute, mentions an Athenian vase of the classic period with a picture of a boy going to school, and his pedagogue (the accompanying slave) holding a cat on a leash. Italian vases of a not much later date show women playing with cats who look just like the cats of today. But apparently, says Engelmann, the exportation from Egypt was difficult and dangerous; cats in Europe were rare till the Christian era—and not long after that they ceased to be gods in Egypt.

When they fell they fell a long way—as far as Lucifer. In Christian Europe cats, particularly black cats, had the misfortune to be regarded as incarnations of the devil; and some people cannot get rid of that superstition to this day, though no doubt they would furiously deny that their dislike of cats is a hangover from witch-fearing ancestors. "Probably no other domestic animal," wrote Hall and Browne, "has been so loved and hated, so petted and persecuted." Even now, few people are neutral about cats; and a good deal of exaggeration can be found in arguments both for them and against them. There are people who have an instinctive horror of all cats—probably an atavistic memory of the great cats of the primal jungle, comparable to the much more common horror of snakes; there are those who cannot forget their demonology; and there are those who say they hate cats because they love dogs. You may like both of course, but people who crave the dog's uncritical devotion and are afraid to meet the coolly detached judgment of the cat, who does not like you unless he finds you worthy of liking, are making a damning admission. Leaving aside all these pathological types, people who say they dislike all cats have simply happened to know the wrong cats.

Not all cats are admirable any more than they are all detestable. "Each individual cat," says Van Vechten, "differs in as many ways as possible from each other individual cat." This may be too sweeping, but generalizations about all cats are as rash as generalizations about all human beings. All cats have tails? Not the Manx cats. All cats have fur? There were hairless cats in Aztec Mexico. Still less can you generalize about the character of "the cat." I have been well acquainted with some fifteen or twenty tail wavers; the majority were admirable—for character or intelligence or both; but several of them were disagreeable or even stupid. My present feline associate, General Gray (known to his intimates by a variety of other names as well), was given to the family (by the wife of a biped General Gray) as replacement for a cat who had been killed. He is one of the best I have ever known, but so was his predecessor; and a cat replaces another cat only to the extent that a wife replaces another wife. She may fill the same place in the household, but you have to get used to an utterly different personality. And those who know cats tend to judge them by the same criteria as human friends. I am ashamed to admit that probably the most intelligent cat I ever knew elicited my respect but not my affection. She was industrious, clever, virtuous; but she lacked charm.

Hall and Browne analyzed the results of a questionnaire in which eight hundred school children told why they liked cats; reasoning that as children anthropomorphize cats and so did primitive men, they might get some light on the early relations of the two species. (As a matter of fact only very young children, or those who do not know cats well, anthropomorphize them.) Most of the children were sure the cat loved them, not just his home, and they were probably right; to anyone who knows cats, the dogma of cat haters that the cat is attached only to places, not to persons, is a malignant myth. He likes places but he can feel great affection for persons too—affection as disinterested as human affections are likely to be. (This is true of most cats anyway; nothing is true of all cats.)*

Van Vechten truly observes that "walking is distasteful to the cat unless he has a purpose in view"; but all one summer General Gray accompanied my then small daughter on her evening walks—long walks, some of them—with no purpose in view but the enjoyment of her company. Once in a while when I am working he comes in and

* The infinite variety of feline behavior is even better known to me than when this was written; for magazine publication of this monograph, in *Harper's* and the *Reader's Digest*, brought me three or four times as much fan mail as anything else I ever wrote—even in those magazines, which seem to be a combination peculiarly adapted to evoking comment from readers. If I had collated all the information offered by my correspondents I could easily have written a book on cats; but none of the evidence necessitated any change in the general conclusions here set down.

rolls for me—not because he wants anything, but because he feels that high contentment which a cat can express only by rolling. He could roll wherever he happened to be; I can think of no reason for his coming from another room to roll in my office, except that he feels so happy that he wants to share his happiness with me.

Most of the eight hundred children said they liked cats because they were nice to play with, only a few because they were intelligent; children are apt to value their human elders by the same standard. As for the intellectuals who admire cats for their intelligence, their philosophic disposition, cat haters would say that this is precisely the same as the children's reaction. Each group reads into the cat the qualities it most appreciates, whether he really has them or not. In some cases this is true. People who are devoted to any pet incline to exaggerate its cleverness; less of that nonsense has been talked about cats than about babies. But many cat stories that seem absurd to ailourophobes are plausible enough to anybody who knows cats, as those who hate them do not. The Associated Press lately seemed to find an element of romance in the story of a cat in Maine which had lost a leg in a trap. His human associate fitted him with a wooden peg—and must have fitted him well, for any cat would spend hours trying to get that sort of contraption off before he ventured to walk on it; and when the cat caught a rat he held it down with his other forepaw and beat it to death with his wooden leg. Fiction? Not wholly. He may have killed the rat, eventually, with his teeth; but any cat who caught a rat would slap it around a bit, and it would be a natural muscular reflex to swing on it with the arm that happened to have a wooden peg attached.

Stories of cats' manipulative skill about the house may also be exaggerated, but there is more in them than those ignorant of the species may realize. E. L. Thorndike, the psychologist, has been scornful of this type of cat story. Thousands of cats, he says, have gone to the door, found it shut, and turned away frustrated, without getting any publicity; but let one single cat reach up and paw the door knob, and immediately he figures in all the books on animal intelligence. Maybe so; but most cats understand how a door is opened even if they cannot do it themselves. A good many cats are either naturally imitative, or else clever enough to try what they have seen human beings attempt with success. I know a cat who dials the telephone, but that is probably mere imitation; her family does not pretend that she has ever lifted the receiver off the hook or actually succeeded in getting a number.

But sometimes it looks like imitation in the hope of success. My cat has never tried to turn a door knob; he can pull a screen door open from outside, with his claws, but when he comes to a wooden door that is closed he simply sits down and scratches at the crack. (He never scratches at the wrong crack, the one where the hinges are.) Experience has taught him that sometimes the door is off the latch, in which case he can pull it open—and also that if he says he wants to get out, and any of the human members of the family are present, the door is likely to be opened for him. He likes to drink water out of the bathtub; if somebody runs a little for him he drinks as much as he wants and then pulls out the plug. That may be the accidental result of a mere impulse to play with a shiny chain; but it seems plausible that he has seen other people pull the plug when they are through with the water in the bathtub, and knows what will happen if he pulls it.

This is no proof of any great mechanical skill in even this one particular cat, to say nothing of the entire species; it is merely evidence of more general intelligence than enemies of the cats are willing to admit. Some of them indeed admit almost nothing—not even those reflective qualities for which the cat is most esteemed by connoisseurs.

IV

The most vigorous attempt to debunk the cat which has come to my attention—its unfavorable conclusions all buttressed by laboratory experiment—is a book published in 1928 by Georgina Gates, then assistant professor at Barnard College, entitled *The Modern Cat: a Study in Comparative Psychology*. Perhaps none of the science of that romantic year need be taken too seriously; much of the physics of 1928 seems to be only antique heresy now, while as for the economics of 1928—! However, let the cat answer the indictment, which is comprehensive enough. The cat has few ideas; she "sees no colors, distinguishes no pitches"; objects are ill-defined to her, she "lives in a blur," with no memories and no anticipations. "She is no philosopher," says Dr. Gates, "no mechanician, no student or critic of human affairs; merely a distant relative, poverty-stricken with respect to the most valuable of all possessions, but cherished for her air of aloofness and that aura of mystery which surrounds her." In short, a poor relation of our noble species.

Now with all respect to the scientific approach, this seems to me to betray very little knowledge of cats outside the laboratory; and it anthropomorphizes the cat more thoroughly than do even the youngest children. It implies that what is useful or pleasant to us must be useful or pleasant to cats too, and that they are deficient in so far as they lack it. The cat is condemned for not being a successful human being. How many human beings could be successful cats?

Certain experiments are cited as proof that the cat is tone-deaf and color-blind. Color-blindness is a considerable misfortune to men and women but much less serious for the cat, who does not have to watch traffic lights; who has other senses to help him distinguish objects and other pleasures to replace those which color gives us. The charge of tone-deafness rests on the researches of an earnest investigator who found that cats could not distinguish (or at least did not find it worth while to show that they distinguished) between different notes on the piano. So what? Why should a cat be interested in the notes of the piano? When he wants music he makes his own.

Anybody who knows cats outside the laboratory knows that their hearing is far superior to ours. Even if they cannot distinguish between the notes of the piano (I remain unconvinced of that), they can detect and identify countless sounds too faint for the human ear, or too obscure for the human understanding. The widespread belief that cats are "psychic" is partly a residue of old superstition, but partly it rests on the observed fact that cats are sensitive to certain impressions which human senses miss. Probably their better hearing is responsible for most of this, their sensitiveness to electricity for the rest of it—a sense which most human beings wholly lack. In the sense of smell the cat's superiority is still greater. It tells him much that we learn by sight, much that we get by conversation or reading, and probably some things we never get at all. Those who despise the cat for his alleged insensitiveness to notes of the piano might ask themselves what he would say of a species so dull, so crude, so poverty-stricken that its language actually has no word for the nasal equivalent of color-blindness;* which is as insensitive to the innumerable delicate distinctions of scent that the cat perceives as he may (or may not) be to the different tones of musical instruments.

"The cat lives in a blur," does he? Well, he does not act in a blur; when he has something to do, somewhere to go, he goes and does it with speed and precision. At a distance, in broad daylight, his vision is probably less precise than ours; but he identifies such objects, and at such distances, as his needs require, by the co-ordination of other senses. And at night—! Stumble over a cat in the dark and he will be surprised, though unless you step on a foot or a tail he will be too courteous to express indignation. Turn on the light, and you can read in his eyes as much pity and disdain for a poor creature who

---

* Rodman Gilder suggests that this blank in our vocabulary be filled by the euphonious monosyllable "snoof."

cannot see in the dark as scientists feel for a poor creature who does not know (or care about) the difference between G sharp and B flat. Dr. Gates remarks that if you put a cat in front of a mirror he will not recognize his own reflection, probably will not realize that this is the image of a cat. Which is true. But if there is another cat, a strange cat, nearby the chances are that he will know it before you do; certainly he will if the other cat is around a corner, or if it is dark.

Most of this depreciation of the cat is sheer anthropomorphizing. We have enormously developed one sense at the expense of all the rest; by far the greater part of the material used by the human mind is collected, in one way or another, by the eye. Unfavorable judgments on the cat's perceptive powers by members of a species whose other senses are far weaker (in the case of smell, almost atrophied) are as uninformed, as uncomprehending, in short as worthless, as the ideas of a celibate on matrimony.

Nobody who knows cats believes that they have no memories or anticipations; they remember and anticipate much that we do not care about and are indifferent to much that interests us; but why not? It is their business to be cats, ours to be human. But what about the most valuable of all possessions, in which the cat is said to be so poverty-stricken? This is reasoning power; the cat's deficiency in which is proved, to Dr. Gates's satisfaction, by one of Thorndike's experiments. He took twelve alley cats, put them before a complicated set of boxes to find a devious way to food, and timed them. Only one found the way easily; as a group they were faster than raccoons, but slower than monkeys or Columbia students.

One must respect the findings of a properly conducted experiment, but need not accept all the conclusions drawn from it. Any educated alley cat (and those who learn slowly die young) knows that food comes in garbage cans, not in trick boxes. Confronted with a novel situation, food in an unfamiliar container, the cats were slow to adapt themselves to their environment. But it does not appear that Thorndike was so inhumane as to push them to the verge of starvation; if he had, probably every one of those cats would have got the food before it starved, which after all is the passing grade for an alley cat. Finding one's way out of mechanical complications is, it must be remembered, more of a human than a feline necessity; and more of a human (or, as the experiment suggests, a simian) aptitude.

But the unfavorable conclusions were based chiefly on the way the cats went at it; they pawed round apparently at random, sometimes trying the wrong way over and over. "Man learns, the cat scrambles," Dr. Gates concludes; but she admits that a Columbia professor who did

not know how to swim, if he fell into so unfamiliar an environment
as deep water, would flounder as awkwardly as Thorndike's cats. "The
cat uses man's second-best procedure, hit-or-miss struggling," instead
of coolly, patiently reasoning his way out. How many men do any
better? Pick up the first twelve human beings you meet, put them into
a human situation of equivalent novelty and complexity, and most of
them would scramble too.

In justice to Dr. Gates, it must be remembered that this was written
in 1928, when the human race seemed to have some grounds for complacency; she could hardly foresee that another decade would teach us
that we are not much better off than Thorndike's cats. There is plenty
of food in the world, plenty of everything we need; but mankind has
got itself into a complicated set of boxes—psychological and emotional—and does not seem able to find the way through. Some men are
patiently trying to think it out; but most of what is going on looks like
hit-or-miss floundering, and often a stubborn persistence in what is
obviously the wrong way.

I will give the psychologists another illustration of the cat's defects
as a reasoner, demanding no payment except the privilege of asking,
"So what?" The cats in the New York Aquarium, employed to keep
out rats, have been taught not to eat the fish. On arrival they are
given electric eels to play with, and after they have had a few shocks
they conclude that anything in the Aquarium tanks (or more probably
anything with the Aquarium smell) is electrified too. Or, as Mark
Twain once summarized it, a cat who has once sat on a hot stove will
never thereafter sit on a cold stove.

And the human race? Most of the shoestring speculators of 1929
had resolved by 1932 that they would never fool with the stock market
again. Yet a good deal of money has been made in the stock market
since 1932. We all despise the people who don't know what we know.
My cat has been trained not to catch birds; but each summer when
he arrives at his country home he meets a new generation of birds who
do not know that he will let them alone. As he lies peacefully under
a bush and listens to their frightened shriekings he wears an expression
of utter contempt—such contempt as a psychologist might feel for a cat
who was slow to find his way through a set of trick boxes.

v

The fact is that ailourology, like anthropology, is a social science;
and we have all learned by now that the exact technique of the physical sciences has only a limited application in such fields. Dr. Gates
indeed appears to suspect this; after her long debunking of the cat she

qualifies by quoting Virginia Roderick's conclusion that "there is no answer to most questions about the cat; she has kept herself wrapped in mystery for some three thousand years, and there's no use trying to solve her now." At any rate the insight of the artist will come much nearer a solution than the meticulous experiments of the laboratory scientist. Anyone who knows cats will acknowledge that the one best thing ever written about them, the concentrated quintessence of so much ailourology as we know, is Kipling's *The Cat Who Walked by Himself*. What that cat thought, what any cat thinks as he walks in the wet wild woods by his wild lone, waving his wild tail, no one can surely say. Not just what we should be thinking, certainly—but perhaps something not altogether alien to our ideas and feelings.

That cats experience the simpler emotions—desire, anger, fear, contentment—no one would deny; but they can have more complex emotions too, both good and bad. My cat, given three seconds to get ready, can run any dog out of the yard; but once a dog tearing in at high speed came on him unexpectedly from behind a bush, and General Gray behaved as other veteran troops have behaved in a similar situation. He ran; and being a cat, he ran up a tree. There he halted and collected himself and looked down at that dog; and you could see the shame in his face, the sense of an imperative obligation to retrieve his self-respect. A moment later he came down the tree and chased the dog out of the yard, as usual.

Charles Willis Thompson once lived with a Persian cat named Thomas Jefferson Topaz, and owned a bulldog named William Howard Woof. The two were great friends and one night they were asleep together in the living room—the bulldog on the rug, the cat precariously extended on the arm of a chair. Too precariously; eventually he fell off, and was painfully awakened when he hit the floor. His reaction, in this humiliating situation, was entirely human; self-respect forbade him to admit that his misfortune was his own fault. He lashed around for somebody else to blame it on, and walked over and slapped the slumbering and innocent dog.

Not only the cat's intellectual but his emotional range is a good deal wider than can be measured by laboratory methods. This does not prove that he is a philosopher, but still less can the scientists prove that he is not. He looks philosophic, he behaves philosophically in his own affairs; he can act with speed and power when he needs to but he avoids all waste exertion, all effort that has no purpose *to a cat;* when there is time he weighs his decisions—no cat ever went through a door held open for him without measured pondering of the arguments for and against the step; he does what he wants to in so far as he can, and except in peril of his life wastes no energy on the impossible. What he thinks of human doings no one knows; but we can occasionally make plausible guesses. One of the most engaging tail wavers in literature is Viktor Scheffel's black tom cat Hiddigeigei. Only a character of fiction, to be sure; you may say it is Scheffel, not Hiddigeigei, speaking when he concludes some derogatory observations on human behavior:

> *Menschentun ist bloss Verkehrtes,*
> *Menschentun ist Ach und Krach.*
> *Im Bewusstsein seines Wertes*
> *Sitzt der Kater auf dem Dach.*

But so I have seen a Persian cat on the roof watch the guests stumble out from a cocktail party across the road; if his verdict was not the same as Hiddigeigei's, then you can read nothing in a face.

Those who know cats best, at any rate, feel that they have a sort of wisdom denied to us; even if we may also have a sort denied to them—of which, God knows, we show little trace at present. Why let yourself be kept by a cat? Because there is little human companionship so satisfying as that of a friend of superhuman dignity and poise, who looks wise, behaves wisely in his own affairs, and regards your tribulations with an affectionate—and silent—sympathy.

The late Clarence Day once speculated on what the world would be like if the species that became dominant had been super-cats instead of super-monkeys. Life would be, he concluded, much more brilliant and beautiful and exciting. How did it happen that this noble species fell behind a tribe of feeble chatterers who in the Tertiary jungles could have been no more than an inconsiderable nuisance? The cats were too philosophic, he concluded, and too individualistic; the simians progressed by their insatiable curiosity and their capacity for co-operation. But this was written some twenty or twenty-five years ago; super-simian co-operation is not conspicuous at present, and simian curiosity has led to the finding out of many inventions, such as submarines and bombing planes. Cats fight, but for reasons that usually make more sense than ours; and they stop fighting when they have settled the point immediately at issue; they have not risen to the concept of totalitarian war. They may yet get a chance to see what they can make of the world; unless, as Harlow Shapley once suggested, we simians leave our planet in such condition that it will be a fit inheritance for no species but the cockroach.

PUREST OF PLEASURES

[*This was written for* Harper's *in 1932 when contract was the rage. The information and the philosophy about bridge were then a novelty; now the game is an accepted feature of the social scene and may stir less curiosity. Still, one reader wrote to say that this piece almost made him want to play a game he had always detested, and the time it was written may lend this article added interest. But perhaps those who don't like bridge, unless they feel adventurous, should pass on to the next item.*]

It seems to be widely felt that in times like these it is ignoble to seek pleasure, or even relaxation; the conscientious citizen of the world ought to be busy every moment trying to help correct the sad state of affairs in general, and has no right to slink back to self-indulgence in his ivory tower. Nobody who has friends in Europe can very seriously dispute that, as a general proposition; when he thinks of the misfortunes that have befallen better men, which he himself has escaped by a mere accident of geography, he cannot help feeling that he ought to be trying to do something about it—even if it appears that there is nothing in particular that he can do at the moment except to contribute to relief funds. Nevertheless, any expert on industrial fatigue will tell you that you will probably do a better job, whatever your job may be, if now and then you stop thinking about it for a little while; and it would seem an excess of Puritanism to abjure this needed diversion just because you might incidentally find some pleasure in it.

The following remarks are an advertisement for the people who find it at what is inaccurately termed the bridge table. (Contract dummy whist is not "contract bridge" any more than a man is the descendant of his great-uncle; but it seems useless to combat an error so long established.) Like miniature golf and mah jongg in their several days, contract is a big business as well as a sport; and a person engaged in the literature industry must feel a certain shame when he reflects that about the only branch of that industry which in the depth of the hard times enjoyed any prosperity is the literature of bridge. One bridge book sold two hundred thousand copies in eighteen months, and I suspect that among its half dozen closest competitors would be two or three other bridge books. "Who gets the girl?" used to be the ever-dependable theme of salable writing; but in contemporary fiction almost anybody can get the girl, so perhaps it is not surprising that this once popular question has been supplanted by "Who gets the bid, and what does he do with it?"

All of this has been a godsend to the bookstores, and of course to the bridge experts as well. Their books sell when other books die unwanted on the counters; they syndicate daily bits of wisdom to newspaper readers all over the country; they teach bridge, and in a thousand towns over the country "pupil of Culbertson" gives the degree of prestige that "pupil of Leschetizky" did in days gone by.

But while, no doubt, the experts all like bridge, and would play it for fun even if they never made any money out of it, it must bring them harassment as well as pleasure; like any other big business men, they have their hours of worry about trade conditions, and when things are going well they wonder how long this will last. I am an average player (at least I hope so; some of my partners might challenge that claim), and what is here said applies to average players—not to the experts or to the enthusiastic incompetents who are as much of an obstruction to the game as is a hay wagon to boulevard traffic. In our own estimation, we average players are the salt of the earth; for we play the game well enough to have some understanding of it and some pride in it, and still not so well that our love of the pastime can ever be contaminated by any sordid hope of gain.

And there are a lot of us; if contract is not the national game, it is second only to golf.

[· · ·]

Also, golf seems to attract persons of a perverse and gloomy nature; some of my friends go out to play it in the same spirit of self-abasement that drove their medieval ancestors to lash themselves with knotted whips. But a man who wants to discourage himself nowadays can do it at far less expense by reading the morning paper.

None of these objections applies to contract. It requires no costly equipment; you do not have to go out in the country to play it; you are playing against other people, not against some theoretical standard of perfection, so if you stay in your own class you will suffer no more than an occasional moderate and salutary humiliation. This, I am convinced, is the first and great commandment for those who want to enjoy contract—stay in your own class. It will spare you mental anguish and it will save you money.

To say that you cannot enjoy a bridge game unless there is money on it is about as reasonable as saying that you cannot get interested in a woman unless she has a husband who might shoot you. If you really want the woman you will need no such irrelevant and supererogatory stimulation; and if you really like the game you will play it as well as you can, whether there is any money up or not. Contract without a stake can be just as good as if you were paying for a dollar a point. However, there are people who feel otherwise—so many of them that if you refuse to play for money you will be considerably restricted in your opportunities to play at all. But stay in your own class and you will find that—since the law of averages can be counted on to give you a fairly even break in the cards from one year's end to another—your game will just about pay its way.

Contract has further attractions for the reflective. Plato held that smell was the purest of the sensual pleasures because it involved no appeasement of pre-existent pain. The joys of the table derive some of their keenness from the preceding pangs of hunger; but no man ever feels himself starving for agreeable odors. "The pleasures of smell spring up suddenly and present themselves in full force to a man who was not previously conscious of any suffering; and when they have vanished they leave no pain behind." Accordingly they are a hundred per cent net profit, and so are the pleasures of contract. The bridge player does not say, "When shall I awake? I will seek it yet again." He may be keenly aware of his lack of love or lack of money, but he does not grow jittery because there is no card game going on. He gives himself over to other preoccupations; and when somebody whispers to him, "Will you make a fourth?" the pleasures of the card table spring up suddenly and present themselves in full force to a man who was not previously conscious of any suffering.

Another merit of the game: as Lord Melbourne might have said, there is no damned nonsense of utility about it. You cannot pretend that it is a form of Service; golfers who are too puritanical to admit that they play golf because they like it will discourse at length upon its hygienic, cultural, and social benefits; but dealing the cards is no great exercise, and the bridge table is no place to meet your customers and talk business while you play. (Unless, of course, you enjoy conversational bridge; in which case you had better stop reading this article, and may consider yourself conspued by its author). There is no good excuse for playing contract except the pleasure you get out of it.

Some attempt has been made to give the game an intellectual snob value; Mr. Culbertson's *Bridge World,* for instance, bursts into the following rhapsody: "If bridge makes strange bedfellows, it is because the pleasures of the intellect are considered superior. Our common meeting ground is the play of intellect in its purest symbolic form." But this is hooey, and a man so shrewd as Culbertson must know it. To him and experts of his class the game does indeed present recondite mathematical-metaphysical beauties for the contemplation of the pure intellect; but these are as far beyond the grasp of the average player as are the high joys of Jeans or Einstein. To play good bridge calls for intellect, but a specialized type of intellect adapted to playing bridge; it is no more a sign of the general brain power flatteringly imputed by the above quotation than is skill at chess. Napoleon was a notably bad chess player; which is a reflection on chess, not a reflection on Napoleon. If bridge brains were good for anything but bridge, you might expect this nation to be ruled by its tournament stars; but except for Mr. Vanderbilt, who sails yachts, I cannot recall that any of them has been conspicuously successful at anything but bridge.

Another expert, Mr. Shepard Barclay, is less flattering to his public but more encouraging: "Bridge is not half so hard to learn as some people fear." Maybe not, but it is a good deal harder to learn than some other people realize. The experts, no doubt, would like to have it both ways: to play well is a proof of intellectual power, yet anybody who buys the right book and applies himself to the right system can learn to play well—a new mode of purveying exclusiveness to the masses. It is true that you cannot play good bridge without a bridge education any more than you can practice good law without a legal education; but mere reading of books and attendance at lectures can no more make a first-rate bridge player than it can make an Untermyer or a Darrow. I believe that anybody of moderate intelligence can by diligent application become a sound bidder; but unless some card sense is born in you, you will never be a really good player, even after twenty-five years of practice. *Crede experto.*

II

The mere existence of contract, and of its predecessors bridge and auction, is proof of this. They are all variants of whist, and they successively supplanted it in favor because they are easier than whist. Any good whist player will be a good contract player when he has mastered the elements of bidding; but millions of people who pass as good contract players because they bid their hands well and play them well (after the bidding has located most of the key cards) would be quite beyond their depth at whist, where the trump depends on chance and the location of the cards has to be inferred from the play.

Whist was so popular in the eighteenth century that (as the learned R. F. Foster records) at Florence whist tables were put in the opera-house boxes, and the music was valued chiefly as "increasing the joy of good fortune, and soothing the affliction of bad." But a game that makes such rigorous demands on the intelligence—or on the card sense, if you prefer—was soon undergoing modifications to make it easier for the average player; at least one of these, Boston, seems to have sprung up no more than twenty-five years after whist had become standardized. In Boston the essential principle of auction was already present; it is a little hard to understand why bridge, with its regression to a very elementary form of bidding, should have intervened. If bridge is really of Russian origin (I believe the Greeks also have a claim on it), its vogue is still less explicable; the game of vint, mentioned in Russian novels long before bridge was played in the West, is considerably more advanced; essentially it is auction without a dummy, and its scoring is in some respects an anticipation of contract.

However, bridge swept the world around the turn of the century, while vint never got outside of Russia; and millions of persons who had been dubbing along at whist found the new game easier and consequently more attractive. It gave an opportunity to cash in on your good hands (when you were the dealer) and escape without loss on your bad hands by bidding the low spade which in those days was never played. Your opponents could do the same, of course; there was more purpose in it than in whist, less chance and less demand on the intelligence. The addition of the "royal spade" bid rid the game of its one obvious weakness—and then, all at once, it was supplanted by auction.

Mr. Foster, that inexhaustible fount of card history, says that auction was invented about 1903 by three members of the Indian civil service at a lonely hill station (readers of Kipling will infer that their fourth had been carried off by cholera) who thought of it only as a three-handed game. But the auction principle had long been familiar in Boston and Five Hundred; maybe one of the three recalled these pastimes, or maybe they learned vint from a Russian spy who had come down over the Pamirs. At any rate, when their three-handed game was played by four hands it was so much of an improvement over bridge that it needed only to be heard of to be adopted everywhere. And then, a few years later, came contract; which is to auction as Clos de Vougeot to home-made wine.

As a purely intellectual exercise the play in contract is far inferior to that in whist; you know too much before the first card is led. But the bidding imports an intellectual exercise of quite another order which is almost as good a discipline in applied psychology as poker. If contract has surpassed the vogue of auction, bringing new recruits to the card table and rekindling the enthusiasm of some of us who had begun to find auction something of a bore, it is because it is a better game, with far more action and far more suspense. In auction a good hand is irresistible; in contract it may be only an enticement to disaster unless you bid it right. No doubt the mere change in scoring has impressed some people with the conviction that contract is more of a game. Writing before the present contract scoring had altogether supplanted the auction values, Foster observed that the stake per point was reduced as the score was increased; "why it would not be just as simple to advance the stakes and keep to the already well-established values is not explained." Here speaks the austere aristocrat; the more practical Barclay provides the explanation. "The higher score appeals to the childish attribute that remains with all adults who are wise enough to avoid growing up completely." However wise such avoidance may be, plenty of adults have managed it with great success; they feel that they are in fast company when they play a game at which you can go down a couple of thousand points on a single hand.

Perhaps contract has certain other advantages peculiarly adapted to these times. Its values, and its interest, are detached, abstracted from reality, from all the heterogeneous and too often unpleasant phenomena of everyday living. I know of no mental exercise which gives so complete an escape from the things you want to escape from. Yet some of its principles have a timely application; in auction you might bid a little and win a great deal, as you could in the empire-building America of the nineteenth century; but in contract you must bid and work for everything you get and risk a disastrous penalty for miscalculation, as entrepreneurs are likely to do in the frontierless and more static America of the future. Vulnerability—the principle that the higher you have risen the more a mistake will cost you—is a concept easily grasped by the American public, which has so often seen the career of a distinguished man ruined by a private peccadillo which would be overlooked in a person of less prominence. (It could be wished that more of our distinguished men might be ruined by their public peccadillos, by their behavior in office.) And finally in an age of confusion and multiplicity, of an all too visible increase in what the physicists call the random element in the universe, there is a nostalgic charm about a game in which for a little while you devote yourself to a fixed and precise objective.

But all this may be fanciful. The great indubitable reason for the popularity of contract is its merit; more than any other card game it approaches the ideal balance between chance and skill. And the secondary and corollary reason is that more talent has been devoted to exploiting it professionally than was ever before expended on any card game. In which connection it is impossible to withhold the blue ribbon from Mr. Ely Culbertson.

III

Rival experts may have had good reasons for disliking Culbertson, but they are all in debt to him, as every manager of a fight club anywhere is in debt to the late Tex Rickard; Culbertson's genius for ballyhoo did more than anything else to make contract a major sport and a big business. In the Culbertson odyssey fact and legend may be intertwined, but the story that he once taught psychology seems plausible enough; for he has practiced it with a brilliance hardly surpassed by Calvin Coolidge or E. L. Bernays. This talent would have made him successful in almost any line of business; that the accident of his marrying a bridge teacher made him apply his gifts to bridge was undoubtedly a piece of luck for the industry.

His competitors might not agree with that; but Culbertson's unpopularity in the trade is part of his showmanship. A man who frankly admits that he is the greatest egotist on earth and then goes on flaunting his ego in the face of his rivals and the public knows exactly what he is doing and why. Jack Dempsey, good-humored and likable in private, built up a public personality that roused the hatred of the crowd, and it made him a rich man; people who know only his fighting face and his professional manner cheerfully paid fifty dollars in the tenuous hope of seeing him flattened out by a Frenchman or an Argentino. Culbertson modest and self-effacing would be only one of the crowd; Culbertson challenging and blatant infuriates his rivals; they trumpet their demand that Culbertson be abolished—and the public sees that it is the pack against Culbertson and concludes that this one man is the equal of them all.

And if there are plain citizens—not competing experts—whom Culbertson infuriates, why, that is more meat for Culbertson; he gets their money too. The latest list of his publications includes five of his own books, one by his wife, and three by other writers explaining the Culbertson system for players good, bad, or indifferent; along with two other books which seem, from the advertiser's description, to be derisive spoofs on Culbertson and all his works. Whether you like him or hate him, he will sell you a book to suit your taste. Such a combination of high impartiality and a nose for profit can hardly be found elsewhere; it is as if the works of Karl Marx were published, in the hope of gain, by the Republican National Committee.

Other bridge writers, plain blunt men, say what they have to say in plain blunt words; but Culbertson goes into flights of metaphor—the submerged reefs of distribution, the protection of the trump fortress, war tactics in open and mountainous country, etc. This may be quite genuine, the way the game appears to Culbertson's restless mind; at any rate it is good business. Read the other experts and you read about a game of cards; read Culbertson and you feel that you are involved in an enterprise of major importance. Even the famous and ridiculous one-hundred-and-fifty-rubber duel with Lenz was good publicity. "Let them hate me," said Domitian, "so long as they fear me"—which any modern publicity expert would amend to "Let them laugh at me so long as they talk about me." The astounding blunders in play which distinguished the first night of that contest may have been due to the well-advertised plethora of champagne; but bad play continued on later and presumably drier evenings, and I suspect that some of it was deliberate—a studied encouragement of the ordinary dub player, who will feel better when he sees those great geniuses Lenz and Culbertson gumming up good hands, even as you and I.

Praise of Culbertson's unique gift for publicity implies no lack of respect for the solider if less showy merits of his rivals. For some of their systems I have little use; but I surmise that if the leaders of politics and industry had bestowed on their trade, in the past twenty years, the amount of serious study and tolerably disinterested thinking that has been invested in bridge by the leaders of the bridge business, this country might be somewhat better off.

IV

But room must be made for the objections of the *advocatus diaboli.* Some of the people who do not like bridge dislike it with a quite inexplicable frenzy. They will tell you that it saps the brain power, if any, of the individual, and disrupts the household by its contentions; it sows discord between wife and husband, between friend and friend; it is nothing less than the terminator of delights and the separator of companions.

Well, most of the complaints about bridge boil down to this, that it is sometimes played by the wrong people. Too much liquor brings out your true nature, whatever that may be; and so does a bad bid, a disastrous takeout, a stupid play by your partner. People who crack under such a strain would crack under whatever strain might be imposed upon them, and I do not see that bridge can be blamed for it. The persons who feel it necessary to conclude each hand with a magisterial correction of their partners (and perhaps their opponents as well) have no place at the bridge table, or anywhere else where they might come into contact with civilized beings; and I do not know that they are more frequently found or more offensively conspicuous at the card table than in some other departments of life.

"Never reproach your partner," says Culbertson, "if there be the slightest thing for which you can reproach yourself." (On the other hand, do not reproach yourself if you think it would give undue encouragement to your partner's baser instincts.) This is not only Christian charity but good sense; the *practical* attitude toward your partner, Culbertson pursues, should be that of a "philosophical, sincere, and sympathetic friend." You share each other's joys, each other's burdens bear; and often for each other flows the sympathizing tear. "Partner, however weak, must feel that you sincerely respect his intelligence and efforts." And if this is odious pretense, if he is so weak that nobody could sincerely respect him—why, that is your fault for not choosing your company. First and foremost, stay in your own class.

You can't always do that when you go out for a social evening and find yourself in an unforeseen bridge game? No; but there is no law requiring a man who can play bridge to play it whenever he is invited. If you play with people you never met before you cannot complain when your partner continually talks over her shoulder to people across the room about her latest round-the-world cruise, meanwhile missing a couple of finesses and overlooking a discard or two. Of course, if you tell the hostess you don't play, and some other guest pipes up with "But you do; I've played with you!"—why, then you are trapped, and may as well resign yourself to whatever fortune fate sends you. But that is no peculiar fault of bridge; it may happen just as well to a man who pretends he doesn't dance because he is alarmed by the weight of his prospective partners. Social life can be made tolerable only by taking a firm stand on such matters; and if indignant hostesses resolve that they will never invite you again, you can always stay at home and read a book.

As for domestic discord, bridge never broke up a home that was not ripe for disruption anyway. If your wife is a very much better player than you, or a very much worse player, you had better not play with her; but you had better not play with anybody else who is very much better or very much worse. In the famous case of the Kansas City

woman who shot her husband for failing to make his contract of four
spades, the news reports omitted the essential points—what cards deceased had held and how he played them. But I suspect that if cards
had never been invented she would have shot him over something else.
Playing against a married couple I knew but slightly, I was shocked by
their recriminations; and when I was dummy I suggested to the proprietor of the restaurant where we were playing, that maybe the game
had better be broken off before shots were fired. "Oh, that don't mean
nothing with them two," he assured me. "They love each other like
you don't see it any more." Evidently their emotional margin was so
wide that they could do without philosophical and sympathetic friendship.

As to the vexed question of bisexual bridge in general, I think that
men who say they don't like to play with women are putting the argument on a wrong basis. The point is that you get full value out of a
bridge game only when it is a bridge game and nothing else; to play
it well requires concentration, and if you are not going to try to play
it well there is no point in playing at all.

It is probably true that women, more often than men, regard a game
of bridge as only an excuse for conversation—including some women
who can play an excellent game when they choose to concentrate on it.
But once again, pick your company and you will have no complaint;
there are plenty of women who at the bridge table are willing to con-
fine themselves to playing bridge, and would rather indulge in conversation over a few drinks. Call it the inveterate prejudice of a pre-
war feminist, if you like, but I have little patience with the men who
complain that "women" do this and that. Even Foster falls into this;
"women," he says, "are great offenders in trifling matters, such as asking the dealer if she passed it, when nothing has been said; looking
over the adversaries' hands as dummy, and then pushing dummy's
cards forward as if arranging them, but in reality indicating which one
to play. . . . There may be some remedy for this sort of thing, but so
far no one seems to have found it."

Well, there is one unfailing remedy—do not play with women like
that. You can find plenty of others—women who are good players and
good sportsmen too.

v

There remain to be answered the weighty criticisms of a couple of
psychologists, who burst into print during the Lenz-Culbertson duel.
"Bridge may develop brains," said Professor Charles Gray Shaw of New

York University, "but the quality of the brains developed is not worth cultivating." Still harsher was Professor Harold Swenson of the University of Chicago: "You couldn't drag a real thinker to the bridge table with a team of horses."

If this means anything except that a couple of professors were picking up crumbs of publicity from the mighty banquet of Culbertson, it means that Professor Swenson's definition of a real thinker is a man who couldn't be dragged to the bridge table by a team of horses. By any other definition he is demonstrably wrong. As for Professor Shaw, he is right this far—that the brains specifically developed by bridge are good for nothing much but bridge; but not so much can be said for his further statement that "the habitual bridge player lacks adequate emotional power and must play to stimulate his nerves."

[· · ·]

Bridge may be a needed stimulus to the nerves, but for us ordinary players its stimulation is intellectual, not emotional, even if the intellect it stimulates is of a specialized and unprofitable type. A philosopher, says Aldous Huxley, is a man who dreams of fewer things than there are in heaven and earth; and it is evident that Professor Shaw has never perceived the real attractions of bridge. Choose your company—people who play not much better than you do and not much worse, people who sit down at the bridge table to play bridge, not to talk about irrelevancies—and you will find yourself transported to another world. The agitations and exacerbations of everyday life drop away from you; for a while you dwell in a remote and austere realm of the pure intellect, uncontaminated by any practical applications; and as your game improves you may catch glimpses of some of those mathematical beauties of sequence, distribution, and arrangement such as perhaps the Absolute perceives when it contemplates Itself.

SHAW AND THE INNER LIGHT

[*This sketch treats some part of Shaw's influence as a prophet. Published in 1935, fifteen years before his death, it is not concerned with his literary genius but rather with his ideas and their reception.*]

An attempt, however diffident, at a retrospective estimate of Shaw cannot be undertaken without filial piety by a member of the generation which in all English-speaking countries was formed chiefly by Shaw and Wells; nor indeed without a more disquieting emotion. We of that generation, who are still uncomfortably surprised when young men address us as Sir, were the first fruits of them that slept, the first graduating class of the School of the Prophets. . . . And as the world of today is on the whole a worse place, and perceptibly nearer the abyss, than the world of 1894, it might seem a logical conclusion that something was fatally wrong, either with us or with our teachers.

It was not so in 1913, and for what has happened since 1913 we sons of the prophets are not greatly responsible. We did not make the war, nor are we the people who will make the next one; Shaw has been popular in Germany, but not with the military caste; and the people whom he influenced in Japan do not govern Japan. In England the Shaw-Wells influence was strongest and the generation that came to maturity about 1913 was most promising; but half the men of that generation are dead, and the rest live only under reprieve. England could be governed, indeed wholly populated, by Shavians, and still be in danger of destruction in a Continental war begun by men to whom Shaw, if they had heard of him at all, was only a misunderstood prophet of the Superman. Granted that the seed sown by the prophets sometimes produced a surprising crop, it was in the main good seed; the trouble was that too often it fell on stony ground. There are not yet enough of the children of light to dominate the policy of any great power, let alone of the world, but that is no fault of the prophets.

[*After this excursus Davis turned to a discussion of the things Shaw (and to some extent Wells) believed, how they preached them, and something of the results as seen so far.*]

Once Shaw thought that abolition of property would be a cure-all; but more fundamental even than Communism in his creed is insistence on the freedom of the spirit. Russia of today may be more to his taste than England of the nineties, but one need not ask what would happen to a contemporary Russian who wrote about the society he lives in as Shaw writes about the society he lives in.

Wells once saw in Lenin's Communist Party the nearest approach to the "competent receiver" for a bankrupt world—a disciplined company purged of all selfish appetites but the lust for power and the pride of omniscience. These are considerable exceptions.

[· · ·]

So in the Communists of 1934 Wells found a "trained obduracy to facts" that drove him to something as near despair as he can feel. Shaw came late to the quest for the competent receiver; in the preface to *Saint Joan* he dreamed of a Catholic Church catholic enough to include Protestants and heretics, a Church which would "inculcate and encourage free-thinking with a complete belief that thought, when really free, must by its own law take the path that leads to the Church's bosom." An engaging idea, but it involves a logical contradiction that was apparent to the Church a thousand years before Shaw was born; consequently there has never been such a Catholic Church, nor is it ever likely, even if you rename it the Communist Party. You cannot combine dogma and evolution.

If in these matters the prophets went astray, nobody else has found the road they missed; and if more people are looking for it now than were looking for it forty years ago, the credit is largely due to Shaw and Wells. For all the differences between them (the chief one is Shaw's distrust of science), the substance of their messages is identical. We must be about our Father's business, without letting ourselves be hampered by trivialities; that business is the establishment of the Kingdom of Heaven on earth; we must be born again before we can enter into the kingdom, but we shall know the truth and the truth shall make us free. Not a novel message; but that may only mean that certain truths are apparent to every mind which reaches a sufficient stature. Unfortunately when truth frees the sort of human beings we have at present, the result is not always what the prophets hoped. Socrates, it has been observed, set men free and the immediate results were Alcibiades and Critias; no wonder their fellow-citizens put their teacher to death. Give Shaw credit for realizing that the truth can be rightly used only by supermen, whom he would produce by education and eugenics.

[· · ·]

Shaw contributed as much as any one man to the economic and political liberation of women, again with unforeseen consequences. He never knew much about women except in their epicene aspects; in *Man and Superman* he mistook accidental and temporary fruits of nineteenth-century English culture for the essential nature of the Eternal Feminine. Whether there is any such eternal and essential nature, God only knows; but at any rate women have not used the vote to impose a tax on bachelors, and if Mrs. Warren's profession is no longer so flourishing, one reason is that there is so much amateur competition.

[· · ·]

These might seem considerable blemishes on a major prophet, but there is more than enough to offset them. If you believe at all in the long-term value of liberty, in the right to search for truth, you must honor a man who has done as much for it as anyone of our time. He broke up the arid crust of mental topsoil that hampered growth; if the humus beneath it was not as fertile as he had hoped, he can hardly be blamed. Get rid of the shams, the pretenses, the encrusted conventions that have outlived their utility, and get down to what is real; that was his message, and he shouted it with such fervor, such insistence, and ultimately such success that it does not greatly matter if he was wrong in a few details. Reality was not always as workable a material as he expected; but it is the material we have got to learn to work with, if we have any faith in human possibilities at all.

"I do not see moral chaos and anarchy as the alternative to romantic convention," he wrote in 1898; "and I am not going to pretend to merely to please the people who are convinced that the world is held together only by the force of unanimous, strenuous, eloquent, trumpet-tongued lying." His opponents, not being all the conscious liars that he seemed to think, replied in kind; and indeed there was some excuse for the reproach of intentional paradox against a man who attacked property and marriage from the economic bombproof built for him by a rich wife, and abused capitalism, imperialism, vaccination, and beefsteak with indiscriminate vehemence. But when he insisted that he was merely one of the rare people with "normal" vision he was nearer right than his antagonists. His assertion that there had been no noteworthy social and ethical progress since Caesar's day sounded absurd in the nineteenth century, but a third of the way through the twentieth we cannot very confidently dispute it. The economics, the sociology, the ethics of *Mrs. Warren's Profession* are as sound today as they were forty years ago; and a world that has seen war will no longer question his picture of it in *Arms and the Man*.

For all his distrust of science and his retrospective admiration, in later years, for medieval Catholicism, Shaw is a quintessential product of the Renaissance and the Reformation.

[· · ·]

One of his most insistently repeated arguments for collective control of property is that only thus can you liberate the spirit and give it a chance to get somewhere. After Shaw's attack on romance read Cabell's defense of it, and you will see that the difference is the difference between a basic optimism and a basic pessimism about human potentiality. For all his surface hedonism and his irreverent treatment of hagiology, Cabell's spirit is that of the medieval Catholic; Shaw's is that of the Protestant whom nothing can silence but the stake. It seems more plausible now than it did forty years ago that the medievalists may have been right; perhaps God (or Nature, or the Life Force, if you prefer) has set insuperable limitations, internal and external, on human accomplishment. Nevertheless some men and some women are so made that they will go on trying till they drop in their tracks, and no man has ever set forth their creed more powerfully than Shaw.

"I sing the philosophic man," says Don Juan in the scene in hell; "him who seeks in contemplation to discover the inner will of the world, in invention to discover the means of fulfilling that will, and in action to do that will by the so-discovered means." How does he discover that inner will? Why, by convincing himself that his own inner will is the world's will despite any evidence to the contrary; he understands the tendency of evolution better than his persecutors. The classic instance in Shaw's works, of course, is Joan of Arc. Mencken, I believe, has remarked that the hero of the Eroica Symphony is not Napoleon but Beethoven; so the protagonist of *Saint Joan* is Bernard Shaw disguised as a peasant girl of medieval Lorraine. He has matured now; he is no longer so defiantly proud of his singularity, so sure that the opposition is a mere pack of leather-lunged liars; but he is as inflexible as ever. But a finer type than Joan, and one more relevant to this age of uncertainty, is Lavinia of *Androcles and the Lion*—not quite sure, at the end, for what she is dying, but sure that there is something worth dying for, even if you can find no better name for it than spiritual integrity. These are the true glory of Shaw's plays, these stubbornly undissuadable followers of the Inner Light. Even in so relatively light a work as *Fanny's First Play* there is a difference in kind between Mrs. Knox and the rest of the conventional suburban parents. In their world the division is between the Respectable and the Disreputable, in her world it is between Right and Wrong; and she can recognize her daughter as one of her own kind, no matter how they may differ on the rightness of assaulting the police. For all Shaw's copious propaganda for collectivism, he is greatest and may be remembered longest as Mr. Valiant-for-Truth, the individualist Protestant prophet, and saint. Sometimes he falls short of saintliness? So did all the saints, sometimes; but it was forgiven them, in consideration of their loyalty to their Voices, their Daimonion, their personal revelation.

There remains Shaw the artist; but nothing that anybody can say about him can add to his stature. In a theater almost wholly given over, when he began, to physical or economic or emotional conflicts, he proved that the intellectual conflicts of characters of sufficient stature could be far more interesting than love-and-money problems, when handled by a dramatist of genius. Above all a comedian of genius; for tragedy deals with problems which are apt to become out of date, the peripeties of comedy have a more durable interest. Even the pilgrims of the inner light will be meaningless, if we fall back into a new medievalism. As Shaw himself wrote, "All the assertions get disproved sooner or later; and so we find the world full of a magnificent debris of artistic fossils, with the matter-of-fact credibility gone clean out of them, but the form still splendid." In comedy there is less assertion; but even comedy needs some intellectual content, and nobody else ever gave it so much as Shaw, unless perhaps Aristophanes.

Unfortunately Aristophanes devoted his genius to the upholding of a social and ideological system that was doomed to crack up no matter how hard he tried to save it; he would have had to be on the same side as Socrates to be as good as Shaw. Moreover, you can no longer understand much of what Aristophanes was talking about without a long classical training. Some of Shaw already begins to date; but not very much—at least in the perhaps ill-focused eyes of one who as he rereads these plays cannot forget the impression they made on him at the first encounter.

Take, for instance, *Fanny's First Play*, which Shaw dismisses as a mere potboiler. Its only serious content, an attack on Respectability and the Home, may be sounding brass and tinkling cymbal to the

young people of today, who cannot imagine a time when Respectability and the Home were important enough to be worth attacking. Yet
they might enjoy it almost as much as their parents did. When I was
young it seemed to me the funniest play I had ever seen; and it still
seems so, after a subsequent experience including such diversely cere-
bral comedies as *Once in a Lifetime* and *Desire under the Elms*. Beside such comedy as Shaw wrote until the war threw the comic aspects
of life into the background, all other comedy is as the crackling of
thorns under a pot.

THE IMPERFECT WAGNERITE

[*Shaw's* The Perfect Wagnerite *popularized, if it did not inaugurate, a type of literary commentary that is today no longer in vogue. At first blush it simply amounts to retelling the other fellow's story in terms of current and very likely vulgar everyday life. Just retelling the story brings to light a kind of "meaning" in the original work that may make sense to your readers. Far removed as this seems to be from the spirit of the "new criticism," I think it can be treated as a specially ambitious form of textual analysis. It develops ambiguities and hidden levels of meaning; the only difference between this and more academic efforts may stem from the over-all attack of the Shavian method.*

[*This article is an exercise in this Shavian type of discussion. If neither the musical nor the literary specialist is likely to value this sort of effort highly, more common readers have often enjoyed it. It may say something about Wagner, or it may say something about Davis, or it may say something about our times: but in any event it should make for enjoyable interrelations among all of these.*]

Now that the Metropolitan Opera Company has survived another crisis, some of us veteran opera-goers can sit back thankfully and reflect on what we should have missed if it had gone the way of other adornments of the fat years. I do not claim to speak for the "opera public"; the New York opera, at least, has several publics. But I am a specimen of perhaps the most truly devoted public of them all —the people who go to the opera house, buying seats when they can afford it and standing up when times are hard, for no social or racial or customary reason, but simply because we like opera. Of course we could hear opera even if the Metropolitan closed; there are minor-league companies that give you a pretty good show for a very moderate amount of money. If you prefer a passably good performance of a good opera to a first-rate performance of a dull opera (and if you do not, you are no true opera fan), those companies can slake your thirst for Italian and French opera, for *Tannhäuser* and even for *Lohengrin*. But in one respect the Metropolitan, to us middle-class citizens who go to the opera only because we like it, is irreplaceable—only there, regularly every season, can you hear *The Ring;* and as we grow older, *The Ring* seems more and more the one indispensable item of the operatic repertoire.

[· · ·]

When it no longer has anything to say to the spectator, that will be a sign that the present human race has turned into something else, better or worse. So long as there are men of our kind, men who can imagine and desire more than they can accomplish, you are lucky if you can come away from the full cycle of *The Ring* without saying to yourself, *"De te fabula narratur."*

But what the devil does it mean, then? says the embittered boxholder who has to appear regularly at the opera house for the sake of his social position, but has never been able to understand what anybody could see in this myth of gods and giants, dwarfs and heroes, with its interminable monologues and wearisome repetitions. Forget the myth, brother, and all the hoyotoho and wagalaweia; *"The Ring* is a drama of today, not of a remote and fabulous antiquity." So wrote, some forty years ago, a London music critic who had also written some plays which were beginning to get productions; his name was George Bernard Shaw. It is still a drama of today, and of every day until the impulse that began with the Renaissance either gets somewhere or finally gutters out. Shaw's interpretation (in *The Perfect Wagnerite*) treats *The Ring* not only as a brief in the case of The Spirit *vs.* The Letter, which it is as surely as are the epistles of St. Paul, but also as a parable of the revolution of 1848, in which Wagner was disastrously involved. Before the revolution, when he was conductor at the Dresden Opera House, he had projected a music drama called *The Death of Siegfried;* after he lost his job and had to escape to Switzerland to save his life he expanded this into a series of four music dramas which turned out to be less about Siegfried than about Wotan. Shaw equates Wotan with the well-intentioned ruler, temporal or spiritual, who must rule by law yet finds his own evolving best intention (personified in Brünnhilde) outgrowing the law. Fricka is the Spirit of the Constitution, Alberich the sort of early industrialist depicted in Marx's *Capital,* Fafner the coupon clipper, and so on. Wotan is unable to realize his good intentions; but the gods (like modern man) can imagine and try to create a nobler species than themselves, the Heroes. So the world is saved at last by Siegfried, the Uninhibited Natural Man who lives wholly by his unconscious, yet finds that in harmony with his best conscious desire.

Whether Shaw would still stand by that interpretation, written in 1898, I do not know. We have learned rather more than was then known about the Uninhibited Natural Man, and the drives of his unconscious no longer seem the surest foundation on which to build the perfect society. Even in 1898 there was one great stumbling block in the way of Shaw's exegesis—*Götterdämmerung*. (This time-honored title seems preferable to any English equivalent.) Siegfried did not triumph; enmeshed in the ancestral curse, he failed, and his death involved the end of the old gods who had created him and the clearing of the ground for a new order in which neither gods nor heroes would have any part—perhaps a dictatorship of the proletariat which had served the Gibichungs, or of some future Hagen who might seize power in their name. Bring the Shavian parable up to date, with Siegfried as Hitler, and it may be a preview of the history of the next few decades.

So far the parallel has been uncannily exact, except that the spectators can see no particular reason to prefer Siegfried to Hagen. In September 1939, when we heard the bands playing a march built around the Siegfried Motive as Hitler made his triumphal entry into Danzig, many of us remembered September 1938, when the sword that Siegfried had forged was brandished in the air, and Wotan's umbrella fell to pieces before the mere wind of its whirling. (The old gentleman has since got himself a new weapon, which may perhaps be more effective; but the treaties and pledges engraved on the shaft of the old one have flown into illegible splinters.) Possibly the parallel will persist to the end, now that an ex-champagne salesman has mixed the Hero a magic drink which made him forget his old loves (ideas, not women); but at this writing we are no farther along than the first act of *Götterdämmerung,* and maybe Dr. Goebbels has rewritten the plot. All we can be sure of is that Hitler makes a better Siegfried than Siegfried himself ever did; he knows what to do with the ring.

None of this could have been foreseen when *The Perfect Wagnerite* was written; but Shaw got around *Götterdämmerung* very ingeniously on historical grounds. Last of the operas in the cycle, it was written first; Wagner had sketched it, out of old mythological materials, before the unsuccessful revolution of 1848. After the revolution, discovering that it needed prefatory explanation, he wrote the other three operas of the cycle in reverse order, filling them with the ideas that were most on his mind at the time. It was years, however, before production of *The Ring* was possible; Wagner put off finishing the music, and when at last he got around to it in the early seventies he must have realized that *Götterdämmerung* did not fit into his great musical-dramatic parable of the revolution at all. Logically the drama ends when Siegfried shatters Wotan's spear, and goes on through the fire to awaken Brünnhilde.

By the early seventies times had changed; Bismarck had triumphed, the Paris Commune had failed; Wagner was dependent on a king's favor and pretty much disillusioned with revolutionaries. "Alberich had got the ring back and was marrying into the best Walhall families," and respectability had humanized him; he was more like Krupp or Carnegie than like the early manufacturers described by Marx and Engels. Wagner realized that between Siegmund who failed and Siegfried who triumphed several generations must intervene; and since it would have been an impossible task to rewrite his whole tetralogy, he let *Götterdämmerung* go as written, counting on the "enormously elaborate and gorgeous musical fabric" to make the listener forget the logical irrelevance.

II

For the nineties, this interpretation was plausible enough; but we know more now about the fruits of Wagner's doctrines, and about the seeds from which they sprang. Wagner's politics and "metapolitics" (as one of his correspondents called them) are subjected to a more searching, and startling, analysis than Shaw ever gave them by Peter Viereck, in *Common Sense* for November and December 1939. Mr. Viereck, who has read far more deeply in Wagner's political writings than I—or apparently than Shaw—says that Wagner was "the most important single fountain-head of Nazi ideology"; which trickled down through Houston Stewart Chamberlain, Alfred Rosenberg, and Dietrich Eckart to a man who could make it work.

The filiation, as Viereck cites it, is striking and convincing; and perhaps the motivation too. Wagner in Paris in the early forties, poor, unsuccessful and unknown, felt "homeless," as did Hitler later in Vienna; he longed (Viereck's phrasing) "to become an organic part of a greater unity"—no trivial part, we may be sure. Of the varieties of Nazi doctrine, the one closest to his views seems to have been the Nazism of Roehm and Gregor Strasser; in 1848 Wagner wanted "a political army of the masses"—just what Roehm wanted in 1934, an ambition that led to his liquidation; and even after 1871, says Peter Viereck, he was still the enemy of property. (Like Shaw he could afford to be, having by that time as much property as he needed.) It is curious that these views, once heresy, seem to be quite orthodox now; Germany has a mass army, far more politicalized than it was two years ago, and property has been pretty thoroughly subjected to the use of the state. But note that they did not become orthodox till the men who might once have climbed to the top with the aid of these doctrines had been put out of the way.

In other respects Wagner's ideas differed greatly from their modern development. He was, says Viereck, no imperialist or militarist; he wanted Germany to be supreme, but in art and thought; the "revolt of instinct against legalism and reason" which, in varying forms, is the basic theme of *The Ring* had in mind more admirable instincts than those that find vent in, for instance, the treatment of prisoners in Dachau. The "uncomposed passage" near the very end of the *Götter-dämmerung* libretto which, in Wagner's opinion, was a summary of the whole tetralogy set Love as the highest good; and it may not have occurred to Wagner that the whole argument for legalism is that when you take off the curbs on instinct you let loose not merely the praise-worthy instincts, but whatever instincts there are.

All of which suggests that *The Ring* is all things to all men. Shaw, out of doctrines potentially more explosive than Wagner himself perhaps ever realized, drew what was congenial to Shaw, and to the en-lightened drawing-room gradualism of the nineties which liked to believe, over the teacups, that it was revolutionary. But presently there came along an artist greater than Shaw—an unsuccessful artist as yet, because he had been working in the wrong medium—who, like Shaw, took from Wagner what he could appreciate; and by the power of his warped genius transmuted it into something very different, and far more formidable.

Wagner might have been thoroughly scandalized if he had seen what he helped to bring into being—at least the Wagner who wrote *The Rhine Gold* and *The Valkyrie,* the Wagner who was primarily inter-ested in Wotan. For Wotan had a conscience; like Bethmann-Hollweg, he was capable of recognizing and admitting that he had done wrong, even if he found it expedient to keep the profits. Wotan would have been ashamed of the Nazis; and so perhaps would his creator.

But Siegfried is something else; and so must have been the Wagner who was capable of creating Siegfried. To Siegfried such concepts as Right and Wrong had no meaning; his universe was divided into What I Want, and What I Don't Happen to Want, Yet. There were periods in Wagner's life when he seemed to have the same attitude, at least as regarded money and women; certainly the man who created Siegfried, perhaps without fully realizing what he was creating, had some appall-ing potentialities which were left for other men to realize.

Siegfried, says Viereck, is "the incarnation of the *Führerprinzip;* in his role as individual he is a mere atomistic mortal, as personification of the German *Volk* he shares its divinity." True, so far as it goes; but the Siegfried that Wagner created out of the much simpler figure of medieval legend is far more than that; he is the incarnation of the Nazi character as we have seen it displayed in action. And here is the mystery. How could even such an artist as Wagner prefigure, with such amazing accuracy, a type-character which was not to come into existence for nearly three quarters of a century?

Among the Germans he knew, conservatives or revolutionaries, there was nobody at all like Siegfried (except perhaps Richard Wagner, or one of the aspects of Richard Wagner that seldom came to the surface); yet in our day, before our eyes, Siegfried has come to life by the million. Was this prophetic intuition such as no other artist has ever displayed? Or—I am rationalist enough to be ashamed of suggesting this, yet it seems a possibility that must be mentioned—was Siegfried always latent in the soul of the German people, and Wagner only the inspired medium who succeeded in materializing him? Or—a more congenial and three-dimensional interpretation—has a considerable part of the German people been formed in the image of Siegfried by long and zealous attendance at the opera house? I leave these questions to the race-psychologists, without promising much confidence in their answer, whatever it may be. *Felix qui potuit rerum cognoscere causas.*

III

So much for the history of Wotan and of Siegfried as political parable and political inspiration. But *The Ring* is spacious enough to admit of more than one interpretation, and what was in the mind of such an artist as Wagner when he wrote it is perhaps not altogether to be grasped even by such a mind as Shaw's. I do not pretend to get more out of it than Shaw got; but I get something different, which no less than Shaw's interpretation may have been implicit in Wagner's vision.

Who cares, you may ask, what I think it means or what Shaw thinks it means? The question is what Wagner thought it means. Unfortunately Wagner has told us what he thought, and Shaw has proved out of his own mouth that he was wrong. Reading Schopenhauer's *Die Welt als Wille und Vorstellung* after he had finished the libretto of *The Ring,* Wagner felt in his first enthusiasm that here was a logical exposition of the very ideas he had set forth in poetry; "now at last," he wrote, "I understand my Wotan." In some respects—emphasis on the superiority of the unconscious to Reason, for instance—Wagner's

philosophy does indeed resemble Schopenhauer's; but in the Wotan
of *The Rhine Gold* and *The Valkyrie* there is none of Schopenhauer's
negation and resignation. He was always in there trying; only when he
was old and tired and beaten did he become a disciple of Schopenhauer.

So never mind what Wagner thought he had written; it. is an old
story (most recently exemplified by the autobiography of H. G. Wells)
that a first-rate writer may not know what he is really doing. It is
also an old story that what you get out of a work of art is largely determined by what you bring to it; the spectator of *The Ring*, says Shaw,
will recognize in it "an image of the life he is himself fighting his way
through." If he is trying to save the world, as was Shaw in the nineties,
or to rule the world, as are other men today, he will read into it a
parable of the world revolution; and he can equally see his own problems reflected in it if he is trying to do no more than show some creditable result for his life's work, and make of himself as decent a figure as
the wear and tear of living will permit.

If you are only an imperfect Wagnerite, a middle-aged middle-class
citizen who goes to the opera because he likes it, you can read in the
history of Wotan (*Götterdämmerung* included) the greatest apologue
ever written of the life of the Average Man. Or if this seems disrespect-
ful to Wotan, call him the typical Rather-Better-Than-Average Man;
the man whose ambitions, by no means wholly unselfish, still aim at so-
cially useful ends; who catches a vision of good things that he hopes
to accomplish, and then finds himself in middle age impotent to accomplish them, paralyzed by his innate shortcomings and by the
ineluctable consequences of his own mistakes.

IV

Wotan's troubles, like those of most young married men, began when
he became a homeowner. Up to that time he had apparently done
pretty well; when we first see him he is the executive of a considerable
organization, he has made some advantageous contracts, and he is successful enough to enlist the services of a smart lawyer, Loge, who can
be depended on to find a loophole in any contract that may prove inconvenient. Wotan also has a wife, Fricka, whom he had wanted badly
enough before he got her (or so he says) to have given his only remain-
ing eye for her. (He had spent the other one for his education.)

Nevertheless, there are already signs of tension between husband and
wife. "I like women too well to suit you," he confesses; but as yet
other women are no problem in themselves; they are only the symptom of a restlessness in Wotan, an itch for variety, that Fricka cannot

share. So, agreeing with Herbert Hoover that nobody ever sang "Home, Sweet Home" to a bundle of rent receipts, she has fallen in with Wotan's project of acquiring a suburban home, in the hope that her husband will be so proud of his establishment that he will stay at home in the evening. (Plenty of apartment wives will recognize her feelings.) So badly does she want the house that she is not much worried about the price; her husband is doing well in the world, he has assured her that they can afford it; with the self-confidence of a rising young executive he has left her out of the negotiations with the contractors—and now she and her husband suddenly discover that the new home will cost more than they can pay.

Wotan gets out of this difficulty more luckily than the average young man—thanks to his lawyer. Usually such talent as Loge's serves the title company; with his professional skill backing up Fafner's brutal violence, the homeowner goes into peonage for the rest of his life. But Wotan pays for his house only by letting himself in for something even more inconvenient than mortgages; he raises the money by the first unmistakably crooked deal of his life, behaving so badly that even his lawyer is ashamed of him. Wotan has overcome his moral scruples, Shaw points out, by working up a moral fervor of the misuse Alberich would have made of the money which Wotan intends to employ for worthy purposes; but presently he meets a woman (a widow with three children, older, more experienced, and wiser than his wife) who recalls him to reality. He has behaved badly because it seemed at the moment that it was the only way out; and thereby he has started a chain of consequences whose end is far beyond his seeing. Always after that he must worry, and be a little afraid.

For the moment Wotan has triumphed, and triumphed very splendidly as the rainbow bridge leaps across the chasm, and the gods cross over it to Walhall on the distant heights. . . . What was once the music of the future is already, to a good many people, the music of the past; and it may be that no one can be deeply moved by it who did not get his emotional set before the nineteenth century went out. But there is an emotion that most men are lucky enough to experience at least once or twice in their lives, an emotion without which no man's life is complete: the feeling of now-at-last-I'm-beginning-to-get-somewhere. The sudden startling glimpse of a rainbow brilliance as some long-sought objective that has cost work and worry, anxiety and apprehension and self-denial and pain, is at last attained—the triumphal culmination of a long struggle, opening the way (so it seems in that exalted moment) to even greater triumphs beyond. These words are pitiably inadequate; no words that I have ever seen in print are adequate to describe this particular feeling. Once and only once, to my perhaps archaic taste, it has been expressed adequately—by the rainbow music at the end of *The Rhine Gold*. . . . Yet presently, interwoven with that music, you begin to hear other themes—reminders of what the triumph has cost, of the hidden forces, irrational and incalculable, that have been aroused. Wotan has done something wrong and he knows it; he keeps up his front, but precisely because he is a fairly decent god, as gods go, he never quite gets over it.

Nor is the stirring up of hatred, the unleashing of a curse, the only cost of Walhall; something irreparable has happened to Wotan's relation to his wife. Before this real estate transaction she may have worried about his restlessness, but she respected him; he might be just a big grown-up boy in some ways, but nobody could deny his business ability. Now Fricka has to recognize that her husband made a fool of himself, that only Loge, whom she despises, saved the family from disaster. Moreover, a marital harmony that had survived ordinary stresses cracked wide open in a money crisis; husband and wife under pressure displayed unsuspected motivations, utterly irreconcilable standards of value; everything each of them did got on the other's nerves, they lost their tempers and blurted out unpleasant truths that can never be forgotten. The quarrel is over, they move into Walhall; but an indispensable illusion has been shattered, Fricka can no longer respect or trust her husband. . . . While Wotan, recalling how maddeningly his wife nagged him when he was worrying his head off about money, finds his thoughts going back to that widow he lately met, and her refreshingly realistic point of view. It could not harm to look her up again—with no sentimental intentions, of course; his interest in Erda is purely intellectual. . . .

You can read in *The Rhine Gold*, says Shaw, the whole tragedy of human history; and you can also read in it such a tragi-comedy as is played out a dozen times a year in every commuting suburb. There stands the House, acquired at such a cost, and not in money alone; still it is a good house, and the young people have taken title and moved in, even though the mortgage hangs heavy over their heads; the quarrel that broke out during the negotiations with the title company has been made up, and now they are going to live happily ever after.

But nothing will ever be quite the same again.

v

The Valkyrie shows us Wotan and Fricka in middle age, successful, prosperous, and miserable. Wotan has continued to do amazingly well for himself, but always there hangs over him the tormenting realization that this may not last, that something he did years ago because it seemed best at the time, without ever foreseeing its consequences, may ultimately ruin him. And there is nothing he can do about it; tied down with promises and commitments, he cannot remove the peril without wrecking the whole social fabric of which he is a part.

As for his domestic relations, he and Fricka maintain the dignified front of a successful middle-aged married couple, but the true situation is plain enough to anybody who knows them well; Brünnhilde, at the beginning of the second act, hurriedly leaves Wotan with the cheerful observation (I translate freely): "You're going to catch hell; here comes your wife." Brünnhilde did not then know of anything particular and recent that Wotan had done to catch hell about, but she knew Fricka, and Wotan too. He still has that itch for variety, yet he has always treated his wife with proper respect; she has a re- markably fine car (which the limitations of stage production seldom permit the audience to see); over certain fields of their common interest she is supreme; her husband seems to have done about everything for her that a man can do for his wife, except be faithful to her. . . . That widow now, Erda—he had gone to see her, drawn by a purely intellec- tual attraction; he wanted to ask her some questions. But apparently she was lonesome, she did not want to talk about abstract topics; and it occurred to Wotan that a man and a woman cannot be sure that they are intellectually congenial till they have got more urgent mat- ters off their minds. This seems to have been his first affair, and no doubt he got into it without ever exactly intending to; but there were others. . . . And others. . . .

The painful scene between Wotan and Fricka in the second act has a bisexual application that could hardly have been dreamed of in Wagner's day, when only women of the aristocracy had much freedom; nowadays there are wives as well as husbands who could play Wotan's part, husbands as well as wives who could play Fricka's. The tragedy is Wotan's, and Fricka has an extremely unsympathetic part; yet Wag- ner as an artist could not help letting us see the psychological springs and explanation of her behavior; she was so rigorously insistent on maintaining the outward front of marriage, even if nothing but hatred was behind it, because her own marriage had ceased to be anything but front. She had to cling to the one thing she had left. It may be that when Wagner wrote her lines he was thinking of the Spirit of Constitutional Law; but it may be also that he was thinking of a woman named Minna Planer Wagner, so uncharitably suspicious of her husband's purely intellectual interests in other women. (Yet this same Minna had once been the gay mistress who so delighted him, the young bride with whom he planned their private Walhall. . . .)

Fricka demanded that Wotan must surrender to her vengeance what he loved best—his son Siegmund, begotten to accomplish what Wotan could not do himself; and Wotan, who had begun by telling himself valorously, "I've got to stand up to her," discovered that he could not stand up to her because she had too much on him. What would become of him if contracts were disregarded? Besides, he does not come into court with clean hands. Siegmund has run off with another man's wife; no wonder, says Fricka, that you stand up for him, you who are always running around with other women. She says enough to let Wotan see that she could easily say more if necessary; so Siegmund must die, not so much because of what he did as because of what his father did before he was ever born.

You need not read any Shavian allegory of education and eugenics into the relation between Wotan and Siegmund. Every man believes, for a while, that he is creating a nobler race to replace himself; that his children will accomplish, by and large, what he himself had intended before he got involved. And I know of no more bitter experience in the life of the average man (or average woman) than the slow realization that your children who once seemed beings of another order, brighter and freer and better, must grow up to become members of the human race; that instead of realizing all the things on which you have somehow missed, they must make their mistakes, meet with their irreparable disappointments, see themselves enmeshed in the consequences of their own well-intentioned blunders—precisely like their grandparents' children, and everybody else's children since time began. Not always is the responsibility for their misfortunes so clear as in Siegmund's case; but any conscientious parent must feel some qualms when he sees his children getting into trouble, ultimately, because they inherited from their parents their share of human frailty.

But Wotan's expiation does not end with the failures of his son. When Brünnhilde, who embodies Wotan's best intention, saves what she can from the disaster, Wotan has to punish her—suppress his own best intention, do something that he knows is wrong, because in the past he has done things that turned out to be wrong, though he never suspected it at the time. A man in that position is about as far down as he can ever get. Maybe you think Wotan deserved it; but not many men, even if they never cheated anybody out of any money and are unfailingly loyal to their wives, can survey their records from middle age without perceiving something that had seemed the best thing to do at the time, but turned out to be disastrous. Wotan is a tragic figure precisely because he is the Average Fairly Decent Man, who generally tries to do the best he can and eventually finds himself entangled in unforeseen consequences. Now he is helpless; he must do what is expected of him, keep up a front. In *The Rhine Gold* he swaggers and blusters and keeps up a front from pride, the pride of the young executive who refuses to admit that he has blundered; but in *The Valkyrie* he sacrifices everything to keeping up a front because he knows how much relies on that front for shelter. He is a man with dependents now—all the gods must fall if Wotan falls; the head of a family, the keystone of a widespread organization. How faulty that organization is he realizes better than anybody else; still he must defend it at any cost, because he cannot think of a practicable alternative that would be any better.

So Wotan, who had once done what seemed best, now does what he has to do, however bad it seems. After he leaves Brünnhilde, Wagner once wrote, the best he can do is to let things take their course. Most men, and most women, sooner or later come to that. Read *The Valkyrie* as anything you like—a parable of nineteenth-century revolution, or of Roosevelt *vs.* the Supreme Court if you prefer; but the man who can sit through it without uncomfortable stirrings of his private conscience is either a paragon of virtue and wisdom or an insufferably complacent fool.

VI

Here, logically, the story of Wotan ends. But Wotan, like most of us, does not end when his existence ceases to have any logical or dramatic justification; he has to go on living.

[• • •]

Wotan survived himself; in *Siegfried* he is nothing but an old fossil, yet he has to go on living till someone is competent to take his place. Like a good many elderly gentlemen of means, he spends his time in travel; he is observant, he picks up a good deal of information, he can answer all the questions anybody asks him and ask questions that less traveled persons are unable to answer; but he cannot do anything about it. He stands by and watches other people striving for what they want, what he wanted once himself; but he is through with striving; things are taking their course, and he has to take their course too. And his wife? We hear no more about her. No doubt, on the rare occasions when Wotan is at home, they get along well enough by keeping out of each other's way; by now they must be too old and tired for either love or hatred.

Yet Wotan has one or two last flickers of energy. He goes to call on Erda for old times' sake, and finds that that once lovely mistress also has grown old and tired, and is disinclined to conversation. ("Good heavens, did the man ever think that what I wanted was to talk to him?") And he meets Siegfried, his grandson who is growing up now, and is about ready to take over the family business; to whom Wotan naturally offers some grandfatherly advice. But Siegfried has no appetite for advice, or for information that might be useful in his business; what he does not know already is not knowledge, and be damned to this old windbag who wants him to stop and talk when he is on his way to see a girl. Whereupon Wotan loses his temper, and feels as a million grandfathers have felt in his place. "What, shall this young squirt, etc.? Not while I can stop him!" But the spear that once ruled the world falls to pieces under Siegfried's sword; its shaft has rotted with time, the contracts so carefully inscribed in it are ancient and forgotten history; the future belongs to a new generation which Wotan, upon acquaintance, does not admire quite so highly as he did when it was still in infancy and could be the repository of all his own unfulfilled aspirations.

Which brings us to Siegfried.

VII

A competent social psychologist might have deduced the whole history of modern Germany, from Bismarck down to Hitler, from this one fact: the Germans are the kind of people who admire such a hero as Siegfried. (Not all of them, to be sure; but a sufficient majority.)* Yet for what Siegfried was, no less than for what his father Siegmund was, Wotan was responsible. He had educated Siegmund very carefully; a rigorous education ("my son is not going to be pampered and spoiled, as I was at his age") but one well calculated to fit him for the profession of hero to which his father had destined him. Unfortunately

---

* Truer than I realized when I wrote it. No nation likes to lose a war; but other nations, when they have lost one, eventually manage to reconcile themselves to the plain fact that they were licked, whatever knavish tricks of their enemies they may blame for the disaster. Only Germany must proclaim the dogma, not to be denied except under penalty of excommunication from the *Volksgemeinschaft*, that unbeaten armies were treasonably betrayed by Jews and democrats within—because three generations of Germans have been conditioned by the Ring operas to the conviction that the German Hero can never be struck down except by a stab in the back.

it turned out that education was not enough to guarantee success; Siegmund never had any luck. Yet he stood up against all adversity with a Calvinistic fortitude; he was a man worth fifty of his son. And while he broke up a home (which needed it) he was no promiscuous amorist. Consider his dialogue with Brünnhilde, who has come to invite him to Walhall, and recites its varied attractions. Are there any women in Walhall? asks Siegmund. Why, yes, says Brünnhilde; we girls are there. But, says Siegmund, can I bring my wife? And upon learning that he cannot—Give my regards to Walhall, he tells her; I'm not coming. The result of this conversation, curiously enough, is to inspire Brünnhilde with an overpowering devotion not only to Siegmund but to his wife; but then Brünnhilde is still a goddess, not yet a woman.

But if Siegmund's education made a man, it did not make a successful man; so Wotan lost his faith in education and let Siegfried grow up anyhow, with consequences which are a good advertisement for a formal schooling. "Having had no god to instruct him in the art of unhappiness," says Shaw, "Siegfried inherits none of his father's ill luck"; but that is a nineteenth-century judgment which Shaw might repudiate today. Siegfried has plenty of ill luck in *Götterdämmerung;* if he had been better educated he might have learned that there are influences which make a man forget what he ought to remember. Cocky, arrogant, bumptious, he grew up not only without inhibitions, but without manners and without knowledge. It is true that a remarkable woman fell in love with him, but he was the only man in sight at the time; a good many superior women have married the men they did for no better reason.

If the young Siegfried is disagreeable, Siegfried in middle age is intolerable. So far luck has been with him, everything he tried has come off, so naturally he thinks he knows it all. After a while he gets bored with country life on Brünnhilde's rock and goes back to town to achieve some more achievements; he is supposed to have learned all that his wife could teach him, but he must have been a dull pupil, for the very first thing he does is to stumble into a clip joint. (The hall of the Gibichungs deserves no politer description, considering what happened to Siegfried there.) Yet it is impossible to be sorry for him when you see how he behaves in the last act of *Götterdämmerung.*

Siegfried, who has got rid of Brünnhilde and married again, is on his way to meet his brothers-in-law when he encounters three girls, and pauses for what he probably considers a little airy repartee. He keeps up his snappy come-backs till they ask him for his ring; and he can think of no better reason for not giving it to them than that his wife might not like it. (Why drag her in?) Then he tells them, at some length, what a remarkable man he is; and when they lose interest in the conversation and walk out on him he says to himself (not the ideal listener, but better than none) that he knows all about women, and would certainly have dated up one of those girls if he were not a respectable married man.

Then he meets his brothers-in-law, and they have a few drinks; and our hero consents to tell them some stories—about himself of course. He talks on and on, till one of the others suggests that they had better have another drink. They have it, and then Siegfried starts right in again—this time, about his prowess with women; at which point one of the listeners loses his patience and reaches for his spear. . . . Breathes there the man with soul so dead that he has not sometimes wanted to do, to some interminable autobiographer at the luncheon table, exactly what Hagen did to Siegfried?

Meanwhile we have heard one last report about Wotan; he is sitting in Walhall amid the cordwood into which he has chopped the World Ash Tree from which he once drew his power, and waiting. This, says Shaw contemptuously, belongs to the old legendary materials with which Wagner began *The Ring*. Old, Mr. Shaw? Legendary, Mr. Shaw? More than almost anything else in the tetralogy, that is a story of today and of every day; it may not fit into the Shavian parable of the revolution that never came off, but it fits with appalling exactitude into the story of the Average Man. For unless he meets with what is ironically termed an untimely end, this is what the Average Man must come to at last—an old, weary, forgotten figure, sitting amid the debris of everything that he once cared about; waiting, with an apathy that does not deserve to be called patience, for an exit that might have been made with greater dignity long before. This is the end of all the striving, good and bad—all the struggles and all the visions, all the triumphs and all the mistakes; all the posturings and boastings, all the hatred and malice and all the love and forbearance too. The normal end of man.

VIII

It is not a very pleasing prospect; and the endeavor to get us somehow reconciled to it has evoked some of the most brilliant flights of human genius. One such is the fifteenth chapter of First Corinthians, another the finale of *Götterdämmerung*. Some people's psychic receiving sets are attuned to the one, some to the other; personally I prefer *Götterdämmerung*, even though no earthly theater can ever produce that last scene quite as Wagner conceived it.

Wagner tells you, as St. Paul tells you, that the immediate tragedy does not really matter; it is part of a Whole, and the Whole is all right. So much of the Whole as we can see at present (not very much, to be sure) offers little evidence in support of that contention; you must be convinced, if you are convinced at all, in some new dimension, on some plane beyond the reach of mere human reason. Wagner transcends reason with music, St. Paul transcends it by faith; but Paul uses words, and combines those words into intelligible ideas, so reason cannot help getting hold of his argument and finding it lacking in cogency. So long as Wagner sticks to words he too is unconvincing; but in the last five minutes he lets the orchestra do his talking, and no man can pick flaws in that argument. Perhaps all he gives you is a species of intoxication; when you have come out from under the spell, when you have left the opera house and gone down into the subway (or into your limousine, if that is where you go), you find yourself back again in a world where the Whole is no greater than the sum of its parts; and a good many of those parts are hard to fit into any totality that makes sense. Perhaps you have only been hearing some music, after all. . . .

Only hearing some music—but what music! Old-fashioned music, it may be; but on the pre-war generations it still has its unequaled effect. The artist has created his own world, and what he says is valid within its dimensions, whether it squares with logic or not. Alberich's curse is as good an explanation as the temptation of Eve for the fact, obvious to anyone who has been around for any length of time, that there is some perhaps incurable inadequacy in men and women, which is likely to bring their best intentions to nothing or worse than nothing; yet we like to feel, even if we cannot quite bring ourselves to believe, that some day, somehow, that failing will be corrected. To enable some of us to feel that for the moment, even if we can no longer feel it when we have come out on the street, the finale of *Götterdämmerung* is more powerful than the assurance that Death is swallowed up in Victory. If the Average Man, at the end of his days, cannot congratulate himself on any particularly impressive achievement, it may give him solace to reflect that one of his kind, once upon a time, evoked from a great artist the noblest of elegies.

FICTION

[*Fiction was Davis's livelihood for fifteen years. Even before
that he had written several novels and a number of shorter
fictional works. His fiction-writing career seems to fall naturally into three divisions: during the first, which lasted
through the first year or two of his free-lancing, he wrote the
five "lighthearted" novels; then for the next two or three
years he worked hard on two more serious novels while also
refining his short story technique; in the last period he did
not by himself write any novels, but most of his income came
from short stories for the slick magazines.*

[*For a sample of the novels, the first selection below is a
long initial segment from his most popular book,* Giant
Killer. *After that there are six short stories, appearing
roughly in the order that they were written. Readers who
remember the magazines of the twenties and thirties, when
these appeared, may be surprised at the relatively unconventional stories or "story ideas" appearing in the conventional
form of the slick story. I believe he regarded mastery of form
as a tool whose value was to permit a writer to work out the
ideas that interested him; applying this principle worked to
make his work distinctive, in slick writing.*]

GIANT KILLER

[*Most of his admirers thought this his best novel, though there are fair numbers of votes for two or three others. The book appealed to all sorts of people, not least to clergymen. (This special appeal was perhaps offset by the prejudice of Fundamentalists against any book like this.)*

[*Whatever it may be that other historical novels are, I think this is a good novel, as such, and that the historical setting is essential to it. It is surely more a novel of ideas than of subjective character study or of historical exposition. However, I think Davis believed the exposition—granted a little modernization of certain ideas to make them easier to convey—was essentially correct.*

[*A more sweeping interpretation was given by Sinclair Lewis in his foreword to the 1943 reprint by* The Readers Club. *"This is a novel which is a sensational report of what the United States of America is trying these days to do,"* he began. *"On the surface, the book has nothing to do with America nor with today . . . It is a lively, well-colored and sometimes ribald restoration of King David . . . As such the book is brilliant entertainment . . . But,"* he said, *"all through the book it is apparent that the author, whether he knows it or not, is thinking how like the Peculiar People of 1000* B.C. *are to that new Peculiar People who make up this America of 1900 plus* A.D., *and that he is telling us our own story."* I think Lewis must have enjoyed the book more for this interpretation.*

[*Following are the first two chapters of Book I.*]

BOOK ONE: SAUL

I

Goliath of Gath paraded on the hillside beyond the brook, swaggering and bellowing; the tall plume of feathers tossed above his bronze helmet, his sword clanked against his bronze shin guards as he stalked and postured on the slope. In the sunset, the burnished scales of his armor shone ruddy and baleful, the broad steel blade of his spear flashed bright and cold. His roarings filled the windless evening; and in all the army of Israel, cowering on the hilltop across the valley, no man dared answer him.

"Come on! Come on! Pick out a man, if there *is* a man in Israel! Pick out a man and send him down to me! If he kills me, we Philistines are your slaves—*if* he kills me!" A derisive cackle went up from the groups of Philistines sprawling on the crest above him. "Come on!" he roared. "Where is he? Saul, King of Israel, send me down a man!"

But there was no answer. Goliath laughed.

"Ho, ho! A man—in Israel! . . . Then send me a woman! I liked your women, when I campaigned in the hill country. Ho, ho! Ask your wives if they remember Goliath!"

He named names, he went into intricate detail of reminiscence; and still no man came down. He spat.

"Call on your god!" he jeered. "Yahweh, god of Israel—your god in a box! Your war god! Where is he? . . . Ho, ho! We took him! We took him in battle, your god and his box too! Israel, Israel! Your god is no god, and your women are anybody's women!"

Still not a sound, not a movement, in the Hebrew lines. And the boy who had been listening from the bushes, on a knoll down the valley, flung himself face downward in the dust and wept.

Only that morning he had left home—a home where nobody appreciated him, in a small town where nothing ever happened—and had gone out into the world to make a name for himself. No one knew that he was setting out on this high quest; he had been sent on an errand, with strict orders for a prompt return. But, once over the hill, he had sung and shouted in pure joy; for now he could prove himself, find some great adventure that would make his fortune.

Here it was—the supreme adventure; he could strike not only for himself but for his people and his god. He could see himself answering the challenge, striding boldly down the hill to meet Goliath while King Saul and the army of Israel cheered him; a bright and glorious picture, that far. But he could see the rest, too, with sickening certainty—the giant's yawn of contempt, then his sudden snarling aggression; the single swift thrust of that broad bright spear. He could see that, and feel it too; as often as the sunlight flashed on the blade his stomach leaped convulsively within him; he shuddered, sick and cold.

He tried to force his arms to thrust aside the screen of shrubbery, he commanded his legs to carry him down the hill; but he could not stir. He reviled himself for a coward, he cursed, he prayed; but at last he lay prone in the dust and wept. He was a failure. His nation was a failure. His god who would not help him, who let himself be blasphemed without reply, was a failure too.

2

He dragged himself up out of the dust at last; the bellowing had ceased; Goliath was climbing the farther slope, going back to supper. Beyond the crest, the smoke of camp fires rose thin against the sunset. In the Hebrew camp, too, across the ravine that flanked the knoll, fires were lighted, dark figures swirled about them. So the obscene farce was over, for today. But tomorrow it would be played again, and the next day—till the giant tired of his sport, and drove Israel before him like frightened sheep. . . . Listlessly the boy picked up the rope of his pack donkey and started down the path toward the ravine. He must do his errand; and then he must slink back home.

But a turn in the trail brought him on a sentry—a gaunt man in the bronze helmet and leather shirt of King Saul's regulars. His bronze-bladed spear pointed at the boy's belly; he snarled a savage "Halt!" And then, as he saw that it was only a boy, he relaxed with a rather sour grin.

"Your name and your tribe and your father's name!" he demanded, in the soft Southern drawl. "And what do you think you're doing here?"

The boy stiffened, in a hot revulsion of pride; but the spear blade was too close for argument.

"My name's Joab," he said sullenly. "My father's dead; I live with my mother and my grandfather Jesse, in Bethlehem of Judah."

"And you've run off to join the army," the sentry concluded. "Better go back home, boy. This is no army to join."

"I'm not running off. I'm only bringing a message to my uncle."

"Your uncle, eh? That would be Eliab?"

"No—my uncle David. . . . But how did you know?" The sentry grinned.

"Oh, I come from Bethlehem myself. Elhanan the son of Jair—ever hear of me? No, I reckon not; it's fifteen years since *I* ran off to join the army. What we thought Saul was going to do, in those days! . . . Your mother's Zeruiah, ain't she? A fine lady like her wouldn't remember me; but I used to work for your grandfather, at sheepshearing and harvest time. It wasn't such a bad town, Bethlehem. Slow, but I've seen worse since I been in the army." He leaned on his spear, melancholy and reminiscent. "David. That would be the youngest of the four boys, as I recollect."

"He's only two years older than I am," said Joab, somewhat heartened by this recognition of his standing back home. "We all grew up together, he and I and my brother Abishai."

"And he's in the army now—that little fellow? Well, well!"

"Not David. My uncles Eliab and Abinadab and Shammah went up last spring, when the King called for volunteers; but David had to stay at home to herd the sheep. My mother sent him to the front last week with some home-cooked food for my uncles—they don't like army rations. He wanted to enlist—but the King wouldn't dare take a gentleman's son without his father's permission. And my grandfather has sent me up to tell David to come back home." Elhanan chuckled.

"Well, if the old gentleman says come back, I reckon he'll come. They don't argue much with old Jesse." His eyes strayed to the pack donkey. "What've you got there? I don't like army rations myself." He strode past Joab, inspected the load, and held up a bulging goatskin. "Wine!" he said severely. "Good wine, too, if your grandfather made it."

"You leave that alone!" Joab blazed. The rage and humiliation that Goliath had aroused boiled over on Elhanan; the boy's knife leaped out. But a casual backhand swing of the spear butt knocked it out of his hand.

"Try to knife a sentry, would you? Lucky I know who you are, boy. Anybody else would have stuck a spear through you." Joab's stomach quivered again. "Don't you know it's against the rules to bring wine into camp?" Elhanan demanded. "War is holy unto the Lord and soldiers are consecrated men. Neither wine nor women till the campaign's over—that's a statute and an ordinance in Israel. Judah's not Israel, so you might not know that; but my sergeant's an Ephraimite. If he'd seen this wineskin—! But I'll just hide the evidence; and so long as you don't say anything, nothing will happen to you." And he hid the wineskin away in the bushes.

Only the pride of Jesse's grandson before a soldier who had been Jesse's harvest hand enabled Joab to swallow the lump in his throat. His wrist ached where the spear butt had struck it; his soul ached with the conviction that he was a coward and a weakling, contemptible and absurd.

"Well?" he said bitterly. "Now will you let me go?" Elhanan sat down, laying his spear beside him.

"Oh, I'll let you go. But how will you get by the sentries without the password? . . . My relief comes pretty soon, and maybe I can get leave to go over to camp for the night. If I can, I'll take you with me.

So you open up that pack, and we'll have supper while we wait. . . .
Come along, now!" as Joab stood glowering. "Never mind who you
are and who I was back in Bethlehem. This ain't Bethlehem, boy;
this is the front. . . . Yes, and just as far front as it'll ever be, in this
war."

In slow bitterness Joab undid his pack of bread and dates and cheese.

"That's a fine way for a soldier to talk!" he snarled.

"Boy, if you'd sat here and listened to Goliath morning and evening,
every day for a week, you'd feel that way, too."

Joab slumped down on the limestone outcrop, hopelessly depressed.

"I know," he groaned. "It's sickening. . . . But—" He shuddered.
"I don't wonder nobody's dared to fight him. Why, he must be nine
feet tall!"

"He may be," said Elhanan. "I never went down there to measure
him. That plume of feathers on his helmet makes him look bigger
than he is, but he's big enough. There's three or four of these giants
down in Gath, I hear. Brothers. Nice family to marry into. . . . Boy,
this is good cheese!"

"Why doesn't Saul fight him?" Joab cried. "He stands head and
shoulders, they say, above every man in Israel."

"Now, you want to remember Saul's a king. He can't take time off
to accommodate everybody that wants a fight. Besides—this kingdom
of Israel may not amount to much now, but where would it be if anything happened to Saul? Tell me that."

"Prince Jonathan—" Joab began; but Elhanan cut him off.

"Jonathan! He's as good a soldier as I ever saw, but the King of
Israel has got to be a politician too. You don't have to serve long in
an army recruited from all the tribes to see that. Jonathan's a soldier
and that's all; and the other princes ain't even that much. A lot of
people have turned against the King since he had that quarrel with
the prophet Samuel; but I tell you we might have a lot worse kings
than Saul."

Elhanan returned to his cheese; and Joab discovered with amazement that he too had been eating while the soldier talked. An hour
ago he had believed he could never stomach food again; but now that
he had absently devoured a loaf of bread, life no longer seemed quite
so hopeless.

"The Philistines must be afraid of us, too," he offered in reviving
spirits. "Their army hasn't attacked."

"That's no army. Only a frontier guard, to make sure Saul won't
come down and burn a few barns while they're getting in the crops.

About two thousand of them—and six thousand of us, regulars and volunteers, when we got here last week. I doubt if there's five thousand, now; a lot of volunteers remember they've got work to do back on the farm, after they take a look at Goliath. I don't mean gentlemen like your uncles; they'll stick till the volunteer regiments disband in the fall. But fellows like me, it takes time to learn not to mind the way your stomach turns over, when the sunlight flashes on the spears."

Joab stared at him in abysmal amazement.

"Did your stomach do that, too?" he gasped.

"Did it? Does it yet? Every time I go into a battle."

"Then how— How do you manage to go in at all?"

Elhanan grinned.

"Well, if you're a soldier you're supposed to fight; that's what they pay you for. So you set your teeth and go ahead; and pretty soon you're too busy to think about your stomach." Joab pondered that.

"And do you mean to say everybody feels that way?" he asked.

"Oh, now and then you strike a fighting fool that doesn't; but most people do. Yes, even Philistines."

And the boy who had begun to regain faith in himself was abased once more by the shame of his people.

"Then why can't we ever beat them?" he cried.

"Oh, we beat them—sometimes. You're too young to remember when they had garrisons all over Israel, even in Saul's town of Gibeah. After the battle of Ebenezer Israel was a conquered province, till Saul started the rebellion and drove 'em out of the hills. But on the plains— Boy, you wait till you see a squadron of iron chariots drivin' down on you! These giants are showy fellows, but the Philistines would beat us just about as often without 'em. . . . Why shouldn't they beat us? Their swords and spears are steel; ours are bronze, all but the King's and Prince Jonathan's. Only our officers can afford armor; but they're rich, they all wear it. Besides—" He spat. "If we don't win in the first rush we don't win at all; we can tell right off if God is with us, if it's Yahweh's day. But these Philistines don't seem to care whether their gods are with 'em or not. They can get the worst of it all morning and still come back to win, giants or no giants."

"It makes me sick!" Joab groaned. Elhanan laughed cheerlessly.

"It's been makin' some of us sick for years. . . . I was down at Beersheba on leave a couple of years ago, and I met an Egyptian girl, and we had some drinks and so on. 'Soldier,' she says to me, 'what a fine big chest you got!' 'Why, yes,' I says, swelling it out, 'it *is* pretty good.' 'My Philistine friends,' she says, 'have told me a lot about the Hebrew army, but they never told me you had such fine big chests. But then of course they only see your backs,' she says. . . . I clouted the little cat over the ear, but she was pretty near right at that."

He was silent, morosely regarding the stars that were beginning to glimmer. Joab heaved a shuddering sigh.

"Then what's to become of us—Yahweh's chosen people?"

"Don't ask me, boy. They pay me to fight, not to think. . . . But sometimes a man can't help thinking, anyway." Elhanan rose, picked up his spear. "Here comes the relief."

Sandals clopped on the stony trail; the sentry's drawling challenge was answered in the nasal twang of the Ephraimites; a squad of soldiers slouched through a gap in the bushes. Elhanan parleyed with the sergeant in an undertone; then, to Joab—

"Go ahead, boy. I'll be right with you."

He laid down his spear, unbuckled his sword belt, and cautiously drew the wineskin out of hiding. The squad had slouched on, but the sergeant lingered.

"What's that?" he asked. Elhanan gave a groan of resignation.

"That, sergeant? Why, that's a sack of barley that I'm taking over to some friends of mine in camp. Want to step behind this bush and take a look at it?" Screened by the shrubbery the sergeant tilted the wineskin and drank deep.

"Barley it is," he agreed, smacking his lips as he returned it to Elhanan. "But be careful nobody sees you. And be back by daylight."

With the wineskin under his cloak, Elhanan followed Joab down the trail.

3

Between the blazing camp fires the boy from Bethlehem walked in wide-eyed amazement. Spears were stacked, helmets were off, pots simmered on the fires; five thousand men, as they ate supper, were abusing each other for being afraid of Goliath; their gesticulations made a ceaseless shadow-play in the firelight. Five thousand men, more than Joab had ever seen in his life; men of every tribe in Israel, from Danites of the distant North, their speech strange with the idioms of their Phoenician neighbors, to a scattering of Jerahmeelites from the desert's edge, far to the south of Judah.

In Bethlehem they knew the southern clans, Judah and Caleb and Jerahmeel—wild jealous tribes who might send men to fight for Saul, but would never acknowledge him as King; they knew the Benjamites, the King's own tribe, their neighbors to the north. But Joab had hardly ever seen an Ephraimite and the remoter northern tribes were only names. Now the northern twang was everywhere; here was the army of all Israel and all the South as well, from Dan to Beersheba—and not one man who dared to fight Goliath.

At that blistering reminder the boy hung his head, no longer interested in this great impotent array; he plodded on, his eyes on Elhanan's heels, till his guide halted, pointing to a campfire near the brow of the hill. Beyond its leaping blaze, the feathery foliage of an acacia was bright against the shadow.

"You'll find your uncles over there," Elhanan grunted; and was gone.

Around the fire lounged half a dozen men, their armor laid aside, taking their ease in belted tunics and sandals—Joab's three uncles, stocky, square-jawed, sullen; two or three other Judean officers whom he knew by sight; and a stranger in a fine blue tunic, with a thin kindly face. No sign of David. . . . Joab came forward into the firelight; and Eliab, the eldest of the uncles, looked up at him and came to his feet with a bound.

"As God lives!" he swore. "You, too? You might as well go right back home! Nobody wants you here!" He scowled, panting. "I'm sick of it, I tell you! You boys trying to edge your way into everything—"

"I'm not trying to edge my way into anything," Joab interrupted. The respect and fear which he felt for his mother and his grandfather dwindled, when it came to Eliab, to the mere perfunctory deference due the eventual head of the family. "Your father sent me up," he said, "with a message for David. Where is he?"

Now Eliab smiled malignly, and his two brothers smiled with him.

"David!" he called. "Come out here!"

There was a stir in the shadows beyond the fire. A young man, not quite so tall as Joab, sauntered out with a rather lordly unconcern; the firelight shone on his unkempt tangle of curly red hair, it gleamed in brown eyes, bright and restless, shadowed with a trace of apprehension.

"Hello, Joab!" He tried hard to be casual; but the pretense broke down before the snarling expectant grins of his brothers. Joab felt a rush of pity.

"Come over here," he said. "I've got a message for you—but we needn't disturb the others." But Eliab seized his arm as he turned away.

"Stay here, both of you! We all want to hear this. Though maybe we can guess what it is." He laughed, and his two brothers laughed with him, acrid and mirthless. "We've been trying for a week to tell him that nobody wants him around here."

"Don't discourage him," said the stranger in blue with a cheerless chuckle. "We need all the men we can get."

"We don't need *him*," Eliab growled.

"You never give me a chance!" said David. "I could be as good a soldier as any of you, if I only had a chance! Why, once when I was herding sheep, a lion came down—" Eliab snorted in disgust.

"A lion? It was a bear, the last time you told it. Next time I suppose it will be a dragon. . . . They sent him up from home with some things to eat," he explained to the stranger. "They thought he'd know enough to come back without being told; I always did, when I was his age. But he's been hanging around ever since, making a nuisance of himself—trying to get a commission, trying to get some officer to take him as armor-bearer, playing his harp, making up songs— He's done about everything, except offer to fight Goliath."

A laugh ran around the circle, but the man in blue only smiled.

"Oh! So he plays the harp and makes up songs?"

"All the time. Especially when there's work to be done. Anything but work, is his motto."

"Why, Eliab, in some countries you'd be proud of such a brother. He's what the Babylonians call an artist."

"Oh, is that what they'd call him? Well, we call him The Pest. Always trying to push in everywhere, get himself noticed—" He turned to Joab. "What did father tell you to tell him?"

"He said to come home and herd the sheep," Joab admitted reluctantly.

"Hah!" Hands on hips, Eliab laughed at David. "I thought so! Who did you leave those sheep with in the wilderness, anyway? It's about time you got back to them. . . . You start at daylight, you and Joab, too. And don't let me see you again tonight. I'm sick of you!"

He sat down beside the fire; and Joab, after a moment of hesitation, picked his way around the lounging circle and retired into the shadows. David was sitting against the tree, his head bowed; his harp—the light sickle-shaped harp that fitted into the curved arm—lay beside him.

"That's always the way!" he muttered as Joab flung himself down. "They never give me a chance. . . . Or you either," he added in afterthought.

"What's the difference?" said Joab wearily. "Perhaps we couldn't use a chance if we had one. . . . After all, we both had our chance today—the most glorious chance any man could want." And, as David looked puzzled— "Goliath," he explained. David shrugged.

"Oh, well! I meant something reasonable. . . . How's everything at home?"

"Worse than ever. Mother and grandfather are furious at you for not coming back, and as usual they take it out on me and Abishai. Especially me; Abishai does everything they ask him to, now that he's in love and hoping they'll let him get married. But I—" David nodded.

"I know," he said. "They're afraid we'll do something new—something that wasn't done by our ancestors. God knows, it's about time somebody did something in this country." Then, more cheerfully— "Has anybody been asking about me?" Joab grinned.

"Your father. . . . But I suppose you mean some of the girls. Well, they haven't asked me. They wouldn't."

"Girls would look at you," David told him, "if you ever looked at them."

"I haven't time for girls. Not till I've done some of the things I mean to do. . . . Or meant to do," Joab amended cheerlessly.

"You're missing something. . . . You haven't seen Rachel, have you?"

"No, I haven't seen her. I let married women alone. . . . And you ought to. If your father ever found out about that—"

David yawned.

"He won't. Nor her husband, if that's what's worrying you. She's clever."

"Clever?" Joab grunted. "She's common—riffraff! David, I don't see what you can get out of a girl like that." In the light of the distant fire, he could see that David was smiling faintly.

"Every woman has something," he said. "Something no other woman has. I've never been disappointed yet. . . . And neither have they, unless they've lied to me." There was a pause; then—

"Who's the man in blue?" Joab asked.

"His name's Beriah; a volunteer officer, of one of the great families of the hill country of Ephraim. He's traveled—to Tyre, and Babylon. . . . Did you hear what he said about me? The Babylonians would call me an artist! And that's from a man who's seen the world, who hasn't spent his life cooped up in Bethlehem. If only I could get to Babylon—!"

"Babylon's a long way off," said Joab. It seemed ten times as far, somehow, since he had seen Goliath. "Sing me a song, David. I need one of your songs tonight. Any one."

"Eliab won't let me sing, when he's within earshot. He found out that the soldiers liked it too well. If I could only stay a few days longer, the King might hear me— But what's the use?" David finished, his spirits sinking. "Back to Bethlehem in the morning!"

The boys lay silent and disheartened; and after a time they heard voices raised in argument around the fire.

"My dear Eliab," Beriah the Ephraimite was protesting, "I said no such thing. I merely argued that from the viewpoint of a man who has seen other countries, as well as our own little corner of the earth, there's something to be said on the side of the Philistines. I prefer my own side, naturally. But I visited the Philistine cities in the last armistice, and I must say I liked the people. The old aristocracy, that is; the masses are only a mongrel mixture of Canaanites, Amorites, renegade Jews, Egyptians— But the old families, the descendants of the invaders who came in from Crete and conquered the country— they're good people, Eliab. We have to fight them, certainly; but we needn't despise them."

"Good people! Their cities are sinks of luxury and vice!"

"Well—" Beriah smiled thinly. "We have vice in Ephraim, and I suspect it's not unknown in Judah; though certainly we haven't much luxury. But there's more than that in Philistia. A spaciousness, a grandeur, a freedom that we never feel, cooped up in our hills. Those splendid porticoed temples; those domed palaces with their gardens; the caravans you see in Gaza, passing through from Egypt to Babylon; Ashkelon harbor, with ships at the docks from Cyprus and Ionia and Tarshish. . . . I tell you, Eliab, it makes Judah and Ephraim seem rather provincial."

"I'm not ashamed of being provincial!" Eliab shouted. "Or of being poor either! We Jews are producers—farmers and sheep ranchers. The Philistines are only middlemen, parasites! They buy and sell, and charge commissions, and lend money at interest. They crowd together in cities, and build themselves palaces, and take hot baths in marble tubs. They load their women with jewels—short-haired, insolent women, who think they are as good as men, women unfit to be named with our mothers in Israel! They stay up late at night, drinking wine out of golden cups while they listen to sensuous music. God hates them!" he summarized.

"I don't doubt that Yahweh hates them," Beriah conceded with a yawn. "Yahweh, we might as well admit, is a rather provincial god. A good enough god for our ancestors in the desert; but it's time we outgrew that old narrow intolerance if we ever expect to amount to anything. I'm glad to see our women taking up the worship of Ashtaroth.

Some of them carry it a little too far; that's usually the way with a new fashion. But Ashtaroth is a strong goddess, the goddess of great nations. Under one name or another they worship her in Philistia, in Phœnicia, in Assyria, in Babylon—"

"You are an assimilationist!" Eliab flung at him.

"Calling names isn't argument. . . . And I'm not an assimilationist!" said Beriah with unexpected earnestness. "I'm all for what Saul is trying to do—unite our weak clans into a nation and make the Philistines keep their hands off of us, give us a chance. But I don't see that patriotism need make us hostile to everything that makes life worth living. Surely we can fight our War of Liberation against Philistine militarism without abusing Philistine culture and Philistine music. Let's try to see both sides."

"You can't afford to see both sides in war time!" Eliab shouted. "And there is only one side, anyway! Our god is better than their gods—"

"Is he? Yahweh is a war god first of all, the Lord of the hosts of Israel. Fifty years ago the Philistines beat us at Ebenezer and captured the Ark of God. They hold it still—on neutral territory, to be sure, if you can call Kirjath-Jearim neutral; practically it's a Philistine dependency. At any rate, the Ark of God is there, and we don't dare try to recover it. I must say, Eliab, a god who can do no better than that—"

"The Ark of God is an Ephraimite superstition!" said Eliab angrily. "God lives on Mount Sinai, not in a box."

"You Southerners take your religion so literally!" Beriah sighed. "You see no beauty in symbolism. . . . At any rate, if Yahweh were such a strong god the Philistines wouldn't beat us continually. Their gods are better than our god—or they are better men than we."

"You are a defeatist!" cried Eliab's brother Shammah. Beriah looked at him coldly.

"I think my military record will bear inspection. I haven't gone down to fight Goliath—but I might, if I had as much faith in Yahweh as you men of Judah. Why don't you go down and fight him? Why does no one at all go down, day after day? Because we've lost faith—faith in ourselves and in our god. We can't change ourselves; but perhaps if we changed gods—"

"I won't change gods!" cried Eliab. "I will have only our old Hebrew god, who brought us up out of the land of Egypt and gave us this Promised Land!" But his fierce heat cooled before the Ephraimite's acid smile.

"The Promised Land!" said Beriah softly. "Yes, our god gave it to us—if we could take it. We drove out the inhabitants of the hill country; but even with his help we can't drive out the inhabitants of the plain. They have chariots of iron. We even lost our hill country once, and if the Philistines ever put forth their strength—as they may do some of these days—we're likely to lose it again, to be conquered and enslaved.

"And meanwhile we cling to our barren hills, grubbing a bare living out of the rocky soil, and swear that this is a land of milk and honey! Poor and ignorant and provincial, we soothe our sense of inferiority by shouting that the things we can't get are not worth having, that they're wicked, hateful to God. Touchy and suspicious and narrow, we make up wonderful tales of the greatness of our ancestors to forget what we are now. . . . The Promised Land! A land of poverty and pettiness, of envy and jealousy and spite that we vent on each other, because we're too weak to turn it on the Philistines! As God lives! Could we, a rural people with a rural god, suspicious of everything that makes life worth living, ever build a Promised Land? Why, any civilized observer—from Babylon, for instance—would say that the best thing that could happen to us would be absorption in a cultured nation like the Philistines!"

Now men sprang up around the fire. "Treason!" they cried. Beriah, lounging on his elbow, only laughed at them.

"Treason? You know it's true. You wouldn't be so hot, if you didn't know it. . . . Tell the King I'm a traitor, if you like; or the General. Saul and Abner know me; they know I'm the only nobleman of Ephraim who still brings his men down for every campaign, year after year. I'm for Saul till the end; but you know as well as I do, Eliab, what the end must be.

"It's not a question of one god or another. I think we weaken ourselves by depending on our outworn god of the desert; but it's more than that. They talk in Babylon—the philosophers at the great temples—of a Law that is above all gods, a great unalterable law that controls the sun and stars in their motions, and writes the fate of men and nations in the stars; a law that brings one nation up and another down in some inexorable succession. . . . I'm afraid, Eliab, that law is on the side of the Philistines."

"The Babylonians are ignorant idolaters!" Eliab screamed. "Our god is stronger than their silly law. With his help we can—"

"Kill Goliath?" Beriah suggested; and Eliab choked, with an uncontrollable shudder. Beriah laughed wearily.

"Oh, I'd like to believe you," he said, "to believe that we are the greatest nation on earth, and our god the strongest god. But there's an argument against that, that none of us has answered. . . . Goliath."

In the great silence that fell about the camp fire, Joab could hear David moving nervously, with sullen mutterings.

"Our god *is* the strongest god!" he growled. "This Ephraimite is a blasphemer!" But Joab hung his head in impotent despair.

"He's right!" he groaned. "He's right. Say what you like—always, at the end, there's Goliath. . . . What can we do, David? What can anyone do?"

He lay down and buried his face in his cloak. But David still sat brooding; and presently he began to strum softly on his harp.

4

King Saul strode up and down in his tent, his scarlet cloak flapping about long hairy legs, his black beard clutched despairingly in both hands. By the table where an oil lamp flickered sat a stocky grizzled man in a bronze corselet, his eyes uneasily following the King.

"Abner!" Saul halted, his eyes lurid. "I can't stand this any longer! Tomorrow morning I go down to fight Goliath."

"You must think of the kingdom," the Commander-in-Chief reminded him. "If anything happened to you, which may God forbid—"

"If anything happened! Could anything be worse than sitting here day after day and listening to that man? You know what it is doing to the morale of the army! . . . Yes, and to my morale too!"

"If you would approve my plan for a flank movement—" Abner began. But the King cut him off with an impatient sweep of the arm.

"A flank movement, around Goliath? Our people are too imaginative for that. They'd be wondering what he was doing behind them; one flight of arrows from a thicket would rout them. . . . No, I must fight him. After all, God was with me once, before I quarreled with Samuel—" He broke off, uncertain.

"God is with you still," said Abner. "Samuel is against you because he made you King; he has never forgiven you for being King, a greater man than he. But—"

"Samuel is still strong, Abner! The country people believe in him. When I do anything, he talks it over with his cronies, and sneers at me—and they go out from Ramah to spread the poison over the whole country, saying that God has forsaken me." He tugged savagely at his beard. "I wonder if God does prefer Samuel!" he muttered. "He never answers me any more, when I inquire at His oracle; His prophets are silent; He never sends me dreams—" His dark eyes burned in torment. "Abner, are we going to fail after all?"

"No!" cried the General. Then, reflectively, "It may not be too late for a reconciliation with Samuel, even yet. He's jealous and conceited; but he is an Ephraimite—and he was a priest at the old temple of Shiloh, serving the Ark of God before the Philistines took it. If we could only recover the Ark, we might recover Samuel too." The King threw up his hands.

"Impossible! The Ark is on neutral territory."

"Yes, the Canaanite cities are neutral," Abner agreed dryly. "But they pay tribute to the Philistines, they keep the Ark for the Philistines. . . . Neutral! Saul, if we made a sudden raid on Kirjath-Jearim, after the Philistines have gone into winter quarters—"

"No!" Saul thundered. "You military men have no respect for the sanctity of treaties! Our ancestors guaranteed the neutrality of the Canaanite cities, swearing a solemn oath before the Lord—"

"And ever since," the General finished, "the Canaanite cities have been a wedge driven into the heart of our country, cutting off Judah from Ephraim. If we held them we could bring Judah into the kingdom too. Must we be bound forever by the diplomatic mistakes of our ancestors, when considerations of imperative strategic necessity—"

"No, no!" said the King uneasily. "It wouldn't do. If I broke that oath, God would certainly forsake me. . . . Besides, that wouldn't dispose of Goliath. Tomorrow morning I am going down!"

The General pondered, stroking his curly, grizzled beard; then he rose and held out his hand.

"Well, Saul, if you must! My cousin—my oldest friend—may the Lord go with you!"

But the King drew away from the offered hand; his eyes were troubled.

"So you're willing to let me go at last! . . . Abner, if anything should happen, swear to me that you will establish my son Jonathan on the throne!"

"Jonathan? But of course! He is the heir—" Saul laughed harshly.

"The heir! What does that mean, in Israel? Our monarchy is new, and less popular every year. The other tribes are jealous of Benjamin; Samuel and his friends are always talking me down, saying that Israel needed no King, that it should serve only God—and Samuel! If I die without some great success, Israel may abolish the monarchy. Or, even if they will still have a King, they may say that my successor should be elected, as I was. But I choose my successor! I choose my son!"

"And I will elect him!" Abner promised. Saul stared at him darkly. "You!" His voice was a hoarse whisper. "You will elect him! Yes, I might have seen it. . . . Oh, I know Jonathan! A good soldier, but no politician. If he succeeds me you will be the true King—yes, as half the time you are King now!" His anger rose gustily. "I give the orders, I bear the complaints of the people; but the ideas are yours—"

"My lord!" the General protested; but the King stormed on.

"Oh, I know you, Abner!" Saul's hand hovered about his sword. "You could never make yourself king; you aren't showy, you lack imagination. It needs a man who has imagination, and who can catch the imagination of the people, to be King in Israel. This unruly nation admires Jonathan the soldier; but you would stand behind him, think his thoughts, move his hands—"

The sword flashed out, swung up— Then, shuddering, Saul lowered it slowly, thrust it back into the scabbard.

"I'm sorry, Abner. These sudden rages come over me—I wonder if God sends them! He knows I have enemies enough, without turning on my best friend. . . . No, I won't fight Goliath. You and Jonathan together might do better than I, but I must try a little longer. If Jonathan only had more insight—or if you could only catch the imagination—I could do that, once."

Through the open tent flap he stared out at the stars. Abruptly he turned back.

"Send word throughout the army," he commanded, "that the man who kills Goliath can marry my daughter."

"The Princess Michal?" Abner asked, his brows lifting. "It is not the custom to give the younger daughter before the firstborn. Public opinion—"

"That's true. . . . Well, then—Merab!" Abner stroked his beard.

"Dare we do that, Saul? We've practically promised her to Adriel. His family is powerful beyond the Jordan. If we offended them—"

"Could anything be worse than this? Offend anybody, if only we can get rid of Goliath! Proclaim it throughout the camp—the Princess Merab is the prize for the man who kills Goliath!"

"Any man? Officer or private?"

"Any man! We can't stand on class distinctions now. . . . That's all for tonight," he finished. "I'm going for a walk."

The fires were dying, now; through the sleeping camp the King strode, his hands clasped behind his back, his face haggard and tormented.

Perhaps he ought to fight Goliath, after all. It would be suicide; he felt that with utter certainty. But it would be a gesture that would

catch the imagination of Israel, that would tinge the nation's memory
of its first King with an ineradicable respect. . . . He shook his head
angrily. Thinking of himself! Never mind that; would the gesture
help the kingdom? It might establish his dynasty, if he died for the
people; it might give Jonathan the prestige that would enable him to
keep Abner in his place. . . . Or it might hopelessly discredit Jonathan;
this peculiar people might think of him only as the son of the man
who failed to kill Goliath.

To die bravely was not enough; Israel needed more than a moral
victory.

For Abner was shrewd; he knew his limitations; he was patient and
unwearying. Dangerous to Jonathan, if he were a secret overlord; but
he could be a useful servant. Jonathan was obtuse, credulous, easy-
going; but, if his father avoided Goliath and lived to train him, he
might yet become the King that Saul had meant to be—glorious and
victorious, the father of his people; schooling them to forget quarrels
and pettiness and jealousy, to act and think together—a great nation,
fit to build, at last, the Promised Land. Saul had seen that vision, had
set his hand to the work; and then the endless wars, victory followed
by defeat, and that fatal quarrel with Samuel—

The King groaned aloud. Always his thoughts went round and
round in a closed circle, back to the same old mistakes, the same bits
of undeserved incalculable ill-fortune—things that had happened once
for all and could never be mended now. Israel was finished; Israel lay
helpless before the giant—and Israel's King, and Israel's God. . . .

Saul lifted his head; down the wind came the music of a harp, a
clear tenor voice was raised in song. He found himself moving toward
the music; other men were moving, too; around the red-haired boy who
was singing, a circle had gathered, and deepened, till it was a hushed,
tense crowd. The King paused—and then the vague solace that the
music had brought him leaped and blazed into new hope.

For it was a song about Goliath: how he stood forth in his arrogance,
defying Israel and Israel's God; how all the army fled from him, dis-
mayed and sore afraid—until a boy came out to meet him, a shepherd
lad. "Who is this uncircumcised Philistine, that he should defy the
armies of the living God? The Lord that delivered me out of the paw
of the lion, He will deliver me out of the hand of the Philistine!"

Now the music was harsh and dissonant; Goliath was mocking the
boy, cursing him by his gods. And in crashing, swelling chords came
the boy's reply— "You come to me with a sword and a spear; but I
come to you in the name of Yahweh Sabaoth, the God of the armies of
Israel! This day will the Lord deliver you into my hand, and I will

give the carcasses of the host of the Philistines to the fowls of the air and the beasts of the field, that all the earth may know that there is a God in Israel!" Then the singer's voice rose in an ecstasy of triumph: "I smote him; I prevailed over him! I slew him!" And at last King Saul knew that this boy he had never heard of was telling his own story, singing tonight what he would do tomorrow; and he wept with joy as the song rose to the climax: "Blessed be the Lord my rock, who teaches my hands to war, and my fingers to fight; my high tower, and my deliverer; my shield, and He in whom I trust! For lo, thine enemies, O Lord, thine enemies shall perish; all the workers of iniquity shall be scattered! But my horn hast thou exalted like the horn of the wild ox; I am anointed with fresh oil!"

. . . Joab, squatting at David's side, was dimly aware of the crowd that pushed and packed itself in around them, of knees pressing against his shoulders, of the stifled breathing of a great company all about. But that only touched his consciousness, and slipped away. He had soared high above the world men lived in, to an empyrean of shimmering magic where boys killed giants, and Israel triumphed over Philistia, and all things ended right. His ecstasy mounted to an unendurable pitch—and then the strings rang in a glorious final chord; the song was ended. . . . And with a crash he came back to the world of reality: a world buried, just now, in a cold oppressive silence through which he sensed a shudder of relaxing tension, the reluctant reawakening of many men to things as they are. His head drooped. After all, it was only a song. . . .

There was a stir behind him; men stepped on him, fell over him, in their haste to get out of the way of a figure thrusting through the crowd—a huge figure in a scarlet cloak, its bronze helmet banded with a circlet of gold. The King! In the firelight his face was bright with exultation; his hands fell on David's shoulders, he drew the bemused boy to his feet.

"At last," Saul thundered, "God has sent me a man! Tomorrow morning you will go down and kill Goliath!"

David stared at him; he blinked and shivered; he tried to speak. Joab knew he was trying to explain that it was only a song; and tomorrow morning he must go back to Bethlehem. But the words would not come. . . . The King broke out in a roar of jovial laughter.

"Don't be afraid of me, lad! Don't think of me as the King; think of me as a father. For when you've killed Goliath you marry my daughter!"

That brought Eliab forward, hastily, his hand raised in salute.

"My lord! Don't take this boy seriously! He's always making up silly songs that don't mean anything!" And as the King glowered at him— "Why, he's no soldier!" said Eliab. "He's only a sheepherder."

David's head flung up; at last he found his voice.

"I am an artist! . . . Temporarily employed as a sheepherder."

"Whatever you are," said the King, "you have faith—in our god, in our people, in yourself. Tomorrow morning you will kill Goliath!"

Now all the brothers gathered round, protesting; they knew their father's unacknowledged tenderness for his last-born son; he would hold them responsible. "He didn't mean it!" they clamored. "It was only one of his songs!" And from behind them, Beriah's voice— "The boy is an artist, my lord the King—not a man of action! Artists always see things as they ought to be."

"But," Saul cried furiously, "he said, 'I smote him!' I!"

"With all respect," Beriah offered, "an artist is not responsible for the opinions of his characters, even in a first-person narrative."

Saul shook his head like a tormented bull.

"I don't know anything about art; I've never had time for it. But I thought I had found a man! . . . Boy, did you mean it? Will you fight?"

David cowered away from his lurid eyes; and Joab, watching in an agony almost as keen as David's own, knew that he was afraid—afraid of this infuriate King, this circle of frenzied men, ready to cheer him if he volunteered for certain death, and to hoot him out of the camp if he behaved sensibly. Against that unendurable picture, David closed his eyes. ·

Now, Joab knew, he could see another picture—a boy armored in faith answering the giant's challenge, striding boldly down the hill while Saul and the army cheered him. A bright and glorious picture, that far. But after that—

David's eyes opened; he stiffened proudly, he looked Saul in the face.

"Yes!" he cried in a rush of ecstasy. "I'll fight him! I'll kill him!"

And as the King embraced him, the crowd broke into a tumult of exultant cheers. So far as they were concerned, Goliath was already slain.

Joab felt that fiery confidence too, above his tremendous awed wonder. David was going to do it! David! . . . But afterward—when they had planned the morning's work in a sort of clamorous mass meeting, and the others had gone away at last, leaving him alone with David, to try to sleep—he found himself thinking, David is going to try to do it. . . .

They were lying at the edge of the hill, where David could see Goliath as soon as he appeared in the morning. Joab sat up, looking

down into the blackness of the valley. David was going to try to do
it. . . . But he was only a boy, and Goliath a man of war from his
youth; his burnished sword shone so balefully, his spear was so broad
and bright— Saul had sent for his own armor and made David try it
on; but they could all see that the bronze corselet and shin guards
would only be in the boy's way. . . .

"David!" Joab whispered. "Are you asleep?"

"No." David sat up; in the starlight, his face was glum.

"David, are you going down to meet him as soon as he comes out?"

"Might as well get it over with."

"Get it over with?" Joab gasped. "You—you're not afraid, are you?"

"No, I'm not afraid. Of course. . . . But— Oh, how did I ever let
myself in for this?" Joab stared at him in cold horror.

"Why, the spirit of the Lord came upon you! A man can do anything when the spirit of the Lord is upon him!"

"Spirit of the Lord!" David laughed savagely. "It was that harp! I
still had the rhythm in my muscles; I could still hear the echoes of my
own music. . . . I forgot it was only a song."

Only a song. . . . Joab shuddered. It couldn't be only a song; Israel
was lost, unless it were a reality.

"You mustn't worry about this now," he said desperately. "You'll
be all right in the morning." (He *must* be all right in the morning.)
"We'll all be cheering you, praying for you—"

"Yes," said David. "So you said."

"David!" Joab flung himself into high resolve. "If he—if he should
kill you, I'll go down and let him kill me too!"

"Uh!" David grunted. "That helps." And as Joab would have persisted in his reassurances— "Oh, shut up, will you? Go to sleep!"

Joab lay down, shuddering with a great cold apprehension; he knew
he could never close his eyes that night. But he had had a long journey
that day, and an evening of draining excitement. Presently he slept.

But David still sat, wide awake, his heart like a stone within him.
His glance fell on the harp, and lingered, baleful and vindictive. And
after a while he snatched it up and flung it far away down the hillside,
in a hopeless frenzy of rage and despair.

5

The morning star hung over the eastward hills when Elhanan the
son of Jair said a thick-tongued good night to his friends and started
back for his post beyond the ravine. They had heard the King's
proclamation throughout the camp, and afterward they had heard
distant cheering; but that did not disturb these half-dozen veterans,

earnest and appreciative drinkers. Let the others shout, if they had anything worth shouting over; but those who had the rare luck to drink old Jesse's wine could enjoy it in prudent silence. Elhanan had enjoyed it copiously; now he picked his way through the camp with tangled feet, walking in unbalanced rushes, more than once almost treading on sleeping men. It was a relief to come out on the hillside with the ravine below him; if he fell, now, he would fall in the way he was going.

. . . So, he mused, the man that kills Goliath can marry the Princess Merab. Saul better bid higher than that. I've seen her, this Princess Merab. Fat girl—no fire in her. I'd never fight a giant for her, Princess or no Princess. That Egyptian girl, now, at Beersheba—she was a hot little piece, even if she did say that about the Hebrew army. . . . Queer the way the stars swing back and forth; I must be drunk. That's it, sure enough; I'm drunk. Why not? The sergeant'll let me sleep it off and I won't have to listen to Goliath. Uncircumcised dog—says our god's no god and our women are anybody's women. But who's going to shut his mouth? Not Elhanan. . . . I make a lot of noise on this hill; the boulders roll out from under a man's feet. Ah! Here's the bottom at last! Now where's that trail? If only the stars would hold still till I got my bearings— What's that? Water! Wet feet! Huh! Thought this brook had been dry for a month. . . . More water—

. . . Elhanan stood still, a cold fear crawling over him. Water—the wrong brook. He had lost his way, come out on the wrong side of camp; up the hill to the right were the Philistines. Already dawn was beginning to break; if a sentry saw him now—! Stumbling, panting, he ran down the brook bed; never mind the noise if only he could get around the shoulder of the hill in time. Over this boulder, around that bush—

A man who had been washing his face and arms in the brook sat up on his haunches, looming big in the dimness.

"What's all the racket about?" he growled. The Philistine accent! . . . Elhanan's teeth chattered; he had left all his weapons on the knoll.

"By Dagon and Atargatis!" the Philistine swore. "Can't a man wash his face without somebody crashing in on him? You've muddied the water, too, just when I was ready to take a drink." He laughed grimly. "I make it a rule never to kill a Jew before breakfast; but just this once—"

He rose—and rose, higher and higher, his monstrous shoulders blocking out the stars, one by one. Elhanan screamed in sudden horror.

"Goliath!"

With a hoarse chuckle the giant came down on him barehanded, his long arms reaching out, his huge taloned fingers groping. Wild with fear, Elhanan ducked under the swinging arms, tried to dive out of reach. His body plunged against the armored shins as Goliath lurched forward with a roar of rage—lurched and stumbled, and fell headlong in a great clatter of metal. His forehead crashed against a sharp corner of the rocky outcrop. He lay still.

Elhanan, pinned down by those mighty legs, waited helplessly for the giant to turn and tear him to pieces. But Goliath lay still. . . . Hesitant, fearful, Elhanan dragged himself out, inch by inch. He stared at the huge inert form. Something was oozing away from the head, a dark trickle across the limestone. Elhanan touched it, tasted it. Blood. . . . Goliath was dead.

In a disintegrating rush of ineffable relief, Elhanan collapsed. Face down in the bushes he wept hysterically; he was sick, long and miserably; at last, in utter exhaustion, he slept.

. . . And in that moment David, keeping shivering vigil above the valley, saw across the eastward hills the first red streak of day. The day when he must die. . . . No! Other men die but it can't happen to me! God will not let it happen to me! Goliath will be sick today! A snake will bite him! There will be an earthquake—a thunderstorm— an eclipse of the sun—

But as the red streak slowly widened that wild hope grew more tenuous; the truth weighed down on him, insistent; it compassed him about, inexorable, ineluctable. He must die. . . . And the artist who had never had to look Necessity in the face, because one refuge was always open, found that refuge closed against him now; his hands groped vainly for the weapon that had always armed him against reality—his harp. The harp that, in haste and anger and folly, he had thrown away, down the hill.

He peered down into the valley; it was still a pool of darkness, no Philistine sentry could see him now. And he couldn't have thrown the harp so very far—

Silently he stepped over the sleeping Joab and crept down the slope.

6

Elhanan's eyes opened. Daylight. His head was throbbing, his bones ached, his throat was hot and dry; he lay gasping in feeble misery, and vowed that he would never touch a drop of that stuff again as long as he lived.

A recollection edged its way into his consciousness. It was fantastically incredible; he tried to frown it away. But it persisted. Presently he turned his head, still dryly skeptical—and stared in stupefac-

tion at a monstrous form, lying prone and lifeless. So it was true. . . .
I've killed Goliath! I've killed Goliath! I'll marry a Princess and live
like a King—

He looked again, frowning, and sat up, peering over the hulking
shoulders. There lay the giant's sword, all bloody; his neck was a
truncated mass of bloody meat; the head was gone. . . . That's queer,
Elhanan mused. I know I was drunk, but you'd think I'd remember
cutting off his head—

He struggled to his feet in wild haste. Up the eastward hill toward
the Hebrew camp—far up the hill—a red-haired youth was swiftly
climbing. Something was slung over his shoulder, something he was
carrying by a black tangle of hair. . . . The head of Goliath. . . .
Elhanan raised a frenzied shout.

"Hey! Come back here! Where you going with that?"

But the red-haired youth—remote, preoccupied, all but out of earshot—only went on climbing. Elhanan shook off his paralyzed horror;
he too began to climb, stumbling and wheezing, toward the summit,
and the dull murmur of the waking camp. But it was too late; he
knew it was too late. Before he was halfway up the hill the boy had
gained the crest; he stood for an instant silhouetted against the sun-
rise, his body thrusting upward like a lance, holding high above him
the head of the giant. . . . And the confused murmur of the camp
recoiled and deepened, and then leaped skyward in a mad roar.

"David! David! He's killed Goliath! Forward—for Yahweh and
David!"

Before Elhanan, still plodding grimly on, had reached the summit,
the first men ran past him—half-armed, in no order at all, but crazed
with confidence and fury. Across the valley trumpets sounded in the
Philistine camp, but Elhanan the old soldier knew that no troops could
stop the Hebrews when in rare incalculable moments they were seized
with this raging frenzy. For the spirit of the Lord had come upon
them; they knew that it was Yahweh's day.

"Stop!" Elhanan screamed. "I killed him! Listen—"

They passed him; they were gone. . . . More men and more, an
interminable swarming; even boys, now, and camp followers. A dark-
eyed boy came leaping down the hill, waving a stolen sword.

"Joab! I killed him! David cut his head off but I killed him!
Listen—"

In a single bound Joab was past him; he had not heard him at all.
. . . Now the rush was thinning; but the valley below was a mass of
men, they swarmed up the farther hill; swords clashed on armor as
the first comers flung themselves on the Philistines. Elhanan stood

still, sick, dazed, dumbfounded. From across the valley came a cease-less roar—"David! David!"

In the wake of the army stumbled a single belated camp follower—a Syrian eunuch, fat and puffing. Elhanan seized him by the shoulders.

"I tell you I killed him!" he sobbed. "Not David!"

"Let me go!" the eunuch squealed. "We'll loot the Philistine camp! Their officers wear gold rings, gold amulets! Get out of my way!"

"But I tell you—"

The eunuch gave a frantic heave, a thrusting push—and leaped over the conqueror of Goliath, lying flat in the dust.

"Stop!" Elhanan bleated. "Listen—"

But it began to dawn on him, now, that no one would ever stop and listen.

So presently he too was stumbling down the hill; not the betrothed of a princess, but an old soldier who hoped he would not be too late for the looting. He did not hear the shivering crackle as his blindly plunging feet crushed a forgotten harp.

II

With songs and shouting, and the throaty jubilant blare of ram's-horn trumpets, King Saul's army marched back to Gibeah his capital, men who had won a battle exulting as if they had won the war. They straggled in a long, disordered column, their spears draped with gar-lands, their shoulders burdened with loot from the camp. Pack donkeys bore captured swords and spears by the hundred, weapons of steel for Israel; Goliath's sword, Goliath's armor, were to be hung up at Yahweh's altar. Greatest prize of all, there were even a few dozen prisoners, battered and dazed, stumbling along with their hands bound behind them; Saul was going to show them off before the daughters of Israel, who had hardly ever seen a captive Philistine, and then he would hew them in pieces before the Lord, a worthy and acceptable sacrifice.

Saul and David rode at the head of the column. In the hills men rode donkeys or camels, when they rode at all; but two fine horses had been taken from the Philistine commander, and Saul and David be-strode them now. The King was majestic in his scarlet cloak, his helmet banded with gold; but it was David whom the eyes of the people sought —David the giant killer. The shepherd boy who had come to camp empty-handed rode now in shining armor; and on his shoulder was a harp of inlaid ebony, with silver strings, that the King had given him out of the tent of the Philistine general to replace the one he had lost.

He rode bareheaded; and the sunbeams slanting through the dust turned his ruddy hair into a fiery golden crown.

From the town women streamed out, wreathed in flowers, clad in their brightest gowns, dancing wildly as they beat their tambourines; singing, to the music of flute and harp, new songs of frenzied exultation with an insistent reiterated refrain—

> "Saul has slain his thousands,
> And David his tens of thousands!"

It seemed to Joab, plodding along unnoticed in the dust of David's horse, that the King was not pleased with that; yet the song only gave a poetic turn to the plain truth. The few days after the battle, and that one night before the battle, had taught Joab that all Saul had accomplished in years was less than David had achieved at a single blow. Men who had fought on in dogged desperation were hot at last with the confident hope of victory.

And the civilians—! Packed on the flat roofs of Gibeah they cheered, flung down flowers; thick oily smoke curled skyward from offerings on a score of altars, a sweet savor in the nostrils of Yahweh who had granted his people victory at last. Through dust and smoke and din, the column marched into the narrow streets; and the crowds surged forward, broke the ranks, mingled with the soldiers, men and women, too, laughing and weeping with joy. Joab was jostled back, down the column. Shivering with nervous elation, he halted to adjust his helmet —a great crested helmet that he had taken, with sword and armor, from a Philistine he had struck down in the pursuit—and whirled about fiercely as a gust of derisive laughter rose behind him.

The Philistine prisoners . . . But they were not laughing at him. Battered, bloodsmeared, without hope, they laughed at the rejoicing city. Their leader sneered in Joab's wrathful face.

"You people take victory hard," he said. "When you get the chance."

And the boy's enthusiasm began to drain away. He marched on, shouting; but the keen edge of his elation was gone. He could see Israel, now, as the Philistines saw it—a trivial people, ludicrously puffed up by this one trivial success. And these prisoners, who knew that they must die within the hour, could still look at Israel, and laugh. . . . The war was not over yet.

By the time the column reached the great open square before Saul's house—a hard-packed parade ground, flanked by the barracks of the regulars—all pretense of order was lost; every soldier had a woman hanging on his arm. For now the campaign was over, the ritual

restriction against wine and women was lifted; after the day of Yahweh would come the night of Ashtaroth. Joab was plodding on, his
mind still on the prisoners, when an eddy in the crowd flung a group
of girls against him—gentlemen's daughters, clad in scarlet, with brace-
lets and anklets of silver. Laughing hysterically, they kissed him, a
soldier returning in triumph—and the last one lingered a moment, her
lips returning to his, hot and avid, her laughter dying as a startled
wonder grew in her eyes. And he was aware that he was a man, who
had killed a man and wanted a woman. . . . She broke away, rejoined
her friends; but he knew he would see her again to-night, at the great
feast when all Gibeah would be drunk with wine and victory. Girls
of her class were brought up in strictness and modesty; but if he came
to her tonight, he could take her—

He did see her that evening, hot-eyed and hilarious with wine; but
he slipped out of her way. He was thinking still of the Philistine prisoners who had been butchered before the great altar, laughing as they
died. . . . He would have no time for women till he had done some
of the things that needed doing—the things he began to believe he
might do, now that David had shown the way.

2

Since the battle he had seen little of David; for now David lived
with the King, he had lifted himself far above the boy with whom he
had once played soldier and stolen melons. But tonight David was
before all men's eyes. Saul brought out the Princess Merab, and joined
her hand to David's in the sight of all the people; he appointed David
to the command of a regiment—a volunteer regiment, about to disband for the winter, but his rank and authority remained. And, before
the altar, Prince Jonathan gave David his own sword and armor, and
they two swore eternal brotherhood.

And David had earned it. Only Joab knew how fully he had earned
it; only Joab knew of that moment in the night before the battle,
when David had almost lost heart. But he had conquered that weakness; faith had brought victory in the morning. . . . Tonight he sat
at the royal table, on the King's right hand, with Abner on Saul's left
and the princes across the table; and in that high company the slayer
of Goliath belonged. In the light of a thousand torches, his face shone
with the high, holy ecstasy of a man who knew himself elect to some
great destiny, who had received peculiar proof that his God was
with him.

So a giant killer should look, a hero chosen of Yahweh to redeem
Yahweh's people. From now on, David was a man set apart. . . . And

Joab, who had killed no giants, must presently go back to a home where nobody appreciated him, in a small town where nothing ever happened.

He had forgotten that, in the delirium of the victory festival. When he remembered it, he looked again for the girl in scarlet, and found her presently hanging amorous on the arm of another man; she looked at him and did not see him. . . . A cold depression settled down on him. All Gibeah was shouting and singing, drinking itself drunken, giving thanks to God and making love to women. Even Eliab and the other uncles were revelling; the disgusted stupefaction with which they had greeted David's exploit had given place to a fraternal pride. But neither wine nor song could lighten Joab's heart. A King who had to consider public opinion would not take him into the army without his grandfather's consent; and he had no hope of that.

The fires went down, the singing died away; all Gibeah slept at last, to wake in the morning with parched throats, and aching heads, and unfamiliar bedfellows. Joab slept alone, and woke too clearheaded for comfort. After breakfast he prowled about the town and saw the few sights—the high place with its altars, the tamarisk tree where the King sat and gave justice. One or two soldiers whom he passed saluted him, for he looked like an officer in the armor which he wore because he had no place to leave it. But he wasn't an officer; he was a boy who must go back to Bethlehem—and the sooner the better. Presently he came back to the parade ground and walked toward the King's house; he was going to see David and say good-bye.

A man in full armor came out of the royal door, and Joab saluted with as military a precision as he could muster. It was Prince Jonathan; he smiled ruefully as he returned the salute.

"I congratulate you!" he said. "I don't know who you are, but you and I seem to be the only sober men in Gibeah this morning. . . . As God lives! What a chance the Philistines missed! A single battalion, just before dawn, could have butchered us all in our beds and burned the town. . . . Well, if they make enough mistakes, we'll beat them yet. . . . What's your unit?" Joab flushed.

"I'm not a soldier, your Highness. I—I happened to be in the battle, and I took this armor from a Philistine—"

"Not without some argument, I imagine," Jonathan suggested. "Good boy! . . . It's a pity you're not in the service. We have plenty of men who can kill, when the spirit of the Lord comes upon them, but not so many who can stay sober through a victory festival and turn up ready for work the morning after. . . . We lack endurance!" said the Prince fiercely. "We win battles but we can't win the war. We take war too lightly; we despise the Philistines for making a business of it, with rules, and a technique; we fight for glory and they fight to win. And they do win." He broke off, sighing. "I wish I'd been in the battle! I'd almost lost hope; but David has made everything possible. . . . See there!" He nodded at a tiny baby boy toddling across the parade ground, his nurse close at his heels. "My son!" said Jonathan proudly. "Meribbaal, who will be King after me—thanks to David! I used to wonder if my son might live and die a slave, cupbearer, perhaps, to the King of Gath. But since David killed the giant—"

Nodding, the man who would be the second King of Israel walked away, to play with the child who would be the third; and left Joab frowning. It seemed to him that a Prince who owed so much to another man would be wiser not to admit it. . . . But the shortcomings of royalty were not his business. He turned, and presented himself at the King's door.

Even in Saul's easy-going establishment there was ceremony enough to impress a country boy. He waited in a vestibule where full-armed soldiers stood on guard, till the slave whom the doorkeeper had sent to David came back and led him through a maze of courts and corridors and arched gateways. They came presently to a court paved with flagstones, green-gold in the sunlight filtering through a grapevine arbor. Here a stair led up to a long gallery; David's rooms were at the nearer end; at the other, behind a latticed door, the women's apartments. As Joab went up he heard a distant high giggle—

Then David ran out and flung his arms about him; not a giant killer highly conscious of his destiny, but a boy greeting his best friend.

"Joab! Where have you been all this time?" Then, glancing at the armor— "Oh, I see! I might have known you'd get into the army." Joab tried to smile.

"The army? No . . . I'm going home."

"Home?" David gasped. "But why?"

"You know your father wouldn't let me serve. Eliab and the others have some freedom—and he can't stop you, now. But I've killed no giants."

"He'd let you serve if the King asked for you," said David. "I'll get Saul to write him a letter—" But Joab shook his head.

"No! You've made your fortune. I must make mine."

"Why can't I help you?"

"Because," said Joab slowly, "you are a man set apart. You fought Goliath when I was afraid. You earned—everything. Till I've earned something—"

"Oh, nonsense!" Before David's high confident laughter all Joab's scruples, his turgid cogitations, did seem rather nonsensical; David made everything look easy. "Take off that armor," he commanded, "and let me lend you a decent cloak. We're going to see some girls."

"Girls?" said Joab in consternation.

"Not ordinary girls. The King's daughters!" Joab drew back.

"What have I to do with kings' daughters?"

"I need you!" said David. "I haven't had a chance yet to talk to the girl I'm going to marry. I'm going to see her now—but she can't receive me alone, of course. Her sister will be with her. And while I talk to Merab you'll talk to her sister—the Princess Michal."

3

"No sign of them yet?" asked old Jesse peevishly. "It's been two weeks."

From his armchair on the housetop he stared across the rolling hills of Judah, purple in the dusk. The dull buzz of voices rose from the close-packed houses of Bethlehem; sandals padded softly on the unpaved streets; a girl laughed in the dark; somewhere in the distance a child was crying. Zeruiah, tall and somber, turned back from the parapet where she had been peering down the fading white streak of the northern road.

"No sign yet, father. . . . Pull your cloak up around your shoulders; it's getting cool. . . . Something must have happened!"

"Now don't be childish! Eliab would have kept them out of the battle. And if anything had happened he'd have said so in his letter."

"Yes. . . . Unless—Just what did he say?"

"Only that God had given us a great victory, and that he'd be home soon with some news."

"And that's all anyone has heard?"

"There was a Jebusite in the marketplace today with all sorts of rumors that are going round Jerusalem—somebody had killed a giant, and Saul was going to give him his daughter— You always hear stories like that, after a battle. As if any of those Northerners could kill a giant!"

"I can't believe Joab would disobey us," said Joab's mother.

"Oh, he's always letting David lead him into some mischief. The boy has no strength of character, Zeruiah. The Lord knows David's bad enough—all this harp playing. But at least he thinks up his own deviltry. Well—with three sons married and settled down, I suppose I can't complain if David never amounts to anything. And yet the boy's bright enough—if only he wasn't always playing that harp—" His stick tapped irritably on the roof tiles.

In the stairwell appeared a shock of black hair, a pair of thick-muscled shoulders; Zeruiah's second son came softly up on the roof.

"Mother! Did you speak to him?" Old Jesse caught the whisper and turned in his chair.

"Is that you, Abishai?"

"Yes, sir." Nervously the boy came forward; his grandfather scowled.

"Your mother tells me you want to marry Tirzah. You're young, Abishai—you're young. And you've got no more sense of responsibility than Joab—always getting into fights around town—" His grimness softened into a dry smile. "But Tirzah's a good sensible girl—and we've got to find some way to keep you boys at home."

"I'd be very glad to stay at home with Tirzah, sir," Abishai stammered.

"Yes, I reckon you would; you're at her house every evening now. . . . But if you get married, you've got to learn to curb your temper. No more fighting. I hear you had a fight today, with that oldest boy of Shemaiah's—"

"Well, sir—" Abishai shifted uneasily. "It was only— There was some talk about David, that maybe he'd run off to join the army; and this fellow said they couldn't use harp players in the army. So I knocked him down—"

"Hmph! Can't say I blame you much for that. All the same— But I reckon we can count on Tirzah to keep you out of mischief. . . . Well, well! I'll speak to her father tomorrow."

"I—I thank you very much, sir. It's mighty good of you."

"Well, marriage steadies a young man. . . . But, Abishai! I'll probably have to pay her father fifty head of sheep as a marriage present. So I want you to understand that when you want a second wife you'll have to pay for her yourself." Abishai grinned shyly.

"I don't want any wife but Tirzah, sir."

"Oh, they all say that at your age. Then when they begin to get on in the world they want to show that they can afford two wives, or maybe three— Showing off, that's what it is. I don't know what the world is coming to."

He fell into morose silence; and presently Abishai ventured—

"May I go now, sir?"

"Go where? Off to see your girl? It would be no more than decent to wait till I've spoken to her father." Abishai was so glum that the old man chuckled. "But I suppose you and she have been talking this over, and she'll want to hear— Well, well, boy—go ahead. When I was young there was an etiquette about such things. But nowadays—"

But as Abishai reached the stairs, a disturbance broke out below. There was a knocking at the street door, the creak of hinges as old Hannah the maidservant opened it. Her voice floated up, respectful.

"Yes, sir?" Then a gasping— "For the land's sake!" . . . A patter of bare feet; twelve-year-old Asahel's voice squealed in delight. "Joab!"

"Joab, eh?" Old Jesse lifted his stiff bones from the chair. "And no David! If that boy has gone and got into trouble; or if this one has run off and left him . . . Joab! Come up here! Give an account of yourself!"

"Yes, sir!" They heard his feet on the stairs; and as he came his grandfather flung wrathful reminders at him.

"You're two weeks late! I told you— Your mother told you—"

"Now, father!" Placidly, Zeruiah cut him off. "Give the boy a chance to tell his story. He may have—"

The rest of it died in a gasp. From the stairs rose a crested helmet, bronze-clad shoulders; with little Asahel clinging to his hand, Joab came out on the roof, his scabbarded sword slapping against his thigh.

"As God lives!" Jesse growled. "Where did you get all that armor?"

Zeruiah's hands clenched. Joab who had left home a submissive boy looked his grandfather in the eye, impenitent, at ease . . . A man.

"I took it from a Philistine, sir. In the battle."

"So you had to get into the battle, did you? Well, what about David?"

"Why—" Joab stared at him. "Why, haven't you heard?"

4

The stupefied silence that followed his tale was broken at last by old Jesse's chuckle.

"Heh! I always thought that boy had something in him! . . . So he's going to marry a Princess, is he?" He frowned. "You'd think he might ask my permission, princess or no princess."

"He's going to write you a letter, sir," said Joab hastily. "He's been pretty busy. The King's taken quite a fancy to his harp playing."

"Hmph! Trying to flatter him, more likely. . . . Oh, David can go his way if he wants to—marry a Benjamite girl and live with princes. But it's a great mistake, to my notion. They're using him, taking advantage of his popularity. They need it. Saul's a failure and people are beginning to see it. Samuel is right—Israel was better off without a King."

"I don't think so, sir." The words came hard; it was the first time in his life that Joab had openly disputed his grandfather. But he went on: "Saul's doing some rather fine things, sir. He's organizing Israel; and Israel is three times as big as Judah and Caleb—all the South. More and more he's getting the tribes to work together, making a nation fit to live in the Promised Land."

He wanted to say more, to try to explain the vision that he was cloudily beginning to perceive; but his voice failed him before his grandfather's stuttering wrath. But before old Jesse could get out the words that would blast the impertinent dissenter, Zeruiah had interposed smoothly—

"Joab, did you see David kill the giant?"

"No, mother. I—I was asleep," he confessed in a rush of shame. "I'd meant to stand by, in case anything happened—but we never supposed Goliath would come out so early. David was the only man awake; and when he saw Goliath the spirit of the Lord came upon him— He told me all about it, afterward. He was awfully decent about my not waking up."

"Never mind," Abishai consoled him. "You'll have your chance, some day. . . . And did David really knock him out with a stone from his sling?"

"He really did. I saw the hole in Goliath's forehead myself."

"It all seems very strange," said Zeruiah.

"Now there you go!" her father fumed. "When once you get your mind set against somebody— Well, Joab, what are you going to do with this armor?"

"Use it, sir, I hope. The King has offered me a commission in the regulars—with your consent, of course." His shaking hands fumbled in his wallet. "Here's a letter, sir, in the King's own hand—"

But old Jesse tossed aside the roll of sheepskin, unopened.

"So you want to go chasing off to be a great man, too? Hmph! You haven't killed any giants."

"No, sir, but I've done a little drilling, this last week; I might—"

"Nonsense! Do you think there's no work to be done here at home, that you have to go tagging off after these Northerners? Now David's gone; and Abishai's getting married; and Asahel's only a child. Who do you think is going to manage the farm if you go running off after a career?"

"There's the overseer," said Joab, burning with the injustice of it. They had never let him manage anything. "Besides, sir, it seems to me the war is about the most important work there is. If we can deliver Israel—deliver Judah too—"

"Judah! The Philistines have never come any farther into Judah than the foothills."

"Because Saul has kept them busy; once they beat him they'll over-run all the hill country. You may not like the Northerners, sir, but they're fighting our battles for us all the same."

But Joab was beginning to lose heart. The truth of all this was obvious, in Gibeah; but down here, where no giants needed killing, where no one's vision carried beyond the hills around the town, he could see that it was less convincing. Nothing sounded important, in Bethlehem.

"But you let Eliab and the others join the army!" he protested.

"For one campaign. They're still free men of Judah; they haven't sworn allegiance to a King, as you'd have to do, if you served in the regulars."

"David has done that, sir." David's father chuckled dryly.

"That's different. You're not going to marry a King's daughter. . . . Now I've heard enough of this. Put that armor away. Your ancestors found work enough in Bethlehem to keep them busy, for two hundred years past; and you can find it too, if you care to look."

Joab stiffened, fiercely defiant; but before he could speak his mother had taken old Jesse's arm.

"Come, father, it's too cold for you out here. Let's go in. . . . Joab, you'd better go to your room and take off that armor; your brothers will want to ask you all sorts of questions. Later on, come and see me."

5

He had thought that his room, the room he had left two weeks ago to seek his fortune, would seem strange to him after this fantastic fort-night. But, depressingly, it was not strange at all. The low bed, the stools, the stand where the oil lamp flickered, even the cracks in the plaster wall—they were worse than familiar; they were foreordained, in-escapable. Through the window came the nocturnal murmur of the town; the oppression of Bethlehem weighed down on him—Bethlehem where nothing was more important than anything else; where nothing ever happened; where nothing would be allowed to happen.

But his brothers distracted him, hanging about him in awestruck admiration as he unbuckled his armor.

"Haven't quite got the feel of it yet," he admitted. "But look at that sword, Abishai! Steel!"

"And did you kill the Philistine that owned it?" little Asahel asked.

"Oh, that wasn't much. The fact is," Joab confessed, "he was run-ning away. I hit him over the back of the neck."

"Think of that!" Abishai muttered. "And David—I can't get over it! . . . What's Gibeah like, Joab?"

"Oh, it's not much of a town. Bigger than Bethlehem, of course."

"And do you live in the palace?" Joab grinned at that.

"Not yet . . . Anyway, it isn't a palace; Saul says he's never had time to build a palace. I live in the officers' quarters, across the parade ground."

"Pretty easy!" said Abishai enviously. From the window, Joab stared out into the blackness of the unlighted town.

"No, it's not easy. I live no better than I lived here, and I work harder learning to be a soldier than I ever worked at home. . . . But there's all the difference in the world. You're not hemmed in, up there. Anything is possible." He slumped suddenly. "That is, if he'd let me go back—"

"Oh, he'll let you go," said Abishai. "Mother can manage that. He didn't want to let me get married, but she brought him around."

"That's different. You're going to stay at home. . . . But I haven't congratulated you yet, have I? Well, you—you're in luck. Tirzah is all right."

Joab was afraid he had put less enthusiasm in that than he intended; but Tirzah's all-rightness was so obvious to Abishai that no more was required.

"Yes, it's great." He grinned awkwardly. "I'm lucky." And with that disposed of— "Joab, have you ever talked to the King?"

"Oh, yes. Two or three times. He's quite friendly, when he isn't in one of his fits of gloom. More friendly than the General. I think Abner's jealous of David. And no wonder."

"Joab, do you remember when we were all boys, playing soldier, and David used to say that when he was King of Judah you'd be his Commander-in-Chief? Remember that? He's not king of anything; but—"

"There will never be a King of Judah," said Joab thoughtfully. "If the South ever takes a King it will go in with the rest. With Saul."

"Talking unionism already?" Abishai snorted. "They've converted you quick."

"You get a different idea of these things," Joab explained, "when you're out in the world. Gibeah—it's only a country town; but they can see a little farther than the next hill. They think, and plan, and try to make things come true. Here in Bethlehem they laugh at any-body with ideas. They laughed at David for making songs. They laugh at Saul, for trying to make a nation. But Saul didn't make himself King—"

"Samuel made him King!" said Abishai. Samuel the prophet was a revered personage, to this devout old-fashioned household. He had once visited them, and conducted a sacrifice. It had been a notable occasion.

"Samuel anointed him," Joab agreed, "but the elders of Israel elected him because they needed a King to lead them against the Philistines. If Israel had stood by him he might have won the war before now. But they lost heart, they began to say that God had forsaken him— But now David has given them back their faith. Now, I believe we're going to win!"

As Abishai caught some of his enthusiasm Joab went on eagerly—

"Look here—why don't you come up to court too? David could get you a commission; and, if mother can get grandfather to let me go, he'd let you go too. The overseer can manage the farm, with Eliab to keep an eye on him. . . . Come on, Abishai! Come up with me, where they do things! We'd go to the wars together, and make our fortunes, and help make a nation—"

But the fire slowly faded from Abishai's face.

"Tirzah's people would never let me take her North," he muttered. "I doubt if she'd want to go anyway." That, thought Joab, was putting it mildly; if he knew Tirzah (and they had all grown up together) she was one to stay where she was, wherever that might be, and to like it. "No!" Abishai decided with a sigh. "You go if you can; but Bethlehem is good enough for me."

It wasn't! thought Joab fiercely. But it would be, after Abishai had lived a few years with Tirzah. . . . He seethed with rage and disgust, and an awful sense of loss; he wanted to tell his brother whom he loved that he was a fool to throw away this great chance for a girl with no imagination. But Abishai was in no mood for such enlightenment, just now.

"Well, I'm not going to stay around Bethlehem all my life!" Asahel declared. "Joab, if the war isn't over when I'm old enough to fight—"

Joab looked down at the twelve-year-old with a tolerant grin.

"I'll see that you get your chance," he promised. "And if I can't, David will. . . . I'd better be going on to see mother," he said uneasily. "She may have some news for me."

6

Zeruiah sat erect and inflexible, her hands clasped in her lap; the bed beside her was strewn with bits of her never-finished work, for she drove herself harder than she drove the maidservants; garments that needed mending, a broken distaff, a roll of household accounts. In the lamplight she was a graven image, her gray hair drawn back, tight and metallic, the deep lines running down to the corners of her mouth

like grooves in bronze. As she regarded him somberly, the boy who
had come to her, subdued to his habitual awed respect, sensed that for
the first time she was treating him as a man.

"Your grandfather will let you go," she said at last. Joab winked
back the tears.

"I don't know how to thank you, mother! I didn't dream you could
do it."

"It wasn't hard. . . . A good deal that you boys have always blamed
on your grandfather has been my doing; I suppose I've been the real
head of the family for years. He had the authority that I needed to
support my decisions, but the decisions were mine. . . . And I've made
a good many mistakes."

"Not this time!" said Joab. "I didn't dare hope you'd see things as
I see them—" His mother smiled.

"Oh, I don't. I haven't much confidence in this scheme of yours.
But you're a man now, Joab. You must go your own way. Make your
own mistakes."

"I'm sorry to leave home, mother." He really was; he was just dis-
covering that acceptance of one thing means rejection of another.
"But this is such a big thing—helping to make a nation, helping the
King, and David—"

"I didn't mean to give you any advice," said his mother. "I've probably given you far too much already. But I'll add just one bit more.
Whatever you do, wherever you go, be yourself—not just a hanger-on
of David."

"Mother, I don't think you've ever been fair to him!"

"You haven't thought I was fair to any of you. Perhaps I wasn't;
you had a strict old-fashioned upbringing. But I've tried to train you
as well as I could for life as I have found it. . . . Life isn't easy, Joab.
It's work. That's why I've never trusted David. Work is what he hates."

"But see what he's done, mother! God must be with him!"

"Yes. . . . That is the way you will find it, Joab. Some people don't
need to work; God is with them. But I'm afraid you and I are the
sort who must work for whatever we get, and perhaps more than we
get. . . . Work for yourself, not David. You've always idealized him.
He was a little older than you, a little stronger; yes, and a little more
clever. And he was my brother—not quite so much under my control.
So you always followed his lead, you and Abishai. Whether it was
stealing melons, or staying out late at night, or what not, he always
organized it and you boys always got the blame."

"He's different," said Joab stubbornly. "He's always had something
the rest of us lacked. . . . Besides, mother, I owe him everything! My

chance to be somebody, to make a name for myself, fighting for our people and our God!"

"If you can always be sure that you're fighting for our people and our God when you're fighting for David," said Zeruiah, "I shall be much surprised. . . . What is this Princess Merab like, whom he's to marry?"

"Well—" Joab sought for courtly adjectives. "She's a well-built girl. What I'd call wholesome looking. . . . Not like her sister!"

"The Princess Michal? Oh! Tell me about her."

"She's slim and keen and eager," said Joab, avoiding his mother's eyes. "Like a flame. And she has ideals—for herself, and the kingdom and our people. She's never satisfied with anything petty and half-hearted. Only the best."

"You seem to have come to know her pretty well, in a short time."

"Why, yes. We've talked a good deal. There isn't much ceremony at Saul's court; the princesses can receive anyone they choose. Not alone, of course; there's always a maid in sight—but not necessarily within earshot. So Michal and I are—friends, I suppose. . . . I never knew a girl like her!"

"Naturally," said Zeruiah, "a King's daughter would have wider interests than a girl in Bethlehem."

"It's not just that, mother. She understands things so!" He began to pace restlessly about. "She's made me see that this war against the Philistines is more, even, than a war for freedom. It's a war for an ideal—to make a nation out of Yahweh's chosen people; a nation fit to make the land he gave us such a kingdom as the world has never seen—a true Promised Land! Our people came into Canaan—and then they made mistakes, they fell into petty quarrels and miserable jealousies; they began to weaken, to lose faith, to give up. But now we can begin again, thanks to David! We can make a nation pleasing in the sight of God—" He paused, rather abashed by his mother's impenetrable eyes. "I don't express it very well," he admitted. "But you ought to hear her!"

"Evidently I should," said Zeruiah. "I was wondering where you'd got all this idealism. Usually you keep your feet on the ground. . . . She seems to be a rather earnest young woman, this Princess." He flushed.

"No, sometimes we laugh and joke together, like children— But she has all the rest too! She's not the sort of woman who'd get in the way of a man's work; she'd be an inspiration. She has ideals, and understanding; and something else. . . . I mean— Well, compare her with a girl like Tirzah. Tirzah's all right," he conceded generously. "She's pretty, and cheerful, and sensible; she'll make Abishai happy. Her home will always be pleasant and comfortable—perhaps too comfortable. But there's something she hasn't got and can't give. . . . I don't know just what to call it—"

"Ecstasy," his mother suggested. "No, Tirzah hasn't that. We don't go in much for ecstasy, in Bethlehem. Our family, especially, unless David gets it out of his songs. . . . But you can't trust ecstasy, Joab. . . . You weren't very old when your father died, but you must remember what a miserable life we led—nothing but quarrels and bitterness. Yet we began with ecstasy, he and I—yes, and ideals too." Her clenched hands relaxed in her lap; she smiled wearily. "I've done the best I could for you boys. I've taught you to work, and look ahead, and do what must be done. David never seemed to take it in very well, but you and Abishai have had a good education—as far as it goes. But I never prepared you for ecstasy. . . . And that was my great mistake. I might have known it would pounce on you some day. Abishai had the luck to fall in love with a girl of his own sort; but you—"

Joab looked at her, startled; then, in happy relief—

"Yes, I'm in love with Michal! I might as well admit it."

"You might as well," his mother agreed. "In fact you might as well blow a trumpet and proclaim it from the housetop."

"Of course," he said, "I haven't dared to tell her so, yet." He laughed nervously. "She's a King's daughter!"

"She knows it, son. Any woman could see it. . . . As for her being a King's daughter— Well!" said Zeruiah. "The King is a gentleman, of course, but his family is no better than yours. Still, he is a King; he'd hardly let his daughter go without a rich marriage present—more than your grandfather could afford. David doesn't need to give a marriage present; he has bought his wife with the head of Goliath. But you—" Joab nodded somberly.

"But," he said, "there are still some giants left, down in Gath."

It would be cruel, thought Zeruiah, to let him see that that was comic. . . . Then, as she looked at his face—as hard and implacable as her own—she knew that it was not comic at all. Whatever it might turn out to be, it was not that. . . . She rose, and embraced him with a sudden hungry intensity.

"I hope you get her, son! . . . Fight for her—and for our people and our God, and yourself! . . . But don't do David's work for him." He sighed.

"You don't understand, mother. No one can understand who wasn't there. David has made everything possible. . . . Everything!"

AMATEUR

The days are gone when graduates of Katonka University had to explain just what and where that institution was. A million-dollar stadium, a dozen costly fraternity houses, at least one player mentioned every year for somebody's All-American football team, a professor publicly discharged for advocating the birth control that other professors merely practise (if you want to know why they practise it, look at the salary list)—these bright and varied glories have put old Katonka on the map. But the fairest jewel in alma mater's crown is that loyal alumnus, United States Senator Chester Balestier.

In the Senate, Balestier is no commanding figure; when he rises to speak the Press Gallery empties, and Senators drift out to the cloak-rooms to tell stories till he has said his say. But the orations delivered to the empty desks go out to every one of his constituents (printing and postage free), and the State Committee praises them in boiler-plate editorials furnished to the country press. Of the hundreds of bills he has introduced, and log-rolled into the statute books, none lives in history as the Balestier Act; but every one lives in the memory of some grateful voter, who got what he wanted and won't forget who got it for him.

So the experts will tell you that Balestier is likely to reach the White House before he is through. No man in public life has more of that priceless quality that politicians call availability—the thing to which tired, bleary-eyed men, assembled in a smoke-filled room to pick a presidential candidate, turn gratefully as the last day of the convention begins to dawn. They don't ask, "What has he done?"; they ask, "What is there against him?" There is nothing against Balestier; he has no enemies, and never will have if he can help it. "One thing is sure," said an old newspaperman one night when a group at the National Press Club was discussing his presidential prospects. "If they resurrected George Washington to run against him, Balestier would carry every state in the union."

They are proud of him for all that at old Katonka; but they are grateful to him too. For he was the first man who put Katonka on the map. Before he ever went into politics he had fought his way into the semifinals of the national tennis championship; and before that, he was the first Katonka man ever mentioned for the All-American football team, in the old days when Walter Camp picked it, and no man dared to pick another. So Balestier can count on the wholehearted loyalty of every man who ever went to old Katonka, and of every woman but one.

But what Katonka owes him is little enough, beside what he owes Katonka. He'll tell you that himself. . . .

Back in the 'nineties Katonka was small, poor, and unknown; most of its students were an uncouth lot, but it had seldom had a less promising recruit than Chet Balestier. He came up from Roundstown, large and raw, immensely earnest and immensely shy. He was earnest because he was the son of a widow, who by thrift and industry had brought him up and saved a little money to start him in college; and he had come to Campusville resolved to work his way through, to study hard and make his mother proud of him, and to avoid such costly and time-consuming diversions as fraternities and football.

He avoided fraternities by unanimous consent. As for football, nobody in that end of the state had ever heard of Chet's exploits on the town team back home—least of all the eastern coach whom old Jarvis Cushing, Katonka's one rich alumnus, had hired to break a long tradition of athletic disaster. For the first fortnight nobody seemed to know that Chet Balestier was in college at all. And then one afternoon, as he was crossing the campus, Dan Hawley spoke to him.

All Dan Hawley wanted was Chet's vote for his candidate for the presidency of the Athletic Association. Dan never ran for a college office himself; he had too many enemies. Besides, he got more fun out of pulling the wires. He elected most of the class presidents and athletic managers, and in that small college he couldn't afford to overlook a single vote. But before he could talk politics to Chet Balestier he had to do a lot of listening.

For Dan Hawley was a senior, a campus celebrity, a Delta Rho. When he noticed the unknown and homesick freshman, Chet simply turned his soul upside down and emptied it, while Dan patiently strolled along with him, muttering an occasional "I see." The substance of what he saw was that college life cost more than Chet had expected, and he hadn't been able to find a job to pay part of his expenses. In the little college town, all jobs were already bespoken. So at the end of the first term he meant to leave Katonka and enter the state university, where jobs were more numerous and tuition was free.

"Some fellows down home tried to get me to go there," he told Dan Hawley. "Lots of Roundstown fellows go to State. But my mother wanted me to go to a church college——"

"Roundstown?" Hawley interrupted. And then— "Balestier! . . . Good Lord, are you the Balestier that played halfback for the Roundstown Bears? Nobody up here ever heard of that team, but I've seen you play; I come from down state too. Why aren't you out at football practise?"

"I won't have time for football. I promised my mother I wouldn't play."

"I see," said Dan, whistling softly. "But look here, Balestier—you said you wanted to work your way through college. Have you tried to get one of those student-watchman jobs?"

"I never heard of them," Chet confessed.

"They've just been started this year. Till this year all these college buildings, representing an investment of maybe a quarter of a million dollars, have had just one night watchman to protect them. Think of that, Balestier! Think of the fire risk! Some of the alumni got so worried about it that old Jarvis Cushing donated a fund to employ fifteen student watchmen. The job pays ten dollars a week——"

"Gosh!" Chet exploded. In those days you could live like a lord at Katonka on ten dollars a week. "Do you suppose I could get a job like that?"

"I can speak to Mr. Cushing about it," Dan promised briskly. "And as that's night work, you'd have your afternoons free for football."

"Oh, I couldn't play football, Hawley. I'll have to study hard——"

"That's all right. All this job would amount to is that you'd lie around somewhere in the college building from supper time till midnight. You could do all your studying then."

"But I promised my mother——"

"Now look, Balestier, you want to do what's best for your mother, don't you? If you could pay all your expenses here in college, think what a load you'd take off her shoulders."

"Oh, of course if I could get that job everything would be fine. But I won't have time for football if I keep up with my studies the way I ought."

"Well——" Dan Hawley shrugged. "Any man in college would be glad to have one of those jobs. I certainly couldn't recommend a man who didn't show the right kind of college spirit."

"Oh!" Chet's eyes widened. "I see. I don't get the job unless I play football. . . . I don't like that, Hawley. It isn't honest."

"Honest? . . . See here, freshman, we aren't hiring anybody to play football. Don't you get anything like that into your head. We only feel that protecting the college buildings is a privilege that shouldn't be given to a man who hasn't proved his loyalty to old Katonka."

Dan paused. Chet's face was working in agonized indecision.

"Tell you what," said Dan. "You think it over, and I'll speak to Mr. Cushing tonight. For all I know, all these jobs are filled."

"Oh, gosh!" Chet groaned. "I hope not. . . . If it would help when you speak to Mr. Cushing, I've got a letter of recommendation from my pastor——"

"I'll tell him that," Dan promised. "It certainly would help."

Jarvis Cushing had been born in Campusville, and had gone forth from Campusville; and had come back, after selling his factories to the trust for two million dollars, to devote his declining years to the bringing up of his motherless daughter, and the putting of old Katonka on the map. Dan Hawley was his chief lieutenant in the student body; old Jarvis liked Dan's cool clearheadedness. If Nesta Cushing were only old enough to marry—— But Nesta was twelve, and a placid coed named Miriam Fuller was wearing Dan's fraternity pin. At that age they don't know the kind of woman they're going to need, old Jarvis was reflecting while Dan told him about Chet Balestier.

"Huh!" said Cushing at last. "I don't mind hiring players to come to college, but I'm damned if I like to hire a man to come out for the team when he's here already."

"He's worth it," Dan promised. "He'll just about double the power of that backfield."

"Don't like all these scruples of his, either. He acts as if he was doing us a favor."

"He's a good kid, Mr. Cushing—just green." Already Dan felt the beginnings of a queer affection—the half-contemptuous, half-envious affection of the clever little man for the slow-witted big man—that was to shape and color all his life. "I think he'll listen to reason, after he's thought it over."

So old Jarvis nodded reluctantly, and next morning Dan told Chet that one more night watchman was to be employed.

"And you could get the job," he added, "if you showed your loyalty to old Katonka. . . . But of course," he sighed, "if you promised your mother——"

Thus began the rise of Chester Balestier.

II

The rise of Katonka University began the next Saturday, when he crashed through the line of an ancient rival for the winning touchdown while the stands roared a rhythmic "Rah! Rah! Balestier!" That was music he had never heard before, and never forgot afterward. And it worked no less powerfully on his mother when he brought her up to Campusville to see the state university game, and let Dan Hawley explain to her that a promise made in ignorance of the circumstances couldn't be called a promise.

Dan told her about college loyalty, but it wasn't Dan that persuaded her. It was Jarvis Cushing, the wealthy Mr. Jarvis Cushing, who sat beside her in the grandstand and howled himself hoarse when Chet beat the state university almost singlehanded. And on Mrs. Balestier's other side little Nesta Cushing was jumping up and down and screaming, "Go on, Chet Balestier!" . . . Chet's mother knew the child would inherit millions; by the time the boy was old enough to think of marrying——

Lost in golden visions, Mrs. Balestier was undisturbed by the news that her son had pledged to that expensive fraternity, Delta Rho.

Three years later Dan Hawley had graduated from law school and married his Miriam, Nesta Cushing had gone East to school, and old Katonka had doubled in size and wealth. Balestier, All-Western half-back, who had got his alma mater's name into the New York papers, was the most famous college student in six states, and every schoolboy knew that he was working his way through. In other colleges stout linesmen and fleet backs had been exposed as ringers and disqualified just before crucial games, thanks to quiet investigations about which Dan Hawley knew more than he ever told; but no one had ever impugned the integrity of old Katonka's student watchmen.

Their jobs paid twenty dollars a week now, but as Katonka prospered college life had grown more costly; Chet Balestier was never quite able to make both ends meet without help from his mother. When she died, at the end of his junior year, she left barely enough money to bury her.

"But don't worry about that," said old Jarvis Cushing when Chet came back from the funeral. "If you need more money than your salary you can have it. I'll take your note, just for the looks of the thing."

"I don't like to be in debt," said Chet, frowning. "I've always worked my way." And then, drawing a long breath— "Anyway, Mr. Cushing, I've decided to go East for my senior year."

"East?" Cushing exploded. "Where?" Chet named an old and famous university; suppose we call it Colonial. Old Jarvis glowered at him. "But you're captain of the team!" he cried.

"Yes, but—I'll never make the All-American out here. Camp never gives more than one place to the colleges west of Carlisle, Pennsylvania, and I'm afraid Heston's going to get it. But at Colonial——"

"You'd probably make it," Cushing conceded. "But what's our

team going to do without you? Haven't you got any loyalty?"

"I think I've done a good deal for old Katonka," said Chet with some hauteur.

Jarvis Cushing snorted.

"You can't play for Colonial till a year from next fall. Transfer students have to wait. How are you going to support yourself for two years? Borrow money?"

"I can earn my way. Some of their alumni talked to me about it last winter. I'm to room with a man—a very fine fellow—who has the advertising concession for the football programs. It's worth six or eight thousand a year, but it's too big a job for him to handle alone. He wants me to help him out. We'll split fifty-fifty."

Jarvis Cushing laughed morosely.

"Those Easterners aren't pikers," he admitted. "When they want something they're willing to pay for it. . . . Well, damn you, if you're up at auction——"

"Auction!" Chet sprang toward him, his· fists clenched. Then— "I can't strike an old man," he said coldly, and walked out.

It was Dan Hawley, of course, who brought them together again.

"Mr. Cushing wants to apologize," he told Chet next day. (There was nothing Jarvis Cushing wanted less, but Dan had made him see that he had to apologize.) "He understands the situation and he wants you to stay here. He practically owns the Central Securities Company up in the city, and he'll give you a job as bond salesman this summer."

"I never sold bonds," Chet protested. "I don't believe I could." (He was young, when those craven words fell from his lips.)

"Boy, you can't help it. They'll give you all the setups—sure sales, sure commissions. Any man that's going to buy bonds at all will jump at the chance to buy them from the best-known football player west of Ann Arbor. You can't lose."

"I'd lose my chance for the All-American. I'd make it at Colonial."

"No, you wouldn't," said Dan smoothly. "Colonial has some rivals who'd like to know how Colonial teams are recruited. If you go there I'll tell them, and you'll never dare put on a football suit."

Chet glared at him; but he knew that when Dan had thought a thing out there was nothing you could do about it.

"Those Colonial fellows will be pretty sore," he offered in a last despairing endeavor. "If they find out that I'm getting a lot of money for staying at Katonka——"

"You're not, my boy, you're not. You're earning an honest living as a bond salesman. Who could object to that?"

"I suppose it looks all right," Chet conceded.

"Of course it does. And if it looks all right it is all right. . . . And you'll make more than money by staying here. Right now you're the hero of this state. I've played around in politics enough to learn that you can cash in on that, when the time comes. Some day we'll send you to Congress—the Sportsmen's Candidate."

So Chet moved from Roundstown to the flourishing city of Centropolis, the state capital; and that summer he made four thousand dollars as commission on his sales of bonds.

Also, that summer, he played in the state tennis tournament.

III

Every country town, in those days when golf was still a fad of effete Easterners, and the movie, the automobile, and the radio were yet to come, had some sport by which the inhabitants beguiled their leisure time; in which such inhabitants as had nothing but leisure time were apt to attain an unholy proficiency. Usually it was baseball, sometimes it was horseshoe pitching; but in Chet's home town, by some accident, it was tennis. He was the champion of Roundstown; at college he could beat anybody else in love sets. But no Western college had tennis teams in those days, so his tennis was practically wasted; he got nothing out of it but recreation. Till that state tournament.

The Centropolis club managed to attract that year an Easterner who ranked in the First Ten—the most important player who had ever appeared on those courts. He loafed through to the final round, and there Chet Balestier beat him. Thanks to that, Chet was invited to play in three other Middle-Western tournaments before the summer was over. Having done so well in the bond business, he decided he could afford what it would cost; and discovered with delighted amazement that it cost him practically nothing. Quite the contrary, in fact.

He lived for tennis, and on tennis, for the next three summers.

In the winter he still sold bonds, but his sales fell off after he graduated from college and no longer appeared in football headlines. Presently he was recalled to a desk job with the securities company, decorative but far from profitable. He bore it for a time in silent fortitude, and then spoke to Dan Hawley; and Dan spoke to Jarvis Cushing.

"Well, what about it?" Cushing grunted. "He's no salesman. Doesn't he expect ever to work for his keep?"

"He earns his keep," Dan observed. "He's the best advertisement this state ever had, so far as sports go—and they're going farther every year. We can afford to take care of him."

"Oh, all right, all right. But I don't see why I always have to give the party."

"We might let you off this time," said Dan thoughtfully. "There's that real-estate development of Findlay's on the North Side. The new tennis club will boost values out that way. I think Findlay might carry Chet for a block of lots, if you put it up to him in the right way."

"I'll do it," old Jarvis sighed. "But I begin to see the difference between a professional and an amateur. The professional comes cheap." Then, more cheerfully—"How's that boy of yours, Danny?" Dan Hawley grinned widely.

"Finest boy in the world, Mr. Cushing. We hope for another in May."

"More power to you," said old Jarvis, silently wishing that Dan Hawley's sons were his grandsons.

Nesta, then, had just finished her freshman year at Katonka. That summer Jarvis Cushing died suddenly. Even in what he called retirement he had taken such good care of his money that he could leave a million to old Katonka and a quarter of a million to Dan Hawley, and still have two or three million left for Nesta.

Chet Balestier hadn't seen her for years; but at her father's funeral he couldn't keep his eyes off her. The child had grown up—a golden blonde, terrifically effective in black, with a slim tense figure that suggested a throttled eagerness. Chet decided that he had been neglecting old Katonka since he graduated; he'd run down to Campusville this fall and see some football games.

On the night after Katonka beat the state university there was a dinner dance at the Theta house. Nesta hadn't danced since her father's death, but she made an exception for Chet Balestier. He had six dances with her in a row; then they strolled out into the crisp smoky autumn night.

"It's a great team," she sighed. "But there's nobody on it like you, Chet. I remember the first game you played in, seven years ago. You tumbled Sir Launcelot off his pedestal that day, and I never put him back."

He looked into her eyes—they were passing under a street lamp— and his heart jumped as he saw that she wasn't joking. Adolescent hero worship—but she was nineteen now; it might not last much longer. . . . They passed into the shadow, and Chet kissed her, for no other reason than that he wanted to kiss her and she wanted him to. He remembered that motivation later, with some pride; for instant afterthought had reminded him that he couldn't live forever on the profit of those North Side lots, and that Nesta Cushing had two or three million dollars.

The next week-end he went down to Campusville, not to see a football game but to see Nesta. He stayed, of course, at the Delta Rho house; it was a little crowded this year, and Campusville had an excellent new hotel. But the brothers were proud to entertain their most distinguished alumnus, and Chet Balestier, who had never paid a hotel bill in his life, didn't see why he should begin now. In the back of his mind, unacknowledged, was a suspicion that if he had come courting Nesta while her father lived old Jarvis would have kicked him out. But her father was dead; and nobody kicked him out of the Theta house, though he and Nesta sat two hours in the parlor with the lights turned low after everybody else had obeyed the house rules and gone to bed.

In February she left college, and they were married. While they were on the honeymoon the ruling powers of the Central Securities Company held conference.

"You can't keep the husband of the heaviest stockholder in a job that pays fifty dollars a week," the president sighed. "Yet it's more than he's worth."

"His athletic following still counts for something," the chairman of the board objected. "If we could make him an extra vice-president with no duties in particular——"

"I think you'd better," said Dan Hawley smoothly. (Dan was general counsel for the company now.) "He'll be too busy to work at his job, anyway, after I've put him into politics. Make him a vice-president; and if you can't figure out how to make the Cushing interest pay his salary, come around to me and I'll show you."

So Chet came back from his bridal journey to find himself a prominent financier. He enjoyed the glamour of that position so much that he was uninterested when Dan Hawley began to talk politics.

"Nobody'd ever vote for a minion of the money power," Chet protested. But Dan shook his head.

"You're wrong, boy. This muckraking game has been overdone and people are about ready for a change. Besides, you're not a minion of the money power. You're a self-made young man who turns his back on the pursuit of wealth to devote himself to public service. I'm going to run you for Congress this fall. Old Laidlaw's held the seat for twenty years and everybody's tired of him. They'll jump at a chance to vote for a young man—especially a young man who almost made the All-American, and went to Newport and beat tennis players from New York and Philadelphia, to the greater glory of Centropolis."

Chet was beginning to think better of his reluctance, but he insisted that he must talk it over with his wife. Nesta, to his astonishment, was enthusiastic; so Chet accepted the nomination, delivered with commanding presence the speeches that Dan Hawley wrote for him, and was not in the least surprised when in November Centropolis gave a huge majority to Chester Balestier, the Sportsmen's Candidate.

IV

A new man can't expect to make much of a dent in the House of Representatives, and Chet's first term was made no easier by his wife. She seemed to think he could reform the world overnight. Even when Dan Hawley explained to her how necessary it was to play along with the organization, she acted as if what was true for ordinary men didn't apply to Chet. But after the first year or two Nesta stopped expecting so much, or at least stopped talking about it. And if Congressman Balestier was a figure of no great consequence in the House, he bulked considerably larger when he went to New York to speak at dinners of the leaders of amateur sport.

"You're doing fine," said Dan Hawley. "Every time they give you a cheer in New York the echo amplifies it back home. One term as governor, and then the Senate."

"Governor?" Chet gasped. "I couldn't get the nomination."

So far as the record goes, it was the last time he ever doubted his ability to get anything.

"Leave that to me," said Dan Hawley.

"I don't know what I'd ever do without you," Chet confessed humbly.

And that, too, so far as is recorded, he never said again.

"Well, old-timer," said Dan Hawley, "I couldn't have done much without you. I've got some ideas about the way things ought to be done, but so many people hate me that I couldn't be elected dog-catcher. And since you and I happen to think so much alike about affairs of state——"

He said it solemnly; and Chet Balestier was never one to probe for grins that didn't appear on the surface.

Dan got him the nomination, and the mistakes of his opponent got him the governorship. (Chet made no mistakes because he took no positions and did nothing.) If some few people suspected that Governor Balestier was the front and Dan Hawley the works, they never said so. His two-year term was uneventful, except for the trolley strike in Centropolis that for three days kept the city in an uproar. "Order must be restored!" the Governor proclaimed in ringing tones, and slipped away to talk to Dan Hawley.

"Call out the militia? You're crazy!" Dan snapped. "Suppose they do burn a few streetcars and smash a few windows. What you want to do——"

The next day the leaders of the union and the heads of the trolley company were called to the Governor's office. Chet Balestier, ex-All-Western halfback, who could have licked any two of them in a rough-and-tumble, locked the door and told them they would stay there till the strike was settled. Within two hours the strikers had got the wage increase they demanded; within two months the trolley company lifted the fare from five cents to eight, with the approval of Governor Balestier's Public Service Commission. This covered the wage increase and a little more, but by that time Centropolis was rolling with easy money brought in by war orders, and people who would have felt the increase in trolley fares a year ago never noticed it now.

That fall the solid labor vote and the solid (though silent) banking influence combined to send Governor Balestier to the Senate.

Back in Washington, with the more dignified position and longer tenure of a senator, Chet breathed a great sigh of relief. He and Nesta both liked the town, and his service in the lower House had enabled them to make friends—the right sort of friends. Nesta's fortune had trebled in war industries; she bought a big house on Meridian Hill, and presently people who had ignored her husband were beginning to pay attention to him in the hope of being invited to her dinners.

A new senator can break into the papers easily enough, but breaking into the inner circle is another matter. Chet, whose resonant voice had broadcast Dan Hawley's ideas to a thousand political rallies, had the wisdom to realize that deeds, not words, were what counted now. He voted with the party on partisan issues; non-partisan issues had a happy way of coming to a vote when he was out of town making an after-dinner speech. He was in New York, addressing a thousand diners on the topic, "Amateur Sport Will Win the War," when the Eighteenth Amendment passed the Senate; he was sick in bed (by Dan Hawley's advice) when the Volstead Act was passed; but he cast his vote (also by Dan's advice) to repass it over Wilson's veto, after a ringing speech that proclaimed his devotion to moral principles. His wife, fortunately, was able to buy up a hundred thousand dollars' worth of wines and liqueurs before the act went into force.

They had settled down, Chet used to reflect comfortably, to the placidity of a happy marriage; she never bothered him any more about visionary reforms. She didn't go with him on his after-dinner speaking trips, as she had done in the first year of their marriage; but she never complained of his frequent absences. The one flaw in their happiness was that they had no children.

Dan Hawley and his Miriam by this time had four. Dan adored them and so did Miriam, but the third side of the triangle was miss-

ing; Dan and Miriam no longer adored each other. For the children's
sake they never formally separated; but Dan spent more and more
time in Washington, where he had a good deal of law business by
now. The failure of his marriage had soured him, but when he was
with Chet and Nesta he recovered his old quizzical good humor.
There were other people in Washington who seemed able to cheer
him up—women he didn't introduce to Nesta when she happened to
meet him in their company.

"He ought to have more sense!" Chet fumed when his wife told him
of one of these chance encounters. "It's outrageous!"

"Is it?" said Nesta moodily. "Pathetic, if you like; he can't get
much real companionship from women like that. Miriam's led him a
rotten life; he needs sympathy and understanding. . . . Like the rest
of us."

"Maybe he does, but first thing you know one of these gold diggers
will shake him down——" Nesta cut him off with a laugh.

"Oh, so that's what's worrying you! Cheer up. I don't think any
gold digger will ever get the best of Dan Hawley."

None the less Senator Balestier, that loyal if frequently nonresident
husband, felt his moral sense affronted by Dan's irregularities. But he
grew more broad-minded after he became acquainted with Madame
Madura.

v

He met her first at one of Nesta's dinners. Esteban Madura had
come to Washington to smooth the way for a loan, which his Latin-
American fatherland had failed to get, so far, because two oil companies were deadlocked over the concessions that went with it. Two
days after the dinner Inez Madura invited Senator Balestier of the
Foreign Relations Committee to tea, alone. And after that——

They were prudent—they had to be; but even so they might not
have escaped detection if Nesta, while their affair was at its height, had
not been making a long visit back home in Centropolis; and if Esteban
Madura had not been preoccupied by affairs of state. The oil company that seemed likely to lose the concession had financed a revolution which turned Madura's party out; and he and his wife were
marooned in Washington. Virtually penniless, Inez confessed at last
with shuddering sobs. Naturally Chet insisted on her accepting a loan
to tide them over; and then another, and another. . . .

Six months later, while Nesta was visiting in Chicago, Chet made a
hasty trip back to Centropolis to see Dan Hawley.

"Dan, I've got to have money. A hundred thousand. Quick."

"Well," said Dan rather coldly, "you've got that much, haven't you?"

"No. I never had that much. Nesta always pays the household expenses. And I had some bad luck in the market last year that pretty nearly cleaned me out."

"Senators shouldn't have bad luck in the market," said Dan. "It shows culpable negligence. . . . Well, if you haven't got the money, Nesta would lend it to you."

"Nesta?" Chet groaned. "Oh my God! . . . Dan, it's for Inez Madura. She and her husband have been bleeding me for months—both of them, working together. If you knew how near I've come to killing that woman——"

"Senators can't afford to be indicted for murder."

"Nor sued for alienation either. Madura will ruin me if I don't come through. But if I do they'll get out—go to Paris. You've got to get me the money."

Dan Hawley's eyes were chill as Chet had never seen them.

"I haven't got it, Chet. And this time I can't raise it."

"Why not?" Chet demanded in a frenzy.

"For—well, call them personal reasons. This time, boy, you've got to find your own exit."

Spurred by extremest need, Chet found it. His old friend Harry Summers, the oil man, whose group was just now promoting a counter-revolution in Madura's fatherland, carried Chet in a venture on the stock market without even asking for his note; in due time he gave Chet the profit—thousand-dollar bills passed from coat pocket to coat pocket in Summers's suite at the Willard—and Chet breathed easily again. His vote made a majority of one in the Foreign Relations Committee for the treaty that gave Summers's group the oil concessions.

Nesta had come home; and Chet, who for months had been nervous, constrained, ashamed in his relations with her, felt that their old harmony was coming back. But one night, when she returned from a dinner which public business had prevented him from attending, she came to his study, cold and purposeful.

"Chet, what's this deal you were in with Harry Summers?"

"How did you know?" he asked, his face turning gray.

"He told me this evening. He'd had too much champagne, and he said he'd supposed of course I knew about it. Which means, I suppose, that he wanted to be sure I did know, with that treaty coming to a vote tomorrow. He swore he'd told nobody else, and he never will; I'm sure of that. He knows you never can tell what a jury may do. . . . But—— Oh, Chet, why didn't you come to me for the money?"

Senator Balestier swallowed, tried to speak. "I don't care what it was for," she told him desperately. "I wouldn't have asked you what it was for——"

By now he had collected himself.

"What it was for? Just an ordinary speculation, my dear. I wouldn't have wanted to make it with your money."

"So you made it with Harry Summers's money. And that treaty——"

"I was going to vote for that treaty anyway. . . . My God, Nesta, you're not implying there's anything wrong about this, are you?"

"No, darling, of course not. But suppose it got into the papers."

"How can it? Nobody knows but us three. Besides," said Senator Balestier comfortably, "the old muckraking days are over. The papers have a new attitude, a healthier attitude, toward the affairs of government. They know the difference between public business and private business."

"So they do," his wife agreed. "And isn't it lucky?"

"Look here, there's nothing wrong about this!" he stormed. "A man can't give his whole life to public service, and still have money enough to live on the scale his position requires. If his friends want to help him—why, it's no more than your father did for me in college. He didn't pay me to come to college and play football; he only made it possible for me to do what I wanted to do, and show my loyalty to old Katonka. . . . Now don't you worry about this. Nobody's going to find out; and even if they did, there's nothing they could take hold of. Everybody knows I'm for the treaty and everybody knows I and Harry Summers are old friends. So long as nobody talks about this stock market deal, it looks all right. And as Dan's so fond of saying, if it looks all right it is all right."

"I suppose so," said Nesta. Then, after a long silence—"By the way, I've decided to take that round-the-world cruise that all those Centropolis people are going on—the Bogarduses and Mrs. Weeks, and Dan Hawley."

VI

Nesta was the only woman Chet had ever really loved; he knew that from the way, the countless ways, he missed her. Other women, he supposed, might have consoled some aspects of his loneliness; women he passed on the street, saw in hotel lobbies, met at dinners, in New York or Washington; women his eyes followed for a moment, speculative. . . . But he was through with all that; never again in his life would he get himself mixed up with another woman. It wasn't right; it wasn't patriotic, for a statesman ought to set an example in secret as well as in public. And it would be disloyal to Nesta whom he loved, who was coming back to him. . . .

This restoration of his moral balance was immensely soothing; more soothing yet was the fact that he would go into the National Convention as the favorite son of his state. This time the President was sure to be renominated, and Senator Balestier could hope for no more than a complimentary vote on the first ballot. But four years from now, with the President shelved, a little luck might bring the nomination to Chet Balestier. . . . And all this while Dan Hawley was cruising around the world! They'd all realize, now, that he could do without Dan Hawley.

He went to New York to meet Nesta at the end of the cruise. It happened that he was to speak there that night, at a dinner of the Association of University Presidents, on "Amateur Sport, the Backbone of Character." It would be one more stone built into the pyramid of his nation-wide reputation; yet when he met Nesta on the pier he had wild dreams of telephoning the chairman of the dinner committee and telling him that he was too ill to speak. It seemed stupidly wasteful to spend even a few hours away from Nesta.

She had always seemed younger than her years, thanks to the slenderness of the sterile woman; but now with a new sparkle in her eyes, the flush of health and zest and vigor under tropic tan, she looked ten years younger than when she went away. Senator Balestier was as nervous, as awestricken, as humbly eager as a lovesick schoolboy; he had no time for more than a nod and a "see-you-later" for Dan Hawley. . . . In their hotel suite, freed at last from the assiduities of servants, he turned hungrily to his wife.

"No," she said with level indifference. "I don't want you to make love to me."

"Tired?" he asked. But he felt a premonitory shudder.

"Not in the least. I'm in love with another man."

The next three minutes were a nightmare. He flung questions at her in hysterical horror; and she answered him, completely candid. Even the things she told him hurt less than her listless unconcern at what he felt about them. But the facts were bad enough. She had been in love with this man for almost a year; she had been his mistress since the second day of the round-the-world cruise. . . . And the man was Dan Hawley. For a moment Chet was dumb with sheer astonishment.

"I know it doesn't seem reasonable," she admitted. "I've known him since I was ten years old and I didn't fall in love with him till I was nearly forty. But I don't intend to give him up now."

"You mean you want me to divorce you so that you can marry him? I certainly won't!"

"No, darling, we're putting no such strain on your generosity. Dan's crazy about his children; if Miriam divorced him she'd keep them and wouldn't let him see them any more than she could help. So that's out. . . . But she wouldn't divorce him unless we drove her to it; Dan's always been very generous with her. She wouldn't live so well on alimony."

"But—what do you mean to do, then?" he stammered. She looked at him with the steady impenetrable eyes of old Jarvis Cushing.

"We're going on," she said. "As we are. . . . Don't worry. We'll be circumspect."

Then he broke down; and it measured the change that Nesta's six months' absence, and the acid memory of Inez Madura, had worked in him that at first he said nothing but that he loved her, he needed her, he couldn't live without her——

Bored, she interrupted him at last.

"I suppose I ought to be sorry for you, Chet. You're making rather a show of yourself, but I don't blame you; I know how you feel. You see, I felt the same thing for years. About you."

"About me?" he repeated. She blazed in sudden bitterness.

"Yes, you! I was wild about you when we were married—and for years afterward. I was only nineteen, and I'd been crazy about you ever since I was twelve. You could have made anything out of me. . . . But you didn't care enough to try."

"Nesta, I never looked at another woman——"

"Possibly not, then. You were too busy looking in the mirror. . . . As for me—well, you took me when you wanted me, and laughed at my silly notions about what my hero could do, and left me to grow up by myself. Which I did. It takes time to kill the sort of adoration I felt for you, but you succeeded, my dear. You succeeded."

"Well, suppose I did——" He blustered, to hide a queasy hollow ache. "Do you mean to sit there and tell me that you intend to go right on with this affair? What do you think I'll be doing?"

"Not a thing," she said. "Any more than I did when you were having your affair with Madame Madura." His jaw dropped.

"Did Dan tell you about that? The dirty——"

"No!" she said scornfully. "He didn't need to tell me. Everybody in Washington knew about it; and most of them told me—as if I hadn't seen it for myself. You won't have to stand what I stood, at any rate. Dan and I will be discreet."

"Discreet?" he roared. "Do you think I'm going to let my wife go on having an affair with another man, under my roof?"

"My roof," she corrected amiably. "I bought it, I furnished it, I pay the taxes and the grocer's bills. And I choose to let you go on living under my roof, as you've lived for twenty years—so long as you don't annoy me. But if you do, out you go. . . . Besides, darling," she reminded him, "this is a moral nation. A prominent statesman can't afford to be even the plaintiff in a divorce suit so scandalous as this one might be. And of course if you make any trouble, I'd file a countersuit against you, naming Madame Madura. That would finish you."

"Finish me?" Chet Balestier was becoming himself again. "But, good God! This will finish me anyway. . . . And I might have been President!" he moaned.

"I told you that Dan and I would be careful. . . . And I promise you this—when you start your campaign for delegates to the National Convention next time I'll take a vacation from Dan; and if you're nominated for the presidency I'll give him up. Permanently."

"You would?" he cried with resurgent hope. "Then you still love me?" She looked at him blankly. "If you'd do that for me——" he explained. She laughed.

"For you? Don't be absurd; I'd do it for myself. I'd rather be the President's wife than Dan Hawley's mistress."

Now, for the first time, he hated her. . . . Also, for the first time, he felt that his mind met hers in complete understanding.

"Well, how the devil do you think either of us is going to get to the White House if you carry on an affair? Especially an affair with the man who'll be chairman of the National Committee if I'm nominated for President? Somebody's sure to find out—at least to suspect——"

"But nobody's going to tell, darling. At least—and this is what counts—nobody's going to print it, unless you're foolish enough to spread it on the record. As you told me once, the newspapers know the difference, now, between private business and public business."

"But if everybody knows it——" he protested.

"So long as they don't print it, my dear, it's going to look all right. And as you told me once, if it looks all right it is all right."

"It was Dan who said that first," he told her harshly.

"I don't doubt it. Dan said all your famous sayings first. . . . Oh, I know he's crooked. But he never fools himself, and he never tries to fool me. If you'd been like that—— But that's all over. There was a time when I couldn't have stood a man who was candid about his crookedness; but I've grown up. . . . Well? Are you going to be sensible about it?"

"No!" he roared. "I know enough to send Dan Hawley to jail!"

"No doubt," she assented. "No doubt, also, he knows a few things about you, though he's never told them to me. Dan has his queer

points of honor. But he'd tell the world if you forced him to; and I
could add a few little contributions—that Summers affair, for instance.
If you don't take your medicine, Chet, you're through with politics."

"I don't care if I am! I'll——"

"You don't care?" she broke in scornfully. "You'd better care! What
would you do if you dropped out of politics? You never supported
yourself for a day of your life! You lived on your mother, on football,
on tennis; and for the last twenty years you've lived on me. If you
lost your seat in the Senate you couldn't earn your keep—and your
friends wouldn't carry you in stock deals, either. No, darling, you're
an amateur. You can't afford to turn professional."

"Nesta—— For God's sake—— Oh, we've both made a mess of things;
but if you'll drop Dan we can start again——"

"Rather late, my dear. . . . I used to wish we could start again—when
we'd been married four or five years, and I began to see where we were
heading. I tried to talk to you about it; but you were too busy to
listen, or else you laughed at me and called me a crazy child. . . . I may
be crazy now, but I'm not a child. I'm forty years old, and I know what
I want, and I mean to get it. It's too late to start again. We're what
we are and we might as well take what we can." She softened a little.
"Come, it's time for you to get ready for your dinner. And brace up!
You ought to look your best, tonight."

Furiously he stamped out, slammed the door behind him. But in
the next room he stood still, irresolute— till he heard a tiny click on
the bedside telephone. It was on the same wire as hers; beyond the
door, her muffled voice murmured. . . . He strode to the telephone, took
off the receiver.

"Biltmore?" she was saying. "I want to speak to Mr. Daniel
Hawley."

He heard Dan's "Hello"; then Nesta's voice, muted to a sensuous
tenderness that her husband hadn't heard in years.

"Hello, dearest. Coming up to dinner with me? . . . Yes, of course.
. . . Chet?" She laughed faintly. "Chet's dining out, I'm afraid, with
the Association of University Presidents. . . . Yes, he's the speaker of
the evening. He'll probably be out quite late."

Senator Balestier dropped the receiver; raging, he strode to the door.
She had put aside the telephone; she lay on a chaise longue, her bare
arms clasped behind her head, her eyes remote, dreamy; her lips half
parted in a smile.

"Nesta!" he roared. "You—— You——"

"So you listened in?" she said. "I wondered if you would. . . . Well?"

"You're going to see him here? Here?"

"We don't dare risk going out together. And we've got to be circumspect—for your sake, darling. After this I'd advise you not to listen in, if you want to preserve your peace of mind." He was scarlet with fury, his fists were clenched. "You ought to begin dressing for dinner," she told him placidly. "And for Heaven's sake pull yourself together. Try to look like the next President of the United States."

He thought he might have killed her, but for that timely reminder.

VII

At the high table, on the toastmaster's right hand, Senator Balestier sat stately, statesmanlike and serene. But behind that unfurrowed brow he was picturing, foreseeing——

No matter how discreet she and Dan might be, people would find out. Their companions on the round-the-world cruise must know, or at least suspect, already; and some of those people came from Centropolis. Presently all their friends would know; ultimately—for Washington was a small town where gossip traveled—every newspaperman would know. They would know that the man who had made Chet Balestier had taken his wife, was still taking her when he chose, making a fool of Chet Balestier under his own roof. They would know and they would snicker——

Chet hardly heard the piled-up eulogies showered on him by the toastmaster who was introducing him; all he could hear was that vast, politely muffled snicker that would presently run all over Washington. . . . But snickers didn't kill; the day was past when a statesman could be laughed out of public life. Everybody might snicker, but nothing would get into the papers; everyone might know, but it need never be publicly acknowledged—unless Chet Balestier made a fool of himself.

No use doing that. A politician couldn't afford to cherish personal grudges. He'd need Dan Hawley when it came to getting pledged delegations to the National Convention, need him still more when it came to persuading delegations pledged to other men to change their vote on the decisive ballot. And he could count on Dan; Dan's final ambition was to make a President. . . . And yet—— Nesta—— At this very moment——

The toastmaster finished; Senator Balestier rose. The assembled university presidents were stirred by the unmistakable sincerity in his resonant voice:

"Mr. Toastmaster, and gentlemen! All that I am tonight I owe to my alma mater."

COUNT NO MAN HAPPY

You might have recognized the house, if you study the pictorial sections of the Sunday papers, or the magazine pages devoted to People in the Public Eye—a big stone house on Prospect Boulevard, the best residence street in Ridgemont. You might have recognized the sunny breakfast room, and you would surely have recognized the man who was just finishing his solitary breakfast—Dr. Victor Compton, whose *Ethics of Tomorrow* had been on the bookstore counters for a year and was still selling a thousand copies a day; who was hailed by liberals as the the apostle of a new and sane morality, and damned every Sunday from a hundred pulpits as Satan incarnate, the corrupter of modern youth.

He didn't look like Satan; tall and lithe and bronzed, with crisp iron-gray hair and a tolerant twinkle in his gray eyes, he looked like a man of the world, who had yet kept himself unspotted from it—the sort of man to whom you could tell your troubles (as his students at the University of Ridgemont had been doing for twenty years). Also, he looked like what is called a man's man. There were women who wished that he were more of a woman's man, that his vast knowledge of woman in the abstract would translate itself into some interest in women in the concrete. But everybody knew that he had never been interested in any woman but his wife.

So when he resigned from the university to write his book about the breakdown of the old authoritarian moral code, and the need of a substitute for Christian ethics, people who knew him could not accuse him of trying to find excuses for his own misconduct. The flawless felicity of his home life had enabled the author of *Ethics of Tomorrow* to retain his friends and his club memberships, in a city where unorthodoxy was the cardinal sin. The clergy might denounce him as a preacher of promiscuity, but you could hardly take that seriously when you looked at Victor and Adele Compton, for twenty-five years a shining model of monogamous bliss. Nor could you plausibly call him a corrupter of youth if you knew the youth on whom he had most influence—Alan, his only child, just graduated from the university with brilliant honors; Alan who was good-humored and astute, sane and gay and eager—as good an advertisement as any moral educator could desire.

Alan came into the breakfast room as his father was lighting his pipe. He too was tall and lithe and bronzed, but the twinkle that ordinarily brightened his gray eyes was gone this morning; he nodded to his father and sat down, moody and distrait. Victor Compton was a little worried. . . . But the boy had been out dancing last night; he had heard him come in at dawn. You needed more sleep than that, at twenty-two.

Alan finished his coffee and grapefruit, lighted a cigarette.

"Mother still asleep?" he asked. "She's a sybarite."

"She's a beautiful woman," said her husband proudly, "and sleep is the best of all cosmetics. Besides, she's earned the right to be luxurious; she worked hard enough, all those years we were living on my salary. . . . You might have taken a little more sleep yourself, son. This summer is your vacation; you ought to rest, before you go to Rome." Alan made a vague gesture. "And when you get to Rome," his father advised him, "don't grind too hard. You're a born scholar and Rome's a scholar's paradise; but your health is worth more than all the prizes the American Academy could give you."

"Dad——" Alan dropped his cigarette in his coffee cup and looked out of the window. "I don't want to go to Rome."

"What? . . . Of course," said his father, still incredulous, "you needn't take that scholarship. If you'd rather go to the School of Archæology at Athens, or anywhere else, we've money enough to send you. But I should think——"

"I don't want to go to Europe at all. Mr. Wales has offered me a job with the Valley Trust Company. I want to take it."

His father would have been less dumbfounded if Alan had said he wanted to turn Mohammedan, or enlist in the marines.

"It's your own life," he said last. "Do what you want, not what I'd have wanted in your place. I don't doubt you could make a banker of yourself, if you tried. But why in the world——? You're a scholar born; it's the work you love, the work you're made for——"

"I'd like to earn a living." Alan's eyes were still aloof.

"We all lived on a professor's salary, till a year ago. And the by-products of scholarship—— Well, I've made half a million dollars out of this book."

"You were lucky." In three words, Alan dismissed the most spectacular literary success of the decade. "I mean you wrote something you believed, and made a lot of money out of it. But nobody ever made half a million dollars out of classical archæology."

"But you don't need to! You don't think your mother and I are going to hold on to every nickel when money rolls in twice as fast as we can spend it? You needn't worry about money; I'll settle a trust fund on you this afternoon—enough to give you an income of ten thousand a year for the rest of your life."

"What?" The boy stared, there were tears in his eyes. "Why, I suppose that would—— Dad, I—I can't thank you——"

"Why should you thank me? It's a pleasure, son. . . . I wanted to be a scholar, too; but I had a wife and baby, I had to keep on teaching. I couldn't take the time for research. I've been a good teacher; I can popularize other men's work—dilute it till the crowd can swallow it. But that's not the same thing. You'll never need to do that. You can look at something and say, This is mine; I did it myself."

He paused, fussing with his pipe. He could be demonstrative with his wife; but it made him self-conscious to display the emotion he felt about his son.

"Alan, when you were growing up, and I realized that you had a first-rate mind, it used to make me sick to think that all your life you'd be hampered by lack of money. And of all that we've got from this book, the thing I prize most is that it has set you free to do what you want." Alan grinned, almost at his ease again.

"I know you better," he said. "You're not just a—a contributor to other people. What you like most about that book is that it was something you believed, and you made everybody listen to it. . . . But I can't begin to tell you——"

The telephone interrupted him. Compton, still unused to a household with four servants, got up from the table and answered it himself.

"Hello. . . . Why, hello, old man! Great to hear from you! . . . What? Not even staying for lunch? . . . I see. . . . If you're in such a hurry you'd better come to the house, not the office. Adele will want to see you. And Alan—— He was about seven when you saw him last. Wait till you see him now. . . . Yes, come right along."

"Hal Bartlett," he said, turning back from the telephone. "Stopping over for a couple of hours on his way back from Denver to New York. You've heard of him, of course—half owner of the Wrenn-Bartlett newspaper chain. He was city editor of the *Press* here, years ago, and they discharged him for printing a story some advertiser didn't like. So he went to New York, and got in with old J. C. Wrenn, and eventually bought the paper that fired him. But this is the first time he's been in Ridgemont since he was thrown out; he seemed to hold a grudge against the town. . . . He and his wife were great friends of ours, when he lived here. That was his first wife; I believe he's had two or three

more, since." Alan was moving toward the door. "Aren't you going
to wait and see him?" his father asked.

"I can't, dad. I—I told a man I'd see him downtown at half
past ten."

"Not Wales of the Valley Trust?"

"No. . . . I guess that was a crazy idea, dad. Don't worry about it.
. . . I'll be out for lunch. Tell mother, if you're going up to wake her."

II

Compton's concern was gone as he ran lightly upstairs. Boys just out
of college had these wild notions; he remembered that he had almost
joined a classmate who was going to grow cantaloupes in the Imperial
Valley. Only Adele's unwillingness to leave Ridgemont had kept him
here, doing the work he was meant for, work crowned at last by this
triumph that was still incredible. He owed everything to Adele.

Her bedroom door was ajar; from the threshold he regarded her relaxed grace as she lay sleeping—still creamy-skinned, still slender, at
forty-four. A bare arm curled about her head; her shingled hair was
soft and wavy, and pure white. An illness had whitened it when she
was thirty, and what they had taken for calamity had proved a blessing; people had thought of her as a white-haired young woman for so
long that they would go on thinking of her as a white-haired young
woman till she was sixty. Her unlined face looked as if she had never
had a worry. She had had plenty, but she hid them behind that un-
ruffled mask and hid other things, too. People who met her for the
first time were apt to think her impassive; but if you knew her——!

Her eyes opened; she stifled a yawn, and smiled at him.

"Hello! . . . Is it terribly late?"

"Not very, but Hal Bartlett's coming up from downtown. He's only
here for an hour or so, and he wants to see us." She sprang out of bed
and kissed him lightly.

"Then run away!" she commanded. "I'll have to hurry if I'm to
receive him at the breakfast table, even in negligée."

Rapid bathing and dressing was an art she had learned when her
husband taught an eight o'clock class at the university. Bartlett had
not yet appeared when she came down, in pajamas of black chiffon
velvet. She poured her coffee, lighted a cigarette.

"Where's Alan?" she asked. "Gone out already?"

"He had some engagement downtown. . . . He had a wild idea that
he ought to start making money, right away. He wanted to take a job
at the Valley Trust——"

"Good heavens!" said his mother. "That means a girl."

"What?" Compton broke into relieved laughter. "Why, of course! Queer that I never thought of it. . . . Well, I told him we'd endow him, with ten thousand a year. He can marry her this summer and take her to Rome with him." But his wife was frowning.

"I wonder who——?" she muttered. "I can't think of any one he's been going with, particularly. . . . Except Brenda Vincent, of course."

"Brenda? But he's only been going with her because her husband asked him to see that she wasn't left out of everything while he was in China. . . . I mean——" said Compton. "You don't imagine there's anything——"

"Your horror," she said, "would astonish the critics of your book. And pain some of its admirers, I'm afraid. You've argued that a childless marriage ought to be dissolved at the wish of either partner—even that there's no need of a marriage ceremony at all, until a child has been conceived."

"That's only theory, at present. Most people still get married; and I've always argued that when a man and a woman have promised to stick together, the burden of proof is on the one who wants to break it up. . . . Besides, when a man goes away for six months on business, and asks a friend to be attentive to his wife, he puts faith in his friend's honor. To betray it—— Well, it isn't done. Alan wouldn't do it."

"I don't think there's any danger," his wife reassured him. "He's twenty-two and Brenda's twenty-seven—a big difference, at their age. Besides, he's seen very little of her lately; which suggests that he's been seeing somebody else. I suppose he'll tell us who it is after he's given her the glad news."

"Yes. Of course." Compton's hands shook a little as he refilled his pipe—and the doorbell announced the arrival of Hal Bartlett.

III

He swept in like a breeze, shook hands with Victor, turned to Adele and kissed her heartily. Her husband blinked; even in these casual days she wasn't given to kissing other men. But few women refused to kiss Hal Bartlett. . . . Absurd to be so touchy. . . . Bartlett sat down looked about him, and grinned.

"This place used to belong to old Harrington of the First National, didn't it? How does it feel, Vic, to live on Millionaires' Row, and be a world-famous celebrity? Not to speak of the blessings you've always had—a brilliant son, and the most beautiful wife in Ridgemont."

"How does it feel? . . . Hal, sometimes it almost frightens me. The Greeks used to think that the gods were jealous of a man who had too

much good fortune; they pulled him down. Solon told Crœsus to count
no man happy till he was dead; you never could tell what might happen to him." He grinned. "I thought things would happen to me,
when this book came out. I'd quit the university already, but I
thought I'd have to resign from my clubs, perhaps even leave town.
But nothing much happened; even the preachers who denounce me
from the pulpit still play golf with me. Ridgemont has been very tolerant."

"So I've heard," said Bartlett. "As you probably know, a lot of
people would still like to get you, but there's nothing they can take
hold of. And why do you suppose Ridgemont is tolerant, for the first
time in its history?"

"Well, I'm vain enough to think it's because they know us. Adele
and I—our friends can't quite believe we're moral anarchists. . . . Why,
even the Bishop—— He shakes his head, of course, when he meets me at
the club; but he's been quite decent about it all."

"The Bishop," said Bartlett, "is honorary president of the Chamber
of Commerce. . . . Don't you see it, Vic? You're the best press agent
this town ever had—the only resident of Ridgemont who's made the
front page of the New York papers since old Senator Pelz died. They
might as well default on a city bond issue as run you out of town."

"Oh, I can't quite believe that, Hal. Of course," said Compton,
"all this publicity was a tremendous surprise to me. I went at this——"
He smiled at his wife. "We both went at it in a mood of self-sacrifice.
It meant giving up the job we'd always lived on; and we thought the
book would sell two or three thousand copies, and perhaps cause some
thinking among intellectuals that might lead to something twenty
years from now."

"You forget," said Bartlett, "that everybody's an intellectual now.
Or at least thinks he is. And almost everybody's promiscuous. But
some people are still so old-fashioned that they want an excuse for it."

"But damn it, man, I don't encourage promiscuity! I merely recognize that it's here. People no longer let the old rules hold them back;
we know that, and I don't like it. I've tried to sketch a new morality—
rational and workable standards that will reduce promiscuity to a mini-
mum. . . . Did you read that book, Hal?"

"Certainly I read it. As I understand it, you think that if men
and women are allowed to do whatever they want, they'll all want to
get married and live faithfully ever after."

"Not all—but most of them. Monogamy is the normal relation, Hal
—the deepest satisfaction, for most people. I hope we can get rid of
promiscuity; but if we must have it, we'd better have it before mar-

riage than after. It makes me sick, Hal, to see idealistic young people keeping themselves continent—yes, they still do it, some of them; the boys even more than the girls—and going into marriage all steamed up with high emotion—and then, at forty, losing their faith, losing their balance, making dreadful asses of themselves. If they've got to shop around they'd better do it before than after. They'll upset fewer apple carts, and they'll have a better chance of finding somebody they can stick to."

"I believe," Bartlett began, "it's your doctrine that the children come first——"

"Absolutely! What a man and woman unattached may do is no concern of society. But the moment a child is born, or even conceived, they ought to consider that child's interest before their own. I don't say that a marriage with children should never be dissolved; but you've got to be sure that divorce would be best for the children. Let childless couples do as they please; but a child makes a marriage."

"Well, it's an interesting theory," Bartlett observed. "What do you think of it, Adele?" Her face was a smiling mask.

"I suppose it would be better than the way things are now. . . . But I don't know; I'm not an intellectual. What do you think of it?"

"I've been too busy practising marriage to go very deep into the theory. When you're paying alimony to three women your judgment is a bit clouded. But I know this much about Vic's ideas—they're still news. That's why I'm here. Vic, how about writing a weekly syndicate feature for the Wrenn-Bartlett newspapers, to run a year? Fifty-two articles, a thousand words apiece, a dollar and a half a word. Even with all your bloated profits, I suppose you could use another seventy-eight thousand."

The Comptons stared at each other; the big money was still so new that mention of such figures amazed them.

"Why, I don't know, Hal," said Compton slowly. "I've said about all I had to say. It wouldn't be fair to rehash the old stuff."

"You could say it to a new audience—reach millions of people who don't buy books. Spread your message."

"If you put it that way——" Compton began, then broke off with a grimace. "I was about to fool myself," he said. "It's hard not to fool yourself, when the money begins to come in. . . . No, Hal, I won't do it. I won't say anything more till I've got something new to say. . . . And do you know why I won't do it?" he demanded fiercely. "As a sort of —well, call it a thank offering. To—to Fortune."

He began to stride up and down, puffing at his pipe.

"Hal, I had a piece of great and undeserved good luck. I wrote this book because I believed it and thought people needed it. I've seen so many people, young and middle-aged, make messes of their lives because they've thrown away the old rulebook, and are trying to do without any rulebook at all. That won't work. I thought I could suggest some rules that might work better. So I gave up my professorship and threw away all hope of another, spent every cent I'd saved, exposed Adele to the risk of poverty—real poverty—at forty-four—all because I believed that this was true and ought to be said. Hal, if they'd told me I'd be burned at the stake for writing that book, I believe I could have got up the nerve to go through with it." He halted, smiling.

"And then," he said, "it made my fortune. Maybe it's superstitious, but I feel that I owe somebody something for that. I won't write any more till I find something else that I think is true, and needs saying. Don't you know I'm right, Hal?"

"Oh, I'm a newspaperman. I'm not sure I know anything except that a good comic strip is more precious than rubies; and that the next best thing, right now, would be a syndicate feature by the author of *Ethics of Tomorrow*. Vic, if you ever do decide to write for the papers, will you give me first call?"

"Of course. I owe you that for the splendid way the *Press* has stood by me in Ridgemont, even when the other papers were against me."

"You don't owe me anything for that. The *Press* is always glad to annoy the vested respectabilities of this town. I haven't forgotten how they threw me out."

"I didn't mean editorial support so much as publicity in the news columns. When the book came out the *Press* quoted it by the page, interviewed me, stirred up people to reply to me, day after day—and all of that was telegraphed all over the country by the press associations. That's what really gave me my start."

"But you still don't owe me or my papers any thanks," said Bartlett. "A good newspaper is as impersonal, in its news columns, as the law of gravitation. Step out of that window and you'll fall to the ground. The law of gravitation doesn't care whether you're going to fall two feet or two hundred. So with an honest paper—if you do something that's news the paper is going to feature it, whether it damns you forever or makes your fortune. It was your luck that when you broke into the news it made you. But you were always a lucky devil, Vic." Bartlett rose. "I've got to hustle for my train," he said. "I hope you people are coming to New York, some of these days."

"Next month—when Alan sails for Europe."

"Then stay a couple of weeks after he's gone. The papers will give

you about a hundred thousand dollars' worth of free publicity, if your
publishers know how to handle you. And the current Mrs. Bartlett
is always glad to see my old friends from back home."

"You'll excuse my not going out with you?" said Adele, rising.
"Ridgemont progresses; we receive in our pajamas, but we haven't got
around to wearing them on the front porch."

She gave him her hands; this time she kissed him spontaneously.
But Victor Compton was beyond absurd jealousies, now.

"Yes," he said as he walked out with Bartlett, "I've always been
lucky. Monogamy would seem the normal state to any man who lived
with Adele. And Alan—— I wish you'd seen him, Hal; he's going to
be a better man than I ever dreamed of being. The best thing I've ever
done in my life was to give him his start. . . . Good-bye, old man."

Bartlett's car drove away; and Victor Compton lingered on the
porch, in the mansion that had once belonged to old Harrington of
the First National Bank, wondering with a rather humble gratitude at
the transformation that had enabled him to refuse seventy-eight thousand dollars for a rather fine point of conscience. Yes, he'd always
been lucky. . . .

He heard the telephone ringing, heard his wife answering it.

"Hello. . . . Yes, this is Doctor Compton's residence. Mrs. Compton
speaking. Who is this? . . . Who? . . The police station——?"

IV

Alan had rung a doorbell on the twelfth floor of Ridgemont's new-
est apartment house, much favored by childless couples of the younger
married set. A girl in a rose negligée let him in. She was slim and
young, but her eyes were haggard; the rouge made patches on her pallid cheeks. He caught her up eagerly.

"Brenda! Darling!"

She was limp in his arms; when he kissed her she turned her lips
away. He let her go; she walked to the window, stood staring out.

"Well——" She turned and faced him. "I guess there's no doubt
about it. Got any bright ideas about what we're going to do?"

"Yes, it's all right! I was ready to take a job downtown—but I won't
have to. Dad told me this morning that he'd endow me, with ten
thousand a year. So I can take you to Rome with me——" She
shrugged irritably. "I suppose we couldn't leave Ridgemont together,"
he said. "But people are going to have to know before long. You
could slip away and join me over there. Then, when John's got his
divorce, we can be married——"

"Is that all you can think about? I don't want to marry you."

He felt an inner simmering—countless tiny tingling explosions.

"You've said you loved me," he told her. "Again and again."

"I might have said anything, then. . . . I thought I did," she conceded. "For a while. This is as much my fault as yours, Alan. John's fault most of all; he ought to have known better than to go away and leave me. But he did go away; and in three weeks he's coming back. And all you can think of is that I ought to get myself divorced so I can marry you."

"You know I'm crazy about you," he told her unsteadily. "I am still—more than ever. When you wouldn't let me see you for weeks, till last night—— It was horrible! . . . This—— Well—— No wonder it upsets you. But I could make you happy——"

"Oh, I'm sick of the sight of you!" she screamed. She was standing by the open window, careless of the neighbors' ears. "You got me into this," she said, "and you've got to get me out. I could find out where to go; Edna Ferrell across the court there would tell me. And then she'd have something on me all the rest of my life. I don't dare. . . . But you could find somebody——"

"Not that, Brenda! We haven't any right."

"Any right! You've been reading that crazy book of your father's! He thinks grown-up people haven't any rights; that they ought to pay all their lives for a little carelessness. Well, I'm not going to! I'm crazy about my husband! I want him! Do you think I'm going to give him up just because you and I lost our heads after he'd left me alone for months?"

"Not so loud! Everybody will hear you!" He strode forward, seized her. She writhed in his grasp, her clenched fists beat helplessly on his chest. "About John——" he said. "I'm ashamed. It was rotten of us to cheat him; but I loved you—and you loved me, then. You know it. I can't be sorry. But if we did a thing like this——"

He broke off; through the open window he had seen a woman at a window across the court, watching them with gleeful interest. Edna Ferrell. . . . His arms relaxed just as Brenda, still struggling, gave him a furious shove. The impact sent them staggering apart; the hollows of her knees struck the low window sill——

He saw two outflung arms clutching wildly at nothing, then two slim legs sticking straight up in the air. He plunged forward, looked over the window sill. Into the well of the court, a hundred feet deep, a bundle of fluttering rose was falling, turning over and over. It struck. An instant of dead silence, then a dull thwack floated up. . . .

He felt his feet stamping the floor as he ran out, felt his fingers pushing the elevator bell. No answer; he could picture elevator boys and hallboys gathering something in the paved court. He didn't want to see It, but he was drawn irresistibly. . . . There was a fire stair beside the elevator; he ran down the steps, flight after flight. The bottom at last. He stumbled out of the stairway door at the rear of the lobby, white, shuddering—the very picture of guilt, conscious and fleeing guilt, to the arriving policeman who intercepted him.

v

Victor Compton sneaked home in the dark, and was grateful for it. So much of these last thirty-six hours had been bright daylight; a man couldn't hide from it, even in a lawyer's office; not even in that cold gray building where he had seen Alan, with iron bars between them. . . . Alan who was held on the charge of murder; Alan who would hardly say a word, even to his father and mother, who talked thickly, incoherently, when he spoke at all. Alan, who was always staring fixedly at something he saw every moment, in daylight or dark—two slim silken legs sticking straight up in the air.

Compton drew the shades on the living-room windows clear down to the sill before he turned on the light. He supposed Adele was somewhere about, but he could do nothing for her; for thirty-six hours she had been a dead white mask; she hadn't said five words to him, or to anyone but Alan; she didn't seem to know whether he was there or not. It might have helped a little if he could have done something for Adele. . . .

He dropped into a chair, touched a lighted match to a pipe he had forgotten to fill. Not much use shutting himself in; even alone, even in the dark, the mad phantasmagoria of these last two days still assailed his eyes and ears. Policemen, lawyers, and always reporters; reporters everywhere. He could shake them off; but he couldn't escape seeing the papers. The papers that had made him.

They were howling at him, howling at Alan, like wolves on the trail. Even the *Press,* usually so eager to annoy the vested respectabilities, was running with the pack this time—leading the pack. The whole story, as Ridgemont saw it, had been summed up in that first headline in the *Press:*

SEX AUTHOR'S SON SLAYS LOVE MATE

Sex author's son. . . . Every paper in Ridgemont, perhaps every paper in the country, was reprinting long passages from *Ethics of Tomorrow.* Selected passages. . . . Impersonal as the law of gravitation;

this was news, whether it damned a man or made his fortune. Beyond question Victor Compton was damned, but that didn't matter now. What mattered was that Victor Compton's book seemed likely to damn his son.

At first Compton had simply been appalled by a horrible accident; he had never doubted that Alan's innocence would be obvious. Why, the whole town knew Alan! But then had come this Ferrell woman with her incredible story; she had heard Brenda tell Alan that she was sick of the sight of him, that she loved her husband; and then, said the Ferrell woman, he had pushed her out of the window. . . . Hysterical, of course; but her testimony went into the record. Still, even when Alan had been locked up by order of a magistrate, his father had never doubted that they could get him off.

He had gone to his own lawyer—Lucius Leigh, his lifelong friend, the best and most respected lawyer in Ridgemont. . . . "Compton, I'm terribly sorry, but I'm engaged on another case that takes all of my time. Can't betray the interests of my client, you know, even to oblige an old friend." . . . Then to Marlowe the second-best lawyer. Marlowe had at least been frank. "Compton, I don't dare. If I happened to get an acquittal I'd have to resign from my clubs. You don't realize how much feeling that book of yours stirred up. It was driven underground for a while; but now that we all see exactly where that sort of doctrine leads——"

Marlowe had been keeping a woman in the South End for years; the whole town knew it; his wife knew it. But that was beside the point.

So at last Victor Compton had gone to Brady. To go to Brady was a confession of guilt; but he belonged to no clubs, he had no reputation, except for getting the guilty acquitted. Brady had taken his check for ten thousand dollars, and then shrugged.

"Ordinarily," he said, "I'd get a change of venue. But there's no use doing that; your book's known everywhere. Ordinarily, too, we might get the District Attorney to accept a plea of guilt in the second degree. That means twenty years to life; but you get out in twelve years if you behave yourself." (Twelve years!) "But no chance of that this time," said Brady regretfully. "The District Attorney's going to run for Governor next year, and he needs a hanging in this case to be sure of the church vote. . . . No, I'm afraid we'll have to fall back on insanity."

"Insanity? But that would be admitting that he killed her! And he didn't! He couldn't! It's unthinkable!"

"Of course," said Brady soothingly. "But there's that Ferrell woman —a friend of both of them, and a millionaire's daughter. And of course Mrs. Vincent's condition supplies a motive. You and I might not consider it a motive, but the average juryman——"

"But if they've read my book, they'd know——"

"Hell, you don't suppose jurymen read, do you? They haven't read your book; they've heard about it. They'll hear bits of it read in court, by the District Attorney. I'll object, of course, but the Judge will overrule me. Not the whole book; just choice bits. . . . No, if we can get some experts to swear he's insane, and even one or two jurors to believe them, we'll be damn lucky. I think we might get him out of the asylum in two or three years, when this has blown over."

"Brady, the boy was in love with her. He's almost crazy now. Two years in an asylum, and he'd really go insane!"

Brady shrugged again.

"It's the best chance. In fact the only chance."

. . . So Victor Compton sat in his living room behind drawn blinds, absently lighting one match after another and touching them to an empty pipe. . . . A ring at the door; voices in the hall. The maid on the threshold——

"The Bishop is calling."

VI

The Bishop of Ridgemont was a man of the world—so much a man of the world that his friends were apt to forget that his professional concerns were otherworldly. For twenty years Victor Compton had known him, as an excellent golfer, a brilliant bridge player, a polished orator at Chamber of Commerce luncheons; as a connoisseur of Burgundy and Madeira in the old days (though his present abstinence was well known). But there was one character in which Compton had never seen him till tonight—the right reverend father in God.

He came forward now, episcopal sternness overlaid by pastoral charity.

"Compton, my friend——" He paused, smiling. "I suppose you won't let me call you my son; you have long been estranged from the Church. But I venture to come in the name of the Church—yes, and of your old friends—in the hope that I may offer you some consolation."

"He didn't do it!" Compton cried. "You know he didn't do it!"

"I should gladly believe he did not. He was a splendid boy."

"Was?" his father shrieked. "He is! We're going to get him acquitted! Don't talk as if—as if he were gone already."

"I sincerely hope you may prove that there has been some mistake.

And I would not add to your burden by pointing out the obvious——"

"That my book's a millstone around his neck? . . . Yes," said Compton. "I know that well enough."

"If you know that," said the Bishop, "some good may yet come of this terrible tragedy. We have had an object lesson that for all our modernism, the wages of sin is still——" Suavely, he suppressed the word. "It's a pity," he said. "These young people, I suppose, were drawn to each other by a feeling that had its deceptive show of beauty. If they had not been ill-advised, Compton——" His voice was resonant in the silent house. "If they and millions like them had not been taught that they could safely discard revealed truth, warnings from on high reinforced by two thousand years of human experience——"

Instinctively Victor Compton struck out in self-defense.

"People were discarding the old code before I ever wrote. I only recognized that, and tried to give them something in its place."

"I have never doubted your good intention," the Bishop conceded. "But when you see to what your teaching leads—— Granted that this was an accident, Compton. None the less, the young people had sinned. A sin that you had taught them was no sin at all."

"That's not fair! I hold that a woman should be faithful to one man, and a man to one woman, at a time; that a childless wife who falls in love with another man should leave the husband and marry the other. Which is what Alan wanted her to do. . . . As for her being his friend's wife, in his friend's absence—— That's a special case; I hadn't foreseen it."

"Every case is a special case, Compton. The Church learned that, long ago."

"Well, as to this special case——" said Compton desperately. "They should have waited till they could tell her husband, frankly——"

"They should have waited? But they were human. And there is the fatal flaw in your theories. You're a good man, in intention; a learned man, in abstractions. But you don't know human nature as the Church has learned to know it. You think that if men and women are permitted to choose their own way they will choose the right. The Church knows better."

Compton stared into the cold fireplace. There were gaps—he was sure of it—in the Bishop's reasoning; questions begged, conclusions assumed as premises. But he was too weary, too distraught, to search them out.

"What does it matter?" he said wearily. "I don't think you're right. But even if you were, what could I do about it now?"

"Recant!" the Bishop thundered. "Abjure your errors! Make public confession—to the newspapers—that you see where your abominable doctrine leads! That would undo some of the harm you have wrought; it might save other men's sons from the disaster that threatens yours. . . . And perhaps, Compton, it might save your son, too."

"Save Alan? How?"

"Compton, all your old friends pity you. And they pity that poor boy whom we all love, and who weakly yielded to an impulse he had been taught to gratify, not to repress. If there is a guilty man it is you, Victor Compton, not the boy whose character you formed! As for Alan—— Nothing the law might do to him could bring back that unhappy girl. The most we can hope for from this deplorable affair is a lesson—a lesson that may save other men's sons and daughters. If you recant, that lesson is made clear. . . . I do not ask you to go all the way, to return to the Church. I would not have any man do what his conscience forbids. But you have been a stumbling block to the weak and ignorant. Remove that stumbling block from their path! That is more important than any infliction of the penalties of the law."

"You mean that Alan——"

"Personally," said the Bishop, "I am convinced that the death was accidental. We have no evidence to the contrary but the words of a frightened, hysterical woman, who can no longer remember just what she did see and hear in that horrible moment."

"Mrs. Ferrell can't remember?" Compton gasped. "Why, then——"

"Mrs. Ferrell," said the Bishop, "belongs to one of our best families, of the old stock. A little worldly, perhaps, a little lax; but still a girl of our own sort. Some of your friends have talked to her father, and he has talked to her. She says she has no idea of what she may have told the police, in that moment of shock. She might have said anything. . . . She might still say anything, Compton."

"But the police took notes of her testimony. They've been printed."

"The notes may be lost before the trial; and newspaper stories are not evidence. The District Attorney is prepared not to question Mrs. Ferrell too closely. If your son says it was an accident, if she says—as she may—that her memory is a blank, the jury will realize that there is no proof of a crime at all. It is not too much to say that men will be chosen as jurors who will be sure to realize it. . . . Indeed there may never be a trial. If Mrs. Ferrell repudiates her first wild words the District Attorney might drop the whole case. . . . So you see, Compton, your old friends haven't left you in the lurch. I can give you my personal assurance that your boy will be released——"

"If I recant. . . . And if I don't——?"

The Bishop leaned back in his easy chair, finger tips gently touching.

"I'm afraid, Compton, it is the general feeling that the lesson of this tragedy must be unmistakably taught. If not in one way, then in another."

"I see. . . . I recant, or my son is hanged." Compton tried to fill his pipe, gave it up after he had covered his lap with spilled tobacco. "You're surprised," he said, "that I hesitate for an instant. So am I. But what I put in that book is what I believe—the truth, as I see it. I believe it's true, I believe it's useful; I believe that if those ideas prevail, people will live better and happier lives. I suppose that faith is—well, my substitute for God."

"Always substitutes!" the Bishop sighed.

"Well—would you recant your faith, for any reason?"

"I cannot admit that the cases are parallel. . . . Consider it in this light, my friend. You have faith in what you regard as truth. So did Galileo. He recanted—yet the earth still goes round the sun. If your truth is truth, and not error, it will still be true even though Victor Compton denies it."

"Yes, but if I deny my truth—— I've heard you preach about Abraham. His God demanded that he sacrifice his son. Abraham was ready to do it, and you said his faith and submission were splendid. . . . But you have no son. I know how Abraham felt."

"Passing over your blasphemy, which I am sure was inadvertent, may I point out a difference between the two cases? Abraham's son was spared, at the last moment; a ram was provided instead. In the present instance there will be no ram."

"And this," said Compton, "is the favor my friends have done me."

"Yes. Your friends, who have watched your progress with pain; your friends, most of whom believe your son is a murderer; your friends, whose sons and daughters you have led astray. I must say, Compton, I think your friends have gone pretty far to help you."

"And you want an answer now—yes or no?"

"Think it over, if you like—till tomorrow. We can't let it go too long; who knows what Mrs. Ferrell might remember, if she were not well advised? Let me know tomorrow, before noon. I shall busy myself in the meantime with writing out a statement, which perhaps you will be good enough to sign and give to the evening papers. I can perhaps suggest a more felicitous phraseology than would occur to you; but it would make a better impression if the statement appeared to be spontaneous."

"It undoubtedly would. . . . Well," said Compton, "I'll let you know in the morning."

He walked with the Bishop to the door; and when he came back he found his wife in the living room. Her white mask had cracked at last; she was glaring at him, with horror and with hate.

VII

"You let him go?" she gasped. "Run after him, and call him back! . . . Yes, I heard you. I'd fallen asleep in the next room. I woke up just now—but I couldn't believe what I heard. I thought I was dreaming, till I heard the slam of the door. . . . And you let him go!"

He dropped into a chair, his head and arms hanging limp.

"I suppose I'll give in," he said at last. "Deny what I believe, swear to a lie, give up trying to help people out of their troubles——"

"Help people out of their troubles? Aren't you going to help Alan out of his trouble? You? . . . You've always said that the children come first. Men and women mustn't consider themselves, they must think of their children. And you hesitate to save your own son!"

"It's not for myself, Adele. It's what I've contributed to a better morality——"

"Morality! What do you know about morality? You've never needed any; you're a one-woman man. You don't know how it feels to be pulled between two attractions, two loyalties. I don't profess to know anything about morality either, but I know there's a way to save Alan. . . . Victor," she said, "have I made you happy? Have you liked living with me—not just at first, but always? Right up till now?"

"Always, my dear. You know that."

"Well—you owe it to Alan. If I hadn't had a little boy who needed his father and his mother both, I'd have gone to New York with Hal Bartlett fifteen years ago. I think I could have held Hal; and I know he'd never have left a son of his in the lurch."

"Good God, Adele! I never dreamed——"

"I know you didn't. I'd never have told you, if it hadn't been for this. I've been glad I didn't go with Hal; I was over that brainstorm in six months. I've been happy with you—happy enough, anyway. . . . But if you let them hang Alan, I'll never speak to you or look at you again."

"I couldn't blame you," he said brokenly. "For of course what I feel—it's personal——"

"It's your pride. . . . If you think more of your pride than your own son——"

"Not my pride," he said. "That's gone; my usefulness too, I'm afraid. Victor Compton and his ideas are pretty thoroughly damned, in the mind of the public, no matter how this comes out. I'd ruin any cause I supported, now. . . . But I still believe I was right; there may be a few other people who agree with me—people my ideas might help. If I deny them, now—— Don't you see, Adele? It's not Alan or me; it's Alan or—well, call it truth."

"Truth?" she said bitterly. "What is truth?"

And, of course, he did not know. He had only faith. . . .

"Well?" she demanded after a protracted silence.

"I don't know," he said. "I'm still thinking."

LOCKSMITHS LAUGH AT LOVE

"I think it would be lovely," she said pensively, "if you and I should have an affair."

"Delightful!" he agreed, dropping her hand in panic haste. Sylvia leaned back against the wall of the restaurant booth, faintly smiling.

"I mean it, Stan." He hadn't doubted it. She meant everything she said, and said everything she meant. "I'm sorry if you're not enthusiastic about it," she added rather acridly.

"Of course I'm enthusiastic! It's only that——"

He paused. Their long comradely friendship had taken on a new warmth of late, since they'd begun making love. . . . But neither of them wanted to get married, yet; and anything else, with Sylvia—— Back home their families lived next door; they had grown up together; he had promised her mother that he would take care of her, in New York.

"It's only," he said, "that I hadn't dreamed you cared so much."

"Oh, Lord, Stan! This isn't 1884! I'm not in love with you, if that's what you mean. I'm not the type that falls in love, the way our ancestors meant it. But if you——"

She broke off. The stuffy warmth of the restaurant was thick with the buzz of voices, the high cackle of laughter. He hated noisy crowds; there had been a time when Sylvia hated them too. But probably she had got used to places like this, going around with Bull Cardigan.

He realized that she was waiting for him to say something.

"You know I've always been crazy about you——" he began dutifully.

"Rot! It's just because I know you haven't that I suggested this. I wouldn't have an affair with a man who was crazy about me, unless I was crazy about him too. It wouldn't be fair. I've always said that."

Her emphasis on the "always" sounded as if she had said it recently, and with a personal application. He scowled; everybody knew that Bull Cardigan was crazy about her.

"But you and I," she went on, "like each other and trust each other and know all about each other; and there's never been any sentimental nonsense between us. . . . Oh, yes, you asked me to marry you once, back home—because it was your duty; because we'd been intended for each other ever since we were babies. It always made me sick, knowing that everybody expected us to get married. As if what we thought about it didn't count."

"I remember what I thought about it the night I asked you."

"There was a moon that night," Sylvia recalled. "And the roses and honeysuckle were in bloom on the porch, and the band was playing in the City Park. You felt a perfectly natural biological impulse."

"Biology's out of my line," he growled. "I'm a physicist. But I still remember how it hurt when you told me you wouldn't marry a man you didn't love."

"Did I say that? But, my dear, I was only seventeen! Of course I used the Victorian phraseology; it was all I knew. What I meant was that I'd be damned if I'd marry the boy that father and mother and the whole town expected me to marry. . . . Oh, I felt biological too, that night. If you'd been anybody else I'd probably have thought I was in love with you; and if I had you'd still be clerking in the bank back home, and I'd be raising babies in a bungalow in the North End. But as it was——"

As it was, she was one of the best girl press agents in New York; and he was the brightest of the bright young men attached to one of the great research laboratories. So it had all turned out for the best, even if it had hurt at the time.

"As it was," she finished, "you went back to college and I went back to school; and the next time we saw each other our little flurry was over, and we've been the best of friends ever since. But lately——"

"What's the matter with lately?" he demanded.

"Not a thing," said Sylvia, reddening. "I was surprised when you first began making love to me again; I'd been afraid all those platonic years had given us a taboo. But they didn't, thank goodness. . . . Only you know, Stan, we can't go on like this." He did know it.

"But my God, Syl! I promised your mother I'd take care of you!"

"I promised your mother the same thing. But I'd much better have an affair with you than with somebody else; and you'd much better——"

"Who said anything about an affair with somebody else?"

"It has been suggested," said Sylvia obscurely. "You needn't think you're the only man who finds me attractive. I've even been asked to take part in a companionate marriage. But I despise this thing of making promises with your fingers crossed, because you're afraid of what people will say! When I get married I'll mean it. . . . But in the meantime—— Well, I'm twenty-five——"

"Oh, well!" he said furiously. "If you just want to have an affair as a matter of principle—a declaration of independence——"

"You know it isn't that! . . . Or do you?" she speculated. "I suppose you've had lots of affairs with women, haven't you, Stan?"

"Certainly," he said with dignity. She laughed in his face.

"Liar! I know better; you're always buried in your laboratory. . . . But if you keep on playing around with Sheila Kron——"

"Sheila Kron? Why, I only like to talk to her!"

"Give the girl time, Stan; you only met her last week. . . . Oh, you needn't look so sniffy; if she wants you she'll get you. You'd be perfectly helpless in the hands of a woman of her age."

"She's exactly one week older than I am!"

"Oh, that's her story, is it? Anyway, she was married before you were out of prep school and divorced twice before you graduated from college. Since then—— Well, the less said the better."

"Now listen, if you're going to talk scandal about Sheila Kron——"

"You needn't rush to the defense of what our ancestors would have called her reputation; she'd laugh at that herself." (He knew it.) "But she'd be blue ruin for you, Stan. She's insatiable of a man's time; no more of your twenty-four-hour experiments if you tied yourself up with her. And when she's through with you she'll put you in her next book of poems, nailed on the barn door for everybody to laugh at."

He knew that, too. Picking out the men who figured in Sheila's poems was the easiest of crossword puzzles.

"So," he said, "this idea of yours was just a missionary impulse? You'd have an affair with me just to keep me away from Sheila Kron?"

"Why not? You're my best friend; I wouldn't want you to fall into the hands of the wrong kind of woman. I'd be good for you and she'd be poison. You're not in love with her, and you know I'm ten times as good-looking as she is; and I wouldn't make demands on your time, and I don't write poems—— Honestly, Stan, I think your mother would thank me if she knew. . . . Not that I'm suggesting that you tell her."

"Well, I'll be damned!" he snorted. And then Sylvia looked up, and gasped, and tried desperately to hide behind her compact.

"O Lord, there's Bull Cardigan! I told him I was working tonight."

Bull Cardigan indeed, coming down the alley between the booths, pausing at almost every one to greet somebody he knew. He filled the alley pretty thoroughly (he had been a halfback at Georgia Tech) and above his broad shoulders his wide face beamed with the well-being of the Wall Street man whose stocks have risen like rockets, while other people's holdings are going down.

"Hello, Stan. . . . Hello there, Sylvia! Got out earlier than you expected, eh? . . . No, thanks, Stan. Can't stop for a drink now. I'm going on to play poker at the Harvard Club. I took a bunch of fellows there for sixteen hundred the other night, and I've got to give them a chance to get it back." (Sixteen hundred was four months' income for Stan; and about four hours' income for Bull, on one of his good days.) "How about dinner tomorrow, Sylvia?" Bull asked amiably.

"Why, I—— I guess so," she faltered. "Stop in at the office at six; I ought to be through by then." And Bull passed on.

"Look here!" said Stan fiercely. "If you're going to have an affair with me I won't have you playing around with Bull Cardigan!"

"An affair with you? But I thought you turned me down!"

"Well, I—— We'd better think it over," he concluded weakly.

"That's what I told Bull," she said.

"Bull? Do you mean to say he's dared ask you——"

"Now listen, Stan. I like Bull——"

"Oh, you do? I hate the big gorilla!"

"Well, I like him!" said Sylvia defiantly. "In a way. . . . And he attracts me—impersonally—just the way you do. No sentiment about it. But I'm afraid of him, too. He's so tremendous and dominating; and he has a terribly crude philosophy about women. When he wants a woman he just goes and takes her."

"Oh, he does, does he? Well, if he thinks he can do that to you——"

"He says I'm different," said Sylvia reproachfully.

"You certainly are! But if you're falling for that old line——"

"Now, Stan, be fair. Bull wants to settle down—with a home at Great Neck, and two children, and three cars, and a speedboat, and a police dog. He's told me all about it. He knows I don't want to get married, but he's so ruthless and overwhelming that I'm afraid he might marry me under promise of seduction. If I had an affair with him I might lose my head and do anything. . . . That's why I'd rather it was you; because I could trust you not to—not to——"

"Not to become too interesting?" he grunted, flinging a bill at the waiter. "Huh! . . . So it's me or Bull, is it?"

"I didn't mean exactly that, but—— I like you both," said Sylvia desperately. "And if he keeps after me—— Anyway," she said, "you needn't act so snooty about it. I know perfectly well, even if you don't, that it's me or Sheila." He stood up.

"You," he said. "And me. . . . Come on." She shrank back, startled.

"But, Stan, I didn't mean right away——"

"Oh, you didn't? Well, I did." He seized her hands, drew her up out of her seat. "Come along!"

She went with him, meekly.

II

The spring night was damp and chill. A taxi slid up to the curb; he put her into it, climbed in beside her.

"Delta Rho Club," he told the driver. She looked at him in consternation. "I've got to get a suitcase," he explained impatiently, "before we can get into a hotel."

"Not a hotel, Stan! It seems so common. . . . Besides, somebody we know might see us."

"Well, I can't take you to my club, and you can't take me to yours."

That exhausted the possibilities, if she wouldn't consider a hotel. He felt an amazing relief.

"I moved yesterday," said Sylvia. (He thought damn.) "Marigold Palmer went to France and left me her apartment on Ninth Street. You've been there, haven't you? Remember that lovely view over the gardens between Ninth and Tenth? . . . But I don't know," she said. "People we know might see you come in——"

He felt reprieved. . . . But if they didn't see him come in tonight, they might see Bull Cardigan tomorrow night. . . . He gave new directions to the driver, and settled back on the seat, as far from her as possible.

He knew he ought to be wildly happy. The woman who was about to yield to him was the woman he most desired, the woman who was his best friend. . . . But she was Sylvia—Sylvia whom he'd promised to take care of in New York. Of course he'd take care of her; he was saving her from Bull Cardigan. But he couldn't help feeling that she was an appalling responsibility. . . . Sheila Kron, now—— An affair with her entailed no responsibility; it was only part of the routine of seeing New York.

Their hands tingled to the touch as he helped her out, but neither spoke till they were going up the stairs.

"I do hope we can get in," said Sylvia.

"Why couldn't we?" he asked with a flicker of reviving hope.

"Marigold has a morbid fear of burglars. She had a big trick lock put on the door, and the key doesn't always work. Once last month, when Bull and I brought Marigold home from a party, he had to get out on the fire escape—it's on the hallway, in this house—and climb over to the window so he could unlock the door from inside."

"Well, maybe we'll have better luck," said Stan dubiously.

But they didn't. No matter how they twisted the key and turned it and rattled the lock, nothing happened. In the unlighted corridor they looked at each other helplessly.

"Where's this fire escape?" he asked with grim resignation.

"Right outside that window, at the end of the hall. . . . But don't try it, Stan! It's four feet across to the bathroom window, and that's too narrow for you to climb in. You have to swing from it to the sill of the living-room window. You could never make it. . . . No, you'll .have to take me back to the club; they'll put me up. And then we can—think this all over."

He regarded that prospect as the shipwrecked mariner regards the smoke of the passing steamer, disappearing beyond the horizon.

"Oh, I can't do it, can't I? Bull Cardigan did it."

"But, darling, that's his stuff!" (She hadn't called him darling for years; she must be creating atmosphere, he reflected morosely.) "Please, Stan! You're a scientist, not an athlete. It—it doesn't matter."

Her trembling hand clutched his arm, but he shook it off.

"Oh, doesn't it?" he growled. Bull had a dinner date with her to-morrow night; and Bull could get in that window— "I just unlatch the door," Stan asked, "after I'm inside?"

She nodded; without a word she followed him to the fire-escape window; her pale anxious face peered after him as he climbed out.

His legs wound round the fire-escape railing; he looked for the bathroom window. Four feet? It looked like forty. Beyond that, and a little lower, the sill of the living-room window that his groping foot must reach; and a four-story drop to a paved areaway below. . . . But Bull Cardigan had done it, and might do it again. . . . Stan leaned out as far as he dared, and lunged forward. His hands caught the bathroom window sill; hanging from that he swung his legs through the air, trying for a footing at the other window—and missed.

He wondered why the jerk hadn't torn his hands away from the bathroom window sill; but they were hanging on for dear life. You didn't appreciate that phrase when you read it in an armchair. . . . He looked up. Sylvia's frightened face stared from the fire escape like a pallid flower blooming in the night. . . . That line was from one of Sheila's poems. Sheila would never get a man into a jam like this. . . . He looked back at Sylvia. Why didn't she call for help? Of course—she was afraid somebody she knew would discover them. Damn her, she'd let him die for fear of what people would say! And she called herself emancipated. . . . Sheila, now, wouldn't care what people would say; everything had been said about her already——

With a tremendous effort he swung his legs again—and this time his foot caught something. He looked; the blessed window sill. One more swing, a slithering lurch of his body along the blank brick wall, and his hand clutched the framework of the living-room window. He let himself down cautiously—thank God the window was open—and a moment later his feet were planted on the firm, the broad, the immovable floor. He wondered why he had never appreciated floors till now. A man stands on them all the time and never thinks about them, till he stands on nothing. . . .

He fumbled for the light switch, turned it on, and unlatched the door. Sylvia stumbled in and fell in a heap in the nearest chair, staring up at him in silence. But Stan was moved to speech.

"Well!" he said. "You're in—and I'm out. You make me sick! I hope I'll never see you again!" Her eyes opened wider, but still she was silent. "You've made a fool of me long enough!" he cried. "You known damn well I'm in love with you—yes, in love the way our ancestors meant it! I'm crazy about you; I always have been. That time I asked you to marry me, back home, you turned me down so hard that I was afraid to say anything more about it; but lately I've been hoping—— Well, never mind that. I know better now. . . . You wanted an affair—but not with Bull Cardigan. You're afraid of him. You wanted somebody you didn't care anything about, somebody you could throw over whenever you got tired. Well, I won't play Madame Butterfly to your B. F. Pinkerton!"

Her hand moved weakly; she was trying to answer him.

"But you can't live up to your own principles!" he jeered. "You nearly broke my neck tonight because you didn't want to go to a hotel. People might see you! People might talk! Huh! Fine free woman you are! . . . Go on—have your affair with Bull! He'll dominate you; he'll sweep you off your feet; the first thing you know you'll be Mrs. Robert Toombs Cardigan, with two children and three cars and a speedboat and a police dog. And it will serve you right!"

The door slammed behind him; she heard his feet pounding down the stairs. And still she could not stir.

III

Morose and hollow-eyed, he came to the laboratory next morning. Here and here only he felt at home, in an austere atmosphere where men measured in millionths of a millimeter, and thought about quanta and wave lengths, not about women. Among coils and condensers, electric circuits and vacuum tubes, you knew where you were. If you did thus and so, such and such would infallibly happen. No surprises, no humiliating disappointments, no appallingly persistent aches. . . .

For eight hours he watched a spot of light reflected from a mirror move across a ground-glass scale, timing it, and starting it over again, and timing it once more. Eight solid hours of that, without thought of food or drink, or Sylvia. When he had finished he spent three hours more plotting the curve of his results, with the help of the most recondite mathematics. And when he had done that, when the results of his experiment lay plain before him, he sat and stared. He had unsettled some of the surest foundations of human knowledge; he had proved that the world's greatest physicists were wrong.

But maybe he was wrong. He might have made a mistake in his figures; and he'd been having trouble all day with the harmonics in the high-frequency alternating currents. . . . Yesterday, he would have been sure that the world's greatest physicists were wrong; but he hadn't discovered, then, how wrong he could be when he had a chance. He was nobody to unsettle the foundations of human knowledge—he who couldn't even unsettle the self-centered callousness of the girl who was dining, tonight, with Bull Cardigan.

He was tired and hungry, his head ached, he wanted a beefsteak and a baked potato. But when they lay before him, at the restaurant around the corner, he couldn't eat them. He swallowed a cup of coffee, but his head ached still. He wanted—— No, he didn't want Sylvia; he was through with her. He wanted a drink, he wanted a noisy crowd—people who talked and laughed, people who didn't matter.

They wouldn't be hard to find. Vic and Mary Salter were throwing a party tonight at their studio on Tenth Street; half the people he knew would be there. Sylvia and Bull Cardigan might drop in after dinner—— No, they wouldn't; not tonight. . . . He didn't care. He never wanted to see her again.

But Sheila Kron would be there, certainly.

IV

Sheila was the first who greeted him. (It was one of those parties where half the guests never see the host and hostess at all.) She had just collected two drinks from the kitchen, and she gave him one of them. On his empty stomach it had instant effect, powerful and gratifying; he looked down thankfully at her flat-nosed face, her colorless hair, her washed-out eyes that mutely admitted that she knew just how homely she was. Men always began by feeling sorry for her.

"And they call this fun!" she said, looking at the chattering crowd. "This smoke makes my eyes smart. Let's get out of it; we can talk on the fire escape."

He helped her through the window; they leaned against the railing in the cool spring night. Below them, gardens filled the whole interior of the block; in the light from the studio windows the back walls of apartment houses took shape beyond the shrubbery—houses that fronted on the other street. He had just realized that the other street was Ninth Street when Sheila began to talk.

"The trouble about parties like this," she said, "is that somebody always ends up at Port Chester."

"Port Chester? What's that?"

"It's a town up the Sound where you can get marriage licenses in the middle of the night. Many a boy or girl has got stewed at a party, and gone to Port Chester in a coma, and waked up next morning in the Pickwick Arms at Greenwich with a wife or husband they'd never seen till the evening before. . . . That happened to me when I was sixteen."

"Poor kid!" he muttered, and slipped an arm about her shoulders. He felt that he was beginning to understand her; she'd had a pretty tough break, on the whole.

"And the strange thing about it, Stan, is that I tried to make that crazy marriage work. I didn't get much co-operation, but I tried. . . . Oh, I know I'm more or less of a joke around town now, but I was full of good intentions when I was sixteen. Everything might have been different if that first man had been the right sort." He stroked her shoulder sympathetically. "It's funny," she said, "for me to be telling you all this, isn't it?"

"Not a bit," he protested.

Yesterday that would have meant, "I suppose you tell everybody." Now he could only muse on the strange sweet fatality that had drawn them together—two bits of driftwood——

"I don't suppose you can understand a woman like me," she said. "You're so aloof and austere. But if you understood how just knowing you has helped me——" He stirred suddenly. She waited for him to ask her how just knowing him had helped her, till she perceived that he was looking at something over her head. "What's the matter?" she asked.

"A burglar! One of those houses across the gardens. . . . Look—there he is, on the fire escape."

She turned and looked, and laughed.

"He's going out, not coming in. Probably somebody's husband came home too soon."

Stan's eyes were used to the dusk, now. He saw a man straddling the railing of a fire escape—a man with wide bulky shoulders. . . . Bull Cardigan. Sylvia had locked herself out again.

"Look!" Sheila gasped. "Oh! He'll break his neck!"

"I hope he does," Stan muttered.

But he didn't. Powerful and agile as a gorilla, he swarmed from the fire escape to the bathroom window, from bathroom window to living-room window, in one quick movement. They saw the light go on; they saw Bull Cardigan pull down the shade, clear to the sill.

Sheila turned to speak to Stan, but Stan had gone.

v

He ran frantically, recklessly, down the narrow iron steps of the fire escape; from the ladder at the bottom he dropped on the pavement of the area; across the gardens he plunged, panting, sobbing. A high board fence blocked him; he leaped, caught the top of it, pulled himself up and swung over. The barbed wire on the top slashed his hands open, but he never knew it. He had forgotten everything except that he was going to throw Bull Cardigan out of Sylvia's apartment, with his own hands.

The ladder of the other fire escape—Sylvia's fire escape—hung above him, beyond his upraised arms. He leaped, caught the lowest rung, hauled himself up. He ran up the narrow iron stairs, counting the floors; the fourth was Sylvia's. He straddled the railing, leaned toward the bathroom window; driven by red fury, he lunged and caught it; as easily as Bull Cardigan, he swung himself over to the other window. He let himself down and in, under the lowered shade.

With a rattle and bang it flew up. Sylvia, standing listless by the table, whirled about and stared at him. She was alone.

"Where's Bull?" he panted, the frenzy of battle still on him.

"Bull? He went home."

"Why did he go home?" Stan felt cheated of the chance to throw him out.

"I sent him home," said Sylvia. "As soon as he let me in. He—— He didn't want to go. But he went."

They stood for an instant, staring; then they moved forward, drawn by an irresistible force. His arms enfolded her; she drew his face down to hers. . . . At last he stood back, staring into her eyes.

"Sylvia! You said you wouldn't have an affair with a man who was crazy about you. . . . But you're going to."

"I said I wouldn't unless——" She laughed hysterically. "Unless I was crazy about him too."

"What? You—you don't mean you're in love with me? The way our ancestors meant it?"

"God pity my ancestors," she said, "if any of them ever felt what I

felt last night, when you hung by your fingers from the window sill. . . .
Darling, I've always been crazy about you; but I didn't know it till I
saw you hanging there and knew it was my fault. Then something
hit me—the way the hurricane hit Florida. I tried to scream for help,
but I couldn't make a sound, I couldn't stir. Afterward, when you
were bawling me out—and how I deserved it!—I still couldn't say a
word. And when you walked out on me I wished I could die——"

His arms released her; she drew back, hurt and bewildered.

"Put on your hat," he commanded. "We're going to Port Chester."

"Port Chester? Where's that?"

"We'll ask a taxi driver. . . . It's a place where you can get a marriage license in the middle of the night."

"But you don't want to get married! Your laboratory——"

"I do want to get married, to you. I know you don't, but try and
get out of it."

"No danger," said Sylvia blithely. "All day long I've been cursing
myself because I didn't say yes that time you asked me back home—
even if it would have meant a bungalow in the North End."

VI

From the fire escape across the garden, Sheila saw all that happened
in the room where the window shade had flown up, and had never
been pulled down. She watched till Sylvia put on her hat and opened
the door, till Stan turned out the light. Then, facing about with a
sigh, she saw a young man's head and shoulders protruding from the
open window behind her.

"Where's Stan?" he demanded.

"God knows," said Sheila cheerlessly.

"I wanted to see him. I thought he was out here with you."

"Well, you can see he isn't. . . . Help me in, Charlie."

She leaned on his shoulder as she came through the window; his
arm about her waist steadied her as she leaped down to the studio
floor.

"Thanks, Charlie dear. Now perhaps you'll bring me a drink, and
we can settle down to one of our old-time talks."

"I'll bring you a drink," Charlie promised, with a preoccupied
frown. "But I wish I could find out where Stan went——"

Sheila heaved a sigh of resignation.

"If tomorrow morning will do," she said, "you might call him up at
the Pickwick Arms at Greenwich."

THE ROAD TO JERICHO

The man at the wheel kept his eyes on the roadway unrolling in the light of his headlamps; but Janice Blair, huddled beside
him, was looking at the faint-lit speedometer that oscillated around
fifty, at the clock that said ten minutes past eleven.

"How far is it now, Don?"

"Twenty miles or so. . . . Getting worried?"

"Of course. Jeff's train gets in at 11:38, and our house is only five
minutes' walk from the station."

"People sometimes miss the 11:38 and have to wait for the 12:27."

"Not Jeff. On nights when he's working late he always leaves the
office in plenty of time. If he gets home and doesn't find me there——"

"Where are you supposed to be?"

"Over in Great Neck, at the movies. He'd know I ought to have
been back from there before eleven."

"You might have stopped in at somebody's house after the show,"
he suggested.

"Whose? If we begin asking our friends to lie for us we might as
well put it in the papers. . . . We shouldn't have gone so far away,
Don."

"Too many people know me in our part of Long Island. Anywhere
within thirty miles of Manorwood we might have bumped into somebody——"

"So we go halfway to Montauk," she said, "and I take the chances."

"Well—I manage the best I can. We won't always have to hide out
like this. Some day business will pick up; then we can——"

"No use thinking about that now. . . . Can't you drive any faster?"

"Not here. If a cop took the number—— There's a side road just
ahead," he recalled. "Cuts over to the Jericho Turnpike. It might
save us five minutes—but you can't tell what you might stumble on to
in these side roads late at night. Rumrunners, or stick-ups——"

"I'll risk it," she said, "if you will. Muriel knows you're out in the
car; no matter how late you get in, you can make up a story that she'd
believe. But I—— Please, Don, take that side road!"

He turned into it—a black strip between thickets. No other cars were in sight, and as the speedometer skipped up past sixty Janice lit a cigarette and stared absently at the road ahead. She would get home in time, now, barring accidents; with that immediate worry lifted she was free to worry about remoter things. . . . She wondered if Don Sharpe still believed that they were going to get their divorces, and marry, as soon as he could afford to pay alimony. What about his children—and hers? Even if Jeff would let her have them, it wouldn't be easy to take them away from their father. Some people seemed to take such rearrangements lightly—but they were the rich, whose children were brought up by servants anyway. When children were used to both parents, needed them both——

She and Don hadn't thought much about that when this began; they hadn't thought much about anything, because there was nothing much they could do. He was the local realtor in Manorwood; he hadn't made a sale in months. And Janice had been doing her own housework since Jeff's second salary cut; even if Don could support her, the cook-housekeeper-nursemaid couldn't walk out on her family. They had meant to get married as soon as business improved and they could free themselves; her fastidious conscience had been soothed by the assurance that their affair was only a prelude. But business had grown worse. . . .

She lit another cigarette, staring at the black road unrolling in the shifting beam of light. . . . Some people took duplicity lightly too, but she hated it. Furtive midday meetings in Manhattan, when she went in to do her shopping; stolen evenings when Jeff was working in town, and she hired a neighbor's maid to stay with the children while she went out—to the movies. . . . Six months of that, and no end in sight.

It was easier for Don; when he went out he knew his wife was with the children. She usually asked three other women in, to make up a table of bridge; twice she had asked Janice. A third time, and Muriel might begin to wonder at the coincidence of her husband's engagements with Mr. Blair's. Still, he knew his children were safe; while Janice, far from home, was harassed by visions of the house catching fire, and the borrowed maid losing her wits in the crisis. No wonder Don sometimes found her moody and unresponsive. . . .

It was worth it—of course; when you found yourself doing something you were ashamed of, it had to be worth it. When it began, she and Jeff were hardly on speaking terms; she had begun to think her marriage would have to be charged off as a loss, to feel that her only hope lay in a new venture. But now that things were going more smoothly at home; and the duplicity she had reluctantly accepted, as a temporary expedient, was becoming part of the routine of life——

She sat up with a smothered scream.

"Don! Stop!" The car sped on. "Didn't you see it?" she gasped. "A car upset by the roadside?"

"Sure I saw it; but it's none of our business. May be a decoy for a holdup, for all we know."

"But, Don!" Madly she clutched his arms; he had to stop as quickly as he could, swerving and slewing across the road. "You've got a gun," she said. "Go back! The lights were still on; we must be the first car that's come past. If people are hurt back there we can't just pass by on the other side."

"On the road to Jericho, Long Island? . . . The Good Samaritan didn't have to get home by 11:38."

"Never mind that. . . . Don——" She pressed her hands to her head, trying to remember what she had seen in that quick flash of the headlights. "Don, I'm almost sure I saw a child. Lying on the ground, as if it had been pitched out——"

"Might have been a dummy," he muttered. She stared at him.

"Yes, it might," she conceded. "And it might not. Suppose somebody had left one of *your* children lying hurt by the roadside?"

"Look here, Janice, you don't realize—— Suppose it really is an accident. *We* can't take anybody to a hospital. We wouldn't get home till one o'clock—and we'd have to give our names. You could make up a name but I couldn't; they'd have the number of the car. If Muriel found out I'd been out with a woman, on a night when you were out too——"

His voice died away before the incredulous scorn in her eyes.

"I see. . . ." Suddenly she opened the door, got out. "Go on home to Muriel," she told him. "I'm going back to that wreck."

For an instant he listened to the click-clack of her heels on the road; then, cursing, he turned the car around, came up behind her as she walked swiftly on—bare-armed, bareheaded, her bronze hair shining in the glow of the headlamps. He stopped beside her; she got in without a word; cautiously they drove up to the wreck. . . . She laughed jerkily as the light fell on that huddled bundle on the ground. It wasn't a child—only a topcoat, turned inside out and flung aside.

"That's that," said Don, disgusted. "We'd better be on our way."

"But we've got to see if there's anybody in that car!"

She was getting out but he thrust her back; flashlight and gun in hand he stepped down, began to explore the nearer thickets. He had

plenty of physical courage, anyway. . . . She got out too, went up to
the wreck in the light of the headlamps. A man lay sprawled beside
the car, his eyes closed, his chest all bloody; his face seemed vaguely
familiar. She bent down; he was still breathing. Vainly she tried to
lift him.

"Don!" she called. The wounded man's eyes fluttered.

"Horse Lombard," he whispered. "Run me off the road, then
plugged me. Tried to make it look like a stick-up. . . ."

His voice died out as Don came up, gun and flashlight ready.

"Janice!" he cried. "You've got blood all over your arms!"

"So I have. . . . I think he's been shot, Don, but he's still alive. Help
me lift him." But Don stood still.

"He looks like a tough customer, Janice. No loss to society."

"But even so——" She was breathing hard. "We can't just leave him
here!" In the silence they heard a distant rapid sputter, saw a single
headlight far down the road. Don relaxed in relief.

"Motor cop," he said. "He'll look after him. Time for us to go."

"He can't take this man to a hospital on a motorcycle."

"Do you want to give our names to the police?" he demanded furiously. "Want to have to tell them what we're doing out here? Want
to see it in all the papers tomorrow?" He turned away. "Come on,
Janice. You can't do a thing without the car—and the car's going home
to Manorwood."

She stood still, incredulous, till she heard the engine starting; then,
in panic, she ran to the car and climbed in. Before the motorcycle
headlight touched them they were safe around a curve in the road.

Once more the speedometer hovered around sixty; the clock stood
at eleven thirty. Shivering, Janice drew on her coat, sat silent.

"Of course I wouldn't have left you behind," Don reassured her
presently. "But I had to get you started someway. . . . Looked like a
gangster killing. We've got no business mixing in with things like
that."

Her silence was implacable; presently he tried again.

"Even Jeff must miss his train once in a while." Still she was silent.
"We'd better get together on a story," he warned her. "If he does happen to have got home ahead of you——" She laughed.

"Do you think that's what's worrying me, Don?"

"You mean he might not ask too many questions? . . . That's so,"
he said, relieved. "He couldn't afford to. For after all, even if he suspected something, what could he do?"

"You mean that even if he wanted to kick his wife out of the house he'd know he couldn't afford to hire another cook-housekeeper-nurse-maid? . . . Thank you, Don; I hadn't thought of that. I doubt if Jeff would think of it either; he's curiously old-fashioned, in some ways. . . . But that isn't what's worrying me." Her words tumbled over one another in stuttering fury. "For six months I've been the mistress of a man who wouldn't go back to see if a child had been hurt—who wouldn't take a wounded man to the hospital."

"But, Janice, I couldn't let you——"

"You weren't thinking about me—not much, anyway. . . . Don't talk to me!"

After that, neither of them said another word till he let her out at the shaded corner, a hundred yards from her door. She felt a familiar relief as she saw that at any rate the house hadn't burned down while she was away. . . .

"What are you going to tell him, Janice?"

"I've no idea. . . . But don't worry; I won't mention your name, anyway. I—I'd be ashamed to, now."

His car rolled away. . . . Since she was late anyhow, she ought to give herself time to think up a story; but she found herself hurrying, feeling the way she ought to have felt six months ago. Miraculously they had escaped discovery all those months; but you had to pay sooner or later for anything you did, and she was paying at last. What Jeff might do, if he found her out, she couldn't guess; but she knew how he would feel. . . . How she would feel, too. . . . She stumbled up the porch steps, still with no idea of what she was going to say to him.

The neighbor's maid rose, yawning, from the living-room couch.

"Everything's been fine, Mrs. Blair. The baby woke up about ten; I gave her a drink of water. And Mr. Blair called up half an hour ago; he'd just missed his train, but he said he'd be out on the 12:27."

"Oh. . . ." So there was a God after all—a merciful God, who made allowances. . . . "Thank you, Nellie. Sorry I kept you up so late; I met some people in Great Neck after the show, and stopped to talk."

II

Five minutes later the maid was gone, and Janice was staring into the bathroom mirror at disheveled bronze hair, a white haggard face, arms dark with dried blood. . . . If Jeff had been at home she could never have explained all that; but now she had plenty of time to clean herself up. . . . She bathed, went to bed—and lay tossing, her nerves in tatters. . . . That man they'd left bleeding by the roadside—she had known his face. A waiter, perhaps, from some roadhouse where Don had taken her? Well, no use worrying about him now; she ought to go to sleep. . . . But all at once she was out of bed, hurrying downstairs to the closet where she had left her coat. Yes, there was a sticky smudge on the cuff——

She cleaned it as well as she could and went back to bed, her heart pounding. She had almost forgotten that stain; what else might she have forgotten? It didn't seem possible, or even right, that she should be let off unpunished. She had taken chances before—crazily reckless chances—and hadn't worried like this; but then she was always looking forward to her next meeting with Don. It would be too sickening to be discovered now. . . .

She heard a taxi stopping outside; Jeff's key in the lock; his feet on the stairs. She doubted if she could sham sleep successfully, so she sat up, turned on the light. His tired face lightened as he saw her.

"Hello! Thought you'd be asleep." He stooped and kissed her.

"I saw a rather gruesome movie; it gave me the jitters.. . . . Too bad you missed your train, dear." (She hated that, but she had to say it.)

"I didn't mind." He began undressing. "Ran into Sam Tolman of Bayside at the station, and rode out with him. He's one of the counsel in the city graft investigation and he says they're really on the trail of some of the higher-ups at last. They put a fellow named Buck Burke on the stand today. Maybe you read about it, in the evening paper. The organization gypped him somehow and he's ready to tell all he knows. He barely got started today; before he's through they'll have enough to send some really big men to Sing Sing." She offered no comment on this prospect of civic betterment; he stopped beside her, stroked her hair. "You look tired, Jan. Poor kid, you work so hard——"

"I don't mind it." Her voice was unsteady. "You work hard too."

"Thank God I've got a job to work at. I've got over being sore at the universe because I'll never be able to retire on stock profits. . . . I must have been insufferable last winter, Jan—grouching around and taking the depression as a personal insult. But it made me ashamed of myself when you took hold without a whimper, doing work we never thought you'd have to do again. I married the best little sportsman on earth; so long as we've got each other and the kids and enough to eat——" He turned off the light, lay down, slipped an arm around her. "You're shivering, Jan. Try to stop thinking about that movie and go to sleep."

But she couldn't sleep when his praise burned her like acid; when her thoughts kept going back to the picture of a man named Buck

Burke in the evening paper—Buck Burke, whose blood had dried on her arms.

III

She was on the porch next afternoon when the newsboy tossed the evening paper into the yard, and before she had finished reading it— or the only part she cared about—the telephone rang.

"Mrs. Blair? This is Don Sharpe." (Talking from his office, where people could hear him.) "I have a client who'd like to rent your house for the rest of the summer. May I come up and talk over his offer?"

"Our house isn't for rent." Her voice shook; she'd always been ashamed of these tricks and expedients. . . . But she had to see him, now. "Still you might drop in," she said, "and tell me about it."

She settled down on the porch; the children were playing in the yard and she had no intention of receiving Don indoors. Five minutes later his car stopped at the curb; he ran up on the porch, pale and apprehensive.

"How about it?" he asked. "There wasn't a single moment when I could have talked to you this morning. . . . Did your story get over?"

"I didn't have to invent one; for once Jeff missed a train. But—— You read the papers, Don? Buck Burke, the key witness in the graft investigation—dead when the policeman found him. Don, he must have died in my arms! . . . No, I'm not going to be hysterical." She sat down, lit a cigarette. "But we've got to decide what we ought to do."

"Do? There's nothing to do but keep our mouths shut, and thank our stars we didn't get mixed up in a story that's all over the front page. . . . Lord, what a narrow escape! The police think a woman was mixed up in it—that phone call that decoyed him out of town. . . . And then when they found your heelprints around the car, and a bronze hairpin——"

"They can't identify that; all bronze hairpins look alike. Anyway, they've got the right man—this Horse Lombard who was picked up on suspicion at Huntington, an hour afterward. The paper said he had the gambling concession at Sylvanus Magargel's political club—and Magargel was one of the higher-ups they thought they'd get through Burke's evidence."

"How do you know Lombard's the right man? They're only holding him while they check up on his alibi."

"Don, he killed Burke. Burke told me so, as he was dying."

He stared at her as if she had told him she had leprosy.

"I didn't hear him say it!" he exploded. "I didn't hear you say it either—and you start forgetting it right now! This may be the biggest scandal since the Becker case. We can't afford to mix up in it!"

"Do you think I want to? But—— This stuff they're digging up about some of the politicians is pretty rotten. Decent people ought to do anything they can——"

"Nobody'd call you decent after you'd had to explain where you were last night, and why. You'd be the key witness then, and the lawyers and reporters would dig up everything you'd ever done in your life. . . . No, you forget about it. They've got the right man without our help; so you just forget it ever happened."

She only hoped she could. . . . He picked up his hat.

"I'd better be going, Janice. . . . When can I see you again?"

"Never—except just around town. . . . Don, I can't go on with it."

"What? Look here, I know a narrow escape like that must have been a shock to you——"

She laughed. "That wasn't the shock, Don. When you wouldn't go back to see if a child had been hurt——"

He fidgeted a little; then—— "Well, I did go back," he said sulkily, "when I saw you meant it. And it wasn't a child. And we couldn't have got Burke to a hospital. . . ."

"As it turned out, we couldn't. But what sickened me was the way you acted before we knew how it was going to turn out. I'd never seen you in a jam before. . . . You look like somebody else, Don."

"But when everything was all right before—— It's not reasonable!"

"Emotions never are. It wasn't reasonable, when you and I had known each other for years, that we danced together at the club one night and felt all at once as if we'd just met. . . . But anyway, I can't go on with it. When poor Jeff is working so hard, and about all he's got is his absolute confidence that I'd never let him down——"

He laughed. "You didn't talk that way about Jeff last winter. . . . But I guess every marriage has its ups and downs. Yours is up just now; and you've had what you wanted and got tired of it, so you're ready to quit and ease your conscience."

"Don, that's not true! I *was* in love with you—but that's all gone now. Call me anything you like, but I can't go on with it." He had risen; he stood over her, menacing. "Don't make a scene on the front porch," she said scornfully. "When we've fooled everybody for six months it would be a pity to start the neighbors talking now."

He glowered at her, stood hesitant.

"And you won't say anything about last night?" he persisted.

"No. . . . After all, they've got the right man; why should I?"

He went down the steps—for the last time; she watched his car roll down the street, disappear around the corner. . . . And now Jeff never need know. . . . She found herself singing as she moved about the kitchen, getting dinner.

IV

Saturday was dance night at the club and all Manorwood was there. Janice saw Don scowling at her furtively, when his wife wasn't looking. Presently, pausing beside him between dances——

"You ought to ask me to dance," she whispered. "Jeff and Muriel will think it's queer if you don't; we've always been such good partners. . . . Besides, I've got to talk to you."

"Jeff suspicious?" he asked uneasily. She shook her head.

"No—but Horse Lombard has been released for lack of evidence."

"Don't you say that name here! . . . Save me the next one, Janice."

They danced; afterward, they went out on the porch to smoke—the club porch, where he had first kissed her. Queer that she could be here with him and feel nothing; that an emotion which could make you behave insanely could turn itself off and on like electricity. . . .

"Don," she said, "I'm the only person who knows that man killed Buck Burke. I'd thought of writing the police an anonymous letter——"

"They might trace it. It wouldn't be evidence, anyway. They need proof, and you couldn't give it without going on the stand. . . . No, you lay off this! You hear?"

"I could go on the stand without giving you away—or myself. I'd been to the movies; afterward a man I—I didn't care to name had taken me for a little drive—— Don, it could sound innocent enough."

"Innocent!" he jeered. "A man you didn't care to name! You'd have to name him; he's a corroborative witness. . . . And did you tell your husband all about it the next morning? Lombard's lawyers would want to know why not. . . . My God, Janice, that's childish! By the time counsel for the defense had got through with you everybody'd know where you'd been and why you'd been there; and when they proved that you'd lied about that, they'd make the jury believe you'd lied all the way through. You wouldn't hurt Lombard, or Sylvanus Magargel; but what you'd do to yourself, and Jeff, and your children—— Not to speak of me," he added drily. "Is Horse Lombard worth it?"

She stood silent a while, looking at the winking lights on the farther shore of the Sound. Lombard wasn't worth it, of course; she wasn't sure civic virtue was worth it. But the self-respect of Janice Blair—— She laughed silently; you couldn't respect yourself if you upset two homes, smeared the growing minds of five little children.

"You have to pay for everything, don't you, Don? . . . I seem to have forfeited the right to self-respect."

"Because we've had an affair? Lots of people have done that."

"No, that was honest and clean—at the beginning, anyway. . . . It's funny, Don. We got into all this trouble because I tried to be a good Samaritan, and help a dying man by the side of the road. . . . Don't worry; I know I can't afford to tell."

Yet she knew that she was still hoping for a miracle—some piece of evidence turning up unexpectedly that would convict Horse Lombard. Without that she must keep on paying, not for her sins but for her virtues. But nothing was important enough to justify what confession would do to Jeff, and her children.

v

The Burke case disappeared from the front page; eventually it disappeared from the newspapers altogether; and it could be conjectured that the District Attorney's office was not too keenly distressed by the lack of evidence against Horse Lombard, who was too close for comfort to men higher up. Yet, as the summer wore on, Janice began to believe in miracles.

It wasn't a miracle, of course, this swift restoration of domestic harmony that Jeff liked to call a second honeymoon. Partly it was a mere reduction to elementals; after the inflated hopes of the boom years, the stinging bitterness of the collapse, they had slowly come to recognize—as had a million other married couples—that they must come back to the simple primitive pattern. A man and a woman living and working together—the man going out to get the meat, the woman staying at home to look after the house and the children; needing each other so much that whether they wanted each other was irrelevant.

But they did want each other; that was the unexpected felicity. . . . Undeserved, too, Janice sometimes thought; she was being let off too easily. Still, that night on the side road she had been ready (like Abraham) to make any sacrifice; and like Abraham, once she had shown her intention she was excused from actual proof. . . . That sort of reasoning was a hangover from Sunday school; when you were thirty years old, and had seen what happened to people, you knew things didn't work that way. Still, they were working that way for her; and when she tried to remember the shamed apprehension in which she had come home that night, expecting to have to face Jeff— when she found that already the memory was fading out—she could only be thankful that somehow, whether she deserved it or not, she had escaped. . . .

Not that she spent much time worrying about such matters; she was too happy. Jeff seemed to feel that he had to make up to her for his long moroseness; she had something to make up to him too, and she could do it spontaneously and completely, now that she was free from the constraint of the months when she had been Don Sharpe's mistress. . . . Don Sharpe's mistress. That was simply incredible, now; when she met him at the club, on the street, he was only Don Sharpe— Muriel Sharpe's husband, an unusually good dancing partner. She supposed, in retrospect, that the affair might have ended much sooner if she had been willing to admit, even to herself, that a woman like her could feel like that—and then get over it. Perhaps a really first-rate woman wouldn't have got over it so soon; but she had; it was all past and gone now, and she could give all of herself to Jeff. What he didn't know couldn't hurt him; and so long as she knew that she was making him happy——

Then a man named Pink Murray was arrested for the murder of Buck Burke.

Janice read that with a sick incredulity, a dizzying shock like nothing she had ever felt in her life; a horrible nightmare, all but forgotten, had suddenly become real. Then, as she followed the story, she saw that she might have expected it; prosecutors might have been willing to give up the Burke case but the reformers, the graft investigators—above all, the newspapers that crusaded for civic virtue and bigger circulations—wouldn't let it drop. Somebody had to be arrested and Pink Murray was the unlucky man. Double unlucky; he was a gambler with a police record, who might have been damaged by Burke's testimony; and he had no connection at all with Sylvanus Magargel, or any other of the higher-ups whom Burke's evidence had threatened.

Even so, Janice couldn't take it seriously at first. But more and more evidence, circumstantial but damning, piled up against Pink Murray. He was indicted, and with unprecedented speed was brought to trial; there appeared witnesses who had seen him that night in Central Long Island, witnesses who had heard him threaten to kill Buck Burke after a quarrel a week before; Janice could perceive that it was expedient that one man should die for certain other people.

But she still couldn't believe it. She read every word about the trial in the papers, and for the first time since June found it hard to sleep of nights; but she knew that Pink Murray hadn't killed Buck Burke. She didn't suppose that a judicial system which let the flagrantly guilty escape would lend itself so easily to the framing of the innocent; she didn't realize what perjury can do when there is plenty of money to buy witnesses; she didn't appreciate the zeal of a youthful District Attorney, fattened on front-page publicity, drunk with ambition, and thankfully sure that he could get this conviction without stepping on important toes. She went on believing what she had to believe to make life livable—till the afternoon when the newsboy tossed the evening paper into the yard, and she ran out to read the streamer headline:

PINK MURRAY GUILTY IN FIRST DEGREE

Presently she put on her coat and went out to walk. It was November; dry leaves blew about the streets, the air was pungent with the smell of bonfires; on the bay front angry little waves whipped the beach. That hot June night when she made Don Sharpe turn back on a side road—it couldn't have happened. She wasn't a woman who sneaked out, when her husband was away, to meet another woman's husband. She was a woman who worked for the man who worked for her, and liked it; who kept his house and took care of his children and slept in his arms. It wasn't fair to make a woman like her, a woman who was doing her job and making her husband happy, pay for another woman's mistakes. . . . She was in the business section of the village now, approaching Don Sharpe's office. She walked in, found him alone.

"Have you seen the papers, Don?" He nodded.

"But Murray will appeal, of course, Janice. He may get off. And anyway, who is he? A tinhorn gambler with a record; if he didn't do this he probably did something else just as bad." He looked at her, and whitened. "Good God, Janice, after all these months you wouldn't kick everything over, just for the sake of Pink Murray!"

"Not for Pink Murray—for Janice Blair. I'd loathe myself forever if I didn't. But I thought I ought to warn you, so that you'd have a chance to tell Muriel first." His eyes shifted. "You've told her!" she gasped. "I might have known you would!"

"I never meant to, Janice. The way it happened——"

"I don't care how it happened." Her hand was on the door.

"Wait!" He started up, caught her wrist. "Muriel won't tell any-body," he said. (Janice could believe that; Muriel was too vain to admit that another woman had distracted her husband.) "And you know all the publicity this will mean——"

"Let me worry about that. You're out of it."

"I'm in on the publicity," he told her. "They'll make you name the man—and I want to tell you right now that I'll deny everything. Nobody can prove where I was on the night of June eighteenth. People in Manorwood never suspected us; we covered up too well. If I deny it, say you must be pinning it on me to protect somebody else, as many people here in town will believe my story as yours."

"Why should you deny it, if Muriel knows and has—forgiven you?"

"It would ruin me if I didn't deny it."

"Ruin you if people knew you'd had an affair? Nonsense."

"Damn the affair. But I'm in real estate. If I helped convict Lombard, if a big organization man like Magargel is involved——"

"I see. . . . All right," she said. "Protect yourself if you can. But I'm going to tell what happened."

"Oh, you are? Have you told Jeff?"

"Not yet. I'm going to tell him first, of course. . . ."

"All right; tell him and see how he likes it. Ask him how he'll en-joy hearing you tell everybody how you cheated with another man. Ask him what it might do to your children. Ask him what chance you'll have of convicting Horse Lombard with me denying everything you say. Just you tell him."

"I'm going to," she said.

VI

But as she went home she felt more ashamed, more apprehensive, than she had felt as she came home on that night in June. It would be harder for her, harder for Jeff too, than if she had had to tell him that night; and she couldn't guess how he might take it. Jeff had lots of stuff but she'd always thought Don had plenty of stuff, till he cracked in a crisis. She and Jeff hadn't faced a real crisis in their eight years of marriage, unless you counted the loss of their money in the 1929 stock crash; and the way he had reacted to that wasn't reas-suring. . . .

At least she could put it off, had to put it off, till everything else was out of the way. She got dinner and tried not to be suspiciously silent at the table; afterward she washed the dishes (Jeff dried them for her) and then went upstairs to see if the children were all right. They seemed to be; at any rate they had fallen asleep. . . . There was always something otherworldly about sleeping children. They were too young to appreciate this now, but when they grew older what would they think of their mother? . . . A mother who let an innocent man go to the chair wouldn't be much good either; but if she did that they would never know it, and what people didn't know wouldn't hurt them. . . .

She came back to the living room. Jeff was reading on the couch, but when he saw her he put down his book, patted the cushions beside him. She sat down—but at the farther end of the couch.

"Jeff . . . I'm sorry, but I've got to tell you something."

He sat still, unnaturally still, as she went through the whole story; only his fingers moved. He had been cutting the pages of his book and the heavy bronze paper knife was still in his hand; his fingers played with it as she went on, his eyes were fixed on it, his face contorted. . . . You could kill somebody with that paper knife; she faced the possibility that he might kill her with it, then and there. . . .

"That's all," she said at last. "I—I'm terribly sorry, Jeff."

He sat looking at the paper cutter; slowly his strong fingers bent it into a horseshoe, an oval, a crumpled mass of metal. He flung it, clattering, into the fireplace, and looked up at her.

"You poor kid! Carrying all that load of secrets around with you for months . . ." But she saw that he was terribly hurt.

"Oh, I hoped you'd never have to know, Jeff!"

"I wish I didn't know. I hate it like hell! I'd never dreamed that you could——"

"I didn't either, till it happened. Maybe some women wouldn't mind it, but I—I'm so ashamed. . . ." By now, he had regained control of himself.

"I'm the one who ought to be ashamed," he said drily. "What a louse Sharpe is! If I was so bad that you could take up with him—— But these last months," he said, "since you broke off with Sharpe. The way you've acted, the way things have been between us—— Did you mean that, Jan? Has that all been on the level?"

"Oh, yes, darling, yes! I'm crazy about you now."

She was crying for the first time in years; he gathered her in his arms but she kept on crying inconsolably.

"All right," he soothed her. "It's all right. If only you feel this way about me now it's all right, Jan."

"All right—except that I've got to tell the whole story in court."

She saw that in his reassurance he had for the moment forgotten that; and with that realization, she almost broke down again.

"Jeff, I won't do it! I've hurt you enough! Pink Murray isn't worth it; I'm not worth it—what it would do to you and the children!"

"Oh, but you've got to do it, of course," he said. "Can't let an innocent man go to the chair. It won't be much fun for any of us, but you've got to play the hand the way it's dealt."

"But it isn't fair, Jeff. The whole town will despise me; they may despise you too, when I tell my story. People's minds do work like that. It isn't fair to drag you into it just because you—you happened to marry a woman like me."

"I don't know what I've ever done to deserve a woman like you," he said slowly. "Plenty of women have had affairs; but a woman who'd risk everything to help somebody who was in trouble, a woman who —who sweareth to her own hurt and changeth not——"

"I'm swearing to your hurt too—and the children's. I've got no right to risk other people's everything."

"The children don't read the papers."

"But when they grow older they'll hear about this. . . ."

"Yes," he said, "they will. And I hope they'll believe what they hear from their father rather than what they get from gossip around town. If they do that, they'll be proud that they're the children of a first-rate woman. . . . You can get somebody to stay with them tomorrow, can't you? I'll get the office to let me off; I want to go along with you when you tell your story to the District Attorney."

"I don't deserve it, Jeff. But if you'll always go along with me——"

SURE THING

There's a great moral lesson somewhere in what happened to Carla Furness, if only you can figure it out. . . .

She was sitting in one of the little booths across from the bar at Louis's, listening to Rex Ainsworth. But she was also looking at him, and it was hard for a woman who did that to pay much attention to what he was saying. He was forty-odd, with sparse black hair and bright black eyes and a black mustache, and a complexion that matched Carla's tinted fingernails; he always wore a flower in his buttonhole, and you could tell by looking at him what clubs he belonged to.

"But you wouldn't need to put up any money," he insisted.

"Somebody would. I couldn't let you guarantee my account."

"Why not? I've got plenty of money and you're broke, now that people can't afford to have their apartments redecorated. God knows when the decorating business will pick up again, but people who study the undercurrents know that the upturn has already begun."

"Has it? Nobody I meet seems to know it."

"The people you meet don't study economic trends. But I do, and I know you can see things beginning to get better. My God, Carla, it's been nearly a year and a half since the stock crash! You don't expect the depression to last forever, do you? The point is that what will go down in history as the recovery of 1931 is just starting; it will be weeks before it's reflected in stock prices, and in the meantime the smart people who know what's going on can clean up. . . . I'm buying five thousand Amalgamated Consolidated for myself; I could buy five hundred for you, and when it goes up——"

"Suppose it goes down, Rex."

"It won't go down," he assured her.

"Everything does. I bought some steel last winter, when it touched a new low. That new low is an old high now."

He laughed. "The trouble with you, Carla, is that you play the market the way you play roulette—just toss your money on the board and pray. So do most people, thank God; that's why trained minds that understand the forces governing price movements can make money in Wall Street. . . . Amal Con won't go down. Most of it's held by a few big fellows who won't let go of it, so this pool will have an easy

336

time pushing it up. It closed today at 28½ and they won't pull out the plug till it touches 70. You'd make twenty thousand clear, on five hundred shares."

"But that's not sporting," she protested. "Like betting on a horse race that you know is fixed—playing a sure thing."

"Every stock speculator thinks he's playing a sure thing; only he usually happens to be wrong."

"How do you know you're not wrong this time?"

"Well—confidentially, of course—a couple of directors of the company are in the pool. I've got the most absolute assurance from the insiders——"

"Yes," she said, "it certainly does take a trained mind to understand the forces governing price movements." He shrugged.

"That's the way the game is played, Carla. No reason why you shouldn't make some money out of it."

She stared silently into her empty cocktail glass. She badly needed to make some money out of something; her business was all but on the rocks.

"Waiter!" he called. "Two more Bacardis. . . . Carla, don't say I can't do this just because we—because we're in love."

"Are we?" she wondered. "Anyway, there's the look of the thing——"

Then the drinks arrived, and the suave proprietor with them.

"Everything all right, Mr. Ainsworth?"

"Everything fine, Louis—even the weather. You don't have any better spring weather than this in Italy. I know; I've been there."

"Louis isn't Italian, he's Spanish," said Carla. Louis frowned.

"Spanish? No! I am Catalan, from Barcelona. Some day you will see a free Catalonia——"

A waiter caught his eye, so they heard no more about free Catalonia. Over his glass, Ainsworth looked speculatively at Carla.

"To resume," he said. "What's wrong with the look of the thing?"

"You know. You've got a reputation—odd man in two divorces. Often a co-respondent but never a bridegroom."

"I'll be a bridegroom if you say the word."

"That isn't all. Everybody knows you've carried a lot of your women in stock deals, just the way you want to carry me."

"That was different. Anyway, you know I'm through with that stuff."

"You'd better be, if I marry you."

"I would be. So why don't you marry me?"

"Well—— You'll laugh at this, Rex; but I really don't approve of

you. I mean—— You were pretty rotten to some of those other women."
He looked at her with a slow grin.

"Carla, you continually surprise me. I suppose that's why I want
to marry you—there'd be something new every day. Just now—— You
look as if you'd been grown under glass, in a Fifth Avenue show window; but get under your skin, and you're just a little girl from—where
was it? Blue Valley, Iowa? . . . Sure, I was rotten to some of those
women. The reason? Chiefly, that I didn't really care a damn about
them. But I couldn't be rotten to you. And you must see something
in me——"

"The same thing all the other women saw, I guess. Not your trained
mind. . . . Anyhow, if you carried me in this stock deal everybody'd
think——"

"Nobody'd need to know about it, except the broker."

"Mayberry? But he knows me; so does his wife. Even if I married
you twenty times over, afterward, they'd always believe——"

"Darling, you're priceless. Why not marry me now, and let me give
you the stock for a wedding present?"

"I couldn't marry anybody while business is so bad," she protested.
"People would think I'd given up trying to make the grade, and taken
you for your money. . . .People in Blue Valley, I mean."

"Why would they know about me? I can't flatter myself that this
reputation of mine that seems to worry you so has reached Blue
Valley."

"There are Blue Valley people in New York. Ben and Edith Fowler
live two floors above me; they always bring the *Weekly Register* down
for me to read, after they're through with it. They know I've had to
let my maid go, and they've read about you in the papers—— I don't
suppose a native New Yorker can understand it," she sighed. "But we
people who came in from the small towns—we're always watching our
old friends, wondering if they're really getting over or just throwing a
front. . . . And here's another thing you won't understand," she said.
"You inherited plenty of money, had it all your life. But we didn't
have much at home and I was taught to take money seriously. If you
carried this stock for me I'd feel as if—as if you had a mortgage on
me. And if Amal Con went down——"

"Carla, you're quaint. . . . Anyway, it won't go down." He glanced
about; the other tables were filling up. "Twenty past six," he said.
"We might as well stay here for dinner. You haven't got a date, have
you?"

"Afraid I have. Andrew Bush is coming in."

"Andrew Bush? Oh, yes." He suppressed a faint grin. "I've met him, haven't I—your old high-school classmate from Blue Valley? The one who works for the telephone company?"

"He used to work for the telephone company, when he first came to town," said Carla with dignity. "But he's one of the Younger Critics now. You must have seen his stuff in the reviews."

"Yes, but that's another business that is not so good any more—being a Younger Critic." Suddenly his eyes were suspicious. "Carla! You said this fellow was coming in. You don't mean you're going to cook dinner for him, in that hole-in-the-wall kitchenette?"

"Yes. What of it?" But she had reddened.

"What of it? You hate to cook; you won't do it, for me. But this fellow——"

"Please, Rex! . . . I'll have to tell you exactly how it is," she decided. "If he dreamed I'd told anybody, he'd never forgive me——"

"And would that make such a lot of difference?"

"Now, Rex, Andy's nothing but—but a boy from back home."

"I'm glad to know that. Does he know it?"

"Of course he knows it. He isn't interested in me; he isn't interested in women at all. Only in ideas. He's writing a book—a very constructive book about the future of America, and whither are we drifting, and the challenge of the crisis, and so on. He writes enough reviews in odd moments to make about twelve dollars a week, and he's learned how to live on that—in New York! Can you imagine it? He's got a furnished room somewhere in a slum—he won't tell anybody where it is—and he doesn't eat anything but crackers and milk and bananas——"

"Except when an old high-school classmate broils a steak for him."

"But he doesn't know I'm going to! He wouldn't come if he did; he's terribly proud. But he needs some real food once in a while; so when he called up I asked him to stop in for a cocktail at a quarter to seven. And I thought I'd say I was too tired to go out and was just cooking a little something for myself, and wouldn't he sit down and help me eat it. See?"

"I see," said Ainsworth, none too happily. "Well—— You'll let me take you home, won't you? Shall we drive through the Park?"

The body of the taxi was mostly glass, but she didn't mind that as they drove through the Park, with his arms around her. When Rex Ainsworth was making love to you you felt that you were really in New York; you had the sense of being in contact with the classic tradition of Petronius and Cellini and Casanova. Most of the passengers in the other taxis driving through the Park were similarly engaged, and had no attention to waste on their neighbors; but on the whole, Carla was rather glad of the walls of glass and the restraints they imposed on Ainsworth. When he kissed her, she reflected dreamily that even if he had been rotten to other women, he was sorry for it now; and he could never be rotten to her. But in the intervals between his kisses, a streak of Blue Valley small-mindedness suggested that probably every one of those other women had thought the same, in her time.

The taxi left the Park, turned eastward down a cross street.

"Rex darling—let me go. I don't want the neighbors to see——" She was thankful that her apartment house was a remodeled walkup, with no doorman, no hallboys. "Please, Rex——"

But he didn't let her go till the taxi stopped. She got out and waved good-bye to him, noticing thankfully that no one was near; she hadn't seen the tall, rough-hewn young man whom the taxi had passed at the corner. He didn't look much like a Younger Critic, though he was; he looked like one who had followed the plow back in Iowa, as he had. He walked past Carla's door; he walked around the block. He had walked around the block four times before he finally decided that the private morals of an old high-school classmate were really no concern of his. If she chose to let a rotter like Ainsworth make love to her in a glass-walled taxi in broad daylight, that was of no importance to a man who was concentrated on the writing of a constructive book about the future of America, and the challenge of the crisis—even though he had known her back home in Blue Valley.

II

And meanwhile Carla was squeezing limes for the cocktail, and putting the steak on to broil. In a smart speakeasy she had looked like something grown under glass in a Fifth Avenue show window; but busy in her kitchenette, in a big white apron, she could have posed for a picture of any woman getting dinner for any man, and wondering why he was late. At last the bell rang; she flew to the door.

"Hello, Andy! How's everything?"

He wondered how she had the effrontery to look so simple and domestic and hospitable when she had just been flaunting her amours before every passer-by; a man with real character, he recognized gloomily, would simply have turned his back on her and walked out. But no man, with character or without it, could have turned his back on the aroma of that steak; especially not a man who lived on bananas and crackers and milk.

"Everything's so-so," he said hoarsely. "How are you?"

"Oh, I'm feeling fine, Andy. Just fine!"

He didn't doubt it, and loathed himself for the poltroonery that kept him from slapping her on the mouth that Ainsworth had kissed. But they had their cocktail; and she explained that she was too tired to go out to dinner so she'd got a little something in; and if he had no other engagement, wouldn't he sit down and take potluck with her? He knew that steak was no potluck; he had no right to let a woman feed him. But after all, an old high-school classmate, to whose flagrantly open amours he felt only a contemptuous indifference, could hardly be classed as a woman.

Just a friend from Blue Valley; that was the only way he could think of her—the only way he had ever thought of her. And there was no harm in staying and taking potluck with a friend from back home.

"How's the book going?" she asked him after dinner.

"Not so well as I'd like," he admitted.

"Why don't you bring up some more chapters for me to read?"

"You didn't think much of what I showed you. . . . And you were right."

"But, Andy, it wasn't bad. It—it's probably a swell book, of its kind. It just didn't seem like you, somehow."

"That's probably in its favor. . . . Damn the book," he said. "Let's talk about something else." Anxiously she wondered why he was so blue.

"How about asking Ben and Edith down to play bridge?" she proposed.

"I don't feel like seeing people tonight. . . . Let's do the dishes. You know your conscience won't let you leave them till morning."

Wiping china and glass and silver, he felt better; working with her seemed as natural as breathing. But when they took off their aprons and went back to the living room, that picture he'd seen through the window of a taxi came back to his inward eye, painted in fiery color.

"Want a highball?" she asked. "Or a rickey?"

"No, thanks. Can't tell what two drinks might do to me; that cocktail was the first I'd had in a month." (He couldn't afford them, of course; and she knew he was ashamed to see any of his other friends, when he was so poor.)

"Andy, I know you're working too hard, and not taking enough care of yourself!" He shrugged away her solicitude.

"I'm all right. How are things with you?"

She wanted to tell him that things with her were simply terrible;

that she wasn't making any money, and was in love—if that was the
word for it—with a man who really looked pretty bad, by the standards
of Blue Valley. But when you're keeping up a front in Manhattan,
with nothing much behind it, you don't make such confessions; not to
people who used to know you back home.

"Oh, I'm fine," she insisted. "I'm even thinking of buying some
stocks, now that the market's scraping bottom."

"Glad you can afford it. What are you going to buy?"

"Well, I hear that Amalgamated Consolidated is selling for a good
deal less than it's worth——"

"What's Amalgamated Consolidated? An investment trust?"

"I—I don't know," she had to admit.

"You don't know? Would you put your money into a company when
you don't even know what it does?"

"But I've been told this is good, by a man who knows."

"Rex Ainsworth?" Andy was purple. "It's rotten enough for you
even to play around with a man like that! But to let him tell you what
to do with your money——"

"I'll play around with anybody I like! And Rex knows stocks——"

"That's good. I'm glad he's not a total blank."

"He's just as much of an intellectual as you are! He—he has a
trained mind; and he reads everything; and he knows Mencken personally—"

"Mencken?" said Andy in abysmal scorn. "Longfellow too, no
doubt?"

"Oh, you make me sick! You don't really believe that nobody over
twenty-five knows anything and that you Younger Critics know it all;
that's just a pose. . . . It wouldn't hurt you if you had a trained mind.
Then you wouldn't have given up your job with the telephone company where you were doing so well and started to write this god-awful
book that I've had to try to be polite about——"

"So that's what you think of the book, is it?" He laughed. "Well,
Carla, I'm glad that at least you had the taste to pick out this—this
intellectual giant when you decided to let yourself be made love to in a
wide-open taxi by broad daylight."

"Andy!" she gasped. "Did you see—— I mean, as if it was any of your
business. . . . Anyway, didn't you ever kiss a girl in a taxi . . . ? No, I
suppose not," she said bitterly. "All you care about is ideas."

"Never mind what I may or may not have done! And I don't care
a damn what you do," he yelled, "so long as you know what you're

about! But when you mix up love—if that's what you call it—and business, you—you put yourself in Ainsworth's hands!"

"In his power, you mean, Andy. You're rusty on the vocabulary of melodrama. . . . I suppose you think he's trying to ruin me, as it used to be called. It may interest you to know that he wants to marry me."

"Worse and worse!" he groaned. "That would be ruin!"

"Well, what do you expect me to do? Live like the Statue of Liberty stuck up on a pedestal? Maybe you can stand that sort of thing, with your ideas to keep you company; but I——" She broke off. "We might as least stop shrieking at each other," she snapped. "I'd hate to have the Fowlers hear us up the airshaft, and write home about it."

That dread possibility reduced him to silence. They stared at each other, taut and pale and quivering.

"Are you going to marry him?" he demanded at last.

"I don't know. What of it?"

What, indeed? . . . He gave a helpless shrug—the shrug of a young man who makes twelve dollars a week, and has staked his future on a book that friendly readers have to try to be polite about—and walked out. . . . She dropped into the nearest chair and sat thinking, and the more she thought the worse she felt. She'd certainly got herself into a jam—mixed up with two men and not really approving of either of them. Andy had been nice in the old days, but he was impossibly touchy and suspicious now. . . . No wonder; he probably wasn't getting enough to eat. She wouldn't be getting enough to eat either, before long, if she didn't make some money somehow.

She took up the telephone, twirled the dial.

"Rex!" she said presently. "Hello. . . . Yes, Andy's gone. . . . No, I don't feel like going out dancing. Sorry. . . . No, I'd rather you wouldn't come over; I'm terribly tired. . . . Listen, Rex. Could you carry that Amal Con for me without anybody ever finding out—anybody at all?"

"Sure, I can fix it up. No trouble. Leave it to me."

"If it goes down," she warned him, "I'd have to give you a note for the money and pay you when I could. Whenever that might be."

She thought he might try to refuse that; but he knew her too well.

"Fair enough," he said lightly. "But it won't go down. These fellows in the pool are friends of mine; they'll tell me when they're ready to pull the plug."

The next day he told her that he had bought her five hundred shares at 29.

"The certificate?" he said. "Oh, that's at the broker's, in a street name; I bought on margin. But never mind. All we have to do now is watch it ride."

III

They watched, and it rode—steadily mounting through the thirties, then into the forties. When Amal Con closed one day at 49, Carla realized that she had a ten-thousand-dollar profit. If she sold now, she wouldn't need to worry about anything for a couple of years—anything that you could get with money. But it would be stupid to sell now, when the plug wasn't to be pulled till Amal Con touched 70.

She kept on watching and it kept on rising. She was glad she had something to think about; for the creeping upturn that Rex talked about grew more and more snail-like. Business was dead; she was at her decorator's shop every day from nine to five, but there was nothing to do but read the stock quotations in the evening papers, and try to remember not to bite her nails while she wondered why she didn't hear from Andy. He probably wasn't getting enough to eat—but she couldn't call him up, or go to see him; she didn't know where he lived, and neither did any of his friends. She had asked them all.

So the days passed—bright spring days. There was a rash of news all over the front pages of the papers—a revolution in Spain, the King in exile, a new government that was going to make all the reforms that had been neglected for five hundred years; but Carla always passed by the front pages with an indifferent glance, to read the stock quotations. And Amal Con kept going up.

Then, late one afternoon, Ainsworth telephoned to her.

"Dine with me tonight?" he asked. "Fine. . . . I suppose you saw that Amal Con closed today at 57?"

"Yes, I did. . . . But Rex, there was a terrific turnover—sixty thousand shares. Somebody must be selling what the bulls are buying."

"Suckers," he said. "People who are taking their profit and getting out. I don't blame them for they don't know what's been planned; but I've been buying another thousand shares every five points up. I give it about another week to touch 70, and then we'll both cash in."

She hoped so, as she locked up the shop that hadn't seen a customer all week. They'd both cash in; twenty thousand for her, half a million, perhaps, for him. With twenty thousand she'd be independent, she could do what she wanted to do; but as she'd been trained to feel about money, she couldn't help feeling a terrific obligation to the man who had made that twenty thousand for her. Which Rex knew, of course. . . . She turned from the door and bumped into Andy Bush on the sidewalk; he looked as gaunt as an alley cat.

"Hello!" she said, her heart thumping. "What have you been doing with yourself, these last eleven days?"

"Was it eleven? I lose track, living by myself. . . . I've been rewriting my book. All of it."

"Why, Andy! What for?"

"You said it was god-awful——"

"What's my opinion worth about a book? I'm not very bright, Andy. You ought to know that, by this time. It's probably a swell book."

"I'm rewriting it, anyway. . . . Meanwhile, I've come to buy you a drink."

"I'll buy you one." And, as he was beginning a protest, she added sternly—— "You know you can't afford it, on twelve dollars a week."

"I made sixteen this week." (Sixteen! And last year he'd been getting a hundred and twenty-five from the telephone company.) "That's living expenses," he told her, "plus a couple of rounds of drinks for you and me."

"All right," she assented, belatedly perceiving that unless she made this much concession to his pride, she might never see him again. "You buy me a drink, or two if you want to; and then I'll buy you one."

And then, she foresaw, he'll take me home; and I'll be too tired to go out again; so we'll pick up a steak on the way, and—— But, good heavens, I can't do that; I've got a date with Rex! Well, anyway——

"You know Louis's place?" she asked. "Just around the corner. It will be a mob scene by six, but we'll get in ahead of the crowd."

But it was a mob scene already; they came in to find the bar swarming, couples and groups weaving their way among the crowded tables, any everybody noisy—far noisier than Louis's patrons were ordinarily permitted to be. But tonight they had encouragement; Louis himself, the suave and decorous Louis, was capering about, the noisiest of the lot.

"Good evening, Miss Furness! Good evening, sir! Have you heard the great news? Catalonia is free at last! Nobody can buy anything here today; it is all on the house, in honor of independent Catalonia!"

So they slipped into a booth that another couple was just vacating, and had one in honor of independent Catalonia. Then they had another, and still another; the waiters, Catalans too, were whisking away empty glasses and bringing fresh drinks as briskly as if they were getting paid for it. Carla, tired but content, felt no need to say anything; and at first Andy was silent too. But presently he began to talk, and talked on and on, incessantly—about his book. She realized that the drinks that had merely relaxed her had gone to his head; probably he hadn't had a thing to eat, all day. . . .

"Haven't I heard enough about that book?" she broke in at last. Then, glancing at her wrist watch—— "I've got to go, Andy. I've got a dinner date at Larue's. Come walk over there with me." (The fresh air would do him good.)

With difficulty, he got his eyes to focus on her; when he spoke, his words came in machine-gun sputters, with long pauses between.

"Walk—overtherenmeet—Ainsworth?" He laughed. "No, thanks. I'll—stayherenhavanother—nhonorofindependent—Catalonia."

"Andy!" She stamped her foot in disgust. . . . She'd read about people who stamped the foot in disgust without ever believing anybody really did it; but there were times when it seemed all you could do. . . . "You're drunk!" she said furiously.

"Wha-at—ofit?" Andy demanded. "Good for a man. Man stays sober—nobodyknowsm. Keeps up a front. Then he gets drunk. Huh! Front goes down. What—hedoeswhen he's drunk—— 'T's his true nature."

"Well, you ought to be ashamed to admit it! What do you do when you get drunk, I'd like to know? Just sit here and rave about the future of America, and whither are we drifting, and the challenge of the crisis! . . . All right, if that's what you like! Stay here and get drunk till they throw you out in the gutter!"

She stalked out, trying to blink the tears back from her eyes.

IV

That was that, she decided as she walked over to Larue's; she wasn't going to see Andy any more. He'd become impossible; whether it was from being a Younger Critic, or from not getting enough to eat, she didn't know, but there was no point in wasting her time on a man who only disgusted her. . . . Rex, now, was always smooth and cheerful; these last months would have been dismal enough without him. When she met him she was miserably aware that to a man with his experience, it would be evident that something humiliating had happened to her; but of course he was too expert to betray the perception. He was smooth, cheerful, amusing as ever; till at last, as they sat over coffee——

"I'm leaving for San Francisco at nine thirty," he told her suddenly.

"They're settling up my aunt's estate out there; I'll be away a month."
She shivered; that was a long time, and New York would be pretty
empty without him. "Come to the train with me?" he asked her.

She had expected that he would make love to her in the taxi, and
was prepared to enjoy it, as she always did, without having to worry
herself about how much it meant. But it would mean something tonight, when she wasn't going to see him for a month. . . . And then, in
the taxi, he let her alone, left her to reflect at leisure on how empty
New York would seem without him. On the station platform, by the
Pullman door, she clung to him of her own accord, her head on his
shoulder.

"Rex dear. . . . I'm going to miss you. . . ."

He took two lavender Pullman tickets out of his pocket.

"You don't have to, Carla. I've got two drawing rooms to Chicago—one for me and one for you. Come along, and we'll get married
there between trains."

"Oh, my dear. . . ." She wondered why she hesitated. "I don't
know——"

"Why not? I'm crazy about you; and you like me—pretty well, don't
you?" he suggested in tactful understatement.

"Of course. But—I hate to give up my independence," she evaded,
wondering just what it was that she was evading. . . . All up and down
the platform men shouted "All aboard!"; Ainsworth stepped into the
vestibule.

"Your independence?" he said. "Who bought it for you? . . . This
is the first time I ever carried a woman in a stock deal for nothing.
Some point of small-town pride wouldn't let you marry me· when you
were broke; so I thought I'd make some money for you, and then you'd
come to reason. Instead of which you prefer to keep what you call
your independence."

"You thought you were buying me?" He shrugged.

"Call it that if you like; it seemed the only way to get you. I've paid
the money—cash over the counter—and it looks as if I don't get the
deed to the property after all." Slowly, the train began to move.
"Coming?" he demanded.

"No!" The train gathered speed; the porter, waiting beside him,
shut the vestibule door; Carla stood on the platform, staring at the
string of Pullmans disappearing in the tunnel.

Quivering with rage, she walked unsteadily back to the station, and
as she crossed the concourse her fury began to drain away. If he had
tried to buy her—— Well, he knew her pretty well, and she must have

impressed him as somebody who could be bought. Her price was higher than that of more obviously purchasable women, but he had expected to get permanent title to the property, not just a lease. He'd paid his money, got nothing for it. . . . No wonder he felt that she had cheated him. And there was only one way she could possibly get out of this tangle with even a shred of decency left.

She stopped at the telegraph desk, wrote a message to her broker:

SELL 500 AMAL CON AT TOMORROW MORNINGS OPENING

Twenty-nine from fifty-seven was twenty-eight, times five hundred—fourteen thousand dollars' profit; and she'd have to give it back to Rex, now that she knew how he felt about the transaction. Which would leave her with just about eighty dollars in the world. . . . She glanced at her wrist watch; nine forty. Louis's closed at ten; she'd have just time to slip in there for a drink, and she had never needed a drink so badly in her life.

The mob was gone, now; the bar was almost empty. But not quite; on an upholstered seat in a corner lay Andy Bush, peacefully asleep.

"Miss Furness!" said Louis, with the gladness of deep relief. "We close at ten; and I didn't want to throw a friend of yours out in the gutter——"

"The gutter's where he belongs," said Carla savagely. But she went over to him, shook him; kept on shaking him till he sat up, blinking amiably.

"Oh, hello, Carla. I must have been asleep. Where'd you come from?"

"Never mind where I came from. We're going home."

"Home's hellhole," said Andy. For an instant he had looked almost sober, but that lucid interval was gone now. "Hellhole," he insisted. "Drather stay here. Louis would give me a bed—nhonorof independent Catalonia."

"You're going home," said Carla implacably. "Come, now!"

But he was so unsteady that a waiter had to help him out to the street; had to prop him up while she got a taxi, and help put him in.

"Where to, miss?" said the driver.

"Where do you live, Andy?"

"Try and find out," said Andy, with a sleepily peaceful smile.

"Oh, you pig! I've got to take you home! You can't stand up!"

"Mallright. Get waked—upinaminute. Then walk home." He took both her hands in one of his and leaned back, still smiling.

"Drive around the Park awhile," she told the driver in despair. "Maybe fresh air will bring him out of it."

So they drove around the Park, and kept on driving. More than once he half came to, but what he wanted to discuss in those interludes wasn't where he lived, or how to get there. At last Carla looked at the meter; seven eighty—and she had less than nine dollars in her purse. She leaned forward, gave the driver her own address; and in a world where there seemed nothing else to be thankful for—— No, that wasn't quite true. But in a world where there was only one other thing to be thankful for, she could still be thankful that she lived in a walkup apartment, with no doorman or hallboys to see a taxi driver helping her bring a drunken man into her chaste bachelor quarters in the middle of the night.

v

Andy Bush woke in a strange room, whose scent was agreeably reminiscent. Somebody had taken off his shoes and coat and tie, and opened his collar, and laid him on the counterpane of a strange bed. He shut his eyes and tried to remember; but the last thing he could recall was having just one more in honor of the independence of Catalonia. His eyes opened again, saw an open door with a shower bath beyond. There was also a closed door; on the other side of it somebody was moving briskly about, and singing.

"Carla!" he called. "Is that you?"

"You didn't expect anybody else, I hope? . . . How do you feel, Andy?"

"Good and ashamed of myself. May I take a shower?"

"That's what it's there for. You'll find towels laid out."

The shower refreshed him, and he found his shoes; but he couldn't find his coat and tie, and he was painfully conscious, as he came out into the living room, of a bristling unshaven chin. There was a breakfast table set for two; and Carla, in blue silk pajamas.

"Feel any better?" she asked anxiously. "I've got some coffee—just made. And I've baked some biscuits, if you think you could eat anything."

"I could eat an ox. I hadn't eaten anything for three days; I'd been saving up to buy you a drink. That's why it hit me so hard. . . . But I haven't any right to eat anything here," he said gloomily.

"Why on earth not?"

"Last night—— God knows how much trouble I must have given you. . . ."

"That's all right, Andy. Sit down and have some coffee." And as he still hesitated—— "Don't be stubborn!" she commanded. "Can't I get breakfast for somebody who went to high school with me, back home?"

"But last night——" he persisted, foggily trying to remember.

"You were fine," she said, smiling. "Now try your coffee."

He tried a cup of coffee, and then another; he tried a biscuit, and then tried about a dozen more. Things began to look better; he lit one of Carla's cigarettes, and dared to look at her across the table. He was brim full of humility, just then, and gratitude, and a conviction of utter unworthiness; but as he looked at her his face must have changed, for she flushed, looked down at the tablecloth. . . . Then the doorbell rang; and he started up, looking for cover.

"Oh, you needn't duck out of sight," she said. "It's only the laundry."

She opened the door—and stood paralyzed, in crimson confusion, as a woman walked in, talking from the moment she crossed the threshold.

"Oh, Carla, I've brought you the *Weekly Register*. You'll want to read it this time, I know; there's such a scandal in Blue Valley——"

She broke off, staring at Andy Bush—coatless, unshaven; staring then at Carla, in pajamas that were obviously meant for sleeping, not for receiving guests.

"Pardon me!" said Edith Fowler emphatically. "If I'd dreamed——"

She vanished, the door slamming behind her. A silence; then——

"And there's another scandal for Blue Valley," Andy groaned. "Edith will get a letter off to her sister by the next mail." Carla turned away from him, looking out of the window; he went to her, put his hands on her shoulders, warm under the thin silk. "Carla!" he said. "Will you marry me?" She whirled about furiously, shook off his hands.

"Because Edith Fowler thinks we—— I certainly will not!"

"Damn Edith Fowler. I was getting ready to ask you when she came in. I'd always meant to ask you, after I finished my book——"

"But you haven't finished it. And you don't care about women."

"Of course I don't care about women! I care about you."

"Do you really, my dear? I——" Her voice broke. "I didn't know——"

"I'm crazy about you. Maybe you think you're in love with Ainsworth——"

Suddenly she was in his arms, laughing hysterically.

"Oh, Andy, do you suppose I'd have wasted any time on him if you'd only—— But I thought all you cared about was ideas." Then, when at last her lips were free—— "Andy!" she was smiling curiously. "Do you really mean this?"

"Of course I mean it. Why not?"

"Well—I'm not sure you really approve of me. After all, I let Rex kiss me in a taxi. It really didn't mean anything, Andy, except that I was lonesome; but I don't suppose you'd understand that. You probably never kissed a girl in a taxi in all your life."

"I may have. But I don't see what that's got to do with it."

"Don't you? . . . Besides, Andy, you're cold sober now; and you told me yesterday that what a man does when he's drunk is his true nature." He was glowering at her, irritated and perplexed; suddenly she broke into helpless laughter. "Darling, don't you really remember anything about last night? You wouldn't tell me where you lived, so I had to bring you here; and in the taxi you made violent love to me——"

"Good God! Did I? And—after we got here——"

"By the time the taxi driver and I got you up here, you were dead to the world. But I must say," Carla admitted blithely, "that your behavior in the taxi was most reassuring. It was nice to know that that was your true nature, after all the evenings you'd been here without doing anything but talk about your book. Still, I couldn't be sure you'd feel the same way when you sobered up——"

"Well, I do," he said, and kissed her again; and again. . . . All at once he let go of her.

"But, Carla, I can't marry you just yet—not on twelve dollars a week."

"That's all right, my dear; we're independent! I've just made fourteen thousand on a stock deal." . . . Last night she had felt that all her profit belonged to Ainsworth; but if Andy needed it—— "And don't say you won't live on it," she commanded. "Any Younger Critic would be willing to let an admirer finance him while he finishes such an important book. . . . And now I'd better slip into the bedroom and get dressed before we have any more callers."

"And while you're doing it, I'll go out and get a shave. My face——" He flushed. "It must feel like sandpaper, doesn't it?"

"Oh, I don't mind a little sandpaper, now and then."

As he went down the stairs he heard a telephone ringing behind him; and when he came back from the barber shop Carla was still sitting there in her pajamas, her face like stone.

"Andy, I'm sorry; I can't marry you. . . . I've done something terrible. Rex Ainsworth——"

"I don't care a damn what you've done."

"But I don't mean that! Rex was carrying five hundred Amal Con for me; and like a little coward, I asked him if he couldn't fix it up so that nobody'd know—not even the broker. I might have known that the simplest way for him to do it was simply to lump it with his own holdings; which he did. . . . Andy, I never had it—never had it at all; and now I've sold it!"

"Well, if a broker lets you sell short without putting up a margin——"

"He thought Rex was guaranteeing my account," she confessed miserably. "He introduced me, and he's guaranteed so many accounts for women. . . . Anyway, they managed to reach him by telephone on a train, and he said he wasn't, so——"

"So you go right into the market this minute, and buy five hundred shares to cover."

"I can't! Andy, that stock is rocketing! I sold at this morning's opening—59. When the broker called me up it had touched 63; I owed him two thousand dollars already. Goodness knows how much I owe by now!"

"You call him up right now," Andy told her, "and tell him to buy five hundred at the market to cover you. Tell him Mr. and Mrs. Andrew Bush will be in this afternoon to see how much they owe. I'll go down to the telephone company and see if they can give me some sort of job. Meet me at Louis's at twelve thirty, and we'll have lunch, and then get married, and then go see your broker."

"And you think I'll let you slave to pay my debts?"

"When you thought you had a profit you were going to share it with me; if you've got a loss, we'll share that. We won't have much to live on while we're paying it off——"

"Who cares?" said Carla. "I can cook. I love to cook, for you."

. . . He came into Louis's at twelve thirty and found her waiting, an evening paper under her arm.

"Luck," he told her, grinning. "The phone company tried two men in my old job, and neither of them had the stuff. So I got it back— a hundred and twenty-five a week. We'll have enough to live on while we're paying our debts. . . ."

"Debts?" She laughed wildly. "Look, Andy—look!"

He took the paper that she thrust into his hands, read a front-page story:

Frantic scenes were enacted on the Curb Exchange this morning when Lucius P. Cavendyne, president of the Amalgamated Consolidated Corporation, declared that the company's earnings did not justify a price of more than $10 a share for the stock, which has been the subject of a feverish bull movement in recent weeks. Amal Con opened at 59 this morning and had touched 64 when Mr. Cavendyne's statement was made. Within ten minutes it had dropped to 15¼——

"It was in those ten minutes," said Carla, "that I put in my buying order to cover. I got it at 21—and I'd sold at 59. Nineteen thousand dollars' profit, and no thanks to Rex Ainsworth! So you needn't take that job; you can finish your book on the future of America——"

"Somehow I feel," he confessed, "that the future of America is going to be pretty much of the same, whether I write a book about it or not. I'm tired of that book; whereas I can do a pretty good job for the telephone company. . . . Let's sit down and have a drink; I need it."

While the waiter went for their Bacardis, Andy glanced absently over the front page of the paper.

"Hello!" he said. "It seems there was some mistake."

"About Amal Con?" she gasped.

"No, no; about Catalonia. It seems Catalonia isn't going to be independent after all."

"Neither are you," said Carla. "Neither am I. And isn't it fun?"

Their Bacardis arrived, and they both thought it was a lovely world. You could hardly expect young people in their happy situation to waste much thought on the sorrows of others—of Louis, who had given away a thousand dollars' worth of free drinks before he discovered that Catalonia wasn't independent after all; or of Rex Ainsworth, who had been assured by his friends on the inside that nobody was going to pull the plug till Amal Con touched 70.

VI

"You ought to have known better," said his broker. (Ainsworth had read the news in Chicago, and had returned in haste.) "Seventy was the figure that was permitted to leak out to the general public; sixty was as far as the insiders ever meant to carry it, I imagine. Anyway, I sold mine at 58 and came out very nicely; while you owe us——" He consulted a memorandum. "One hundred eighty-two thousand, seven hundred and thirty-seven dollars."

"And no cents?" said Ainsworth. "Thanks for that, anyway. . . . By right, Carla Furness owes you some of that. I'd bought five hundred for her."

"Had you? When we phoned you on the train, you said you hadn't."

"I know," Ainsworth conceded. "I was sore at her, then. How did she come out? . . . What? Nineteen thousand ahead? There's certainly a great moral lesson in that," said Ainsworth sadly. "By the way, may I use your telephone?"

"Go ahead. . . . What's the great moral lesson?" the broker asked. "Not to mix stock deals and love affairs?" Ainsworth called a number; then, as he waited for an answer——

"Why," he said, "you might draw a number of moral lessons from it. For instance, that if you get under the skin of the slickest, most metropolitan-looking woman, you might find nothing but a little girl from a small town, full of small-town scruples. . . . Hello! Hotel de Venise? Miss Doraine, please—Marilyn Doraine . . . Or you might say," Ainsworth went on in mellow speculation, "that the lesson is that a man who's usually cast as a co-respondent is out of character if he tries to play the bridegroom. Or maybe the lesson is only that God loves the young and foolish, and gives them all the breaks. . . . Hello! Oh, hello, Marilyn. This is Rex. It's quite a while since you asked me for advice about your investments. Suppose we get together at dinner this evening, and talk things over."

THE HOME GROUNDS

He wasn't at all the sort of man she had meant to marry; but neither was anybody else, unless perhaps the Prince of Wales. Eunice Belden had danced with the Prince of Wales at Cannes when she was nineteen; but nothing came of it, except that it left her a little more dissatisfied with the men she met back home in Rivermont.

Rivermont is quite a place, of course—not the metropolis it used to be in the old steamboat days, but it can still claim a population of half a million, at least between censuses. It's been quite a place ever since the War of 1812; you know who's who there, and who isn't. The Beldens have been among the whos, right from the beginning; they would never dream of marrying outside their own class. And the men Eunice knew in her class, the boys she had grown up with—they were pleasant enough, but they lacked salt. They went into the old banks or old law firms downtown, and became solid citizens, pillars of society; but Eunice wanted something more than that. She was worth something more than that and she knew it; with her tact and social aptitude, her Parisian education, her real talent for languages, she was fitted to be an ambassador's wife; and she doubted if any man could satisfy her who wasn't fit to be an ambassador.

So, though she thought once or twice that she was in love, nothing came of it. At twenty-two, she even let her engagement be announced to Douglas Ewing, whose family had been intermarrying with the Beldens for a hundred years; but before he could get her to the altar she began looking him over, and he didn't quite measure up. Neither did the other men who from time to time attracted her. She was twenty-six, and had begun to wonder if she would ever find a man who measured up, when she accompanied her father to the Democratic National Convention in Chicago, and met Pete Ripley.

She and her father had front-row seats on the platform behind the speakers' stand; Adrian Belden rated that much for his past contributions to Democratic campaign funds. Eunice could look down over the flag-draped railing into the press stands, where coatless, perspiring men slugged away at noiseless typewriters, or dashed off to buttonhole some dignitary for a whispered conversation that seemed to be profoundly important. One man in particular she found herself noticing every day—a thin, dark young man, with a complete self-possession that fascinated her; he seemed so unobtrusively and yet so thoroughly convinced of his capacity to handle any situation into which he might be thrown. She found herself hoping she would meet him at one of the dinners or dances that were being given all over Chicago for delegates and their women; but she hadn't met him when the last afternoon came, and the convention was marking time with vaudeville acts and windy speeches while its candidate was flying out from Albany to accept the nomination.

Eunice sat by the flag-draped rail, looking superbly poised and cool—ash-blond hair, clear skin, light summer frock; but inwardly she wished to heaven the convention were over so that she could go home. Dinners and dances were all well enough, but she got enough of that in the winter, at Rivermont and Palm Beach; there wasn't much point in coming to Chicago in such weather for more of the same. Of course—she flushed at the remembrance—that wasn't why she had come to Chicago. Her father had been one of the engineers of the great stampede to Newton D. Baker that was to start whenever the convention became deadlocked. If Baker went to the White House Adrian Belden would in all likelihood become an ambassador, and his motherless daughter would be an ambassador's hostess after all. But the convention, unfortunately, had never become deadlocked; the thundering herd that was to stampede to Baker had stayed peacefully in its own pasture; and Adrian Belden and his daughter would go home to Rivermont with nothing to show for their trip but a receipted hotel bill. . . .

At this point in her musings Doug Ewing came up to her; he had been one of the Roosevelt floor managers, and just now he was on top of the world.

"Like to go out to the airport, Eunice, and meet Roosevelt?"

"Thanks, my dear; it's much too hot. . . . Yes, I know it's stifling in here; but I'd rather stand it than move."

He shrugged and went on. . . . Baldish, complacent, he looked faintly like her father; you could see that he'd spent his life being a Rivermont gentleman. A worthy type, the Rivermont gentleman; but it had no surprises for one who had grown up with it. And Doug Ewing was still a bachelor, still in love with her—or perhaps it was only that because they had been engaged four years ago he felt that he ought to be still in love with her, till some other woman should distract him. At any rate, he was still around; if nothing else happened to her, if nobody else happened to her, she supposed that some day she might——

She heard a strange voice behind her, saw a strange young man—thin and dark, with an air of completely confident self-possession that had none of Doug Ewing's complacency. He was talking to the national committeewoman from her state; Eunice deliberately faced about, and the committeewoman had no choice but to introduce Mr. Ripley, Washington correspondent of the New York *Record*.

"Not *the* Washington correspondent," he amended with a grin. "My chief's the statesman-journalist; I'm only one of his bright young men."

And then he looked at Eunice, and Eunice looked at him—and he settled down beside her, in her father's vacant chair, as if that was the place of all places where he ought to be. Coatless, his sleeves rolled up, a working man in working clothes, he was utterly at his ease—as American as a buffalo nickel; but Eunice wasn't surprised to learn, as they talked, that he had spent a couple of years in his newspaper's Paris office.

They talked on, and presently—— "Nothing's going to happen here for hours," said Pete Ripley. "I know a place not so very far away where the beer is excellent, and there's a radio to warn us when anything is likely to be doing in the convention hall. What about it?"

"Let's go," said Eunice.

So they spent the next hour or two over seidels of beer in a Czech restaurant, talking as inextinguishably as the speakers who were killing time in the convention hall, but far more to the point. And when he brought her back, and left her at the gate of the platform—— "There's a party at the Blackstone tonight," she said. "Supper and dancing. Will you come?"

"I'll have to work pretty late, but I'll be there when I can. . . . By the way," he confessed, "I never did get your name; that woman only called you Eunice. . . . Belden? And didn't you say you came from Rivermont?" She nodded; his face changed. "I came from down around there myself," he said. "But I'm coming to the party anyway," he finished cryptically.

He was very late; and you wouldn't have known that the cool, controlled Miss Belden was inwardly all jitters till she saw him at the door. They had three or four dances in succession—he didn't seem to know that any other women were there, and she shrugged away the other men who wanted to dance with her, after he came; then they sat out a while, talking. And when the party was breaking up——

"Are you going straight back to Washington?" she asked him.

"I have a week's vacation; I'd thought of visiting my home town."

"That's near Rivermont, isn't it? Will you come and see me?"

"You know I'll come and see you," said Pete Ripley. His voice shook a little, but Eunice didn't mind that; she felt rather shaky herself.

Two or three days later he called her up from a Rivermont hotel, and she asked him to come to dinner. Did he know the house? . . . But of course he did; everybody who had ever been in Rivermont knew the Belden mansion. It had been built about 1840, by an architect who wasn't quite sure whether he was imitating Windsor Castle or a Gothic cathedral. The Beldens had never dreamed of tearing it down; it was part of their history, and of Rivermont's.

"Pete Ripley's coming to dinner," Eunice told her father. "You met him in Chicago, for a moment. He's a Washington correspondent."

"Ah," said Adrian Belden. "Remarkable men, these Washington correspondents. Statesmen-journalists." Eunice smiled.

"Pete says he's only one of the bright young men; but I doubt it."

She left her father gasping. Pete! The way her voice had sounded when she spoke the name—— And she barely knows the man! thought Adrian Belden in consternation.

Pete Ripley, at the moment, was also in consternation—dressing for dinner in his downtown hotel, and literally shaking in his shoes.

II

You see, Pete came from Greenville, where his father used to run the harness store. Greenville is all right, if you happen to like it—just about the same as a couple of thousand other small towns, with this exception: it's only thirty miles from Rivermont, too far away for a commuting suburb and too near to have a civic consciousness of its own.

To Pete Ripley, as he grew up, Rivermont was The City, the sum of all urbanity, past and present, the focus of the universe. He bought his clothes in Rivermont, he read the Rivermont papers (there was a good deal in them about the Beldens and a good deal about Greenville too, for it happened to be the town the city papers picked on when they wanted to make sport of the outlying rustics); and he had gradually absorbed the conviction that no man from Greenville could ever be really at home in that great metropolis. Even in New York and Paris he still thought of Rivermont as The City; he had kissed a duchess in a Park Avenue penthouse and played bridge with an unemployed king at Biarritz, but when he crossed the threshold of the Belden mansion he came near pulling his forelock.

Eunice saw that he was nervous, of course, but she set it down to a more gratifying cause. But things began to go wrong, beginning with the cocktail before dinner. Pete needed a bracer, so he tossed it down— as people did toss down those prohibition cocktails, quickly, so that

they wouldn't taste the gin—and was ready for another. He had forgotten that people like the Beldens still had cases of pre-war gin in the
cellar, and that their single cocktail before dinner was meant to be
sipped and savored. Adrian Belden was incapable of lifting his eyebrows at a guest, but his immobile face somehow gave Pete—and
Eunice—the impression that inward eyebrows had been lifted. At
dinner, when Belden tried to draw him out, Pete had none of the ease
he had shown in Chicago; before the slightly stuffy imperturbability
of a Rivermont gentleman he seemed like a college boy. Eunice found
herself wondering desperately if this one, too, would fail to measure up.

So, after dinner, she announced that she must show Pete the view—
astonished at herself, almost ashamed of herself, but unshakably resolved that they were going to bring this thing to the point. . . . There
was a long sweep of lawn down to a stone wall on the brink of a
bluff; below, far away, were the lights of downtown Rivermont. The
constraint dropped away from them as they strolled across the dewy
lawn in the starlight, but he took care not to let his arm brush against
hers. Beside the wall they paused; he looked at her, her eyes met his
steadily—— With a gasp of desperation, like a pious brigand looting a
sanctuary, he took her in his arms; and she wondered why she had
ever thought that his dinner-table baucheries mattered. . . .

"This is what matters," she whispered, when she could speak again.

"Yes. . . . But it's so—preposterous," he groaned.

"Preposterous?" He could feel her stiffening in his arms. "Why?"

"Well, for one thing, I don't make any money—what you'd call
money. I used to get a hundred dollars a week; last month I was cut
to eighty-five, and I may be cut again. Two people could live on that
in Washington; but not the way you've been used to living."

"That's all right; I have money. . . . I had money," she amended. "I
own some office buildings downtown that hardly pay taxes and interest
now. But that doesn't matter. We Beldens are used to depressions;
we were ruined in the panic of 1837 and we came right back. I could
find enough money——"

"You don't think I'd live on it, do you?"

"Why not, if it was my contribution to a partnership?" (But, almost
unconsciously, she had withdrawn herself from his arms.) "Part of
my contribution," she corrected, flushed and smiling. "Look, my
dear—there are things in marriage besides love; there's respect, and—
and accomplishment. Both of us together, doing something that
neither could do alone. I want to make something of my life—use what
I've got, do the things I know I can do. I'd be a first-rate ambassa-

dor's wife—but you never can tell who's going to be an ambassador, in this country."

"I can tell you I'm not," said Pete. "So what?"

"No, you're not going to be an ambassador—not just yet, anyway. But you Washington correspondents really are statesmen-journalists, even if you laugh at the word. You're brilliant, and ambitious——" She couldn't recall that he had ever said so; but a man about whom she could feel this way must be ambitious. "And I could help you so much!" she said. "I have tact; I know all the right people; I'd give dinners that nobody in Washington could afford to miss——"

"I'd miss them; the hardest part of my day's work comes between six and nine in the evening. Even my chief, who doesn't work any more than he has to, never knows when he can get home for dinner."

"Oh. . . . I'd thought——" But never mind that vision of a statesman-journalist whose clever wife built him up until the President, in some future crisis, would be compelled by public opinion to appoint him Secretary of State. "Well?" she said. "As you put it, so what?"

"I wish I knew. . . . Eunice, I'm crazy about you—but aside from everything else, a Belden doesn't marry a man from Greenville."

"Greenville? . . . Oh! That place up the river? I don't see why that should make any difference." With a surge of elation, he realized that it didn't. Rivermont and its newspapers took the Beldens at their own valuation; an alliance with them would ennoble even a man from Greenville. "I mean——" she said. "You never did anything awful in Greenville, did you?" He shook his head. "Well, then!" she said, smiling. "I can't see that I'd disgrace myself by becoming Mrs. Peter Ripley."

"Mrs. Homer Ripley. Pete's only a nickname."

"Homer?" she said. "But—people aren't named Homer."

"Not the sort of people you know. But I am."

"But couldn't you change it—legally—to Peter, or anything else?"

"I wish I'd done that, in time. But I need it now; it's a trade mark. Sometimes they sign my stories in the paper; and they sign them with the name that's on the payroll—Homer Ripley. . . . Not," he added defiantly, "that any newspaperman ought to be ashamed of being named for Homer. He was a pretty good reporter, in his day."

. . . That name on her cards—Mrs. Homer Ripley. . . . Mr. and Mrs. Homer Ripley request the honor of your presence—— But they couldn't give formal dinners, if he had to work over the dinner hour. . . . Mr. and Mrs. Homer Ripley of Washington are at the Breakers—— But he was a salaried employee and winter was his busiest season; he couldn't spend it at Palm Beach. . . .

"Eunice!" he said fiercely. "I've been making you do all the work. I do want you——"

His arms reached out for her; but he had waited just a moment too long.

"Please, Pete! Not now. . . . Silly of me, I suppose. Silly of you, too, to feel so apologetic and—and feudal. . . . But perhaps I can understand," she said thoughtfully. "The Belden mansion, and the Belden tradition, must look rather formidable from Greenville; and you've been seeing me on—on my own grounds. . . . Ever go to ball games, Pete? . . . Then you know there are teams that win consistently on their home grounds, where they know every clod of dirt and blade of grass, but aren't so good in strange territory. I suppose some people are like that." (She had never supposed that she'd be thinking of marrying one of them, but——) "Have you been to Greenville yet?" she asked him.

"Not yet. There's nobody I particularly care to see, except my uncle. I'd thought I might hire a car and drive out there tomorrow."

"You needn't hire a car, Pete; I'll drive you out in the roadster. I want to see you on your home grounds. . . . We'd better go back to the house; father might wonder what's keeping us."

When they came out she had expected that they would go back to announce, triumphantly, what had been keeping them; but even in this unforeseen turmoil of emotions, she wasn't going to risk throwing her life away on a man who didn't measure up.

III

The drive up the river restored her spirits, and his. Alone with her he was quietly sure of himself—the sort of man who could kiss a duchess with aplomb, or tell a king what he thought about a misleading discard. And Greenville, Eunice discovered, was a town like any other town—not at all the comic-strip village you read about in the Rivermont papers. But its native son, on his home grounds, wasn't Pete Ripley, the rising young Washington correspondent; he was only Homer, whom everybody remembered as a gawky kid around town. The citizens stared, not unreasonably, at the roadster and the girl in it; but their expression suggested that whoever she might be, she couldn't be so much if she was running around with Homer.

They stopped in at the harness store, and met Pete's uncle. He was cordial enough, but Eunice could see that he didn't feel that Pete was ennobled by association with a Belden; he felt that even a Belden was faintly declassed by association with his nephew. So she refused an invitation to come up to the house and have a bite to eat; they had

planned, she said, to stop for lunch at a roadhouse down the river. . . .
But when they got there, and the food she had ordered was set before
her, she couldn't touch it.

"I'm sorry, Pete," she said miserably. "It just won't do."

"Greenville was too much? . . . Oh, I know I'm not good enough
for you——"

"Pete, there's only one thing on earth that keeps you from being
good enough for me—the fact that you think that. I don't care what
people think in Greenville—or anywhere else." (Not even what her
father thought; his opinion of Pete had been very thinly concealed.)
"I could even stand the Homer," she conceded, "after I got used to it.
But if you think that—— I want a man who measures up to me, and
looks me in the eye."

"I could do that in Chicago. Down here—— Eunice, I do want
you——"

"I know you do. And most girls who felt the way I feel about you
wouldn't stop to argue. But you've got to have respect to make a marriage last, and I couldn't respect a man who didn't respect himself.
What they think of you in Greenville doesn't matter; but when you
act as if you agreed with them——"

So Pete took an afternoon train to Washington; and Adrian Belden
couldn't conceal his relief at learning that he wasn't coming to dinner
that evening.

"I've asked Doug Ewing to drop in," he explained. "He's the new
state chairman; and I thought the boy might appreciate a little advice."

IV

Roosevelt carried the state by half a million, but Adrian Belden's
advice didn't have much to do with it. Eunice doubted if even Doug
Ewing had had much to do with it, in a landslide year; but Doug got
the credit. . . . Her father subscribed to the New York *Record,* for the
fulness and impartiality of its political news, and Eunice read it dili-
gently—especially the stories signed by Homer Ripley. He knew his
stuff; he was a thorough reporter and you could see that he understood the men and the forces he was writing about; in his field, he had
a sure touch of mastery. If he'd only been able to feel that way, that
night on her lawn—or the next day, in Greenville—— But it still hurt
to think about that.

So Eunice went to Palm Beach that winter, as usual; and as usual
met two or three men who seemed worth looking over, and were extremely anxious to let her look them over. But she was still unattached

when the mid-February epidemic of bank closings brought her home in haste—to find that her alarm was needless; all the big banks in Rivermont were sound. It was rather late to go back to Florida, so her father suggested that she accompany him to Washington to see the inauguration. He had been one of the three hundred prominent citizens mentioned in the *New York Times* as cabinet possibilities, and one of the two hundred and ninety who hadn't got the job; but he felt that he ought to be in Washington on March fourth.

"I know several members of the new administration very well," he observed. "No doubt they'll want to confer with me on some of the more urgent problems. My name has been mentioned for an embassy; nothing is settled yet, but——"

The prospect of being an ambassador's hostess buoyed Eunice up till she talked to Doug Ewing, just before they left for Washington.

"I've tried to tell him," Doug sighed, "that people who bet on the wrong horse before the convention are out of luck; but he won't believe it. . . . Confidentially, Eunice, there may be an ambassador from Rivermont; but it looks as if I'd be the man."

"You?" she gasped. But his grandfather had been an ambassador; he had money, breeding, intelligence; he'd make a far better ambassador than most. "My congratulations," she said. "You've earned it, Doug."

"Yes, I think I have. But I'm not sure that I'd want it—alone. If you'd go with me——"

"My dear!" She sighed uneasily. "We've been over all that."

"But not all this. It's a new situation. I know you're—unemotional, Eunice; I wouldn't expect too much." (Every man thinks you're frigid, she reflected, if you're cool to him.) "But I also know," he pursued, "that you're—well, looking for a job, to put it frankly. I can give you the sort of job you want—and I'd need you. I haven't been in Europe for years and you go almost every summer; I don't know anybody over there and you know all sorts of people who count; my French is atrocious and yours is perfect. You'd double my value, Eunice. And I think we know each other pretty well—we're the same sort. . . ."

"We'd probably get along very nicely," she agreed. . . . Almost like marrying your brother, but she could do wonders for Doug. And— Madame l'Ambassadrice. . . . "I'll think it over," she promised. "Shall I see you on the train?"

"I'm going on the Roosevelt-Garner Club Special, but I'll call you up as soon as I get in. You'll be at the Willard, as usual?"

"No, father's decided at last that we might as well move over to the Carlton. I'll count on you, then, for the inaugural ball."

v

At half past six in the evening of Friday, March third, the head of the New York *Record's* Washington bureau came up to a young man who had just flung his last sheet of copy at a telegraph operator.

"All clear on that story, Pete? I've got a lousy little job for some-body, and nobody else is free. Adrian Belden of Rivermont is at the Carlton; he's an old stuffed shirt—and a great friend of our owner. We've got orders to get his views on the banking situation—as if any-body cared a damn what that old fossil thinks, on a night when the United States is coming apart in the middle and breaking loose at both ends. Still, those are orders; so hop to it."

Ten minutes later Pete was edging his way through the buzzing swarm in the Carlton lobby—local dignitaries from everywhere, with their women; all lavishly dressed; all wondering what was going to become of the country, and of themselves. Half a dozen people who knew him stopped him before he reached the desk to ask him what he knew, what he thought was going to happen; but he evaded them all, and told the clerk that Mr. Ripley of the New York *Record* was call-ing on Mr. Belden. And presently Mr. Ripley was directed to go right up to Suite 1010.

He knocked at a half-open door, walked into a sitting room. Nobody was there but a girl with ash-blond hair, in a shimmering pale-gold evening gown; there was a cocktail shaker on a table, and two glasses.

"Hello, Pete!" She was smiling with a cordiality that couldn't be called impersonal; it acknowledged him as an old friend from the Chicago convention. "Father's somewhere downstairs," she said. "He asked me to mix him a cocktail, but we'll get another glass when he comes back. . . . How are you?"

"Fine. If anybody in the United States is fine, this evening."

"Isn't it dreadful?" Eunice agreed. "Father was furious when he saw that sign over the desk—no checks accepted. Of course I told him it wasn't meant for people like us, but as soon as he dressed he went down to see the manager about it. He never carries more than enough cash for tips and taxi hire and so on."

"There are people," said Pete drily, "who haven't been carrying even that much lately." Suddenly she was crimson.

"I know. . . . I know but I'm afraid I didn't realize," she said bit-terly. "People like me, to whom nothing really uncomfortable was happening or ever could happen—— Or am I wrong about that too?

All this talk about breakdown and revolution that we've been hearing for so long—I never took it seriously—perhaps not seriously enough. . . . What do you think, Pete? You traveled all over the country last fall . . . oh, yes, I read your articles," she confessed in some confusion. "And you know things, and people. What do you think?"

"I think this country has still got plenty of stuff," he told her, "if only Roosevelt will do something with it. I think right now it doesn't matter much what he does, so long as he does something. Later it may matter, but now——"

"Yes," she sighed. "If anybody would do anything—— But we're forgetting our cocktails, Pete."

She lifted her glass, smiled at him across the brim with pleasant friendliness—nothing more. Pete needed a bracer, but he remembered this time that Belden cocktails were meant to be sipped and savored. . . . Queer that you could sit calmly talking to a girl when you wanted to jump up and grab her; that they could talk things over like a couple of old friends, when the last time he'd seen her——

Then her father came in, looking considerably more perturbed than you would expect of a Rivermont gentleman. He was still more perturbed when he saw Pete Ripley; for an instant, he seemed to feel that the mob from the Faubourg St. Antoine was battering at the gates of the Tuileries. But as soon as he learned that Pete wanted his views on the situation, and meant to print them in the paper, he became authoritative.

"I think it's outrageous!" he exploded. "When the manager of a hotel like this refuses to accept the check of a responsible person like myself—— They'd never have done that at the Willard; I've been going there for thirty years. But I chose not to go there this time, and of course it's hopeless to try to get in there tonight."

"It's my fault," said Eunice. "I insisted on our coming to the Carlton." Adrian Belden shrugged away the suggestion that his women-folk could ever be at fault.

"None the less," he insisted, "it's outrageous! Hotel managements should use some discretion."

"Well, of course, Mr. Belden," Pete interposed, "you can see how they feel. When Hoover almost took the country off the gold standard this afternoon, and Roosevelt will probably have to do it tomorrow——"

"What?" said Adrian Belden. "My God, who told you that?"

"A man who knows." For a while Adrian Belden couldn't speak.

"Unthinkable!" he said at last. "The American financial system is fundamentally sound. At least, I know the Rivermont banks——"

"Rivermont isn't the whole United States, Mr. Belden."

"True," said Adrian Belden, with the air of a man confronting the unpalatable and inevitable at last. "Well! Hrrmph! I don't feel that I care to be quoted at the moment, Mr. Ripley. . . . Will you excuse me? I want to call up Doug Ewing and find out what he knows."

He vanished into a bedroom, and Eunice turned to Pete.

"What does it all mean?" she asked helplessly. He shrugged.

"You know as much as I do—and maybe we both know as much as Hoover and Roosevelt. But there's no use getting excited about it."

"I suppose not. . . . Are you going to the concert tonight?"

"Me? I'm working tonight—all night, for all I know."

"But I'll see you at the inaugural ball tomorrow night, won't I?"

"I'm working then too—not to speak of all day. But," he said, desperately feeling that he was sticking out his chin, "I might drop in here tomorrow morning on my way to the Capitol. . . . That is, if—if you'd care about seeing me, Eunice."

"Of course I care about seeing you."

She'd meant to say it warmly, but impersonally—as it ought to be said to an old friend from the Chicago convention. But her voice came out in tatters; and all the friendly indifference that she had built up at such effort—that he had built up, following her lead—crashed around them. As if they two could ever be indifferent. . . . Then her father emerged from the bedroom.

"Doug Ewing's up in the air too," he announced. "He's been trying to see Roosevelt, but I take it that bright young men aren't being seen tonight, even if they're important state chairmen." He couldn't wholly repress a trace of satisfaction at this putting of the bright young men in their place. "He said he'd meet us at the concert hall," he pursued. "I don't know but that I'd better send you over there alone, Eunice. On a night like this I really ought to call on one or two of the more prominent members of the new administration, and give them my view of matters for what it's worth. . . . Meanwhile, I suppose we'd better get some dinner." He looked at Pete. "Er—perhaps you'd care to dine with us, Mr. Ripley." That was an abdication, and Pete knew it.

"I'd like to, Mr. Belden. But I've got to get back to the office."

VI

At ten o'clock on the morning of March fourth Pete walked into the Carlton lobby; and presently, in the milling crowd, he found Eunice, her ash-blond hair glowing softly against the collar of her chinchilla coat.

"Oh, hello!" she said briskly. "I'm starving. Father and I ordered breakfast upstairs and waited for an hour and a half without getting it—and there's simply no use trying to get into the dining room. So we were just going out to look for a restaurant that wasn't too crowded. He stopped at the desk to tell them what he thought of such service—— Here he is."

There he was—Adrian Belden, resplendent in silk hat and morning coat; conscious of being, and of looking, a Rivermont gentleman. It had been a pretty good type, the Rivermont gentleman, thought Pete Ripley; a pretty good type, in its day.

"Ah, good morning, Mr. Ripley. It seems that we must go out for breakfast. Perhaps you will—— Oh, you've breakfasted? At least, if you have time, you might join us in a cup of coffee. I must stop in at a bank first, however, to cash a check."

"You can't," said Pete. "The banks are closed."

"Not the Washington banks!" said Adrian Belden, with the air of one who felt that a bad joke had gone far enough.

"The Washington banks, the New York banks, every bank in the country. Even the Rivermont banks." Adrian Belden turned white.

"You mean to say that nobody's check is good anywhere? Nobody's credit? . . . My God, what's to become of us?"

"Maybe Roosevelt knows," Pete suggested. "Let's hope so, anyway. . . . Meanwhile, Mr. Belden, if you're embarrassed for petty cash—and if fifty dollars would help——"

"Why—er—it would, for the moment, to be perfectly frank with you. For the moment. But the way our hotel bill is mounting up——"

"That's all right," said Pete. "I'll speak to the manager; he knows me. You'll find they'll take your check, Mr. Belden."

"What? You really could—— Extremely good of you, Mr. Ripley. I don't know how to thank you. . . . Now, about breakfast—— What—must you be off? Well, I trust we're going to see more of you. . . ."

"Get a taxi, father," Eunice commanded. "I'll join you in a moment." She turned to Pete, took hold of his coat sleeve. "You can't spare fifty dollars," she said, "when nobody knows what may happen."

"My credit's good in my home town, so long as anything's good. . . . But it was pure luck that I had it," he confessed with a grin. "I drew it out of the bank yesterday to buy some Scotch, and never had time to see the bootlegger."

"But, Pete!" She was apprehensive—worrying, he perceived, not about the country, or about herself; worrying about him. "If you speak to the manager about our hotel bill," she said, "and he takes father's check—then you're responsible, if the check isn't good."

"It's good. The Rivermont banks are perfectly sound."

"Well, I know father thinks so. But—he might be wrong, Pete." (And that, he knew, was another abdication.)

"I was afraid he might be," he confessed. "So I went over to the Treasury last night and asked Mills. He says the Rivermont banks are all right."

"Oh," said Eunice. (Her father had tried to reach Mills last night, and Woodin too; but they'd been too busy to see him.) "Pete! Will you dine with me tonight—just me? I know you can't tell when you can get off, but they must let you eat some time, don't they? . . . All right; I'll wait for you. I won't go to that ball till I've seen you, no matter when. . . . I—I mean—— That is, if you like to——"

"I'd like to," he told her. "You wait for me."

She waited, that evening—her body still chilled from the long hours on the wind-swept benches in front of the Capitol, her spirit still warm with new hope—and not all of it came from the inaugural address. She waited and waited; and at twenty minutes past eight, Pete called her up.

"Eunice, I've got to be over at the White House offices at nine. No time to wait for hotel service, and I haven't eaten anything since morning. You order your dinner, and I'll grab a cup of coffee and a sandwich at a lunch counter and then come up and talk to you for a minute. That's absolutely all the time I can get."

"Where's your lunch counter?" she asked imperiously. "1559 F Street? All right; I'll come right down there and grab a sandwich and a cup of coffee with you."

In the lobby, as she was hurrying out, she met Doug Ewing—very resplendent and ambassadorial in full evening dress. But worried.

"Where are you going?" he asked her. "It's too early for the ball."

"I'm dining out. I'll see you later, at the Auditorium."

"Let me drive you to your dinner; I've got to talk to you. What's the address? . . . 1599 F Street? What sort of place is that?"

"A lunch counter," she said amiably. "I'm dining with a busy man."

He was still trying to figure that out as they got into the taxi.

"What's the matter, Doug? I feel so much better since I heard Roosevelt telling us not to be afraid. So does everybody—even father."

"So do I," he admitted, "as far as that goes. But right now I've got three hundred and seventy-nine members of the Rivermont Roosevelt-Garner Club over at the Raleigh, and no money to pay the bill with. . . . But never mind that. It's all right about the embassy. Illyria, I think."